I became lost in the superb watercolor scenes rendered by Ross Greening. They evoked my cranial memories of military cockpits, the bountiful luxury of boring holes in the sky, and the smell of engines coughing smoke as the props begin to spin in a powerful blur. It rekindled the feeling of easing back on the stick to climb free as a bird from the earth's imprisonment.

The intensity of air battles, such as the Tokyo raiders and all who followed experienced, would become lost if not for films, and far better, if not for the words rendered so poignantly in Ross's account along with the magical strokes of his brush. Where so many thousands of souls at Arlington, in the Pacific, in Europe, and in the depths of the world's oceans cannot be heard, Ross is there to speak on their behalf.

—*William J. O'Dwyer, historian and author*

Ross Greening's talents, originality, and concise leadership clearly benefited all downed airmen incarcerated at our Barth-on-the-Bay wartime holding center. He directed our lives rather than just commanding us.

Our captors accorded him as much recognition as we did. Just differently! During that coldest-ever winter of 1944–45, one day while "walking our fence line" for exercise, I reached the main gate at the same time as four, long-leather-coated, henchmen-sized Germans were commencing their compound guard duty.

Surprise; the giant among them was as easily recognized as Joe Louis in those days—it was the former world heavyweight boxing champion, Max Schmeling! All of us believed that this celebrated German paratrooper sergeant had lost his life in one of the Mediterranean campaigns. Surprise again; he brought art supplies from his movie star wife's ample stores with which to replenish Greening's empty shelf. And, he mentioned "in passing," his plan to revisit New York as soon as hostilities ended.

—*Lewis A. Wickens, former POW*

Ross Greening was a man of many talents, all of which he did very well. He was a true American pilot, an outstanding military leader, a real war hero, an exceptional artist, a fine writer, an accomplished inventor, and a dedicated family man. He was a Jack of all trades and a master of many.

—*Col. John P. Doolittle, USAF (ret.)*

I am very pleased that the memoirs of C. Ross Greening are now in print. As the Historian for the Doolittle Tokyo Raiders, I first became aware of his many talents when I learned he was the inventor of the famous "20-cent bombsight" used on this epic mission. He was an artist whose works were the basis for a post-war, nation-wide exhibition showing the ingenuity of Americans while prisoners of war. Readers will find that he had an unusually interesting life, although it was much too brief.

—*Carroll V. Glines, author of* The Doolittle Raid

Not As Briefed

From the Doolittle Raid to a German Stalag

Not As Briefed

From the Doolittle Raid to a German Stalag

Colonel C. Ross Greening

Compiled and edited by Dorothy Greening and Karen Morgan Driscoll

WSU
PRESS

Washington State University Press
Pullman, Washington

Washington State University Press
PO Box 645910
Pullman, Washington 99164-5910
Phone: 800-354-7360
Fax: 509-335-8568
E-mail: wsupress@wsu.edu
Web site: www.wsu.edu/wsupress

Library of Congress Cataloging-in-Publication Data

Greening, C. Ross (Charles Ross), 1914-
    Not as briettle : from the Doolittle raid to a German stalag / by Colonel C. Ross
Greening ; compiled and edited by Dorothy Greening and Karen Morgan Driscoll.
       p. cm.
    Includes index.
    ISBN 0-87422-239-7 (alk. paper)
    1. Greening, C. Ross (Charles Ross), 1914- 2. World War, 1939-1945—Personal narratives, American. 3. World War, 1939-1945—Aerial operations, American. 4. Bomber pilots—United States—Biography. 5. United States. Army Air Forces—Biography. 6. World War, 1939-1945—Prisoners and prisons, German. 7. Tokyo (Japan)—History—Bombardment, 1942—Personal narratives. 8. World War, 1939-1945—Campaigns—Italy. 9. World War, 1939-1945—Art and the war. I. Greening, Dorothy, 1912- II. Driscoll, Karen Morgan, 1941- III. Title.

D811.G412 A3 2001
940.54'4973—dc21   2001026160

CONTENTS

DEDICATION

ON BEHALF OF ROSS GREENING—

This book is dedicated to the Italian citizens who protected and nourished Ross Greening in body and spirit while he was an escaped POW during World War II. These wonderful people exhibited the finest form of heroism by repeatedly risking their lives for him simply out of human decency. In spite of their own difficult circumstances, they often gave more to him than they kept for themselves. They saved his life, filled his heart, and became part of his family. He always was indebted to them.

Verona locality—

Rita Pavoni, daughter Elsa, and a son, of Pescantina.

Mr. and Mrs. Antonio (Toni) Peduzzi, daughter Nela (Nellie), and son Italo, of Pescantina.

Angelina and Quirino Righetti, sons Rinaldo and Italo, and daughters Emiliana, Edda, and Danila, of San Peretto.

Mr. and Mrs. Bustaggi, sons Angelo and Guiseppe (Beppi), and daughter Nela, of San Peretto.

And to the orphan boy, to Dr. Roberto Pavoncelli, and to other residents of San Peretto di Negrar, Pescantina, Viscontina, and Verona.

Cividale locality—

Mr. and Mrs. Pietro (Pete) Comugnero and Luigi Comugnero, of Masarolis.

Herma Zamparutti, of Masarolis.

Padre Don Amelio Pinzano, of Masarolis.

Elio and Elena Borgnolo, son Claudio, and daughter Renata, of Valle.

Lilia, a "little sweetheart," of Pedrosa.

Amabile, another "little sweetheart," and the other mountain children.

And to residents of Udine, Cividale, and the four mountain villages of Masarolis, Pedrosa, Reant, and Valle.

DOROTHY GREENING—

I dedicate this book to my sons, Allen Ross Greening and William Charles Greening. They lost their father when they were very young. This book will help them tell the world what kind of man he was.

KAREN MORGAN DRISCOLL—

This book is dedicated to my mother, Shirley Greening Morgan. She was proud of me for doing this. That was all the help I needed.

FOREWORD

When given the opportunity to introduce this very appealing story about an old friend, college classmate, and fellow airman, my first thought was of Ross Greening's regard for forewords in general, as exemplified by an episode from his prisoner of war days. A friend and fellow POW tried to convince Ross that a careful reading of a "foreword" was essential to understanding the essence of a book. Ross, however, took the position that a foreword was simply a boilerplate statement and a complete waste of time to read. Under the stress of long imprisonment, the discussion became heated with a little physical contact—an act completely alien for two of the most gentle of men. Thus, I bear in mind what Ross most probably would've said about my foreword.

I remember well one evening during our ROTC encampment at the Presidio of Monterey, when I sat with Ross on a cliff overlooking the Pacific Ocean. He discussed his attraction to flying, and his intention to apply for the U.S. Army Air Corps flight program upon graduation from Washington State College, but this posed a conflict with his love of art. After his first training flight at Randolph Field in Texas, however, he didn't have a second thought about his choice of careers.

He was a natural pilot, and quickly developed a great love for planes and flying. Ross had complete confidence in his abilities and flew anything he could get his hands on. He was a careful pilot, but found great enjoyment in testing the performance characteristics of the aircraft he flew. As a result, he made other men under his command better pilots.

I remember Ross most clearly as a great friend dating back to our college days when we were on the WSC track team and worked on school publications that featured his popular cartoons. With his boyish grin, natural exuberance, and quirky sense of humor, he was the kind of fellow that everyone wanted to be around; there were few dull moments. We had no money in our pockets at the ROTC camp, so Ross would set up an easel in the company street each Saturday and draw caricatures or portraits of the cadets. When he made enough money, we set out for the beach at Carmel.

One time he talked an Air Force dentist friend into taking the ugliest, most unsightly teeth ever pulled, and placing them in a bridge. Ross put this bridge in his mouth and then delighted in going out in public where people couldn't keep their eyes off this good looking man with terrible teeth. This was vintage Ross Greening.

After World War II, I had the good fortune to spend many hours with Ross while he talked about his wartime experiences, but he always did so in a jocular and self deprecating way. While I knew he went through difficult times, I had no idea of the depth of his suffering and the hardships he experienced until I read this book. This is a story of incredible courage and determination.

It is a story that everyone should read, particularly the young people of our country who haven't witnessed the high cost of freedom. Ross Greening was a warrior in the finest tradition of the U.S. military, and I'm proud to have been his friend.

Harry E. Goldsworthy
Lt. Gen. USAF (ret.)

ACKNOWLEDGMENTS

HOW THIS BOOK CAME TO BE—

When I can't sleep, I wander the house looking for something to read. One night I found a big box of old, dog-eared carbon copies of typed sheets that described my uncle's wartime experiences. They'd been loaned to my husband for a video project. I already was well acquainted with Ross's paintings and I'd heard stories about his life, but I was unaware that this written account existed. I couldn't find any starting point or even page numbers, so I just randomly picked up a pile of pages and started reading.

There wasn't any sleep for me that night. Even with the pages out of order, the story was fascinating. The words came alive and I felt as if I were transported back to World War II, living past events alongside Ross. The details were rich and the emotions heartrending.

When the morning sun appeared, I rubbed my bleary eyes and decided I'd organize and type up this account to preserve it as a part of our family history. I was afraid these old pages would slip into oblivion if I didn't do so.

When I was well into this task, I happened to take down a framed photo of Ross that my mother had given me. On the back, I was surprised to find a letter from him that she had taped there. It was sent to me when I was 13 years old. Ross was very ill at the time and mother had urged me to write him a letter.

Ross had answered my letter, complimenting me on my writing, and adding, "Maybe you can help me write my book someday."

When reading this letter again after forty years had passed, I decided then and there to help Ross write his book.

Later, I learned that many people who'd known of his experiences had told Ross that a book should be written about him. In about 1955, Ross was introduced to a professional author who was interested in writing the story. Ed Mack Miller and Ross hit it off right away and with Ed taking notes, the two stayed up an entire night, while Ross recorded his story on Dictaphone. Regrettably, both men passed away before the book could be completed.

Despite her grief, Ross's wife, Dot, spent a year listening to her husband's voice and transcribing the disks into a complete typed copy. Then, over the years, she tried time and again to find a professional writer, but without success, largely due to the manuscript's extensive length. Everyone who read the material agreed it deserved to be published, somehow.

Ross's words were wonderfully stated. As I saw it, my job was to thread the story together from Ross's handwritten diaries, letters, and transcribed oral materials, and to edit them. Sometimes it was hard, but it always was fascinating. The effort took about five years.

After I sent a rough, partial draft to Dot, unknown to me she had passed it on to Randall Johnson, an old friend and classmate of Ross's at WSC, and the designer of the famous Cougar head logo. Randall, in turn, had passed the manuscript on and, to my surprise, we were in the pipeline for publication by the WSU Press!

This is how this fine book came to life after lying in a box for 47 years.

PERSONS DESERVING A HEARTFELT "THANK YOU"—

Ed Mack Miller was a fine author and became a great admirer of Ross. He recognized what an excellent storyteller Ross was. Miller's enthusiastic, marathon listening session produced the majority of the powerful text that is included in this book.

Col. Jake Miller, USMC (ret.), was a classmate and lifelong friend of Ross and Dot's. Shortly after Ross's death, he probably worked harder and put more time into trying to get a book out about Ross's experiences than anyone else. The love and energy he put into this effort is deeply appreciated by the family.

Randall Johnson, Ross's classmate and fellow art major, remains a lifelong friend of the Greening family. His vision that a fine, publishable book existed within the pages of an extremely rough, incomplete draft is a testimony to his creative mind.

Shortly after graduating from college, Ross persuaded his classmate Harry Goldsworthy to leave his Department of Agriculture job and join the U.S. Army Air Force. Now a retired three star general, this lifelong friend also played a part in helping get the book published. His wise guidance and prompt generous help proved invaluable.

When Randall Johnson wished to have the manuscript seriously considered for publication by the WSU Press, he turned to Dr. James Quann, former WSU Registrar. Quann continues to conduct long-term research regarding the his-

tory and biographies of WSU's military veterans. Quann discovered that Ross was WSU's most highly decorated WW II veteran, and he felt the manuscript draft was good enough to begin working with the WSU Press to have it accepted. He also conducted a successful financial campaign to allow for the extensive color reproduction of Ross's paintings in the book.

Lt. Col. Carroll V. Glines, USAF (ret.), the official historian of the Doolittle Raiders, has published numerous books and articles. He currently assists the Doolittle Museum in encouraging and advising persons who are writing military and historical memoirs. Glines meticulously read the section regarding the Doolittle Raid and provided wonderful advice. He's been a longtime friend of Dot Greening's and his friendship is deeply valued.

Jack Lang is one of the New Zealand soldiers with whom Ross shared some of the most hazardous and stressful wartime experiences, and also some of the most joyful memories. The depth of their friendship was something the rest of us can hardly fathom. When Jack read a draft of my text, he said it seemed as if Ross were right beside him, telling the story. I was extremely relieved and pleased. I wanted assurance that I'd preserved the tone of Ross's words as I transformed casual letters, official reports, introspective diaries, and ad lib speeches into smooth rhetoric. For this book, Jack also provided a copy of a watercolor painting that Ross had given him. I am deeply thankful to Jack Lang for his help and enduring friendship.

Jack also generously shared a precious, fragile copy of the diary written by Bob Smith, the other New Zealander who shared a life on the run with Ross and Jack. Bob passed away many years ago, but the testimony of his deep friendship with Ross lives on in Bob's wonderful words, which are included in the Appendix of this book.

Sometimes, when it's needed most and you are very lucky, exactly the right person comes into your life. Maj. Bill O'Dwyer, USAF Reserve (ret.), was that person. Bill is a professional writer on a wide array of subjects, including aviation and military history. Bill encouraged me, saying that this project deserved to be published and not just become a family record. He authored a wonderful six-page article for *Flight Journal* magazine in October 1999, promoting the forthcoming book. He proofed a preliminary draft with more care and respect than I ever expected. He advised me, cheered me up, solved problems, and promoted the book. He deserves more thanks than I can ever say.

My father, Capt. Edward Maxwell Morgan, USN (ret.), and my mother, Shirley Greening Morgan, gave me all their love and support throughout this project. Nothing mattered more to me; my mother lived long enough to know *Not as Briefed* soon would be published.

Ross's other sister, Virginia Greening Nisker, also provided invaluable assistance. She proofed the final draft and, with her firsthand knowledge, cleared up some details for us. She has been wonderfully supportive and enthusiastic about the project.

Ross's nephew, Hans Zeiger, took a keen interest in the manuscript, proofed an early draft, and caught more problems than anyone else other than my editor. He sent me several typed pages of wonderful suggestions that I appreciated and used. He was at the ripe old age of 15 when he did this. I think he has a career in publishing open to him if he wants it.

Ross's sons, Allen Greening and Chuck Greening, constantly provided support and encouragement. They contributed a good deal of material used in the book, met with the

Twelve-year-old Karen Morgan. Portrait painted by Ross Greening at Laird's Lodge, Montana.

editor to help select photos and other illustrations, and assisted with proofreading.

My son in law, Erick Paetsch, graciously contributed his time and legal expertise to the project, which gave us confidence to proceed.

Only people who spend a few years working on a book can know how vital the patience and support of their spouse is. Acknowledging my husband, Andy, for his love and help feels like thanking the air I breathe. Thanks Andy for being there for me.

When I dreamed of this book being published, I visualized a format full of color paintings and photographs, and with sidebars presenting interesting information. I also hoped for a certain kind of person to edit the text. Someone who would respect Ross as I did, and who at the same time would see the historic importance of the book and help with the necessary research to get everything correct and clear. If I could have created that editor myself, he would have been Glen Lindeman, Editor of the Washington State University Press. He became devoted to this book, poured his own time into it, helped me bring it to a polished form, and respected my wishes far more than I deserved. The format is exactly as I dreamed it should be. Glen, dear friend and partner, thank you very, very much.

Dot Greening has been the "keeper of the flame" of Ross's memory for all these years. No one could have done better. She has given innumerable talks to civic groups and school children, kept up a lively correspondence with Air Force friends, attended almost all of the Doolittle Raider reunions, and handled numerous requests to use Ross's materials in books, articles, and art shows. She never gave up hope that a book about Ross's life would be published. I admire her tremendously and thank her for entrusting me with compiling and editing such a wonderful story.

At Dot's request, I'll include her statements here about my part in the book. Dot said that many, many people had told her that Ross's material was wonderful, but too long and complicated. There were more events in this man's life than was reasonable for a book. The last rejection by a professional military historian came just as this project began.

Little did Dot realize that the book could be published after all those pros turned it down. Ross did it himself, helped by his niece who gathered up the old papers and dog-eared manuscripts and started typing, with a blind faith that a story such as this deserved to be a book. Then with tears in her voice, Dot thanked me once again.

Many people graciously contributed to defray the additional, but necessary, design costs of including Ross's beautiful artwork in full color in the book—

By far, the Doolittle Tokyo Raiders Association provided the largest single donation.

Other major donors were Jim and Barbara Quann, Bill and Doris O'Dwyer, Randall and Jeanne Johnson, Harry and Edith Goldsworthy, Grant and Grace Dixon, Del and Mid Rowland, John and Priscilla Doolittle, and Carroll and Mary Glines.

Significant support also came from the Tokyo raiders themselves and their families. Among others, they included R.G. Emmens, Robert and Portia Hite, David M. Jones, Edith M. McClure, Roy and Kay Stork, Marcine J. Barr, Mary Davenport, Jacob DeShazer, Frank Kappeler, Mary H. York, and John C. Gray.

Lewis A. Wickens and other former POWs likewise provided assistance, as did Greening family friends, associates, and supporters, including Robert and Jean Goldsworthy, Seth J. Marshall, Jr., and numerous others.

All of these persons helped make *Not as Briefed* possible. To all, I and the WSU Press thank you.

Karen Morgan Driscoll
June 2001

Ross Greening (front, center) served as student ROTC commandant at Washington State College.

CHAPTER ONE

EARLY YEARS

I've always wanted to fly airplanes. I saw my first one when I was four. I grabbed my tricycle and gave chase not realizing the futility of catching that fascinating machine. Several blocks from my house, I collided with my dad who was standing in front of his bank in Miles City, Montana, watching the same plane. Every effort to stop me failed so he bundled me into the car and drove to the field where "the bird from heaven" had landed. It was a huge Army bomber. From that time on, I resolved I'd never rest until I could fly one of those machines!

When I was six, my parents took me to an aerial demonstration at a field near our home, and, with my older sister, I took my first flight. A few years later, I was thrilled beyond description to witness a parachute jump by a daredevil named Charles A. Lindbergh.

My dad was a banker, state senator, and cattle rancher. He had banks in several little Montana towns including Miles City, Roundup, Hardin, and Melstone. My mother, sister, and I came down with the Spanish flu when I was

Four-year-old Ross Greening and six-year-old Shirley Greening celebrating the end of World War I in Miles City, Montana, on November 11, 1918.

about four years old, but we were among the lucky ones and we all survived.

In 1925 when I was eleven years old, my father's banks and other investments failed because of the depression in rural areas and we moved to Tacoma, Washington. I became quite interested in art, but flying was still my main love. I was involved in my first crash at age thirteen when an International OX-5 in which I had bummed a ride pancaked into a Japanese-American farmer's raspberry field. By the time I was in high school, I also was interested in sports and played football, ran track, and got pretty good at throwing the javelin, setting a record or two.

I attended Washington State College in Pullman, majoring in fine arts and minoring in physical education and military science. In 1933, between my first and second years of college, I took a summertime voyage to the cities of Yokohama, Kobe, Shanghai, Hong Kong, and Manila aboard the SS *President Cleveland* cruise ship as a seaman, scullery man, and pantryman. I washed about

50,000 dishes that summer, and had a wonderful ride all around Yokohama in a rickshaw for 3 cents. I also took my first drink of hard liquor, a Singapore Sling, and saw a man I had just been talking to, fall seventy feet down a hatch and land on his head and die. It was so hot I had to wring out my bed sheets each morning, but I became hooked on traveling during that summer.

I had never dated much during high school. I preferred to spend my time with a couple of buddies who also were

First plane ride, June 1921.

women haters at that point and we went camping all over Puget Sound, roaming the woods or going out in a rowboat and shooting dogfish with our 22s at night or fishing during the day. I had a little three-legged dog named Spottie, who was my best camping pal and frequently we went off alone hunting.

During my freshman year in college, my Theta Chi fraternity brothers insisted that I bring a date to the Pledge Dance, since, after all, I was making all the decorations for the event. My older sister, Shirley, was in the Tri Delt house and she took pity on me and fixed me up with a sorority sister named Dorothy Watson, who was very popular. I found out later that my sister told her that I didn't dance and didn't like girls. Whoever went with me would probably have a mis-

erable time although I was a wonderful boy and loved to do things outdoors rather than go to dances. In spite of that wonderful introduction, for some reason or other, Dot decided to go out with me.

Just like my sister said, I couldn't dance, but Dot showed me some steps and pretty soon we were having a good time. We got to talking and the conversation got around to the out of doors. I learned that Dot really liked sports and fishing.

Over the next couple of years I mostly dated Dot, but I did go out with one other girl, and for awhile I was having trouble deciding which one I liked the best. One time I invited Dot to a dance in nearby Moscow, Idaho, about ten miles away. We were going to double date with a fraternity brother who was bringing a blind date and another couple in the same car. You can imagine how I felt when I discovered that my fraternity friend's blind date was the other girl I had been dating! In spite of that, we all had a good time at the dance, but coming home our old jalopy broke down in the mud outside of Moscow. We all had to do some walking and the gals were in their long dresses and party shoes. Dot thought it was a lark, but the other girls, particularly the one I'd been dating, couldn't see anything funny about it and they were really poor sports. I decided then and there that Dot was the one for me because she was such a good trooper and would be more fun to be with, able to take the bad with the good. We went together steadily from then on until I graduated in 1936.

During my senior year in college I hitchhiked from Pullman to Vancouver, Washington, to take the physical exam for flight school. On the road I met a fellow named Hubert Zemke, who was on his way to take the exam also. We became good friends and were both destined to be pilots.

After graduation in 1936, I was offered an opportunity to work in Walt Disney's studio as an apprentice cartoonist. However, I wanted to fly, so as soon as I graduated, I applied

Javelin thrower for the Washington State College track and field team, Pullman, Washington.

to the Air Corps Flying School at Randolph Field, Texas, and was accepted. I kept up with my art while I was in flight school and made portraits of my roommates along with lots of sketches of flight school activities. I survived the course even though, on my initial night flight, I dove my Seversky BT-8 into the ground and woke up with the doc waving my lucky rabbit's foot under my nose.

He said, "If this gadget got you through the mess you've been in, it certainly must be better than smelling salts!"

I had been too enthusiastic in trying to dive for the ground as soon as I observed a signal to avoid delaying the rest of the planes behind me. I rolled my BT-8 over and dove, but failed to recover. The plane hit wheels and nose together in the middle of a field. The engine broke off, the plane flipped over on its back, skidded a few feet, and came to rest, a pile of junk. I was thrown from the front of the aircraft through the instrument panel. Somehow, I wasn't seriously hurt and managed to graduate, June 9, 1937, and was assigned to the Twentieth Pursuit Group, Barksdale Field, Louisiana, where I flew P-6s and P-26s.

During this period, I persuaded Dot to marry me. At the time we were to be married, I was the proud possessor of a 1935 Plymouth sedan, of third-hand vintage. I threw my things in the car and took off from Louisiana for Olympia, Washington, 2,700 miles away, where we were to be wed. I stopped only once for two hours in the entire 2,700 miles. However, it took the better part of three weeks to return after our marriage.

I figured that I could afford $400 from my finances for our wedding trip. After the ceremony, we took off in a cloud of dust through Oregon, and then on to California. The weather was perfect at first, but the further south we went the colder it became. We were sightseeing in San Francisco and Los Angeles when Dot started to get the flu. We decided the best thing would be to head straight for Louisiana as quickly as possible. We proceeded out across the desert with a case of grapefruit to help Dot ward off her flu bug. Unfortunately, my Plymouth began wobbling and shaking, and soon we were weaving from one side to the other, through perilous passes and on dangerous roads. We had the car checked in almost every garage we came to, and had the wheels realigned and balanced. Nevertheless, as we went through the Arizona mountains we came close to going over cliffs off the side of the road. Meanwhile, Dot was becoming sicker and sicker.

In El Paso, as we were leaving town, we heard a clatter and bang behind us and then the car settled down on its right rear wheel. I looked back and saw the remains of the springs scattered down the highway. We secured a 1936 Chevrolet spring at a garage, which was the only one we could find to fit our 1935 Plymouth. It made the right rear ride high, but Dot's flu was getting worse so we headed off across the Texas panhandle anyway. Each night, we stopped early to let Dot soak in a bathtub and packed her in hot towels and blankets to help her get through the night.

We reached Fort Worth on Thanksgiving eve. We figured, if luck was with us, we could make it the remaining 200 miles to Barksdale where we could enjoy a fine Thanksgiving dinner at the mess hall. A holiday dinner at one of the messes was something to be treasured in those days. I was the mess officer so we probably would enjoy a seat of honor.

When we departed Fort Worth early in the morning, the car still wobbled. Traffic was fairly heavy as we drove along the turnpike. Suddenly and without warning, the right front axle snapped off and the wheel slid underneath the front of the car, as the bumper fell on the wheel. The car skidded across the left side of the road, dodged through a tight hole

in the traffic, and plowed into a bank on the other side. Fortunately, we weren't hurt, but we were a bit discouraged at this point.

We needed to get the car fixed and our total resources at this point were $17.50. We finally found a garage and the repairman told us the wheel was pinned underneath the car in such a way that it had not broken the hydraulic lines. However, we needed a new axle and he didn't have one available. We headed for the dump and found a 1936 Plymouth axle.

After installing the axle, our bill was $16.50, which left us with $1.00 to get to Barksdale. About 125 miles from Barksdale, I heard a characteristic hiss. We had a slow leak in the rear tire. I limped into a gas station and had it repaired for 25 cents. With the remaining 75 cents, I put all the gas I could into the tank and headed out again. After numerous stops to have the tire pumped up again and again, we approached the gate at Barksdale. I saluted the guard as we headed for the closest friend's house. Just as we went through the gate, the engine missed and we were out of gas. We coasted to a dead stop in front of my friend's house just as the rear tire went completely flat. Dot was so sick I had to carry her into the house. Waiting for me there was a mes-

Wedding day, November 11, 1937. From left, Mrs. Jewell Ross Greening, Ross Greening, Dorothy Watson Greening, Virginia Greening, and Charles Greening.

sage from my dad, who was the manager of a bank in Tacoma where I had my account. The message said I was not to worry because in his capacity as bank manager he had covered our $190 overdraft! It was a wedding trip to remember.

In 1938, I was transferred from Barksdale to Hamilton Field, California, and assigned to the Seventh Bombardment Group, Eleventh Bombardment Squadron, which was being equipped with B-17s, the first to come off the Boeing production line. In 1940, volunteers were requested to open McChord Field in Tacoma, Washington. Since Tacoma was my hometown, I volunteered for this assignment and was attached to the Seventeenth Medium Bombardment Group. To my surprise, due to a shortage of officers, when we arrived I was immediately assigned to six different jobs. I was the base public relations officer, the assistant S-2 or intelligence officer, the assistant adjutant, the base photography officer, the base provost marshal, and the base operations officer.

McChord boasted one of the largest barracks in the world at the time. It was designed to hold approximately 2,000 enlisted men including headquarters and other offices. The large, central heating plant, intended to provide heat for most of the buildings on the base, was located about 1/4 mile to the west. Before opening the barracks, we had to test the heating plant to see whether or not it was adequate to heat the huge building. A number of the base's officials were standing by for this test. A call was sent to the plant to turn on the heat. The officials stood anxiously around the vents in the barracks, waiting for a flow of warm air. It didn't come. We called the heating plant again and rushed back to the air vents, but still no heat.

We consulted the base engineer and he deduced that there must be an obstruction in the tunnel from the plant to the barracks. They decided to have someone crawl through the tunnel to find the blockage. An enlisted man went to the heating plant to enter the tunnel and hopefully emerge somewhere in the barracks. To his amazement, he found that there was no tunnel—in their haste to establish the base, the engineers apparently had forgotten to construct one. By then, the landscaping and streets had been put in. This all had to be torn up. It was an embarrassing day for the engineers.

The Seventeenth Bombardment Group was the first tactical outfit assigned to McChord Field. It came from March Field, California, and was equipped with old Douglas B-18s. We had a few Northrup A-17s and A-17As for proficiency flying assigned to my squadron. One day, one of the A-17s that was a transient from Patterson Field, Ohio, disappeared. The pilot complained that when he went down to operations to take off, his plane couldn't be found.

A few hours later, the A-17 was seen approaching the field in an erratic pattern. The pilot made a pass at the runway, bounced the wheels, and then gave it the gas and went around. He made several more passes at the field in a sloppy manner. As base operations officer, I warned all of the other planes in the air to stay out of the traffic area until this A-17 landed. It made another pass, but too slowly. The plane hit the ground and bounced into the air as before, but in a high nose attitude this time, much too high for safe flying. When the pilot applied the gas to go around, he tried to put the nose down. The plane crashed and burned at the end of the runway.

Quickly switching from being base operations officer, I assumed my base provost marshal role and rushed to the scene of the accident with a number of guards from the barracks. Guards were placed around the wreck to keep people away. Then I received instructions from Colonel Walsh, the base commander, to prohibit anyone from taking photographs of the wreck. About this time, two more of my six jobs came into play. I was to photograph the scene as photography officer, and to prepare press releases for the local media as public relations officer. As provost marshal, I noticed a newspaper photographer in a car standing on the hill nearby taking some pictures, even though we had posted

signs saying it was forbidden. I instructed the guards to confiscate the newsman's camera and I took it to the base adjutant's office. The base adjutant was gone, so in his absence, utilizing my fourth hat as assistant adjutant, I held onto the camera myself.

Later that evening, the photographer who had had his camera confiscated came to the base adjutant's office and in this capacity I received him. He requested that his camera be returned to him.

Being rather young and full of myself, at this point I got a "bright idea." As acting adjutant, I informed him that he would have to go to the public relations officer, who had information about the camera. I told him how to get to the public relations office, but by a devious route. When he left, I rushed to the public relations office. Shortly, I heard a knock and in came the press photographer. He had a peculiar look as he eyed me, but I introduced myself as the base public relations officer and didn't tell him my name. When he asked for his camera, I told him that it had been given to the base provost marshal, since he was in charge of the guard who had confiscated the camera.

Ross with sister Virginia at Mt. Rainier, Washington.

I sent him off again by a round about route and rushed off to the provost marshal's office to take over that role. I got in my seat just as the photographer arrived. This time he had a very serious look about him. When he requested his camera, I told him that I'd been instructed to return the camera, but the film needed to be removed and therefore it had been sent to the base photographer. The office was a block away so I dispatched a very befuddled press photographer to the

base photographer's office while I madly rushed off to don my other hat. This time when he arrived, I had the camera on my desk and the film removed, but there was no doubt in his mind that a prank had been pulled and without hesitation he recognized me as the wearer of all of the other hats.

His comments were not complimentary and he didn't take the joke well. In fact, he wrote a pretty defamatory article in the newspaper about me. Meanwhile, I kept my hand in art by painting numerous portraits of squadron mates and watercolors of planes and incidents in the air.

After a number of the tactical squadrons of the Seventeenth Bombardment Group and the Eighty-ninth Reconnaissance Squadron arrived, I was assigned as a pilot. Douglas B-23s, a faster, lighter, and more maneuverable aircraft, replaced our Douglas B-18s. As an "old" bombardier, pilot, and navigator, I was assigned as an instructor in bombardment.

In 1941, while flying off the coast of Washington in a B-23, my engineer accidentally tripped the handle of a hatch and almost fell 8,000 feet into the Pacific Ocean. I saw him starting to go out the hatch and dove from the flight deck and managed to grab his ankles. He was beaten up by the air stream and shook up by the whole experience by the time that the crew and I pulled him safely back inside.

View of Randolph Field, Texas, from 6,000 feet.

In late 1940 and 1941, the B-23s were replaced with North American B-25s. The Mitchell bombers were purchased by the U.S. Army Air Force direct from the drawing board due to the great demand for an up-to-date combat aircraft. The entire program had to be expedited, so the Seventeenth Bombardment Group and Eighty-ninth Reconnaissance Squadron were chosen to fly the aircraft from the factory to McChord, and some of them from McChord to Patterson Field, Ohio. We were ordered to conduct accelerated service tests for gasoline consumption, speed runs, and various other things.

Capt. Spyder Eckman and I were part of three crews selected for the non-stop transcontinental flights. We went to Mitchell Field, New York, to begin our hop, which was to March Field, California, non-stop at 15,000 feet or below. I had a crew of four men. The visibility and ceiling were zero when we took off, but the top of the overcast was only about 3,000 feet up. We made our flight to March Field in fourteen hours and encountered hail, rain, and just about every kind of bad weather and were exhausted when we arrived. We learned that the other two planes had been unable to make the trip due to the weather. We had a bite of lunch, refueled, and began our flight back. The return proved to be far more hazardous than the trip out—we flew nine of the twelve hours on instruments. We were supposed to make this return flight at 15,000 feet, but a large part of it was at 20,000 or 25,000 feet. We had an old type of oxygen mask that was very tiring to use, particularly in our already exhausted condition.

At one time we became lost in the Oklahoma City vicinity. We were so confused that we considered our navigation adequate if we could determine which state we were in. We broke out of the overcast at Pittsburgh, Pennsylvania, and continued on toward Mitchell Field. Over New York

Cadet in training at Randolph Field, Texas.

NOT AS BRIEFED

City we received a weather report that Mitchell was still socked in and we couldn't land there, so we returned to Dayton, Ohio. From March Field to New York and then on to Dayton took a total of twelve hours. I was so tired when I arrived in Dayton that I had difficulty getting out of the plane. As I came in from the hangar line, the traffic officer informed me that a new P-39 fighter just had been flown in and that I was welcome to take it out if I wanted. I got a few bites and flew the P-39 for two hours. This amounted to a total of twenty-eight hours of flying in a day and a half. It was the longest stretch of flying I ever did at one time in my life. Nevertheless, I enjoyed every bit of it.

After completing the accelerated service tests, I participated in extended Army maneuvers in Louisiana, Texas, and the Carolinas. While in Texas, we used quarter pound bags of rancid flour as "bombs." During maneuvers, we were to attack any vehicles and troops we could find and drop our "bombs" on them. The bags of wormy flour were easily spotted on a roadway and, of course, the troops had no trouble identifying whether or not they were casualties after we had made an attack.

General George Patton, who had his headquarters set up in a small town along the Louisiana-Texas border, was a commander of the troops. When B-25s dropped rancid flour sacks on Patton's troops and headquarters, he strenuously objected. One of the referees designated for these maneuvers notified him that the headquarters was not included as a target for the B-25s, and assured him that it wouldn't happen again. The referee had just spoken when my B-25 came screaming over the rooftops at tree level, scattering flour in all directions. One stream of flour bags came directly through General Patton's mess tent and cleaned all of the utensils and food from the tables. I understand the referee got up and left without saying a word.

After the Texas venture, we were ordered to the East Coast for further maneuvers. I wrote to Dot in Washington State telling her to come to Ellington Field, Texas, where we thought we would remain for a few days. She took off in a car with another officer's wife to drive across country. After a long day of driving, they checked into the only hotel around, which was a seedy place with a lady managing it who looked rather peculiar to them. The manager seemed surprised that they didn't want single rooms. After they had checked into their room, they gradually began to realize from the noise, men and women going in and out of rooms rather frequently, and other activities that this "hotel" had another business purpose. After barricading the door to their room with all of the furniture, they spent the night awake, afraid to stay, but afraid to leave. It was funny to us afterwards, but not at the time for two rather innocent young wives!

A day before Dot was to arrive at Ellington, I learned that we were going to be sent to Augusta, Georgia. Through the State Patrol along her route, I dispatched a message to her, but made the mistake of saying, "Meet me at the airbase at Atlanta, Georgia," instead of Augusta. To compound the problem, when we arrived at Augusta we learned that a hurricane was in progress and we were immediately sent to Savannah. At Savannah we found we still couldn't adequately protect the planes, so we went on to Tampa, Florida.

Dot, traveling alone by this time, arrived at Atlanta, which was not even a completed airfield. It was under

construction and no one there knew anything about my unit. She began calling every base she could think of trying to locate our missing squadron, but with no luck. That night at a small tourist house, she cried her heart out in spite of the kind attempts of two elderly ladies running the place to comfort her. A couple of days later a sergeant at Langley Field heard of my whereabouts and traced us from Augusta to Savannah and from there to Tampa. Dot's call to the base at Tampa was transferred to the Officers' Club and then to the cocktail bar telephone. I happened to be standing there, heard the phone ring, and answered it just to be helpful to the bartender—only to hear Dot's voice on the other end!

Maneuvers lasted until December 1941, when we were notified to return to our assigned home base in Pendleton, Oregon.

Gouges in turf and wrecked BT-8 at Randolph Field, Texas.

On December 6, Maj. Jack Hilger, our commanding officer, and our entire flight were caught in a thunderstorm just west of Maxwell Field in Alabama. After a half-hour of floundering in the storm, we decided we had to return to Maxwell where we landed in a downpour. The visibility was so bad that we lost two planes in crackups when landing.

One, flown by Lt. Jack Sims, was unable to stop and headed straight for a golf course, which was attached to the Air Command and Staff School. At that moment, the commanding officer of the base was out inspecting the number eight green, which was almost in line with the runway. He was concerned about the damage the rain might be causing. To his horror when he looked up towards the runway, he saw Jack Sims' sliding, skidding airplane appear out of the rain and come directly towards him. He dove for his life into the bunker as the B-25 skidded slowly across the green, gouging a foot-and-a-half deep hole with the nose wheel as it ripped the cup squarely from its position. The plane went on across the green and plunged over a bank towards the river, where it came to rest hanging in the trees below. The crews of both crackups escaped serious injury, and that night in the Officers' Club bar we lamented the loss of our first B-25s.

The next day we proceeded on our way towards Pendleton Field, Oregon. Late in the afternoon, we approached the Grand Canyon. Just for the fun of it, we dove down below the rim of the canyon in formation, all twenty-five planes. We were a happy bunch diving in and out of the canyon that day. Lt. Bob Emmens was riding the rim, being a little more conservative than the rest of us.

Suddenly, he called us on the radio saying, "Listen to H.V. Kaltenborn, he has some very important news."

He gave us the call frequency to tune into with our radio compasses. This was our first word of the attack on Pearl Harbor. As if obeying a spoken order, the entire formation reassembled and somberly left the Grand Canyon and flew in formation straight for Pendleton, where we arrived shortly after dark. The Pendleton populace, noting the arrival of the bombers, assumed that the Army Air Force had sent them for the protection of the base, but it was really just a coincidence.

The next morning, we feverishly prepared for a possible Japanese coastal attack by readying fifteen planes for a mission over the ocean. Our squadron was the first to leave, but the weather was extremely bad. Three of us—Lt. Henry Schwane, Lt. Joe Skeldon, and myself—managed to penetrate the overcast and make it to the coast. All twelve of the other planes landed in different spots in various stages of emergency across the State of Washington and down the Columbia River Gorge.

Our plan was to fly off the mouth of the Columbia River and some 200 miles out to sea, patrolling for possible Japanese aircraft carriers operating in the area. In the early days of the war, we suspected anything and knew little or nothing. Out at sea I spotted what appeared to be a dead whale. We had heard previously that anything could be used as camouflage by Japanese submarines, so without further ado we took a bombing run on this dead whale. We never found out positively that it was anything but a whale. We landed in weather so severe that Lt. Ted Lawson, flying on another patrol, had to set his B-25 down on an Oregon beach.

When I met Schwane in the operations shack after our landing, I said, "Hank, I bombed a whale. What did you get?"

He said, "Oh, I bombed a submarine."

I did a double take and then realized that Henry was serious. He actually had bombed the first Japanese submarine in American waters in World War II.[1]

We returned to Pendleton the next day by flying along the river up the Columbia River Gorge. It was disconcerting to make such a flight because you could never tell when you might meet somebody coming in the opposite direction through the pea soup fog.

Dot was staying in a motel in the Pendleton area. She had a real scare a few days later when a plane, reported to be mine, crashed right next to the motel. She heard the plane coming, heard it just miss the building, and then heard it crash. It wasn't until evening that they determined the smoking mess was a transient B-26 and not my plane. By that time I was long overdue coming back from a coastal patrol. A wind of almost hurricane proportions had blown our plane far out to sea and we didn't return until late that night.

After numerous attempts at conducting submarine patrols from Pendleton, it was determined that Oregon and Washington's mountainous areas were too difficult to cross at that time of year and our squadron was sent to McChord Field at Tacoma.

Later during my assignment at McChord, one of my flying mates from another squadron of the Seventeenth Bombardment Group, Lt. Everett "Brick" Holstrom, successfully sank a Japanese submarine almost within the mouth of the Columbia River. He sighted it so suddenly that he had no opportunity to turn on the bombsite. He merely estimated where to drop the bomb, lucked out, and blew the submarine directly in half, and watched it sink. That was the second submarine victory for our Seventeenth Bombardment Group.

Dot Greening.

The weather made our patrols ineffective much of the time out of McChord, too, so we were ordered back to Pendleton. While there, I attended a gunnery camp at Spokane, Washington. Christmas 1941 with my wife in Spokane was wonderful and it turned out to be the last we were able to enjoy together for several years. ✪

NOTE

1. According to available Japanese records and other sources, however, it never has been proven conclusively that any Japanese submarines were sunk off the Washington-Oregon coast at this or any other time.

U.S. ARMY A.C. "SCATCAT."
TRANSPARENT PURSUIT P-99¼.

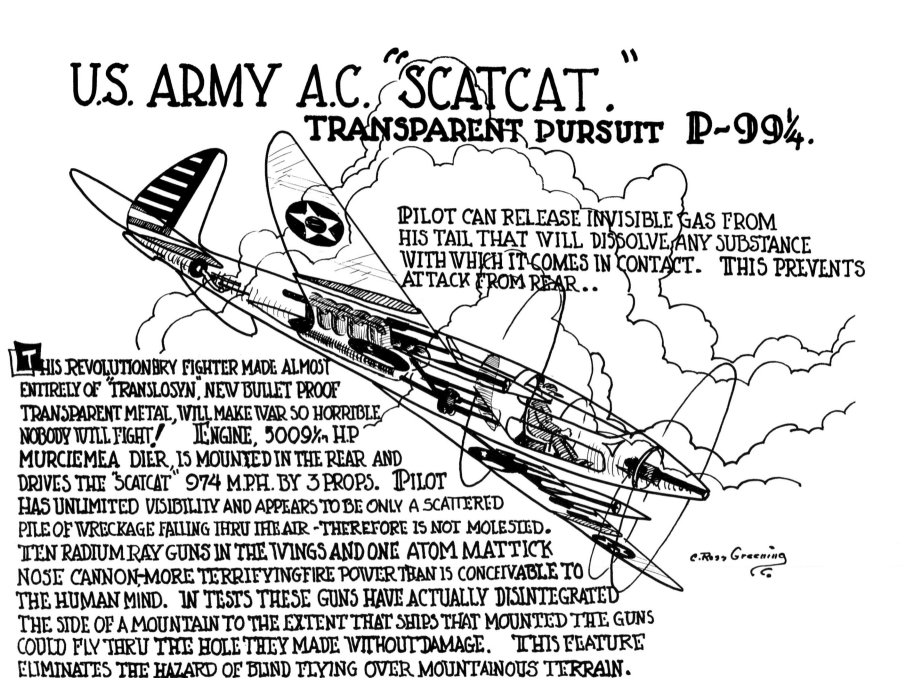

PILOT CAN RELEASE INVISIBLE GAS FROM HIS TAIL THAT WILL DISSOLVE ANY SUBSTANCE WITH WHICH IT COMES IN CONTACT. THIS PREVENTS ATTACK FROM REAR...

THIS REVOLUTIONARY FIGHTER MADE ALMOST ENTIRELY OF "TRANSLOSYN", NEW BULLET PROOF TRANSPARENT METAL, WILL MAKE WAR SO HORRIBLE NOBODY WILL FIGHT! ENGINE, 5009½m H.P MURCIEMEA DIER, IS MOUNTED IN THE REAR AND DRIVES THE "SCATCAT" 974 M.P.H. BY 3 PROPS. PILOT HAS UNLIMITED VISIBILITY AND APPEARS TO BE ONLY A SCATTERED PILE OF WRECKAGE FALLING THRU THE AIR - THEREFORE IS NOT MOLESTED. TEN RADIUM RAY GUNS IN THE WINGS AND ONE ATOM MATTICK NOSE CANNON - MORE TERRIFYING FIRE POWER THAN IS CONCEIVABLE TO THE HUMAN MIND. IN TESTS THESE GUNS HAVE ACTUALLY DISINTEGRATED THE SIDE OF A MOUNTAIN TO THE EXTENT THAT SHIPS THAT MOUNTED THE GUNS COULD FLY THRU THE HOLE THEY MADE WITHOUT DAMAGE. THIS FEATURE ELIMINATES THE HAZARD OF BLIND FLYING OVER MOUNTAINOUS TERRAIN.

C. Ross Greening

CHAPTER TWO

HOOKING UP WITH DOOLITTLE

After completing gunnery school in Spokane, I was offered a higher position to fly B-25s in one of the cadres being organized from the Eighty-ninth and other squadrons of the Seventeenth Group. We were transferred to Columbia, South Carolina. By this time we were two months into the war and things were not going well for us in the Pacific. Pearl Harbor had been attacked, Wake and Guam had fallen, and the Philippines were taking a beating. The Japanese were steamrolling the Allies out of the Pacific.

The Seventeenth Bombardment Group was well trained in B-25s, having been through a year of maneuvers. We were one of the first bomb groups to fly this aircraft. We learned that Capt. David Jones and other men had been diverted, in their flight to Columbia, to have special modifications made to their planes at Minneapolis Mid-Continent Airlines. We didn't know it, of course, but this was just the first step in an important assignment for us.

The remainder of us were billeted in a tent city at the airport in Columbia. One day, I was talking to Maj. Jack Hilger when a B-25 flew over the field in a very distinctive manner, like the way Alexander Seversky had flown P-35s and P-43s in exhibition flights. This B-25 peeled off over the airstrip, made a sharp nip-up, and landed on the runway in front of where Jack and I stood.

I recall saying that whoever that was, he sure was an excellent pilot.

That pilot proved to be Jimmy Doolittle. We all had heard about him and admired him immensely. Maj. Hilger had introduced Lt. Col. Doolittle to the group when Lt. Bob Emmens and I were out on a flight. Doolittle was visiting the Seventeenth Bombardment Group to ask for volunteers for a very hazardous mission. He could not say what the nature of the mission was. When Emmens and I returned from our flight, we learned that the entire complement of volunteers already had been picked. We were extremely disappointed at not having had a chance to volunteer.

Seeing our long faces, Maj. Hilger asked us if we would like to assist as training specialists even though we couldn't go on the mission. We agreed and I found myself at Eglin Field in the Florida panhandle shortly thereafter, getting the armaments for the B-25s arranged for the mission. My wife was able to join me and we stayed in the Valparaiso Inn with the rest of the crew and their wives, where we had a delightful time while our unit trained.

Some time later, Doolittle announced in the operations shack that the bombing mission would be dangerous and it was doubtful if we would get back alive. Shortly thereafter, I was approached by Lt. Kenneth Reddy, who said he had a personal problem. He was concerned because the pilot of his plane wanted to get out of the mission some way, even if it meant injuring himself. Lt. Reddy wanted to know what he should do. I told him that I would take care of it.

I informed Doolittle that I wished to replace the pilot. That's how I became the pilot and flight leader of plane #40-2249 with Lt. Reddy, Bowie, Texas, as co-pilot. Making up the rest of our crew were Staff Sgt. Bill Birch of Long Beach, California, as bombardier; Sgt. Melvin Gardner from Lynden, Arizona, crew chief and gunner; and Lt. Frank Kappeler of the San Francisco Bay area, navigator. It was a good crew, and a combination hard to beat. Our plane was in poor condition by this time, but lots of hard work soon made it one of the best in the line. We named it the "*Hari Kari-er*" and an insignia of a naked angel carrying a bomb was painted on the fuselage. It attracted attention every place we stopped.

During the days following the attack on Pearl Harbor, there was much discussion in the press about how the United States should bomb Tokyo in retaliation. Large sums of money were offered to the first individuals to carry out such a raid. The amounts of cash mentioned in various newspapers throughout the country varied from a few hundred thousand to a million dollars. (After the raid, the offers mysteriously disappeared but, of course, we wouldn't have taken them anyway.)

It never occurred to me that I might be involved in such an action until Doolittle notified a few of us that our top secret mission was to bomb Japan. Among those told included Capt. Edward "Ski" York, the operations officer for the entire group; Maj. John Hilger, the executive officer under Doolittle (who was the commander); Capt. David Jones, the navigation officer responsible for information about targets in Japan; Lt. Travis Hoover, the supply officer; and myself, the armament officer.

Later, I learned that a naval officer had conceived the previously unheard idea of launching Army Air Force bombers from an aircraft carrier in a surprise attack on Japan. From the early days of the war, President Franklin Roosevelt had wanted direct military action conducted against the Japanese homeland in response to the Pearl Harbor raid. A secret

study followed to determine whether it could be accomplished. The study considered B-18s, B-23s, B-25s, B-26s, and others as possible aircraft to be flown on the mission. It didn't take long to determine that the B-25 was the aircraft to use because of its short takeoff capability, long range, and relatively good bomb carrying capacity. In January 1942, the Navy's chief, Admiral King, and the Army Air Corps' General Arnold examined the plan and came to agreement that it could be carried out.

By launching from a carrier 400 miles off the Japanese coast, the B-25s could attack the main industrial centers of Japan and then continue to either

Lt. Charles Ross Greening.

Russia, the Chinese mainland, or ditch at sea. It was hoped that a successful raid would reduce Japanese morale while increasing American spirits. The psychological aspects of the bombing were, of course, the primary goal, but planners also hoped that the destruction of specific targets and the resulting confusion would slow down Japanese industrial production. They further hoped that the raid would cause Japan's leaders to recall combat aircraft being used against the hard-pressed Allies in the South Pacific and reassign them to defending the homeland. Except for the few of us who had to know what the mission was in order to plan it, the rest of the men had no knowledge about the nature of the operation during our training, other than that it would be particularly hazardous.

We conducted all of our training at Eglin Field. The newly commissioned aircraft carrier, *Hornet*, was ordered to take part in the mission by carrying the B-25s on its deck. Our planes had flown in the Louisiana and Carolina maneuvers in 1941 and were somewhat beaten up from that activity. They were not equipped for aerial combat and required special adaptations for the upcoming mission.

The details of the modifications are contained in a special study I prepared for the Armed Forces Staff College titled "The First Joint Action," since this was the first joint mission conducted by the Army Air Force and the Navy. Included among the many modifications was the installation of special fuel tanks. One tank with a bullet-sealing liner was mounted in the top part of the bomb bay. Another tank—a large rubber envelope—was placed in what normally was a crawl way in the bomb bay. This rubber envelope, when emptied of gasoline, could be deflated and folded, so crewmen could go back and forth between the front and back parts of the aircraft. Later, we put in another gas tank in place of the bottom turret, which was removed because the guns would be useless in a low altitude attack. We also had bullet-sealing wing tanks.

The B-25s carried an average total of 1,141 gallons of gasoline, of which, we figured 1,100 gallons would be available for use. We trained by flying from Eglin Field to Fort Myers, Florida, then across the Gulf of Mexico to Houston, Texas, and then back to Eglin Field, which we presumed to be a distance of 1,900 miles. We figured we needed to fly at least 1,900 miles to accomplish the mission satisfactorily. Each of the aircraft had to have its compass "swung," instruments calibrated, worn equipment replaced, and blast plates installed by the gun turrets so gunners wouldn't blow off the sides of the aircraft when firing the guns.

In many cases, the gun turrets were installed at Eglin. When we provided specifications to the Eglin Field people, they told us it would take approximately one month to modify each of the twenty-four aircraft. Doolittle informed them that wasn't good enough. He said he would give them less than a month to modify all of the planes. Due to his careful planning and constant drive and leadership, the Eglin staff was able to modify all of the aircraft on time.

There were a number of peacetime regulations that gave us problems. We were training out over the ocean with up to 90 percent of our fuel exhausted, considerably out of range of radio or rescue, and at an altitude much lower than what was permitted. This all was against regulations. We received repeated complaints from the base commander, who was not allowed to know anything about our secret mission. He visited daily to complain about our group's violations. Since we couldn't tell him anything, we continued our training as we saw fit. Finally we decided to take him on a low altitude flight. We skipped over the waves for several hundred miles, ran up and down the beaches, and simulated attacks on small villages in Florida. The base officer was so excited by this thrilling type of flying that he completely forgot about the complaints and wanted to go on future flights.

For practice takeoffs, there were a couple of outlying airstrips marked with carefully measured lines. These lines replicated the distance required for a B-25 to successfully lift off from a carrier's deck. A Navy airman, Lt. Henry Miller from the Pensacola Naval Base, was assigned to our group as a liaison officer. He assisted us by explaining Navy procedures and protocol, and described the physical features of a carrier. We took our planes out daily to the outlying airstrips and practiced short takeoffs. Using a tape measure and stopwatch, with observers both in the aircraft and on the ground, we recorded the exact number of feet, wind velocity, load condition, and air speed required to get a B-25 off a carrier deck. We measured and recorded every aspect that we could

in order to launch a plane into the air sooner and more efficiently.

Only two accidents occurred during practice. An engine on Lt. James Bates's B-25 developed problems during liftoff. Fortunately, he was able to land safely. However, the wheels were partially retracted and the plane came in on its belly. The Navy's Lt. Miller was aboard, but it didn't frighten him any more than it did the rest of the crew. Another plane piloted by Lt. Dick Joyce was lost when its nose wheel folded up while taxiing in after landing at Houston, Texas.

Markers were set up in the bay near Eglin Field to give us definite mileage fixes so we could calibrate our airspeed indicators. We swung our compasses and dropped a number of bombs at a practice range. Some of us, including Doolittle, released our first live bombs during this training.

According to the plan we envisioned, we needed to bomb targets from an extremely low altitude. Our planes, however, were equipped with the Norden bombsight, which was designed to operate efficiently at 4,000 feet or higher. The Norden sight could be used at lower altitudes, but not with its automatic features. Furthermore, it lost its effectiveness below 4,000 feet during the extreme maneuvering of a short bomb run. It was expensive too, costing over $10,000 each, and was highly classified. We didn't want to risk having it fall into Japanese hands.

As a result, I decided we needed a substitute (see page 28). As the mission's armament officer, I set about designing a new bombsight specifically for this mission, one that could be effective at altitudes of 100 to 1,500 feet. Sgt. Edwin Bain, my assistant technician, and I gave this problem a lot of thought. We obtained scrap Dural aluminum. First we made drawings and then at the shop cut a 7" x 7" quadrangle to install on the Norden mount. We inscribed a 90-degree arc facing forward with markings 10 degrees apart. On this quadrangle we fixed a vertical 5 1/4" x 7 1/4" piece of aluminum. This had a rounded top and it pivoted horizontally on the quadrangle plate. There needed to be a pointer to

work with the front arc so that a relative directional bearing could be obtained. Thus, in the upper rear quadrant of the upright piece, we marked off another 90-degree arc so we could get an up-and-down slant angle. The attached sighting bar on this vertical plate was a piece of right angle aluminum with a simple V notch for the rear sight, and a pointed front sight that would fill the V just like a rifle sight—a crude one.

Sgt. Bain and I thought it would work, but because it was so simple we couldn't be sure. All the bombardier had to do was pivot the horizontal plane and tell his pilot on intercom how many degrees right or left to steer to line up on the target. The gun sight, of course, was aimed from the bombardier's window at the front of the plane.

Later, we made improvements by connecting the gun sight to the remaining linkages that served the Norden sight. This permitted a bombardier to give course directions to a pilot through the PDI (Pilot Direction Indicator) instrument without relying on voice communication. The turning of the sight either right or left by means of a handle would deflect the PDI needle to the right or left, directing the pilot to follow the prescribed heading. With a B-25 on an attack course, all the bombardier needed to know was the plane's speed and altitude to set the vertical angle of the gun sight. When the target came into his lined-up bead, the bombardier prepared to "pickle off" his bombs.

All a bombardier did next was set a dropping angle taken from a series of tables fastened to the Norden bombsight base. It was a double drift attachment hooked onto the base, which permitted us to determine proper dropping angles for any sized bomb, at any altitude, in any wind conditions, and at any ground speed. This was all computed automatically once the wind speed was known. A bombardier only needed to set the dropping angle on the vertical plate, then aim the bombsight in the direction of the target just like he would a gun. As the airplane flew to the target, of course, he would have to raise the tail of the sight to keep it on the target. As it contacted the stop or dropping angle on the vertical plate, the bombardier released a bomb, generally with good results. The bombsight was named the "Mark Twain" in reference to the "lead line" depth finder used on the Mississippi River paddle wheelers in bygone days.

I helped demonstrate this crude sight to Doolittle on his first bombing run. Kenneth Reddy served as co-pilot. Initially, the bombardier used the Norden bombsight. Being in the same aircraft with Doolittle, he was nervous and made a mistake with the Norden sight, forgetting to raise the forward vision prism when dropping the bombs. Consequently, the bombs fell almost a mile short of the target. We made a couple of additional runs and the bombardier came reasonably close, but only with considerable manipulation of the bombsight and with some confusion in the cockpit.

For the test of the "Mark Twain" we substituted co-pilot Ken Reddy for the bombardier. Reddy had never dropped a bomb in his life. He sighted the Mark Twain on the shack we used as the target, looked at the double drift indicator to get his drift angle, and aimed the gadget as if he were shooting a gun. We must have built a certain amount of luck into the sight along with its simplicity because Reddy hit the shack squarely on the nose with his first bomb. Then to prove it wasn't an accident, he hit close to the target on the next two runs. Based on our testing, Doolittle made the decision to remove the Norden sights from all of the planes and replace them with the Mark Twain. We later determined that the materials for each of these homemade sights cost approximately 20 cents.

We planned to destroy any of our planes that might land or be forced down in enemy territory. Small, incendiary bombs were issued that could ignite a plane and cause its destruction. Security was a primary concern throughout the training and the mission. It was decided that complete radio silence was necessary, and we were trained to remove the transmitters and coils from the command sets. They wouldn't be replaced until after bombing the Japanese main-

Ross with crew in pre-war days.

land when we needed to communicate with each other and the landing sites. The sending of unintentional broadcasts when pilots thought they were only on intercom had given away aircraft before.

A camera was installed in each plane to take frames at set intervals and in various directions to pictorially record the targets as they were bombed. (Regretfully, as it turned out, little film was recovered from the mission. I had a personal 8-MM movie camera and took twenty-five feet of film during the raid, but this too was lost. It is unfortunate that we weren't able to retain better photo coverage of the attack.)

For special emergencies, each crewman was issued a pint bottle of whiskey in addition to other items such as canteens, hatchets, and weapons. That bottle, I believe, was the one thing each of the boys took with them later when bailing out. For security, we did not brief the crews about targets until after they were aboard the *Hornet*. Even our wives remained uninformed about the real purpose of the mission. They were told that we were ferrying planes to an undisclosed destination and we would be back in about six weeks.

Our times at the Valparaiso Inn during training were good ones even though it was a beaten up old building. It was a fine place to spend those last days with our wives. Whenever one of the lads was finishing his flight for the day, you could be sure he would buzz the Valparaiso to raise the shingles a bit just before landing at Eglin. It was against regulations, but in those days we figured rules were only made to be broken. The plan was to train all of the crews even though only a certain percentage would actually fly on the mission. Almost all of the men were taken aboard the *Hornet* for security reasons. The extra airmen would serve as replacements if needed.

There was only one possible breach of security that I knew about during our training in Florida. On Dot's bus trip to Eglin, there was a middle-aged woman who was interested in just about everyone on the bus, especially a sergeant from our crew. This didn't cause any suspicion at the time because many people were curious about our training at Eglin. Later, when we were having dinner at a little steakhouse on the highway, Dot recognized her again. This time she was questioning other members of our outfit in a suspicious manner. I left, went to the base, contacted the FBI, and arranged to have her and the sergeant she was questioning put in the local clink until it could be determined if she was a security risk. Later, she was removed from the base and told not to cause any difficulty in the future. To my knowledge, she was not a subversive agent, just someone using bad judgement.

There was another security slip-up later in San Francisco when we were preparing to leave on the *Hornet*. A Navy serviceman on shore leave approached a news correspondent and said he could provide details about an intended raid on Tokyo for the right fee. Fortunately, the correspondent was patriotic and appreciated the need for security. He refused the offer and threatened to beat the head off the sailor if he told others. The correspondent reported this incident to the Navy. I don't think the story ever leaked out, and I don't know how the sailor got his information.

Our wives obviously were quite concerned about the mission and it was fairly risky having them with us at Eglin Field. Since this was our first combat mission, and some thought it might be our last, I am glad we were given this privilege of allowing our wives to be with us. At night, we gathered in the dining room and dance hall at Eglin. We had drinks and good food and enjoyed life as much as we could.

Some of us took a fishing trip far out in the Gulf of Mexico. We discovered, when we arrived at the fishing spot, that we had forgotten all of the fishing gear. Fortunately, we had remembered to bring enough beer, whisky, and music to have a wonderful party and enjoy some swimming. Some of the other crews flying that day decided to simulate a low altitude bombing attack against merchant shipping, using our boat as the prime target. Several of our boys dived overboard to escape the "attacks." Believe me, facing one of those low altitude runs wasn't something you could take lightly.

After several weeks of training, twenty-two crews left Eglin in the latter part of March 1942, with everything on the B-25s in readiness except for having the compasses swung. Later during the mission, we would regret not having done this.

Our destination was McClellan Field at Sacramento, California, where final modifications were to be made to the planes and the last training missions would be conducted. Meanwhile, the *Hornet* was anchoring at Alameda Naval Air Station across the bay from San Francisco. The trip from

Eglin to Sacramento was supposed to be non-stop in order to make a last gas check on our B-25s, but most of the planes had to land at Kelly Field, Texas, to avoid foul weather, while Doolittle put down at Biggs Field near El Paso. (After the Tokyo raid, we learned that there was one unreported landing. Lt. Bob Gray put down on a Texas highway next to his home, stopping just long enough to see his folks.)

When we set out again, the trip west from Texas to Sacramento proved interesting because of the special war-time security regulations regarding weather reporting, radio transmissions, and landing field lights. We needed a code word to receive weather information. We encountered bad weather from El Paso westward. Three ships in our flight went directly over Mt. Whitney, but couldn't see it in the clouds. The Sacramento valley was entirely fogged in, and we couldn't determine what the ceiling was under the mist. We made radio calls, but were not given weather stats because we didn't know the code.

When we arrived in the Sacramento vicinity, we asked the tower operator just to tell us if we could get under the ceiling, without disclosing any information that could be intercepted by the enemy. He thought it could be safely done, so we dropped down only to discover that they wouldn't turn on the runway lights for security reasons. The entire coast was blacked out that night due to the threat of enemy submarines. By flying close to the ground and flashing the landing lights, I was able to pick out the runway and landed first. I taxied around so the other planes could see at least that much of the runway from my lights. I thought these security regulations were ridiculous. The possible loss of our aircraft and crewmen could have been worse than any damage a submarine might have inflicted, especially as far inland as Sacramento.

We were scheduled to have a final engineering check done at Sacramento's McClellan Field, which just had started operating as a depot for planes embarking for overseas combat duty. The base's systems were not completely established when we arrived. Just before leaving Eglin, it had been determined that we needed some extra guns and they had been ordered for Sacramento, as well as new propellers for all of the planes. The old props were worn and out of balance, and new ones would provide added efficiency for the long mission. My machine flew at 225 miles an hour with the old propellers. With new props and polishing up the plane a bit, I got 275 mph with the same power settings. Other modifications were planned as well.

The first upgraded and checked-out planes made practice takeoffs at a remote airfield up the valley near Williams, while the rest of us remained in Sacramento. The McClellan Field personnel insisted that they had to dismantle our engines, take everything apart, and check plugs and carburetors, because that was base procedure. This was unnecessary because we already had done this, and besides, we had carefully calibrated the settings for most efficiency in a long flight. We finally moved our own maintenance personnel in, and made the base crews work under our crew chief's supervision, to the extreme dismay of the base commander.

During off-hours before shipping out, we spent a good deal of our last days at the Senator Hotel and a few bars and nightclubs in Sacramento. One night, Davy Jones, Ski York, and I saw an old gentleman sound asleep in the hotel lobby near the door. Davy thought he should give the fellow an old fashioned hot foot, so he stuck a match in the toe of the man's shoe between the top leather and sole, and lit it. There was no reaction from the old boy, so Davy did it again, in both shoes. Again no reaction, so he put an entire matchbook in the sole and lit it. It went off with a blaze.

Just then, a lady who had been watching the prank said indignantly, "Why don't you leave this old man alone!"

Immediately the man opened his eyes in a bit of a drunken stupor, and said, "Go on, you ol 'bat, leave these guys alone. Let them have their fun," and then went back to sleep.

"Jungle Jim" Hallmark, one of our pilots, had his own sort of fun at the Senator Hotel. After cashing his per diem check, he went to his sixth floor room and pitched one-dollar bills out the window to the street below. Dean took great delight in watching people pick them up, sneak the bills into a pocket, and scurry off for fear someone was watching. Sometimes he would yell down for them to return the bills. They immediately ran off and tried to lose themselves in the crowd. He was having his fun in a rather expensive way.

On April 1, 1942, we were ordered to fly to Alameda where the planes would be loaded aboard the *Hornet*. After landing, we would be told which planes would be taken aboard and which would be left behind. Prior to departing from Sacramento, the usual paperwork was presented to each pilot for comments regarding aircraft maintenance performed at the base. The ceiling was only about 800 feet with a dense overcast, so we also needed an instrument clearance.

Jack Hilger and I were standing nearby when an officer from base operations presented a maintenance form to Doolittle. In broad, large letters, Doolittle wrote "Lousy" diagonally across the form.

The officer said, "Col. Doolittle, you can't make a remark like this. I won't sign your clearance unless you make this thing out in detail."

Doolittle replied, "Well, you can take your information and your clearance. I'm going to leave clearance or not, as I've got a very important engagement in Alameda."

He turned on his heel, climbed aboard his plane, and took off. When Doolittle's B-25 left the runway, he pulled straight up into the overcast and disappeared. A few seconds lapsed, then we heard the engines wind up as he started a tremendous dive. Doolittle came back down through the overcast and executed an excellent buzz along the hangar line, right in front of the operations officer's eyes, then pulled back up into the overcast and disappeared in the direction of Alameda.

The officer turned to Hilger and me, saying, "Who the heck is that guy? He is certainly headed for a lot of trouble."

Hilger and I didn't disagree with him.

The rest of our planes began departing for Alameda as fast as they could get off the ground. Unfortunately, I couldn't get an engine started. When we examined it, we discovered that the Sacramento maintenance crews had failed to tighten the spark plugs beyond finger tight, consequently the cylinders were not creating any compression. We had to de-cowl, get wrenches, and tighten the plugs. This held us up for an hour and a half. We were panicking, feeling that we would be left behind, and we were mad at the maintenance men.

After the rest of the B-25s left, all of which repeated our leader's performance and buzzed the field, I was the recipient of the operation officer's ire. He said an unpleasant fate would befall our entire group as a result of our flagrant violation of operation and flying orders.

After taking off, I buzzed the field too. ✪

CHAPTER THREE

ABOARD THE USS "HORNET"

When I circled the field at Alameda and first sighted the USS *Hornet* at the dock, she looked about as big as a postage stamp. We were the last ones hoisted aboard, and the *Hornet* moved out into San Francisco harbor for the night. That evening, Ski York, Davy Jones, and I went on leave in San Francisco. We returned to the carrier early the next morning, April 2, 1942. We knew that the next time we touched land it would be in China or as prisoners of war in Japan, unless something even more drastic happened to us. Sixteen crews and their planes were selected to launch from the carrier, but all of the crews that had trained and the support personnel were put aboard for security reasons, and as replacements if needed.

It was a thrill when the *Hornet* set out. Laden with sixteen Army Air Force bombers, she sailed under both of the San Francisco bridges and headed for the open sea, escorted by two cruisers, four destroyers, an oiler, two PBY flying boats, and a blimp. A mission of this type never had been attempted before—the record number of "firsts" we were attempting quite chilled our blood.

At Barksdale Field, Louisana, Ross takes Dot on her first airplane ride, early 1938.

By way of background, the *Hornet* had been commissioned in late 1941, with Captain Marc Mitscher as skipper. Some key members of the staff included Commander George Henderson, executive officer; Commander Pat Creehan, chief engineer; Commander Eakers, navigator; Commander James W. Smith, gunnery officer; Lt. Commander Stanhope Ring, director of the *Hornet*'s air group; Lt. Commander Samuel Mitchell, CO of Fighter Squadron 8; Lt. Commander "Gus" Widhelm and Lt. Commander Alfred Tucker of the dive-bombing squadrons; and Lt. Commander John Waldron and Ensign George Gay of Torpedo Squadron 8. Two months later, Gay would be the sole survivor of the *Hornet*'s fifteen torpedo bombers that attacked Japanese carriers during the Battle of Midway on June 4, 1942.

Shortly after one of the *Hornet*'s shakedown cruises, she had returned to Norfolk, Virginia, where two B-25 bombers were loaded aboard by crane. She then sailed out to sea and the B-25s were placed at the end of the flight deck, allowing for a maximum distance for takeoff. Army pilots

NOT AS BRIEFED *"In November 1943, a flight of P-40 Warhawks started 'beating up' a German munitions train caught unloading at a siding in north Italy. After four ships had made strafing passes, fourteen cars exploded, destroying the fifth P-40 making his attack. The explosion was so great it rocked violently Lt. Steve Turner's ship at thirty-five hundred feet. It was such incidents as this for which there could be no briefing. The unknown quantity, the uncertain element in every aerial combat episode was always summed up afterwards, 'not as briefed.' Lt. Turner of Lancaster, Massachusetts, later became a P.O.W. as a result of a combat fight over Yugoslavia."* Not as Briefed

boarded the planes, successfully launched them, and flew to Norfolk. The *Hornet* remained in Virginia for final arrangements, then sailed in company with a convoy to the Panama Canal. From there, the carrier proceeded alone, training flight crews. By the end of March, she entered San Francisco Bay and hardly had docked when our group of B-25s started appearing. Sixteen planes were towed from the airfield to the dock and hoisted aboard.

As we rolled over the waves, our mission was carefully studied and we were constantly briefed. Targets were assigned and every eventuality was considered, so we had a fair idea of what to expect. The Navy would provide weather forecasts and launch us no further out than 600 nautical miles from Japan. We all felt ready to go and our morale was high. None of us had ever been in combat before; it all would be new to us. Doolittle planned to leave a couple of hours early, and in the dark set fire to Tokyo's Shiba ward, in order to serve as a beacon for our planes attacking later in the night. The Navy assured us that we would be taken to within 400 or possibly 500 miles from Japan. A greater distance would significantly reduce our chances of reaching airstrips near Chuchou and elsewhere in eastern China, where preparations were being made to receive us.

Davy Jones was quartered with Gus Widhelm, the CO of one of the Navy's dive-bomber squadrons. Gus had a marvelous record collection, providing many evenings of entertainment for those of us liking music. At the time, however, Gus didn't do much listening to the record collection himself because he had a lot of new blood on board for his poker games. By the time we launched our attack, he had emptied the wallets of most of the Army flyers who played poker. The Army rear guard left aboard the carrier, however, later recouped some of Gus's winnings before arriving in Pearl Harbor—they won back $1,500 plus another $100. Sometimes there is justice. Unfortunately, those of us who went on the mission never had a chance to win back our losses.

I later saw Gus after the Tokyo raid and learned that when taking off on a mission, he let "Nearer My God to Thee" play continuously on his record player. On his last mission from the *Hornet* in the Battle of the Santa Cruz Islands in late October 1942—when the carrier went down—Gus's record player was on as the ship slid beneath the waves.

We studied the carrier's flight deck, its movements at sea, and the Navy air arm's procedures. We also researched twenty years of weather reports for the western Pacific, Japan, and China. Each day, we inspected our planes to insure that the salt air was not causing damage or rust, and every third day we "ran up" our engines. We only had one mechanical difficulty. During a "run up," one of Lt. Don Smith's engines developed a split washer. The washer's purpose was to separate the blower blade when shifting the blowers. Smith's engine was liable to fail, particularly if the blowers were shifted during the target run-in. This type of repair was supposed to be done by depot maintenance and was prohibited in field situations. Nevertheless, because of our predicament, we decided to fix it on the ship.

The Navy's maintenance men built an A-frame on the pitching deck of the carrier and lifted the heavy, 1,700 horse-power engine off the plane and took it below. The repair was a difficult task accomplished with the able assistance of the Navy. In the machine shop, new parts were made for the blower section and installed. The engine was remounted the day before we took off. Don Smith was the most worried man aboard, fearing his plane wouldn't be ready to go. If the repair hadn't been finished in time, his plane would have been pushed overboard, rather than leaving it on deck as an obstacle to the Navy's flight operations.

The submarines *Thresher* and *Trout*, occupying patrol stations in advance, sent valuable weather information to the task force. Northwest of Hawaii, the *Hornet* and its seven accompanying ships had been joined by the carrier *Enterprise* and two more cruisers, four destroyers, and an oiler. The *Enterprise* sent out daily scouting planes to prevent possible interception of our task force by the Japanese.

Watching the *Hornet* being refueled by the tanker *Cimarron* while under way proved interesting. On April 16, the first attempt had to be abandoned due to extremely heavy seas. Large cables had fastened the vessels together, but the rough seas snapped the lines like threads, which gave me a deep appreciation of the ocean's power.

The refueling was accomplished the next day just before a thirty-knot, gale force wind came up. I was standing on the *Hornet*'s stern looking down on the *Cimarron*'s afterdeck, when a large wave rose up and covered the *Cimarron* aft, washing a sailor overboard. The fellow was so close that it seemed I could almost reach out and grab him. A sailor on the *Cimarron* threw an additional life preserver

to the lad before he was too far out, but that was the best they could do. It was surprising to me that everyone promptly went about their business and seemingly forgot the poor lad lost overboard. I noticed later, however, that one of the destroyers put to and, by the time it was on the horizon to our stern, had stopped to pick the sailor up. I can't imagine he enjoyed the remainder of the voyage, because a destroyer pitches and rolls so much more violently and heavily than a tender does.

About this time, a special ceremony was conducted on deck. Some years earlier, the Japanese had awarded a number of medals to Americans, symbolizing Japan's everlasting friendship with the United States. Our ceremony, attended by all of the Army airmen and many Navy personnel, was for attaching the medals to a bomb to return them to the Japanese. Lt. Ted Lawson was the lucky one who got to drop that bomb. The friendship symbolized by those medals definitely had run out. There were men aboard the *Hornet* who had friends and relatives killed or injured in the Japanese attacks. They were allowed to write personal messages on the bombs. One of my crewmen had lost his brother. When he scrawled out a message, I had to turn away so he wouldn't see the tears in my eyes.

In the rough seas of April 17, the destroyers and the two tankers departed to await rendezvous with the main task force after the B-25s were launched. There was no announcement aboard ship, but it was obvious by the increased beat of the carrier's engines that the final dash to the launch point had begun. Our speed was twenty-seven knots, making for about a forty-knot wind on deck. To me, it seemed like a cyclone. Our intended launch day was April 21.

During the trip, there had been much speculation among a number of the boys about landing at alternate places to those designated in our plans. We noted, in particular, that Russia was closer to Japan than China. Russia, however, was not at war with Japan and had refused permission to let us land in the Vladivostok area. Already in

a death grip with invading German armies, the Russians feared Japanese reprisals. Several of us secretly concluded, however, that should we run into trouble or have insufficient gas to get to China, we might attempt landing in Russia, since the boss hadn't exactly said yet that we couldn't go there.

The final briefing on April 17 was held in the officers' dining room when Doolittle gave his last instructions. He made a final offer to anyone who might want to withdraw from the mission. Then he gave three warnings. The first was that no one could go to Russia. The second was that non-military targets, including the Temple of Heaven, were not to be bombed. And third, that this was the last briefing before takeoff. From this point on, we were to be ready to go as early as the evening of April 19.

In anticipation of our imminent departure, the B-25s were loaded with bombs, machine guns, ammunition, and essential equipment. Loading a 500-pound bomb on the deck of a pitching carrier was a new experience. Our planes were designed to be loaded on stable ground and the bomb hoists were adjusted from within the bomb bay. The bomb loader stood inside and put the shackles on as a bomb was hoisted into position. On a pitching carrier, however, it was hazardous because the loader's head was positioned between two 500-pound bombs shifting back and forth.

The gas tanks were ready for topping off shortly before takeoff. If filled before that time, the pitching of the ship would have spilled gasoline on the deck. All of the planes were stowed aft on the top deck, ready for takeoff. This meant, however, that many of the carrier's guns couldn't be used for anti-aircraft defense, and, of course, the *Hornet*'s own planes stowed below deck couldn't take off to protect her because our aircraft were in the way. The *Hornet* relied on the *Enterprise* and the other support vessels for protection until after the B-25s were launched.

Feelings ran high among the airmen. Some of the fellows not scheduled to go tried to offer money and bargained with those who were, hoping to change places. It didn't really matter, however, because Doolittle had selected the crews being sent and he was unlikely to allow changes.

Early in the morning darkness of April 18, radar unexpectedly picked up probable enemy patrol craft, but the task force changed course and apparently avoided contact. At 6 AM, just about daybreak, a patrol plane from the *Enterprise* sighted an enemy vessel. Then, at about 7:30 AM, a Japanese patrol craft came into view of the task force.

I left my stateroom to pass through one of the hangar doors onto the flight deck. I came outside just as the guns began firing. It was exciting to hear and see "real" fire for the first time. I observed a patrol vessel on the horizon surrounded by rising geysers of water. After several salvos, I saw the gunners hit dead center. We learned later that the vessel actually did report our presence to higher authority, but the report was doubted and a confirmation was requested. This was their undoing; there wasn't enough time to make a confirmation before the patrol craft was sunk. The *Enterprise*'s dive-bombers helped finish off the patrol vessel for a conclusive intercept and attacked others in the locality.

As the *Hornet* pitched and rolled, general quarters suddenly sounded and pandemonium broke loose. I thought, perhaps, we already had sailed to the 400-mile mark, but this proved incorrect. Our premature detection by patrol vessels probably had resulted in mainland Japanese command posts being alerted by radio.

Thus, by 8 AM when we least expected it, the call came over the loud speaker, "Army pilots, man your planes!"

I had been writing a letter to my wife and just had time to seal the envelope and hand it to a sailor. I thought it might be a drill, so I calmly took my things to the plane. When I heard the engines warming up, however, I knew this wasn't a practice run. The decision had been made to launch our bombers prematurely. I heard the bull horn signaling for our immediate departure. By previous agreement between the Naval and Air commands, the Army aircraft were either to be launched immediately or pushed overboard to clear the decks so the *Hornet* could defend herself with her guns and planes. The risk to the carriers from alerted Japanese air and naval forces was too great to proceed any closer to the mainland. I don't mind admitting that cold chills were running up and down my spine.

We scrambled to the planes. As mentioned, when I had reached the flight deck I heard the cannons of the cruiser to our left commence booming, firing at the target two or three miles away with deadly accuracy. It was raining slightly and the sea was extremely rough. The wind practically blew me aft to my plane. Airmen and sailors ran in all directions. Our boys scooted around collecting their bags and storing them in the aft sections of the aircraft. The carrier boys took their positions. It seemed unreal, but I was glad to be going. I was tense from waiting and a bit seasick. Getting airborne would relieve my seasickness if nothing else.

I believe the suddenness of the departure actually might have made the launch more successful than if we had taken off according to schedule. We forgot our queasy stomachs and the anxiety that gets to a man when anticipating danger. We were worked up to a feverish pitch by the abruptness of events and didn't have time to think about things. It was a testimony to our good training because we reacted the way we were supposed to.

I made my way to each of the aircraft to check the bombs, insuring that the arming wires were set and each crew had incendiary devices to destroy their aircraft if forced down in enemy territory. When I delivered an incendiary bomb to Doolittle's plane, I saw him standing in the navigator's compartment, his face quite set. He looked a bit pale, but very determined.

Just at that moment, Frank Kappeler, whom I sent to the bridge to check on our position, came to me and said, "Captain Greening, we are over 800 miles from Tokyo. I didn't know we were going to be this far away."

It was broad daylight, thus we had lost the advantage of attacking in the darkness, and we didn't have weather reports for our destinations. I told Doolittle what the distance was. He merely nodded his head and didn't say a word. He'd already given us our final briefing. It didn't take any more than a glance to realize that he had nothing more to say. He was ready for action and expected us to be ready too. I gave him an incendiary bomb. That was the last time I saw him until we met again in Chungking, China.

When handing Davy Jones an incendiary device, I saw he had a resigned, disgusted look on his face. He reported that a bomb bay tank had developed a leak and his plane was pouring gas onto the deck. Meanwhile, the aviation fuel in the carrier's supply line had been shut off in case of an enemy attack, so there was no way to top off his tank again. He was due to take off ahead of me since he was #5 and I was #11. I ran back and instructed the crew chief to take gas from my B-25 and carry the cans to Jones's plane. I thought I might be able to replenish my fuel with some more five-gallon tins. Fortunately, when our time came, the carrier's gas lines had been turned on again and we were able to top off our tanks and grab a few more five-gallon tins.

Engines were started only on the three planes in line immediately following the one that was taking off. As soon as one plane lifted off, another pilot in the line-up fired up his engines and waited to taxi out. Behind each of the wheels, a Navy man followed along with a set of chocks, held by long sticks so he wouldn't get too close to the propellers. The ship's navigator on the bridge displayed the true compass course of the carrier in large black numbers on cards.

When in the air, we could fly along the length of the carrier deck using a white line from stern to bow to determine drift and compensate for wind, and take a reading on our compasses to see if it checked out with the navigator's cards. During the voyage, we had noticed that our compasses gave erratic readings due to magnetic disturbances caused by the ship. We feared some of the compasses were permanently

out of alignment, but once airborne, we thought they were "fairly" accurate.

I'll never forget the sight of Doolittle's B-25 when it started its roll down the deck for takeoff. The flagman, standing on deck immediately to the left of the plane, was waving in a circular motion, telling the Boss to get his engines revved up. Doolittle's flaps were full down. The scream of those two engines, the excitement and urgency, made an incredible sight. I was lying face down on the wet deck, clutching tie-down plates to keep from being blown back by the terrific wind. When Doolittle's B-25 began to move, it seemed unreal. When it leaped into the air at a sickening angle, took the stiff wind in its teeth, and headed out over the water toward Tokyo, above all the noise you could hear men cheering on the bridge, the decks, and even in the B-25s. I had chills running up and down my spine from excitement.

It was a parting of good friends. Considering our circumstances, I don't think there was a man leaving who really believed he would complete the flight safely.

The props of planes not yet fired up were turning over slowly in the high wind. The *Hornet* ran at approximately 27 knots, facing into about a 25-knot wind—thus the air blew at approximately 52 knots over the deck. The planes only had to gain a speed of 20 more mph to become airborne. What we thought would be our most difficult hazard, the takeoff, turned out to be among the least of our problems. We had relatively little difficulty getting off the carrier deck. The biggest concern was when the carrier pitched and rolled, which caused a plane to cast from side to side. This could be corrected, however, with a slight use of the brake or rudder propeller. Two sets of wheel markers composed of sand and cork had been glued on the deck to provide traction for the wheels while the engines ran up. We thought that a wet deck might actually cause planes to slide from the force of the revved-up engines.

Doolittle's takeoff immediately proved to be a lesson for us. Even though it was successful, it was steep. This sort of

takeoff was planned, but since it hadn't been done on a carrier before, we didn't know how close to stalling this attitude would be. Lt. Miller, the Navy liaison officer, remained alongside the signalman for the rest of the takeoffs, signaling to us not to pull back on the wheels so hard. Because of the high wind, we could take off with more of a normal stance. The nose-high attitude of the second plane flown by Lt. Travis Hoover, however, was even more extreme than Col. Doolittle's, but he corrected before stalling. It was a concern for each of us as we left the deck.

Ted Lawson took off as #7. He put the flaps down, then pulled them back up, and in the excitement forgot to put them down again. We watched his plane disappear below the bow of the ship, then come waddling back up like some big bullfrog, right on the water ahead of the carrier.

When I taxied into position for takeoff as #11, it seemed to me that my right wing couldn't help but hit the carrier island. There was about seven feet of clearance. I'll admit I was tense. I could see many faces peering down from the bridge and navigation rail on the carrier's island. All of the crewmen whose aircraft hadn't been brought aboard were there. I wondered how many still were willing to change places with us now. We were 800 miles from Japan—twice the distance we had bargained for, and 200 more than was considered really feasible for the amount of fuel we carried.

The carrier's bow pitched more violently than I'd ever seen before. I heard later it even alarmed some of the veteran Navy aviators. When the pitch caused the front deck to drop down, the horizon disappeared and nothing but ocean was visible to me through the cockpit windows. Water splashed along the deck and the wind tugged at every control surface. When the flagman gave the rev-up signal, I pushed the throttles up to wide-open position and held the flaps full down, then held on for the go-ahead.

When the flag dropped, I released the brakes. Just at that moment, the carrier started a slight roll to the left, causing my plane to veer towards the left rail. I corrected this, keeping the left wheel on one of the two white lines used for alignment along the full length of the deck. With a force I hadn't experienced before, my B-25 seemed to rocket into the air about a hundred feet before the end of the deck. A terrific wind wash from the carrier's bow made the plane pitch up high, requiring a hard push forward on the stick to keep the nose down. This kept us from zooming on at the same uncomfortable angle that I had seen other planes do. Lt. Miller, who was standing by the flagman with a large blackboard, was warning us about it.

We intended, if possible, to have flights of three planes each join up to make the run in. My flight was composed of my plane, Lt. Bill Bower on the right, and Lt. Edgar McElroy on the left. As soon as the *Hari Kari-er* was airborne with flaps and wheels up, I made a slow turn to the right to pass back over the carrier, checking course and drift. I then proceeded at low altitude and speed so McElroy and Bower could catch up. They fell into position for the long flight to Japan.

On that April 18, 1942, morning, the launching order and times were: Lt. Col. James Doolittle at 8:20, Lt. Travis Hoover at 8:25, Lt. Robert Gray at 8:30, Lt. Everett Holstrom at 8:33, Capt. David Jones at 8:37, Lt. Dean Hallmark at 8:40, Lt. Ted Lawson at 8:43, Capt. Edward York at 8:46, Lt. Harold Watson at 8:50, Lt. Richard Joyce at 8:53, Capt. Ross Greening at 8:56, Lt. William Bower at 8:59, Lt. Edgar McElroy at 9:01, Maj. John Hilger at 9:07, Lt. Donald Smith at 9:15, and Lt. William Farrow at 9:19.

Unfortunately, when the last plane to depart was being moved into launching position, a Navy chock man slipped and fell. When he got up, the chock was not on the wheel and the plane rolled backward. The prop hit him and severed an arm. (It eventually was reported to me that the crew took up a sizeable collection for the maimed man.)

All sixteen planes had taken off in approximately one hour. Some intervals were only three minutes apart. We felt that wasn't too bad for pilots who had never done such a thing on a carrier before. ✪

MAYHEM FROM A MITCHELL *"Greening's own ship, Hari Kari-er, strafing a Jap patrol boat east of Honshu, April 18, 1942. Homing for China from Tokyo, numerous targets of opportunity were available on the Japanese sea. This was the first of three confirmed sunk by Col. Greening's crew. Three others were probables." The man running for the deckhouse also became a casualty of the Hari Kari-er's gunfire. Not as Briefed*

CHAPTER FOUR

ATTACK ON JAPAN

We flew right on the water, as low as possible to avoid detection. We weren't sure if the Japanese had air or sea patrols to protect the mainland. Actually, a lot of elements were uncertain concerning this mission. Much of our training had been conjecture—some based on previous experience, and some on a certain amount of deduction.

Doolittle had said his best estimate was that if we bombed Japan in the daytime, we could lose upwards of 50 percent of our aircraft. If we bombed at night, not as many would be lost. Consequently, we'd planned to arrive over Japan in darkness. Unfortunately, circumstances had forced us to take off early on the morning of April 18, meaning that we would be attacking almost at high noon when Japanese air activity would be at its greatest. It was obvious to me, and I am sure to the others, that we were in for a difficult time. We would be fortunate to get out of this mission alive.

While flying close to the deck out over the ocean and so far from the United States, everything seemed unreal. We only had the word of the Navy that we were nearing Japan. I felt I could wake up any minute and be in my bed at home. However, just enough reality was pressing in to force me to give up the idea that this was a dream. We relied on our reflexes, hoping that the weeks, months, and years of training for just this sort of thing would pull us through. None of us had been under fire before or in any combat situation, with the exception of Brick Holstrom's brief encounter with a Japanese submarine at the mouth of the Columbia River.

Plenty of things raced through our minds. We talked about some, and others we kept to ourselves. I've heard about people seeing a lifetime of events passing through their minds in just a few moments, but we had 4 1/2 hours to reflect on our lives. It was tough to concentrate on the flying we had to do.

From the information available, the staff had determined the best targets and which crews should attack specific sites. In most cases, however, the selection of targets was left up to the crews, who determined which places were most suitable to their particular talents. Thus, every plane had an assigned target, and each crew had been briefed about all aspects of the attack. Our crew, in plane #40-2249, had selected oil refineries at the Yokohama docks. This was largely on my recommendation because I had visited Japan in the summer of 1933 when I was a teenage seaman aboard the SS *President Cleveland*. The vessel had docked at Yokohama and I thought I could recognize the area. (As it turned out, I recognized nothing.)

As already mentioned, the mission's basic tactic had been that Doolittle would proceed alone and bomb a flammable section of Tokyo, creating a beacon in the night to help guide following planes to their targets. Obviously, we

SO SORRY, PLEASE *"This Mitchell, flown by Lt. Everett Holstrom of Tacoma, Wash., nailed the first credited sub victim of World War II near the mouth of the Columbia River, December 1941."* Not as Briefed

now would be attacking in broad daylight instead, but we instinctively implemented the rest of the plan. Doolittle was followed by Lt. Hoover's group of three planes, who would attack the northern part of Tokyo. A second flight of three B-25s led by Capt. Davy Jones would strike the central part of Tokyo, and a third flight under Capt. York would attack southern Tokyo and the north-central part of the bay area. My flight, the fourth set of three bombers, was scheduled to strike Yokohama and the Kosukan Naval Yard at the western side of Tokyo Bay, and not far from Tokyo itself. The fifth group led by Maj. Hilger planned to proceed south of Tokyo to the Nagoya vicinity, before splitting up to bomb Nagoya, Osaka, and Kobe.

Our planes were spread out over a fifty mile front to create the impression that there were more of us than there really were. By using these tactics, we hoped to delude enemy ground fire and air opposition. We also thought detection might be lessened if our aircraft were widely dispersed.

My flight passed so low over the ocean that at times it seemed we would drag our tails in the water. We flew just

above the waves, but occasionally rose to a few hundred feet to check drift and attempt to get a more accurate estimate of our arrival time over Japan. A merchant vessel some distance from our position seemed to recognize us as the enemy because it engaged in evasive maneuvers. Some crewmen later reported that they flew right over this vessel, but elected not to attack it because they wanted to put all of their bombs on the target areas.

When finally nearing Japan, we watched for landmarks, such as Mt. Fujiyama or Tokyo Bay, but without success. On approaching the coast, we spotted several sampans that may have been patrol boats. We did our best to stay low and away from them. I recognized the same smell from the mainland that I encountered when aboard the SS *President Cleveland*, nine years before.

I was surprised to see hills and small mountains at our landfall instead of the flat terrain we expected around Tokyo Bay. Most of the planes arrived over Japan about sixty miles north of where they had intended because our compasses were out of adjustment. McElroy took my wing signal and headed south. Bower dropped back slightly as he cut across toward a valley. My intention was to fly up this valley as close to the ground as possible, which would give us maximum protection from detection. I looked down at the first village we passed above at the shoreline. It remained peaceful and few of the occupants seemed interested in our planes; some people looked up and waved as we flew by. We rose up over a hill to try and see Tokyo Bay. On the downhill side,

Greening and Sgt. Edwin V. Bain developed the "Mark Twain" bombsight for the Doolittle raid. Here a replica is visible in the bombardier's nose position of a B-25 on display at the Air Force Museum, Wright-Patterson AFB, Dayton, Ohio. Karen Driscoll

Bower continued on while I turned to the left to search out our target.

It's difficult enough to fly under 500 feet in peacetime, but even more so when you're excited, in strange terrain, and fearing for your life. It's hard to think clearly and do things rationally and deliberately.

Ken Reddy, my co-pilot, made a marvelous suggestion. "Capt. Greening, let's be nonchalant about this… What do you say we have a sandwich? …We can say when we go home 'We were eating a sandwich when we were bombing Tokyo.'"

I took a bite of sandwich.

That bite went unchewed and unswallowed until well after the bomb run and we were flying toward China.

During the run in, we constantly monitored the radio compass frequencies hoping to get a navigation fix on a Tokyo broadcast. Several of our other boys reported hearing a broadcast in English that claimed Japan was invulnerable to attack. That transmission was suddenly cut off when our bombs hit the targets. The Japanese wanted to avoid having their radio broadcasts serving as navigation beacons for American planes.

I don't think I'd ever flown so low in my life, dodging down creek beds and ducking between trees rather than going over them. I'm not sure it was necessary, but it gave a sense of security. Those minutes seemed like hours.

We approached an airfield full of training planes. I was just about to ask Sgt. Birch, our bombardier, to fire the nose gun at these aircraft, which were parked in two beautiful lines. All were training aircraft except for some fighters at either end. As we started our pass over the field, I suddenly realized the foolishness of opening fire. It would be a cinch to give us away and alert the Japanese about our boys com-

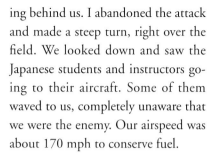

ing behind us. I abandoned the attack and made a steep turn, right over the field. We looked down and saw the Japanese students and instructors going to their aircraft. Some of them waved to us, completely unaware that we were the enemy. Our airspeed was about 170 mph to conserve fuel.

Suddenly, I heard Sgt. Gardner firing in the top turret. I started to yell at him for test-firing his guns, which would give us away. I looked out of my right window past Ken Reddy and saw the first of four Japanese fighters pass our wing tip. The fighter was on fire. Gardner had scored a direct hit. About that time a second plane passed by. None of the fighters were painted except for their insignia. They fired six guns forward and apparently used incendiary bullets, leaving long lines of white smoke at each burst. The fighters didn't approach our tail. During training, I had directed that a set of dummy "guns" be installed in each B-25's tail, since we were vulnerable to attack from behind. These stout wooden sticks appeared larger than the twin .50 caliber machine guns in the top turret. I think the Japanese pilots wanted to avoid them.

We were extremely excited. Kappeler, the navigator, wrote little notes like mad to tell us what was happening, since Reddy and I couldn't see to the rear or hear him when he yelled at us. I think he tried to say they were making passes from one side to the other. Reddy and I had the engines wide open. Soon, a second fighter crashed and burned after falling under Gardner's deadly aim. This discouraged the other two, and they started dropping back out of range.

Unfortunately, Gardner didn't hold fire and started using up ammunition faster than we could afford. Soon, a gun temporarily jammed and the turret motors burned out from continuous use. The back of the plane filled with smoke and

"My sister, Shirley, flew from Hawaii to San Francisco in this China Clipper when our dad died in 1940. San Francisco was socked in with fog and the pilot finally landed on the water after ducking through a hole in the fog and then flew under the Golden Gate Bridge."

Self portrait.

the turret froze in position. The fighters noticed this and pressed the attack again. We couldn't defend ourselves and would be shot down unless we took evasive action or went faster than the 275 mph we now were going. I flew as low as possible. If they got beneath us, we would be duck soup because our lower guns had been removed for the mission.

The *Hari Kari-er* was east of the Tokyo area by this time. I am not sure if a target I identified off in the distance was the one we were supposed to attack. I wanted to drop the bombs soon, to reduce weight and allow the plane to gain speed. I tried to be composed (still with that bite of sandwich in my mouth). I saw two columns of smoke coming from where the fighters had crashed and looked back to take pictures with my movie camera. I shot a few feet of film, but wasn't able to hold the camera steady. Kappeler was a little

JIMMY LEADS THE WAY *"Lt. Col. James H. Doolittle taking off Number One from the U.S. aircraft carrier Hornet, April 18, 1942, for the first raid on Tokyo… Months of practice paid off in a successful mission. No ships were lost over the targets… although eight of the members of two crews were captured in China after crash landing, three members of which were later executed by the Japanese Army and one died of disease in a prisoner of war camp."* Not as Briefed

I Like To See That Rising Sun Go Down *"A-20 Bostons skip-bombing two Jap transports in the South Pacific. Extremely effective against shipping, this perilous pastime requires cool, pre-determined courage on the part of the pilot; this bomb-run takes him into the mouth and down the barrel of every anti-aircraft gun on the target."* Not as Briefed

dubious about what I was doing. He could see the fighters coming in to attack, but Reddy and I, covered from behind by protective armor plates, weren't able to see them. To make it clear to me, Kappeler reached around the armor plating and grabbed me by either ear to forcibly turn my head in the direction of the fighters. Considering how low we were to the deck, all of this was pretty hazardous.

We cleared the treetops by only a matter of feet or possibly inches, and passed alongside some taller ones. Ahead were high-tension power lines. In the excitement of the moment, I thought if I flew under the power lines the fighters might not notice them, follow us, and hit the lines. I succeeded in getting under the power lines, but the tactic

didn't work. I flew so low over an agricultural plot that I can't understand how I missed hitting a farmer plowing with his ox. I wonder what he thought when our B-25 suddenly went thrashing past his head, with two Japanese fighters shooting at us in furious pursuit. As we flew over homes and buildings, some people still came out to wave at us.

About this time, one of the fighters registered a line of ten or fifteen hits on our plane from the trailing edge of our right wing up to the prop. I knew we'd be easy prey unless we dropped our bomb load soon and gained speed to outrun them. I think my voice squeaked when I asked Birch to prepare to drop the four 500-pound incendiary cluster bombs. We hadn't reached Tokyo Bay yet, but I could see a

COL. HUBERT ZEMKE *"C.O. of the 56ᵗʰ Fighter Group, a Thunderbolt outfit based in England. From Missoula, Montana, Col. Zemke had nineteen and a half victories in the air and eight and a half on the ground—the twenty-eight making him the ranking American ace in the European Theater of Operations. (The halves were shared victories with his wing man.) North of Hanover on October 30, 1944, the Colonel's ship split apart in a thunderhead but he parachuted safely to the ground to become a prisoner of war."* In his senior year of college, Greening met Zemke when hitchhiking from Pullman to Vancouver, Washington, where both took exams for flight school. Greening considered "this one of his finest works." Not as Briefed

getting any higher. It was a welcome relief seeing the release light flash four times, indicating the bombs were on the way.

Incendiaries are not supposed to explode, but a jarring blast shook our ship causing Reddy and me to hit the cabin ceiling. Our bombs had struck gasoline tanks or something similarly volatile. Reddy hit hard enough to cut his head. Blood streamed down his face. The plane's nose dropped from the concussion, pitching us at a steep angle towards the ground. Reddy and I hauled back on the yoke to keep from striking trees. When the bomb load dropped, we became 2,000 pounds lighter and our airspeed increased from 275 to 300 mph. This was all we needed to leave the two Japanese fighter pilots behind wondering if they were parked.

I might point out here that Allied forces up to this time hadn't identified the type of fighter we encountered. Our later reports and the drawings I made were the first identification of this plane by any American airmen. The report was questioned for a year, until it finally was confirmed that the Japanese were producing a new fighter called a "Toni."

I believe the fighters would have shot us down if we had continued to our assigned target. It surprised us to look back and see the tremendous conflagration we had started. Oily black smoke gushed up in billowy clouds about a thousand feet. We thought we had done our part in bombing Japan, even though we felt badly about not hitting our assigned target. The refinery was located east of Tokyo at Sakura.

concentration of buildings ahead and figured we'd better use it as a target while we still could bomb anything. Our precious gas was being consumed at about 300 gallons per hour, and we still had to fly to China.

When crossing an open field and approaching the buildings, we noticed refinery pipelines and tanks camouflaged by thatched roofs, appearing to look like a cluster of houses. We rationalized, if we were going to bomb a refinery this one would do just fine. I climbed only to 700 feet to drop our eggs because the pursuit planes were too close for us to risk

At 300 mph, we pulled away from the fighters and then slowed down to 275 mph to conserve fuel. China was about 1,400 miles away. Unfortunately, whenever we slowed down, the Japanese fighters closed in and we had to increase our speed again. I managed to stay ahead of them and turned out to sea. I hoped to lure them over the open water where by a stroke of luck they might run out of fuel. The minute we left the mainland, the fighters broke off the attack. It felt good to pass above the shoreline and race out over the waves to get away from the fighters.

Other planes were in the air over the Tokyo area; some I'm sure were B-25s. I saw a light plane, apparently a Piper Cub type trainer with two people aboard. They were just a little above us, but wiggled their wings in greeting as we went by. I'm sure they mistook our plane as one of their own.

Japanese patrol boats ringed the mouth of Tokyo harbor. Dead ahead we saw a large oil slick. In the middle, it appeared there was a man clinging to a log. We flew directly over and thought we saw a dead man in a leather jacket with his head hanging down in the water. We assumed it was a dead B-25 crewman. We were angry and scared, and decided to shoot up the patrol boats in the area. The first one we encountered obviously was a military craft. A man standing on deck saw us approach and must have recognized us as the enemy. I told Birch to open fire as soon as possible with the .30 caliber nose gun. A pattern of bullets swept across the deck and hit the surprised sailor in the chest. He rolled off into the water. I don't think he knew what hit him. We looked back and saw the boat burning furiously.

When we attacked the next patrol boat, a Japanese sailor threw his hands up as if to surrender. I guess he expected us to stop and take him prisoner. We shot him and left this boat smoking too. We attacked a third patrol craft, and then pre-

BAIL OUT OVER CHINA *"[Greening's] ship had been in the air 14 1/2 hours after leaving the carrier* Hornet *and had traveled 2,450 miles as well as successfully engaging four Jap 'Toni' fighters and shooting down two."* Not as Briefed

pared to shoot at another that was some distance away. However, it didn't have the same silhouette as the others. As we closed and almost were in range, peculiar streaks of smoke began coming at us, passing above and around our plane. Flashes of fire ringed this vessel and with a little more careful observation we realized it was a Japanese destroyer. They were not about to let us shoot them up with a mere .30 caliber machine gun. We quickly broke off the attack and headed for China. ✲

The Hari Kari-er dropping incendiary bombs on a refinery at Sakura, Japan. Washington State Historical Society, Tacoma, Washington

CHAPTER FIVE

NOT AS BRIEFED

During the encounter with the "Toni" fighters, the *Hari Kari-er* received hits on the right wing. While flying along off the east coast of Japan, we heard the engine missing. We wanted to check and see if something vital had been hit, but felt it wasn't safe to let our flight engineer, Sgt. Gardner, out of the top gun turret to do so. We noticed a cloud deck at 2,500 feet, and decided to climb into it and inspect for damage. It was a wonderful feeling hiding in the clouds. There was no serious harm to the plane; however, the right engine occasionally kept missing.

Frank Kappeler took a reading with the drift meter to determine wind direction and course. He discovered that luckily we had a thirty-knot tail wind. This meant we just might make it to China after all. Up to that point, it seemed fairly certain that we'd be ditching and then rowing across the East China Sea if we ever hoped to get to the mainland. It seemed amazing that Japan and the most dangerous part of the mission was behind us. I finally swallowed that bite of sandwich stuck in my mouth.

After we dropped to the deck, other planes were visible off to the right, but we couldn't be sure what kind of aircraft they were, or risk flying over on the assumption they were ours. We stayed out at sea far enough so that only the distant shoreline and hills of the east coast of Japan were visible. In passing some islands, we were concerned about anti-aircraft defenses that we might encounter. The overcast became thick and we knew bad weather was ahead.

I saw what appeared to be a fishing vessel, with a number of small, yellow rowboats around it. As we came closer, the rowboats headed back to the mother ship, apparently for protection. Being unsure about whether this Japanese vessel was picking up crashed crewmen, we decided not to attack it in case some of our friends were aboard. There were patrol craft in the area and we did a little more shooting.

It alarmed us whenever the engine backfired and missed. It ran rough for about thirty minutes. Then, to our great relief, it began functioning smoothly as we left the southern tip of Japan and headed out across the East China Sea.

Our next concern was setting a course to Chuchou in Chekiang Province, where we planned to refuel and proceed to Chungking for further instructions. We had been given a homing frequency to direct us to a landing field by radio compass. About four hours from our destination, however, it became obvious that we weren't going to make contact. We learned later that Col. Clayton Bissell, the Army's chief air officer at Chungking, had sent out a crew to set up the radio system at the airfields. Before establishing the homing network, however, the plane crashed. Because of this and other complications, no signal was sent out.

By now the rain was intense and the clouds darkened as night fell. We were exhausted from flying all day, couldn't get a celestial or radio navigational fix, and fuel was running short. We knew the mountains in China were 4,000 to 6,000 feet high. Of course, they were entirely unfamiliar to us. The field at Chuchou in eastern China supposedly would be lighted for our benefit.

While still over water, we decided to gain altitude, then reduce power to a minimum, lower the flaps to full down, and put the plane in a nosedive to distribute as much fuel as possible from the rear tanks to the wing tanks. When completing this maneuver, gasoline flowed into the standpipes, which drained into the wing tanks. We recovered an additional sixty gallons of fuel. During this time, I left the power off and the flaps down until we were just above the ocean again. However, visibility was bad and it was difficult to see the water. We decided to climb above the overcast and take a celestial fix, but the plane began icing up and we realized this wouldn't work. By now, we were flying on instruments and Kappeler was navigating by dead reckoning.

We flew on in the rainy darkness, uncertain whether we were over water or land. I had Gardner put the radio coils back in the transmitter. We signaled other aircraft, but received no answer. I scanned the radio dial a couple of times, seeing if I could pick up a broadcast to provide a clue as to where to proceed. The only thing we heard was cello music with a horn accompaniment, apparently Russian, which we listened to for a while. It made the situation seem even more ominous and unreal.

As the fuel gauges dropped toward zero, I had the crew gather near and we discussed our predicament. It was my opinion that we should bail out and continue on the ground to safety. On slips of paper, Kappeler provided each man with a sketch indicating the approximate locations of towns in respect to our position. We broke out the emergency rations and water. After filling the canteens, we drank the remaining water, and ate as many candy bars as we could. The rations were distributed equally and we made sure that we

The Hari Kari-er crew after the bail-out and reuniting in the village of Wei Chow Fu. This is one of the best photos taken of the Doolittle raiders in China: left to right, S/Sgt. William L. Birch (bombardier-gunner), Lt. Frank J. Kappeler (navigator), Capt. C. Ross Greening (pilot), Lt. Kenneth E. Reddy (co-pilot), and Sgt. Melvin J. Gardner (engineer-gunner).

carried other emergency gear, including first aid kits, pistols, and extra clips of ammunition.

When bailing out, we would jump as close together as possible to increase our chances of landing near each other on the ground. If we didn't meet up after parachuting, it was agreed to walk downhill to the first stream, continue down it to the first river, then down to the first town. There, hopefully we could join up and assist each other in getting out.

Flying in the rain and black of night, not knowing where we were, didn't make this seem like a good idea. But I thought it was the only thing we could do.

Sgt. Gardner voiced a counter proposal. "Captain, if we can see a light, why don't we dump out the flares and try to put this thing down in a rice paddy?"

I asked the crew what they thought about this. They agreed to try it. If a light was visible on the ground, we would circle down over our flares to what we thought was the height of the hills here—4,500 feet. If this failed, we could proceed with the original plan and bail out at higher altitude. We saw a light on the ground after our discussion ended. I immediately put the plane into a left turn, descending from 10,000 to 4,500 feet. We leveled out, but couldn't see the light again. Our course was at 220 degrees, toward our proscribed destination.

I flipped on the landing lights, trying to see ahead through the fog and rain. Suddenly, treetops brushed our wing tips and a hill appeared to jut up directly in front. Pilots flying at night know that if the landing lights are reflecting off the ground, you are too close for safety—particularly with a hill looming up fast. Instantly, Ken Reddy pushed the props open while I pushed the throttles wide open. We stood that B-25 on its tail and climbed to 10,000 feet. We promptly decided to bail out as originally planned.

The crew gathered in the navigator's compartment while Reddy and I turned on the automatic flight control. We were squared away for our final discussion before abandoning the *Hari Kari-er*. Only twenty gallons of fuel remained. We kept our heading at 220 degrees on automatic pilot to avoid Japanese-held territory.

I told Ken to get out of his seat. Without thinking, he did it in the usual way by unbuckling both the chute and seat buckles. He said, "What in the heck am I doing!" and quickly sat back down and strapped on the chute.

I felt saddened and weak in the knees about abandoning the *Hari Kari-er*. I turned on the radios, de-icers, and other equipment so she could go to her glory with everything running full blast. It felt so unusual to get out of my seat with the chute on. Five men wearing parachutes in a navigation compartment made it damned crowded. We did the best we could to inspect each other's gear. I had the ship stalling along at 125 mph to reduce the windblast as we dropped out the escape hatch.

I asked Gardner to open the hatch. He lifted the floor plate, pulled the release lever, but the lid wouldn't drop. Gardner gave it a couple of husky kicks, but it still didn't open. Then he and Birch together practically jumped on it. It popped out so fast that it was imperceptible to the eye. Instead of a door in the floor, suddenly there was a gaping, black hole with rivulets of rainwater streaming past. I told the crew to jump in order of rank, with lowest rank first.

When Sgt. Bill Birch bailed out, he flicked his hand in a friendly salute, saying, "So long, Captain, thanks for the ride." He stepped down, disappearing into the night.

Shortly, all the crew was gone and I was by myself. Never before had I been alone in a B-25 in flight. It was lonesome and weird, particularly being over China at night. I took a last look at the lit-up instrument panel. The lights were brightly blazing and the *Hari Kari-er* was running better than she had for quite a long time. The engine wasn't even missing. I felt tempted to crawl back into the pilot's seat and see what I could do, riding it out until the gas was gone and maybe landing her. But, a look at both fuel gauges reading zero convinced me it was best to follow my own instructions and get out while the *Hari Kari-er* was still flying.

Maps and other items were stuffed in my coat front. I cast one last glance at my movie camera and decided it wasn't good to eat. I left it in favor of scooping up an armload of the remaining provisions lying on the navigator's table. Holding these in my right arm and my gun belt in the left hand, I faced the rear, put my feet through the hole, and by force of habit attempted to find the first step of the ladder. But the first step wasn't there. It was 10,000 feet below.

I remember hearing the engines as the plane bore off into the night, making its own way to the end of the mission. The engine sounds diminished rapidly. As I fell, it became quieter except for the rushing wind, which caught my feet and I somersaulted backwards. I had a terrifying thought that the chute had failed to open and I had better rip open the chute case. Then I realized I was holding onto the

provisions instead of pulling the ripcord. In the few split seconds that I thought about this, I had the crazy idea of letting the provisions go, pulling the rip cord, and then grabbing the provisions again since they would fall at the same speed I did. I put this plan into action and let go, pulled the cord, and grabbed for the provisions. It must have looked like a grocery store explosion. There were groceries all over the sky in China. The chute opened with a boom, just as I heard the ship's final roar fade into the night.

My head ached terribly because I had been suddenly jerked into an upright position. The force of the chute's violent opening had straightened out the clasp that held my gun to my belt, so I stuck the pistol in my pocket to keep from loosing it.

It was a strange sensation being in such blackness that you can't see the parachute above you, your hand in front of your face, or where you are falling. It was cold and raining. I still had my gun, canteen, and first aid kit. I felt around, found my flashlight, and shined it downward. Immediately, I saw two flashes of light in the fog below. I yelled, but apparently was too far away to be heard. Nevertheless, it was reassuring to know someone else was down there. I later learned that Ken Reddy was immediately below me. He had shined his flashlight upward and shouted to me, but he couldn't hear me just as I couldn't hear him.

I suddenly smelled China and its fields, fertilized with human waste. The wind caused the chute to swing about sickeningly. I became nauseated and lost my breakfast and that bite of sandwich I took over Japan. I shined my flashlight up at the parachute. It looked like a small dot far above me. The swinging motion, rushing wind, and weird sounds during the descent were confusing and upsetting. It seemed I was in the air for an awfully long time. I kept shining the flashlight down in the fog, trying to see where I would be landing.

Suddenly a large black opening seemed to appear below me. It wasn't until my face smacked into a tree that I real-

LT. FRANK KAPPELER SPEAKS—

We had mixed feelings about the raid when we got together and talked about it. We knew we had accomplished our mission all right but we sure hated to have to report that we had to give up one perfectly good airplane. The "Hari Kari-er" lived up to its name and committed hari kari all right— something we hadn't expected when we named her. Ross Greening summed it up for us when he said, "Well, I think they'll call the mission a success. But there's one thing you'll have to admit," he added.

"What's that?" we asked in unison.

"It was one of those that will have to go down as 'Not As Briefed.'"

We agreed with him.

—Quoted in Carroll V. Glines, *Doolittle's Tokyo Raiders* (Princeton, NJ: D. Van Nostrand, 1964), 239.

ized this wasn't an opening, but the silhouette of a large hill. The tree held me, suspended by my chute. The flashlight was torn from my hand, spiraled to the ground, and bounced further downhill, till it stuck in some bushes about seventy-five feet away.

I don't know how long I hung there. I recall listening to the rain and trying to understand the circumstances in which I found myself. I heard three shots in the distance, but I wasn't about to respond by shooting my pistol. I don't know why. The next morning, I learned that the shots came from Reddy, who was signaling to us. I just hung there and tried to contemplate my predicament. A number of things went through my mind—I thought about the absurdity of events occurring in the world at the time, and the utterly incredible manner in which I had arrived on a hill somewhere in China (I hoped it was China!). I shed a few tears, feeling sorry for myself, and the world in general. I thought about home and family—whether or not I'd see them again, or if they would ever know what the crew and I had just gone through.

After awhile my legs became numb and I began focusing on getting out of the tangled chute. This required some care and much time, and the only cutting instrument I had was a small penknife that had belonged to my father. I used it to cut half of the shroud lines. Then, by gingerly working the chute, I pulled it off the top of the tree and descended until I could reach the trunk. As I grabbed the trunk, I slid down further, dragging the parachute behind me until I reached the ground. I discovered I'd been only about twenty feet up. The flashlight, because of where it fell, had given the illusion of a greater distance. I switched off the flashlight to save the batteries and tried to figure out what to do next.

The tree stood on a steep slope and I couldn't keep my footing. Strangely enough, this was the first time I'd been on the ground since leaving San Francisco and I still had sea legs. I decided I'd be better off staying in the tree. I laboriously worked myself back up to the lower branches, tying up the parachute the best I could to form a hammock. Then I slipped into the bag formed by the fabric and wrapped my body around the tree trunk, where I remained suspended for the night. It was a most unusual hammock, but served effectively as a rain shelter. Even so, I got very cold that night.

As I tried to sleep, night sounds began to work on my mind. A small creek wasn't far away. The whole time, that babbling creek made me imagine the most fantastic things. It actually talked to me, saying, "They went this way." "They

went that way." "You go this way, I'll go that way. Keep your gun. You catch him as he comes round the hill."

It bubbled away in such a manner that it made me think of voices, repeating over and over the same things, until I almost went out of my mind. I had my .45 out, ready to shoot, though I don't know what I would have shot at. The next morning, I found it difficult to get out of my improvised hammock. I almost was trapped. A hammock made from a twenty-eight foot diameter parachute is a deep pit to climb out of.

I started downhill, finding it so steep that I slid and crawled to keep from falling. I came to the creek and it looked clean, but considering how human fertilizer was used in the fields, I was not about to take a drink. I proceeded downhill as best I could and came upon terraced agricultural plots. Sitting down on a terrace wall, I thought how unusual it was that such an inaccessible locality was cultivated. The wall was about as many feet high as the horizontal width of the cultivated area behind it, which indicates how steep the pitch of the hill was.

As I sat there, I saw motion near the bottom of the canyon below me. I saw a person in a brown uniform with a white bandage, about a quarter-mile away. I whistled and yelled, and he immediately whistled back. A good, old American whistle! It couldn't be anything else. I yelled at the top of my lungs; it was Ken Reddy, my co-pilot! The bank was so steep that I wrapped my parachute up tightly and pitched it out. It fell to the bottom of the ravine, almost at Reddy's feet. I then scrambled down the hillside to Reddy. We welcomed each other with genuine joy and affection.

He also had spent a miserable night on the hillside, having hit his head on a rock and injured his knee, which puffed up like a watermelon. The cut on his forehead was deep and swollen. We made a crutch out of a section of bamboo, bound his knee, tied his head up with a piece of parachute, and headed out on foot, following the instructions given to the crew the night before. For some reason, however, going

downstream didn't seem right to us. We came to a small road or path. It seemed better for us to go uphill, so we did. We came to a little hut with a Chinese farmer standing in the doorway.

We used the words that we thought would identify us immediately, "Lushu hoo Megwa Fugi" (I am an American).

The farmer looked startled, withdrew inside the hut, and shut the door. We continued uphill until, at the top, we heard shooting as if some sort of battle were occurring. We decided to retrace our steps and follow my original instructions. We went downstream.

In about an hour, we came to a small village. It appeared that the farmer had alerted the village about us because there was a sizeable crowd standing on the outskirts awaiting our arrival. A rather intelligent looking young lad seemed to stand out at the center of the crowd. We approached him and tried to identify ourselves. Our magic words didn't work on him either. He escorted us to a schoolhouse. It was open to the elements—portions of it didn't even have a roof. Inside on the walls, there were maps and pictures, including photographs of Chiang Kai-shek, the Nationalist Chinese leader.

Of course, we saluted the Generalissimo and immediately gained the faith of the villagers. We drew pictures depicting bombs and parachutes, pointed to Tokyo on a map, and then pointed to the bombs, then to the parachutes. It wasn't long before they deduced that we had attacked the enemy, parachuted into their area, and were asking for help. Of course, we indicated we were hungry. People were eating what appeared to be rolled-up pancakes, with some kind of filling in the center. They immediately gave us some, which, unfortunately, was unpalatable to us. Reddy swallowed a bite or two then immediately threw everything up.

We each had a canteen, so I took a swallow from mine and Ken drank from his. Ken produced a cigar he had saved for this raid. He offered it to the villagers, but they wouldn't take it, so he and I smoked it. I'd never used tobacco, but was willing to puff on the cigar to keep something in my stomach even if it was only smoke. We spent about an hour in the village getting acquainted. We indicated that we needed to proceed down to the first river and then to the first town. They agreed to show us the way. Our guides were an elderly, one-eyed man and the town postmaster, who also was the village headman. They took us on a walk through the hills the likes of which I never experienced before and didn't ever want to again.

Ken had extreme difficulty walking. His leg obviously was badly hurt, and his head was bound up as tight as possible to keep from bleeding too much. The injury over his right eyebrow was swollen and he couldn't see out of the eye. Nevertheless, he didn't complain and did a marvelous job in making his way along unassisted. We offered to help him several times, but he always refused us.

We began what proved to be an extremely long walk. The population living in these mountains was sparse and poor. The hills were steep and the trails narrow and difficult. Before long, we tired and were unwilling to proceed, but our escorts insisted that we keep going because it was dangerous in this locality. This proved correct. At the next village, a large, excited crowd told us that we needed to hide. They helped us into a small, dirty, insect-infested attic of sorts. I thought if we encountered a Japanese patrol, it probably would be a small one and we had a chance of eliminating them with our .45s. We hid for a while, then the villagers came and got us because the threat, real or suspected, had passed. (I found out later when taking a practice shot with my .45 that it wouldn't shoot. The firing pin was too short. This would have been embarrassing if I'd met a Japanese patrol.)

At each village, they offered us food. We didn't want to give the impression that we didn't like the food, but we were entirely unaccustomed to it and couldn't keep it down. We craved cold, clear water, but needed to save the water in our canteens for an emergency. We needed something to drink.

At one of the villages we entered, I was given a large bowl of clear, cold liquid. Reddy received a bowl too. We tipped them up and took big swallows before realizing it was powerful distilled rice wine. At about 120 or 150 proof, it almost removed the lining from your mouth. The shock to our systems was more than we could take. We spit wine in all directions. I think the villagers were a little dismayed and unhappy about our discourteous reaction to this most cherished gift.

In each village, we noticed the many "honey pots" located all around. These were for holding and fermenting human excrement. Occasionally, a farmer came up with a pair of slinged buckets on a shoulder, dipped them into the honey pots, and took the fertilizer to the fields. We couldn't, however, tolerate the odor.

At times, our escorts became alarmed and led us at a dead run through the hills. We learned to comply the best we could. My shoes were not meant for hiking and were wearing out fast. Coming to a river, they put us under the decking of a boat, but after floating about two miles we landed and continued walking. At each village we were paraded and given gifts and food. We quite enjoyed being the center of attention. Occasionally, we came upon a messenger who advised our guides about the situation ahead. Obviously, word about us was being sent forward in some manner. Each time a messenger arrived, there was an extensive greeting and discussion, followed by a short rest. The Chinese took out their small pipes, stuffed them with a bit of tobacco, took one puff, blew out the ash, and added another bit of tobacco, repeating the procedure.

It seemed that we walked for endless miles (we found out later it was about forty miles). My joints ached and swelled, and I became feverish and exhausted. I didn't think I could take another step, but every time we suggested resting, the Chinese insisted that we continue because of the danger. I didn't think I could walk that far, but I guess you can do most anything under the right circumstances.

By nightfall, we came to a river and were loaded on a truck and driven to the small town of Wei Chow Fu and put up in the town's best hotel for the night. The hotel had been completely evacuated for our benefit. The Chinese militia in the area had thrown the other customers out—lock, stock, and barrel—to insure that we had privacy. They gave us strong coffee with canned milk and lots of sugar. This did us a lot of good, providing strength.

The bedroom apparently had been designed from an American picturebook of styles from a hundred years before. It featured a large feather bed and a long pillow running the full width at the head, all beautifully rounded and fluffed up. I was so exhausted that I barely made it to the bed. I fell on it in a heap, only to bounce off with a clatter. The bed consisted almost entirely of wood and was covered only with a thin layer of rice hulls in a sack. Obviously, the picture in a magazine or other source had shown the correct shape of a western bed, but had not described the materials. I imagine the Chinese thought we were strange people indeed to sleep on such a thing. Our escorts slept on the floor. If we had used any sense at all, we would have done the same thing. I just remember that I hit the bed with a bump and passed out.

I awoke stiff and sore in every joint and with a high fever, but I was greeted by one of the finest sights I've ever seen. Standing in the doorway were the rest of the crew—Mel Gardner, Frank Kappeler, and Bill Birch. They had followed the instructions explicitly, proceeding downstream to the first town. They too spent the night here, and now were standing before us safe and sound, with the exception of a few bruises and strains. We greeted each other with an enthusiasm that only those who were there could possibly appreciate.

The officers in charge of the guerilla bands were intent on treating us well. We were fed an "American" breakfast of eggs and ham, plus fried snake, beer, and other things I can't describe. Before breakfast, however, they wanted us to pose on a bridge that they said was of fine engineering and

completed within the last 150 years. We agreed and the five of us were photographed on the structure. This picture later became one of our most prized possessions. Lt. Dick Joyce picked up the photograph when coming through the area a few days later.

The Chinese decided that we shouldn't remain in the village any longer because of Japanese patrols. We climbed aboard a truck along with an escort of guerilla soldiers armed to the teeth. They were young and obviously unaccustomed to traveling in a motor vehicle because they became carsick. Whenever a person or vehicle appeared ahead, our truck stopped, the soldiers fell out, formed a line of skirmishers, and advanced until they positively identified the people ahead. They took no chances.

The truck stalled at one point and wouldn't start. Gardner, being a mechanic, easily diagnosed the trouble, but wasn't allowed to fix it. The Chinese fiddled with the engine, until it seemed like we were going to stay there for the rest of the war. Finally, they agreed to let Gardner take a look at it. He had the engine running in ten minutes. The Chinese were amazed at his ability to repair the truck, which they thought was found only in China. Actually, it was a Dodge that had been sent from America to China. Though a recent model, it looked about twenty years old due to operating in this rugged environment.

Our destination was only about forty miles away, but our Chinese escort took us some 187 miles in order to pass through areas only lightly patrolled by the Japanese. Unfortunately, the Japanese had begun a brutal retaliatory campaign in response to the Tokyo raid. Somehow, they seemed to know about the movements of the Chinese. After a full day of travel, we arrived in Chuchou, where we had intended to land. We learned that the mountains here actually were 6,500 feet high, which was 2,000 feet higher than we expected. This explained our close call with the treetops before bailing out.

When we arrived at a barracks, a strange looking man wearing Chinese clothes that were much too small for him greeted us. He also had a long, Fu Manchu style mustache. It was Capt. Davy Jones, whom we quickly dubbed as Fu Man Jones. His uniform had been badly torn, so he had been given Chinese clothing. He also let his mustache droop down the sides of his mouth to help disguise himself as a native. Jones and his crew were here, as well as Lt. William Bower and his crew. That evening, Maj. John Hilger and his crew also arrived. As Americans who had just bombed Japan, we were provided with the finest accommodations available. The extra clothing provided to us felt somewhat like cardboard, but it was thick and warm. The beds were too small, but nevertheless much appreciated.

We were quartered near a large airfield subjected to almost continuous bombing since the Tokyo raid. We suggested to the Chinese officials that some effort be made to oppose the Japanese air attacks. They told us to forget the idea. It cost the Japanese thousands of dollars to make bomb holes in the airstrip that the Chinese could fill for just a few cents each. During one period, we observed that the Japanese dropped forty bombs, of which twenty-two were duds. We examined the bomb fragments and believed they were made from American scrap metal.

Much of our time was spent in an air raid shelter near the airstrip. Interestingly, Chuchou had direct telephone links to Chinese sympathizers at the Japanese airstrips from which the attacking bombers were departing. We overheard these communications, and sometimes the Chinese let us listen in on the phone. You actually could hear the Japanese warming up their engines for takeoff in the background. The informers gave the expected time and altitude of the raiders. Even such details as the pilots' names were passed on to the Chinese. We could almost check out our watches with the planes' reported arrival times. The informants undoubtedly were phoning right from a Japanese operations shack.

We were warned by Chinese officials not to antagonize the Japanese. If we should even by accident hit one of their planes with our .45-caliber pistols, this would incur the wrath of the Japanese to a degree that the local population couldn't sustain. The Chinese would suffer far more if there was stepped-up retaliation, than if they just endured the bombing.

We couldn't stay at the airfield for long because informants undoubtedly had reported our presence to the Japanese. We were moved to a small mountain retreat about ten miles away, where there were barracks and an air raid shelter built into the rock. When escorted through the streets and roads into the mountains, we saw how difficult circumstances were for the Chinese in this locality. Strafing Japanese planes had killed many. Frequently, bodies were stacked like cordwood along the roadside until they could be taken away for burial. It was a depressing sight to us. We hadn't encountered anything like this before.

The air raid shelter adjoined a Chinese barracks, where they offered us food and comforts. Unfortunately, the quality of their best was far below what we had known in America, thus we didn't always appreciate their efforts. The food tasted terrible to us, beds were too short, and we were cold. I'm afraid we didn't make a good showing for ourselves. I can imagine that the Chinese there didn't think much of Americans.

The Chinese took a number of photographs of us, most of which they kept for themselves. When posing for the camera, it was interesting to see them hold up signs that proclaimed the true and everlasting friendship between the Chinese and American people. We stayed here approximately a week, most of the time in the air raid shelter. It seemed as if Japanese planes attacked constantly. The news reports about our bombing attack were encouraging. It appeared we had caused the greatest panic in Tokyo since the 1921 earthquake and the raid inflicted enormous damage.

Other bailed-out crewmen that had been found in the hills joined us on April 22. The stories the lads told kept us entertained for nearly the whole time. Some accounts were amazing. For example, Sgt. Waldo Bither, at 35 the oldest man on the mission next to Doolittle, had bailed out and landed in a fairly flat place, but in complete darkness. To settle his nerves, he smoked a cigarette and pitched the smoldering snub away. Instead of hitting the ground, the twisting and turning butt fell completely out of sight. Bither had landed on the edge of a high cliff. He wasn't more than a couple of yards from the edge. Incidentally, he also had accidentally opened his parachute while still in the plane and had to repack it on the navigator's table before bailing out.

On April 23, Lt. Bob Gray came in with two of his men from plane #3. Lt. Charles Ozuk, however, was missing and Sgt. Leland Faktor had been killed during the bail-out. We received several phone calls that night, but the connection was poor and we couldn't fully determine what they were about. We did learn that some bodies and men had been picked up near the ocean beaches. Everyone blamed the Navy (unfairly as we later found out), believing that they hadn't held to their agreement to get us in closer to Japan.

On April 24, Lt. Ozuk came in with both legs badly gashed. He had hung all night in his parachute on the side of a cliff. His left leg had a cut at least 4 1/2 inches long and 3/4 inch deep. It took him six days to complete the trip to Chuchou. Lt. Edgar McElroy and crew arrived safely, but the train they were on had been machine gunned, leaving two people dead. Lt. Lucian Youngblood arrived early on the morning of April 25.

Rain fell on April 26, consequently there were no Japanese attacks. At a dinner reception, General Tang of the Chinese Army explained how grateful his people were for what we had done. That evening, twenty of us left on a train for Kweilin, traveling at night to avoid Japanese raids. The next morning, we switched to a bus, which was a safer way to travel should the Japanese attack. At times we were only

sixty miles from the front lines. It took all day to travel to Mingtu over extremely rough roads. The Chinese food and lodging were the best yet.

We continued on about 140 miles to Kiang. A ferry at the river had been washed away, so we crossed over in small boats. We were met on the other side and taken to two receptions. The provincial commissioner provided an excellent meal and 140-proof wine. Everybody toasted everyone. When we met the governor, I had to make a speech. We were introduced to many fine people and stayed at a wonderful hotel in Kiang.

The next day, several men became ill from the unfamiliar food, but not seriously. I rode around Kiang's streets in a rickshaw. Another bus drove us to Hengyang, a distance of about 240 miles. This took about sixteen hours over difficult roads. When we arrived, our hosts furnished us with the finest accommodations yet. Each community was trying to outdo the others in welcoming us.

On April 29, we were notified that an American transport from Chungking was flying in to pick us up. This news boosted morale 100 percent. It was a beautiful sight when that C-47 soared in over the airfield at about 2:30 PM. We hadn't seen an American plane since bailing out. The plane's pilot was Capt. Richardson and the Army's regional air commander, Col. Bissell, accompanied him. The Colonel wanted us to get into the C-47 as fast as we could. Richardson didn't even shut off the engines or taxi to the other end of the field. After the excitement of getting aboard and taking off, we discovered that there were two Chinese in the plane. These men had accompanied us for many days. Though it wasn't intended, it was fitting that they should get a free trip.

The flight to Chungking took about 2 1/2 hours. The C-47 flew along a river valley near the city and toward an airfield. Richardson lowered the wheels and flaps, clearly appearing to make an approach to set the plane down. However, he suddenly pulled up the wheels and flaps and contin-

ued on for a couple of miles to a well camouflaged airstrip and landed there. Hardly had the engines stopped before ground crews pulled the plane into a hillside hanger and dropped a camouflage net over the entrance.

We were quartered at the American Embassy in Chungking and had dinner with General John Magruder. At the end of the evening, Bissell informed us that he would have good news to give us tomorrow.

The next morning, Bissell walked into the room where the officers and enlisted men were assembled. Accompanied by General Magruder and his staff, Bissell announced that all of us had earned the Distinguished Flying Cross. I found I couldn't breath very well. At the time, it was the biggest thrill of my life.

After congratulations and cigars, we learned that we were going to Calcutta to be outfitted with new equipment and clothing. Secrecy about the attack on Japan still had to be maintained, however, and we were to keep our knowledge about it to ourselves. Some of the boys still were unaccounted for, but presumably were in Japanese hands. Congratulatory messages were received from President Roosevelt, General Marshall, and General Arnold. The Chief of the Chinese Air Force, General Mou, also paid us a personal visit, and we were invited to parties.

May 1 was payday. To my amazement, we received our regular paychecks even in far off China. Twenty of us were invited to dine with the Generalissimo and Madame Chiang Kai-shek. We left at one o'clock in the afternoon accompanied by Bissell and two Chinese generals. When introduced to Madame Chiang Kai-shek, we thought she was one of the most gracious individuals we had ever met. I was the senior rank in our little group, consequently I was required to give an impromptu speech at the dinner. I presented Madame Chiang with a set of Air Corps insignia. I had a bit of an embarrassing time fumbling around trying to find somewhere to pin them on her.

We saw the Generalissimo only for a short period during dinner. He entered the room, apparently harassed and hurried, and made a very short speech that wasn't translated. Then he came over, shook hands with me as the ranking representative of our group, and left. Later, we learned he wasn't pleased about the attack on Japan because it had brought on additional aggression by the Japanese against his troops and people. He also had been planning operations against the Japanese, but the forward areas necessary for these activities now were lost or threatened due to the Japanese retaliation.

We spent an enjoyable half-hour with Madame Chiang after the Generalissimo left. We gave her additional gifts, including a Seventeenth Bombardment Group insignia and my flight cap. This was the first of many meetings with important people, but it left a lasting impression on all of us.

After returning to the American Embassy, we were surprised that evening when Madame Chiang with a detachment of Chinese soldiers came to visit us. She presented us with medals for distinguished service, which, we were told, were difficult to earn and rarely awarded. The impressive appearing Chinese Order of the Celestial Cloud was issued to each of us according to our rank.

On May 3, the same C-47 that had brought us here arrived with another group of airmen and Lt. Col. Doolittle, only now he was "General" Doolittle. Bissell informed me of the promotion, which skipped the rank of colonel entirely, but it was to be kept a secret for now. We visited with them for a few moments, and then our group was loaded aboard the C-47. We proceeded to an airstrip at Yunang, where American volunteers flew P-40 fighters against the Japanese.

The following day, we continued to Dinjon, India, where the plane circled the airfield, waiting for landing instructions to be relayed by signal flares. Our ship had fired its flare, but hadn't received an answering signal from the tower. Suddenly, a large black column of smoke rose up from the field. Our pilot approached to land anyway, without a

signal. Just as the C-47 touched down, two P-40s zoomed by in the opposite direction, taking off on the same runway.

As our plane rolled to a stop, a British soldier yanked open the rear door and screamed that an air raid was in progress. He said we should take off immediately for Cedeea and wait there until it was safe to return. Before we knew what was happening, he grabbed the Tommy guns from our hands and slammed the door shut. Capt. Richardson spun the plane around and took off in the other direction, believing Japanese fighters or bombers were expected at any moment. We reached Cedeea safely, and soon received word to return to Dinjon.

At Dinjon, we learned what had happened. A new control tower recently had been built at the base. When our C-47 circled the field and released an identification flare, the tower operator shot off an answering flare, but in his haste he forgot to open a window in the new tower. The flare bounced off the window and set the structure on fire. An alarm was set off, sounding like an air raid alert. When the tower operator saw people running for the air raid shelters, he asked one of them, "What's going on?" He was told an attack was coming. He joined them, not realizing his role in the whole affair. The tower burned to the ground.

We refueled and flew on to Calcutta, intending to land at DumDum field, but the British had camouflaged it so well that we couldn't find it. Our pilot circled for twenty minutes, but couldn't spot the airstrip until he was able follow another plane in.

We were put up in Calcutta's Great Eastern Hotel. We were a pretty crummy looking bunch by this time. I had a piece of a parachute patching the seat of my pants, and other boys had missing or torn clothing. The temperature was extremely hot and the only new uniforms available were British jungle jackets and shorts. On May 5, we spent the day outfitting ourselves at various tailor shops. Until May 11, we had the run of the city. We visited every nightclub and any other entertainment and amusement spot that we

could, and were guests at a swimming club where we met many Brits and became good friends.

I finally could write a letter to my wife, though I still had to keep the mission a secret.

While in Calcutta, we caught up on the news. The war was going badly for the United States and our Allies. We were being pushed back on all fronts. The population in Calcutta was boarding up, preparing for an invasion by the Japanese. Fighter airstrips were being established right in the middle of Calcutta in the local parks. B-17s of the Eleventh Squadron of the Seventh Bombardment Group made periodic visits to the DumDum airfield, loading bombs and refueling for attacks on Rangoon and other targets in the Japanese advance. The U.S. Army's General Stilwell was making his historic march out of Burma.

Next we flew to Allahabad where the Ninth Squadron of the Seventh Bombardment Group was based. We provided them with whatever information we could about the Japanese. Here, meeting up again with a number of American boys, we had many bull sessions about our experiences.

In Allahabad, it was so hot during the day (118 or 120 degrees) that it was barely possible to work on a plane, or in fact even touch one. It was nearly unbearable for those of us not used to it. A few days later, we proceeded to the regional U.S. Army Air Force headquarters at New Delhi, but had hardly arrived before Jack Hilger, Davy Jones, and I received orders to return to China for further duty. We were to prepare airfields, armaments, and general logistical support to General Halverson's B-24s, which were expected to arrive there in preparation for bombing Japan at a later date.

We were flown by C-47 to Dinjon and quartered at a tea plantation in the jungle about ten miles from the airfield. As I walked to a small cottage on stilts and went up the steps, something from over the door jumped down and landed on my head. It was a tame monkey, objecting to my entering the cottage. It took some time to disentangle the monkey,

but it was an introduction to the wildness of the Indian jungle.

We set out by jeep in the morning darkness, heading back to the airfield to catch a flight to China. We drove along with only the dim blackout headlights to guide us. In the usual American way, we were driving too fast. Suddenly, we bumped into something we couldn't identify, but it was huge and towered over our heads. I thought we had hit a large jungle tree that was the size of an elephant's leg. My impression was correct, in fact, because we had run into an elephant that was trekking through the jungle. The elephant peered down with beady eyes, but fortunately didn't retaliate. After we calmed down, we proceeded to the airport.

At Dinjon, Hilger and I boarded a B-24 Liberator, the first to fly into China. We anticipated that this could lead to some more interesting experiences for us. This type of plane carried a very large bomb load and the Japanese undoubtedly would object to it being moved closer to their homeland. The pilot allowed Hilger and me to spell him a bit on the flight "over the hump" to China. The plane had a full crew in addition to us. Unfortunately, there weren't enough oxygen tubes on board. While flying at 19,000 to 21,000 feet, we passed the tubes around to stay conscious. I sometimes thought it would be better just to skip the oxygen and pass out, so I could forget the fear that those high, misty mountains put in me.

As was usual on this route, we experienced difficult flying conditions. The B-24 climbed to 24,000 feet with reasonable ease; however, at that altitude we encountered severe icing. When the pilot applied the de-icing boots, only one operated, putting the weight of the plane out of balance. The aircraft stalled and went into a series of spins, once to the right, then to the left. We dropped from 24,000 to 17,000 feet before recovering. The maps and charts indicated that the mountains here jutted up to 19,000 feet. This was somewhat disconcerting, because our rapid calculations showed we were flying 2,000 feet below that level. The pilot put on the power as gingerly as possible, trying to ease us back up to a safe height. The other nine men aboard added several gallons of sweat to his efforts. We finally got across the Hump, staggering along at minimum speed and in an unusual attitude, with one wing heavily iced up and the other free of ice. We were lucky.

As we approached Kunming, the ground was obscured by overcast and the mountaintops showed through the clouds. Thinking we were in the correct locality, we deduced that the airfield was in the valley below. Our pilot decided to "let-down" under the clouds and get a visual fix. We broke out much closer to the ground than we expected. When we looked toward the end of the valley where a town was supposed to be, we saw nothing but small, scattered villages. We searched the area and studied the maps, concluding that this wasn't the correct valley. We were 120 miles off course.

Somehow, Dame Fortune guided us through the mountains to Kunming, where we finally circled and landed. General Claire Chennault, the commander of the all-volunteer Flying Tigers, invited us to his operations room. He pointed out a number of likely looking Japanese targets.

He said, "Boys, if you'll take this B-24 and let us load it with bombs, we can go out and wipe out half of the Japanese army and most of their air force. We guarantee that we'll give you coverage and get you back home without any trouble."

Back in the United States, Ross shows decorations earned in the Doolittle raid to his mother and Dot.

We had been given definite orders and thus were obliged to refuse his invitation to take another crack at the Japanese. Of course, Chennault was disappointed about our decision, but he provided fuel and allowed us to proceed on to Chengtu, a field situated west and a little north of Chungking.

At Chengtu, we saw an amazing sight. Without modern machinery, the Chinese were building an airstrip that would be a credit to any American engineering effort. The runway was thick, sturdy, well constructed, and plenty long enough for the heavy bombers that planned to use it as a base of operations. The approaches were good and the camouflaging was exceptional, even in the construction stage. The amazing thing was that 120,000 Chinese laborers were building it by hand. Thirty thousand of them were needed merely to provide food for the workers.

Jack Hilger and I were given decent quarters in a building adjoining the airfield, where we set up our base of activity. Our quarters had a shower modeled after a picture of an American design. Externally, it looked just like an American shower, but the technical details behind the design were Chinese. Water came from a large wooden tank located directly over the showerhead, which was filled by a line of Chinese water-carriers, passing buckets by hand from a nearby well. The heating system consisted of a charcoal brazier placed on a section of pipe. Water heated in the pipe went directly to the showerhead, so showers were scalding

for a few seconds, followed by cold water. Just the same, we appreciated their efforts and enjoyed showering.

Aside from occasionally taking the B-24 up to keep the Japanese from anticipating when it would be on the ground and thus plan an attack to destroy it, our mission consisted of preparing ordnance and fuel supplies for the upcoming arrival of Halverson's B-24s. The bombs had been made by the Chinese, but copied from Russian, American, Italian, and German designs, which varied in every manner, shape, and description. Some were fat, some long, and some thin with long tail veins. Some had two lugs for suspension in the bomb bays, and others had one.

We ended up cutting lugs off some bombs and welding them onto others in order to adapt them to our bomb bay shackles. I was alarmed by the old-type, fulminate of mercury primers and detonators for the bombs because they could be set off just by the heat of your hand. I marked with chalk where the lugs were to be cut and replaced, but I usually found a reason to be on the other side of the field when the acetylene torch man went to work. Fortunately, the casings were well built and we didn't have any detonations.

Bombs were loaded on the B-24 for testing at a nearby range that we had asked the Chinese to establish. A Chinese general accompanied us on the first run. Our B-24 carried bombs of each description, in addition to a water-filled practice bomb. Several days prior to the test, the people in the area had been warned to evacuate. Unfortunately, this simply acted as an invitation to many curious Chinese. On the day of the test, the area next to the target was jammed with peasants. As the B-24 circled at 7,000 feet, preparing for the first drop, we realized that people had crowded into the target area. We informed the Chinese general about this and recommended abandoning the test.

He replied, "I suggest that you go ahead and drop the bombs, as we advised them to get off the field. Besides, I don't think we'll kill very many anyway."

Between ourselves, we decided not to drop any high explosives, but we did choose to release the water-filled practice bomb. It was so poorly constructed, however, that when it left the bomb bay, the air flowing around it drained it of water. The tumbling pile of junk fell a half-mile short of the target. The inquisitive Chinese thought it strange that the bomb didn't explode. We had no chance to recover the materials, because the peasants hauled away every scrap before we got there.

A few days later, while working on the various types of bombs and looking over some aircraft that the Russians had provided to the Chinese, we saw a C-47 circling the field for a landing. It brought us a garbled message ordering a number of the Doolittle raiders back to the United States. I noticed one name beginning with a "G" and ending with a "g," which contained the same number of letters as mine. I deduced it was me, as had my superior officers. I was to report in New Delhi and see if in fact I had been ordered back to the States. Because Japanese advances were threatening the airfields and word had come that General Halverson's bomber group was assigned to action in Egypt for an indefinite period, there was little purpose for staying in China at this time.

We soon were airborne in the B-24, returning toward India. We landed in Kunming again, where I ended up in a dispensary for a few days with malaria. Then, we took off to fly over the Hump. This time both de-icers worked and we carried an extra oxygen tank and were much more comfortable. On approaching Dinjon, we encountered the start of the monsoon rains. It was one of the most intense rainfalls I ever experienced. The B-24 had every appearance of being underwater even at the altitude we were flying. It was impossible to see the wingtips. Rain leaked through every crack and large puddles washed around in the plane. At Dinjon, I spent another night with the monkey.

We next boarded a C-47 equipped for high altitude flying, but had a worrisome time due to a violently shaking engine, 100-mph headwinds, and a dust storm near Allahabad. The engine had been recovered from a belly landing and straightened with a sledgehammer. Thus, the propeller was out of balance. We flew at 19,000 feet with no oxygen. I had an excellent view of Mt. Everest when passing close by the Himalayas, but I couldn't get a picture because my camera froze up at that altitude.

When passing through Allahabad, I met my engineer-gunner, Sgt. Melvin Gardner. He was scheduled to embark the next morning on a bombing mission in Burma and proceed on to Kunming, China. I told Gardner that I would wire him if he was on the list to return to the States.

At New Delhi, I elected not to continue in the C-47. Sgt. Bill Birch, my bombardier and good friend, however, chose to proceed in the same plane. On takeoff, the C-47's accumulated discrepancies caught up with it. Getting not much higher than a hundred feet in the air, the pilot was forced to make a belly landing in an Indian field, unfortunately killing a sacred cow. The angered Indians chased after Birch and the others. Birch was a good track man and made it back to New Delhi in good time.

After arriving in New Delhi, I was happy to learn that twenty-seven of us from the Doolittle outfit had orders to return to the United States, including Sgt. Gardner. I wired Allahabad, asking to have Gardner withdrawn from any operations so he could be sent back to the States. Unfortunately, the message was pigeonholed just a little too long. Gardner took off with a flight of B-25s that bombed Lashio, Burma. When Japanese planes attacked them over the mountains, they dove into the clouds. All but one of the B-25s crashed into the mountains. Gardner never was heard from again.[1]

At New Delhi, a Boeing Stratocruiser came to pick us up. Among our group was Ted Lawson. He had crash-landed his B-25 just off the Chinese coast, resulting in a dreadful leg injury that required amputation. With the great strain

Ross asked for continued duty in a combat theater and was made a group commander of a B-26 marauder outfit sent to North Africa. He also was promoted to Lt. Colonel. U.S. Army Air Forces

and extreme difficulties he had just overcome, it isn't hard to understand why I didn't recognize him at first.

On the trip back, it was quite remarkable to realize that we were completing the last leg of a trip around the world—just for the purpose of having bombed Japan for thirty seconds. Stopping at Cairo, I visited the Sphinx and Pyramids. Proceeding through South America and the Caribbean, we landed in Florida and called our wives, who were waiting at Myrtle Beach, South Carolina. They left by train for Washington, D.C., where we met them.

We waited ten days for an opportunity to visit with the President, but he was hard pressed for time because Winston Churchill and his staff were in the country. General Hap Arnold officially pinned the Distinguished Service Cross on twenty-three of us at Bolling Field in Washington, D.C., on

June 27, 1942. After the ceremony, we departed to our hometowns, after which time we toured and gave speeches to sell war bonds.[2] When back in the States for awhile, I was saddened to learn about the score or more of men who had been captured by the Japanese, interned in Russia, or died in China during the mission or in subsequent assignments.

I next was reassigned as the operations officer of the Seventeenth Medium Bombardment Group at Barksdale Field, near Shreveport, Louisiana, but I was loaned to the Ninety-fifth Squadron at the same airstrip as its commander. By now, I was flying the high-performance B-26 Marauder, a twin-engine bomber that was smaller than a B-25. On my first morning serving as squadron commander, I scrambled into a B-26 following a flash warning about a submarine sighting off the Gulf coast. On takeoff, the newly commissioned co-pilot forgot about the heavy bomb load. He pulled the landing gear up too soon. It was a bad crash—one propeller even hit the control tower a half-mile away. Fortunately, we came out of it okay.

My co-pilot from the Tokyo raid, Lt. Ken Reddy, was living with Dot and me during this time. Regretfully, he and five other crewmen were killed on a cross-country flight near Little Rock, Arkansas, on September 3, 1942. I identified his battered body by the scars on his head resulting from the bail-out over China. On November 20, 1942, another Tokyo raider, bombardier Lt. Robert Clever, who was scheduled for the African campaign, died when a B-26 spun-in on takeoff near Versailles, Ohio.

I had been transferred to Fort Wayne, Indiana, to prepare our B-26s for the Allied invasion of North Africa. During this period, I received a citation from Madame Chiang Kai-shek for my participation in the Tokyo raid. I didn't have the foggiest notion what the Chinese characters on the large scroll said. Dot and I decided that the best way to find out would be to take it to one of Fort Wayne's Chinese restaurants.

When we were seated in a cafe, we unrolled the scroll and asked the waitress to please translate it for us. She looked it over carefully for a few moments without saying a word, then took it into the kitchen. We heard a discussion in Chinese, then the cafe manager returned bearing the scroll.

He said, "What would you people like to have to eat? We want you to have the best meal we have in the house on us."

We replied that we were happy to pay, but just wanted to know what the scroll said.

He acted embarrassed when he translated it. This decoration, given by the Generalissimo and Madame Chiang Kai-shek, was one of the highest awards that could be bestowed on someone of my similar rank in the Chinese Air Force.

We had a rousing party with wine and all the trimmings. I think it was the best Chinese food I ever ate. ✪

NOTES

1. Tokyo raiders, Sgt. Omer Duquette and Lt. Eugene McGurl, also died in this same action, June 3, 1942.

2. *Seattle Times*, Summer 1942—Missing Flyer's Fiancee Honored: "A pretty, dark-haired girl stood in Victory Square yesterday as one of the heroes of the Tokyo air raid, Maj. Charles R. Greening, told how his tail gunner 'saved my life' by shooting down two Japanese fighter planes.

   "Then he paused. 'That gunner, Sergt. Melvin Gardner, now is reported missing. But...his fiancee is right here at Victory Square!'

   "He drew Miss Virginia Harmon, whom he had found in the crowd of spectators only a few minutes before, to the microphone. She looked down at the sea of sympathetic faces of people aware that here was a bit of unrehearsed drama.

   "Afterward... she confessed, 'I couldn't say a word. I was too scared.'

   "'When I read in Friday's *Times* that Major Greening would be at Victory Square I just went down to the square and cornered him,' Miss Harmon said. 'I knew if anyone could tell me about Mel he could.'

   "Major Greening did tell her about Mel. 'He's a rare man,' he said. 'And keep your hopes up.'...Miss Harmon, 19-year-old Seattl[ite]... met Gardner last July 27 [1941] when she was on a vacation trip to Spokane."

CHAPTER SIX

NORTH AFRICAN OPERATIONS

The crew and I experienced a couple of close calls during the trip to Africa in late 1942. In Puerto Rico, the plane's flaps crept up on takeoff and I had to dive over a cliff at the end of a runway to reach flying speed. At a field in the South American jungle, the tail dragged in some trees during take-off. We had to abandon that plane at the next base.

After flying across the Atlantic to Accra, my squadron continued north to Marrakech, Morocco. We were among the first U.S. Army Air Force planes to arrive in this area, where a French Foreign Legion general invited my operations officer and me to a banquet. We were the honored guests and sat to the general's right in a sprawling mass of tents covering the festive grounds. We were entertained by native dancers, magicians, and clowns, followed by a review of the soldiers. Taking my camera, I took motion pictures of the men standing at attention as we walked down the review line, which probably was something new for the troops.

Some of the fellows in my squadron had picked up various pets, including orangutans, monkeys, and two small chow-type puppies. Unfortunately, we lost one of the dogs before reaching our base at Telergma, Algeria, where we were billeted in tents. However, the other canine, known as Sgt. McGillicuddy, became the mascot for one of the crews, and, in fact, for the entire outfit. He flew on missions with a specially rigged parachute, had sergeant stripes painted on his front legs, and wore a dog tag. The dog tag was exactly the same as ours, except his blood type was specified as K-9-P. Sgt. McGillicuddy always arrived at his crew's plane before a flight and was assured a seat.

Christmas 1942 was a particularly lonely and miserable time for me. Before, when away from home at

On April 18, 1943, the Doolittle raiders on duty in North Africa celebrate the first anniversary of the attack on Japan. Gathering at the farmhouse were General Doolittle (commander of the 15th Air Force), several of the raiders, and some of the men who trained for the mission, but did not launch from the USS Hornet. Ross stands at the rear.

this time of year, I'd felt much the same, but now it seemed more intense and permanent, giving me a constant stomach-ache. Having just left the States, I could tell it just wasn't possible for folks there to fully realize what a terrible thing this war was. News from home sure meant a lot. I saw fellows cry when receiving a letter or package.

On a fateful day when our squadron bombed a hot target near Gabes in southern Tunisia, the plane carrying our mascot, Sgt. McGillicuddy, was shot down. The plane crashed in flames within enemy lines somewhat west of Gabes. We all felt very sad at the loss of the six-man crew and our mascot.

A couple of months later, Free French troops inspected the downed plane when advancing through the area. They reported finding the dog tags of seven crew members in the badly burned wreckage. We were asked to identify the dog tags and report this information back to French headquarters. After we did so, we learned that the crew members were awarded the Croix de Guerre for bravery. Among those decorated was Sgt. McGillicuddy. I believe he was the only dog to posthumously receive a foreign decoration for air combat during World War II.

In North Africa, we found ourselves nearly deprived of alcoholic beverages, except for an acrid, red Arab wine that wasn't very palatable to us. We hit upon the idea of removing copper tubing from a wrecked B-26 to construct a still. We were expertly advised by Lt. Cornelius from the Kentucky mountain country. In order to start the still percolating effectively, he claimed he had to remove his shoes. Never in his life had he been able to run a still unless he was bare foot. "Cornelius's corn" became a popular distillate.

We used Arab wine, ran it through the still mixed with orange concentrate from Red Cross parcels, and came up with "liquid lightning." We opened a bar at the Telergma officer's club and brought the club's budget into the black with $2,500 in profits in only six weeks. We employed the services of Lt. Cornelius with complete freedom from inter-ference by "revenuers." Finally, the liquor still blew up, putting a quick halt to our business.

Shortly, we contacted a local French brewery, which became a secret source of beer for us. The quality was poor, but it was beer. We had to provide the brewery with some supplies, including sugar, and in return we received good quantities of brew. Unfortunately, it lacked one quality considered vital by Americans. It wasn't cold! There wasn't anything even similar to refrigeration at our base camp.

Finally, we hit upon the idea of making slings for the twelve-gallon kegs and hanging them in a B-26 bomb bay. I flew the plane to an altitude where the cold, rarified air would, in about three hours, chill the beer to a satisfactory temperature. On the approach to the field, we called the control tower, advising all ground crews and personnel from the bomb groups to be on hand with canteens because the beer was cold and ready to drink.

While flying missions, I wasn't hurt, but I saw men get seriously injured or killed. I couldn't figure out what kept me from being one of them. Every time we'd go out, we'd call it, "One for Clever and Reddy." We were pasting the Huns pretty good, and they knew we wouldn't give up until we'd won. I couldn't understand why they didn't want to try and

A LETTER HOME, JANUARY 1, 1943—

If anyone thinks it is warm in Africa they are crazy. I have never been so cold in my life. At night it seems unbearable at times …I certainly wish there was some way we could show people at home what the fellows have to go through here… One of my gunners was shot three times through the chest and passed out for a moment—as soon as he came to he got back on the guns and shot down a German pursuit plane that was shooting at our ship. He will live but is close to the brink.

save what they had left and quit. Our missions were proving effective again and again, but every now and then the Germans got in a lucky hit.

My ship finally was shot up on a raid. No one else's was, and I felt better then because I no longer was the only one who hadn't been hit. When it happened, I thought we'd go down. A heavy AA shell burst ten feet in front of the plane during the bomb run. It shook us up, but did nothing worse than punch a few holes in our B-26. In reply to their efforts, we promptly bombed them to kingdom come.

I now had over 125 hours of combat time and had been on constant duty without even one day off. I was growing weary of it all. Only six officers from the original squadron were still with me. Things hadn't been as tough on us as for the poor German lads, but I couldn't get used to seeing good friends being lost, even though we were winning.

One day, the fellow in the plane right behind me was shot down. He was a very good friend. I was leading and we did our best to give him cover. We downed the enemy ship that shot him up, but it wasn't soon enough. I didn't quite feel the same afterwards, and cussed and prayed all in the same breath.

I missed my wife so much that I wanted to crate up a load of bombs, knives, hand grenades, hatpins, poison, and whatever in my little bomber, and take off and finish this war once and for all. I wanted to go home, sit beside Dot in front of the fireplace with a jug of beer and our dogs, and never move again except to go fishing for a bit. I'd received an Air Medal and another was coming up, but personally, I'd rather be with my wife than have all of the medals they could give me.

Eventually, I visited the front lines and saw firsthand the beating that the Germans took while trying to hold on in North Africa. Thousands of wrecked and burned vehicles, as well as knocked-out tanks, dotted the countryside. Here and there I came upon crashed planes and burned camps. Buildings were blasted to bits. Most memorable were the

German graveyards where hundreds of soldiers were buried. In one burned-out tank, I saw the skeletons of the crew. They weren't removed until the Americans occupied the area.

Ships and vessels of all sizes were sunk along the coast and in the waterways. Bridges had been blasted and tank traps still remained at various points. This all was hard to believe. A lot of German equipment had been captured intact. Thousands of their land mines and booby traps had been removed by our sappers and stacked along the roadways.

My squadron had been without fresh meat for about six months, even though we tried to procure some through supply channels. Finally, we received word that it was available at Cape Bone where it was being disembarked. However, the supply people there were condemning the meat because there weren't any refrigeration facilities inland where it was designated to be sent. Apparently, they were condemning it right into their own refrigerators.

On July 16, I called some of our men together, and told them that we were going to acquire fresh provisions. I said, "I have Plan A and Plan B. Plan A will involve the same number of vehicles and I'll be in the lead vehicle. The difference in the plans will start when I come out of the field office at Cape Bone. If I'm not smiling when I come out, Plan B goes into effect."

Plan A, which entailed going through normal channels, didn't work out and I left the Cape Bone office without a smile. Therefore, we ended up exercising Plan B. When we got back to our base, our four six-by-six trucks were loaded with fresh meat that hadn't exactly been given to us. Bombs also had been in short supply, so that same day we procured what we needed for our upcoming mission in the same manner—that is, by force.

On the morning of July 17, 1943, the squadron was briefed for a 500-plane raid on the railroad marshaling yards at Naples on the Italian mainland. By this date, the Allies finally had driven the Axis out of North Africa, and our boys

had invaded Sicily, pushing the Italian and German troops halfway across the island. Our mission was to interdict Axis supply lines along the west coast of Italy. This would be my twenty-seventh mission since arriving in North Africa.

After the briefing, I went back to my office at the little Digeta airfield in Tunisia. I removed all of the items from my pockets that might provide information to the enemy if I was captured, and put them in an envelope. I tossed it to Maj. Hanford, our ground executive officer.

I suddenly realized I'd lost my rabbit's foot! I'd carried it on every flight since I'd learned how to fly. I wasn't superstitious, but I couldn't help thinking about the many close calls that I'd had while carrying it with me. I was the same as many others; I went along with superstitious beliefs just in case there might be something to it.

Since the rabbit foot was gone, I fingered my wallet with two months back pay in it for a moment, then tossed it to Hanford, saying, "Send this home to my wife."

At the time, I thought I was joking. I really don't know why I asked him to do that. I'd never done this sort of thing before. I usually didn't joke about my prospects prior to a dangerous mission.

Hanford didn't crack a smile. I'll never forget the way he looked at me. Evidently, he didn't think much of my joke as I left the office.

"A couple of letters are here for you," someone said shortly thereafter. "Do you want me to hold them or will you read them now?"

"I'll read them on the way in to the target," I replied.

I went back to pick them up and noticed my cigar box. I selected two cigars and stuffed them along with the two letters into my shirt pocket. One cigar, according to my routine, would be smoked on the way in, and the other on the way back. The second was intended to be the more enjoyable smoke.

"Good hunting," Hanford shouted as I left.

The strain of being at war begins to show.

The wing commander, General Webster, and his chief of staff, Colonel Doyle, were going along with the squadron. At the briefing, I had talked the general out of joining me in the lead aircraft because my B-26 already was overcrowded with necessary personnel. He agreed to fly with the leader of the second element.

Our formation was looking good at the rendezvous point. The fighters joined us right on time and our group of bombers was snug and tight. To the rear, I saw succeeding sections of bombers and fighters dropping into place exactly as briefed. Our group had forty-eight planes in the air that day and I was really proud of them. All of the crews were performing according to plan. Most had learned their jobs the hard way and now were seasoned combat veterans with many months of hard and brutal fighting under their belts. There had been some bad days during the past few months, with high losses and few replacements, and, of course, miserable living conditions and little rest. However, it had all contributed to our present efficiency.

The formation headed out over the Mediterranean Sea, climbing slowly to allow the bombers, with their heavy loads of 500 pound bombs, to maintain position. The air was smooth and the mission was on schedule. Two fighter groups were included—one to go with us to the target, and the other to screen radar stations in Sicily, then sweep over enemy airstrips, hoping to flush out a few ME-109s or ME-110s before heading home.

My crew consisted of Maj. Diamond, pilot; Lt. Koch, bombardier; Lt. Batchelor, navigator; and three gunners in addition to myself as the formation commander. I gave the signal for the formation to test fire the guns and make last-minute checks. I watched the ships move out slowly, each gun winked a few times, then the planes settled back into their positions.

Maj. Diamond called to his gunners on the inter-phone: "OK! Test guns when ready."

As each gunner tested the guns, a comforting shudder swept through the ship, followed by their return calls.

"Tail guns, OK Sir."

"Waist guns, OK Sir."

"Turret, OK Sir."

We also test fired the six nose guns, which filled the cockpit with smoke and sounded like tanks crashing through a can factory. The formation pulled back together and we concentrated on our navigation and reviewed the plan of attack. Meanwhile, a couple of the ships had signaled and turned back due to mechanical difficulties. They were replaced immediately by spares flying alongside for that purpose. The tail gunner gave a running commentary on the progress of the formation, since we couldn't look back to see it ourselves. The mission was right on schedule.

When all of my checks were completed, I reached for a cigar and clutched the two "V-mail" letters I'd temporarily forgotten about. One was from my mother and the other from Dot. I lit my stogie and commenced reading, occasionally pausing to check the cockpit instruments or observe the formation. Mom told me about her job as an office worker in the Tacoma shipyards, which she had chosen to do as her part in the war effort. My younger sister, Virginia, was helping make B-17s at the Boeing plant in Seattle. My other sister, Shirley Morgan, was doing her bit for her husband, Lt. Max Morgan, a Navy flyer patrolling for enemy submarines in the Caribbean. Mom said Dad would've been proud of all of us if he were alive. With him gone, though, she couldn't help being lonesome.

I re-lit the cigar and opened the letter from my wife. Dot also described activities on the home front. She worked for the Red Cross in Hoquiam, Washington, while living with an old college chum, Kay McCollom. Kay was the wife of

ASSOCIATED PRESS, *June 4, 1943— Maj. Charles R. Greening of Tacoma, who devised the 20 cent bombsight which he and fellow airmen used in the celebrated bombing of Tokyo last year, has reported a new technique for destroying enemy aircraft. Bomb them in flight. Mrs. Greening said today her famous husband described in a letter from North Africa how his bombardier dropped a bomb on a German plane in the air.*

"He said they were attacked by a bunch of German pursuit ships," she related, "and one of them flew directly underneath his plane. The bombardier let loose and scored a direct hit."

one of my best friends and former fraternity brother, Lt. Col. Loren "Mac" McCollom. He also was a pilot, flying fighters out of England. Dot told me about her visit to a fortune-teller in Port Townsend, Washington, who told her she could expect some "exciting news" on July 21 of this year.

"Of course," Dot said in her letter, "this can only mean you're coming home!"

"Home!" How appealing that word sounded—yet how fantastically distant. My thoughts of home quickly dissolved as the first islands north of the Gulf of Naples appeared through the haze. This was close to our initial turning point for the run-in to the target. All of the ships flew in perfect formation, like a mother hen with chicks running beside her. Engine power was increased and we commenced slow evasive action as the first flak bursts puffed below us. I pulled a

APPROACHING ASCENSION *"Two B-26 Marauders approaching Ascension Island located in the South Atlantic. Pinhead size, Ascension made the long over-water hop from Natal, Brazil, to Dakar, Africa, a safer one."* Not as Briefed

tin hat over my head in anticipation of the few minutes of hard work about to commence, but then took it off because it bothered me.

When leveling out at 13,000 feet over the coast of Italy, I gave the signal for a right turn over the initial point. The fighters pulled away to the left to avoid the flak beginning to mushroom up from below. Our group made the turn easily and each flight maneuvered into position for the bomb run. We proceeded south toward the target. I had my first glimpse of Mt. Vesuvius south of Naples, which was sending up a column of smoke from its crater. Vesuvius had fascinated me since I was a boy, when I'd read stories about the destruction of ancient Pompeii. I was eager to observe the volcano while on this flight.

The flak increased, becoming the worst I had ever experienced. Maj. Diamond called to bombardier Koch, "On course. Open bomb bay doors."

I focused my thoughts on the bombardier, who had warmed up the bombsight and turned on the bomb-rack switches. Now he was carrying the ball. A few minutes remained before we needed to fly the ship straight and level for the bomb drop. Therefore, we took slow, evasive action, trying to avoid the flak that was coming closer and intensifying every minute. I tried to shoot some movie footage of the flak and of Mt. Vesuvius, but I lost that battle of nerves and tossed the camera to the floor. I intermittently turned the IFF radio transmitter on and off, hoping it would interfere with the radio reading of the anti-aircraft guns.

All at once, the main flak attack commenced. It was furious and terrifying. My throat was dry and tight, as burst after burst blackened the sky, making crashing sounds like the head-on collisions of trains. Black puffs instantly appeared, hung momentarily, then swiftly swept past us. Diamond's eyes were riveted on the instruments, waiting for the bombardier's signal to follow the direction indicator. Suddenly, a large burst exploded under the tail, cutting our control wires and shaking the plane so much that I thought it was going to pieces.

With the control wires gone, we were forced to use the trim tabs to continue the bomb run. In the back of my mind, I knew this plane would never get us home. My heart pounded. I was breathless and sick to my stomach. I felt crash after crash of exploding flak, tearing our ship up like birdshot through a crippled pheasant. We needed just one minute of straight, level flight to release the bombs. Sixty seconds seemed like sixty minutes.

I glued my eyes to a signal light that would flicker when the bombs left the rack. It seemed they'd never go on. For an awful moment, I thought the bomb bay was damaged by flak and we wouldn't be able to drop the bombs. Just when I was about to call Koch, the bomb lights suddenly flicked four times. I glanced back and saw the big eggs separate. Four 500-pound bombs were on their way to the target. Now all we had to do was figure out a way to get home.

We nosed down slightly to drop below the flak, but the bursts seemed to double in retaliation. Then, I spotted two well-aimed salvos—one string on our right, and another to the left. The bracketing was good.

"Boy! Not bad shooting," I screamed over the roar of the engines. "They have us square. If we don't turn, the next salvo should be it!"

Lt. Diamond replied with a helpless tug on the floppy control column.

Then it came—a direct hit to the right engine! A thunderous roar on our right was followed by terrible shaking. I recall seeing the engine, with the cowling gone, just barely hanging on the wing. The right side of the cockpit was smashed in, the wind roared, and the instrument panel gauges danced crazily in the smoke and tangled wire. My breath stopped completely from fright. The heat was terrific, like a blowtorch blasting through the cockpit. Why weren't we burned or hurt?

The plane vibrated horribly because the battered mass of junk that had been a fine $15,000 engine still hung to the mounts. The wind blasted through jagged holes in the fuselage. Parts of the plane dropped off, falling back through the formation behind us. The intense flak continued. Our plane lost position in the formation. Obviously, we were riding a dead duck.

"Let's get out of this thing!" I yelled at Maj. Diamond, but he just sat there at the controls. I believe he was staying to try and help the rest of us get out.

No further formalities were in order. It was time to get out and start the long walk home. Koch, in the bombardier's nose position, wanted to get past us in the cockpit, so he could bail-out. I reached out to call the gunners in the tail section, but found that my radio junction box was blasted away. Koch peered up through the bombardier's crawl-way, his eyes pleading with me to get out of the way and let him escape.

As I scrambled out of my seat toward the rear, with Koch close behind, I pulled the bomb bay emergency bottle to hold the doors in open position. Batchelor, looking bewildered, stood in the navigator's compartment waiting for orders.

"Hit the silk!" I shouted while pointing at the bomb bay.

As I pointed, there was another blinding flash and everything happened at once. The engine fell free, a wing started coming off, and the plane began to burn. Another flak burst exploded almost directly in the bomb bay. The explosion was deafening and shell fragments crashed through the full length of the ship.

Batchelor shouted, "I've been hit with a hammer!" and clutched his right leg.

Koch, Batchelor, and I clambered onto the bomb bay catwalk to jump. I glanced back and couldn't see Diamond. Figuring he'd been hit, I started back, but just then the plane snapped violently into a left spin, throwing the three of us out.

As I fell, the thought flashed through my mind that Axis fighter planes recently had machine-gunned five bailed-out Americans as they hung helplessly in their parachutes. I wanted to delay opening my chute until fairly close to the ground to avoid the same fate, but my clenched fist already was putting permanent fingerprints in the rip cord handle.

Then I saw our B-26 dropping in a big flat spin right alongside of me. A B-26 falls and spins at about 120 or 125 mph. Unfortunately, that was about the same speed I was falling. The plane's wing swung by my face with a strong rush of wind. It made a couple of more passes at me, nearly connecting each time. At 10,000 feet, I decided I'd better open my chute to get away from the plane. Yanking on the cord, I felt the gratifying tug of silk hitting the wind, suspending me in the air.

I saw the ship spinning down directly below me, scattering parts and trailing smoke. The wreck hit the base of Mt. Vesuvius and within a split second erupted into a furious blaze, emitting an oily mass of black smoke in the sky. Meanwhile, the noise of the enemy's AA guns and the exploding bombs from our formation were terrible. I saw only five chutes from the other six crewmen and I shuddered, visualizing Diamond burning in the wreckage below.

I glanced at our bomber formation and suddenly noticed, back toward the target area, that a massive ball of flame was plunging earthward. I thought, "What sort of weapon was this?" I'd seen bombs and rockets dropped on our formations by Axis aircraft, but this was something new. The ball of flame was so huge that I couldn't conceive of any aircraft big enough to carry such a weapon. I thought it was some new, gruesome, German bomb. (A little later, another downed airman would tell me what it was.)

The blazing mass landed directly on a large oil storage tank in a refinery area. The storage tank immediately exploded. Thus, after the gigantic ball of flame fell to the ground, a massive explosion went right back up into the sky. The blast formed a huge smoke ring that completely encircled me. I was at about 7,000 feet, but the explosion almost reached me. I hardly believed what I was seeing.

As I watched our formation continue the mission, I was proud to see the number two man assume the lead, as I'd told him to do. The other planes tightened up behind him. It's difficult when the lead plane gets shot out of formation. Sometimes, a squadron goes in all directions, but my group stayed together nicely. It was gratifying to see the guys do this.

As they flew on, I was left hanging alone and forlorn in the harness. For some stupid reason, I thought about the things that I'd left behind, including several bottles of whiskey in my tent. I knew that Jack Henderson, who liked good whiskey, would be there to lament my loss by drinking it up. In my confused state of mind, I decided I'd wire him to have him save my things for me.

I heard a flat, "whok" sound. I suddenly realized it was enemy artillery—88s or 105s—firing at the formation. One round, making an awful sound, passed so close to me that it tore holes in the chute. These noises when heard inside a plane are muffled and not quite as frightening as when out in the open. Flak burst directly under me, actually lifting my entire weight out of the harness and nearly collapsing the

Naples, July 17, 1943.

chute. Several large rents appeared where shell fragments penetrated the fabric. Why I wasn't hit, I'll never know. I desperately wished I hadn't opened my chute so soon. It seemed like it would take an eternity to reach the ground.

Again, a flaming ball fell behind me, which I presumed was a bomber going down. No chutes appeared near it. The target area was a conflagration of destruction and ruin. I looked about frantically for enemy fighters that might machine-gun me as I descended. I forgot about this worry, however, when I dropped lower and a heavy barrage of machine-gun bullets from the ground cracked around me. Bullets clipped the shroud lines and one hit me in the knee. Though I felt it, it didn't hurt for some reason. I tried to swing in the chute, so I'd offer as poor of a target as possible. I panicked, realizing how helpless I was.

I slipped the chute as best I could to control the direction of my descent. To make matters more difficult, however, the seat-type life raft that was part of the chute had fallen out from under me when I jumped. Thus, I'd dropped down in the harness and the chest straps were choking me. Being out of breath and with my heart pounding fast, I didn't have much strength, and sheer terror was robbing me of what little was left. I pulled as long as I could on the chute, then glanced down to see where I would land. To my horror, I looked squarely into the smoking crater of Mt. Vesuvius!

At the time, Vesuvius was building up for an eruption. As I tried to judge my fall in the oscillating chute, I could see the vent where smoke billowed out. I was on the ocean side of the volcano, drifting directly toward the crater. I thought for sure that I'd drop into it. I wanted to dump the air in my chute, fall straight for a time, and land short of the crater, but I was afraid that I'd land on the burning wreckage of our plane. I could hear the ammunition in it going off like popcorn.

In spite of my desperation, I was mesmerized by the fantastic view into the volcano. Suddenly, the crater rim drifted past and, alarmingly, the ground rushed up faster and faster toward me. I dimly recall an ugly ridge of lava rock beneath my feet. I made a last effort to reach a small smooth area just beyond. A split second before landing, I remembered my premonition about having bad luck this day because I'd lost my rabbit's foot. Then the lights went out.

It was a new beginning for me when I awoke.

I don't know how long I was unconscious, but it seemed as if I were awakening in bed at home. I didn't know who I was, where I was, or why this big mountain was here. There was a kind of silence all around me, with smoke billowing up. I had a vague memory of a volcano, but no name connected to it. The farthest thing from my mind was the war.

My wind-filled chute was dragging me along. I heard a groan, and looked around, thinking, "My God, I'm setting on some guy. There's a leg underneath me, sticking out the side. Who in the world did I land on?"

Then I realized it was my own leg, disjointed at the hip and sticking out at a horrible angle. The groan was mine also. I removed my harness and tried to get to my feet amongst the volcanic rocks. I didn't start hurting until I tried to stand up. The effort was useless because both legs were numb. My clothing was torn and my face was covered with blood.

Shaking my head, I tried to make sense out of this completely foggy picture. It seemed like a bad dream. The huge mountain above me billowed brown-black smoke. Below me were foothills, with agricultural fields and villages. Huge columns of dark smoke rose from a city to the north. I was totally bewildered by the thundering explosions and my head was swimming. I passed out again—nature's anesthetic for pain.

I don't think I was out for long, however, when I felt a warm breeze briskly pass over my head. I opened my eyes again. The bad dream had returned, looking just the same. My legs were cramped with pain by now, my throat was parched, and I was burning with fever.

I stuck my head up over a rock. Suddenly, I heard a "splat" about six inches behind my head. I thought the rock was exploding. I dropped back down and waited. This was too much for me to figure out. I raised my head again, and "whak" came another. Someone down there was shooting at me!

I must have blacked out again, because the next thing I remember was the hazy sight of a person with a hot, sweaty, red face pushed into an odd looking helmet. Where'd this guy come from? How long has he been here? He was looking at me over the sights of a gun! Why? I had no idea, but at least someone was here. I needed help and, in my confusion, was glad to see him. I held my right hand out to greet him.

The soldier must have been confused also, because without pausing he placed his rifle against some rocks and came over to shake my hand. I felt sure he was going to help me. Suddenly, he rushed back, snatched the rifle, and pointed it at my head again. So far nothing made sense. I didn't know who he was, but I knew the gun meant business. I didn't know he was a German soldier.

After standing there, observing me for a few moments, the strange soldier shouted in a guttural and thoroughly unintelligible tongue. His wild gestures indicated he wanted me

to get up and follow him. All I could do was shrug my shoulders and point to my aching legs. He eased up close to inspect me and saw that I couldn't move. Then a couple of more men showed up. After studying my legs a bit, one put a rifle between my legs and pried, while another sat on my knee and popped my hip back into joint. It hurt horribly, and I remember an awful "whack" when it went in. I thought they'd broken my leg. But they hadn't, so they must have known what they were doing.

The first soldier motioned for me to climb on his back, piggyback style. The trip down the mountain was a nightmare. I remember holding his rifle so he could use his hands for support as we slid and fell over rocks. My whole body screamed in pain. I vaguely recall other men joining us, pulling at my left leg and doing everything they could to make my trip down more painful.

During the descent, I did my best to figure out the situation. I now realized these men were German soldiers, but I couldn't understand why I was with them. I couldn't recall any of the events that would explain why I was here. I figured I must be a prisoner of war, but still couldn't remember who I was. I worried that the Germans would think I was really stubborn if I wouldn't give them my name.

It wasn't long until more people met up with us. They grabbed me and helped hauled me up a steep trail to a motorcycle with a sidecar. Men jammed me into the sidecar and piled in on top of me. The rough ride down was accompanied by much excitement and shouting. After what seemed an eternity of bouncing and jolting, we pulled into a garage beneath a house.

I was dumped onto a table in the basement. An argument ensued between some civilians, the Germans, and some other strange soldiers, but I focused only on my aches and pains. I finally realized that I had a face cut, a bullet wound near my knee, two sprained ankles, a badly twisted left leg, and numerous gashes and bruises.

The Germans disappeared and a civilian graciously bathed my wounds and cuts with alcohol. I absent-mindedly looked at numerous pints of beer stacked along the wall. I was given a bottle that tasted flat and weak, but under the circumstances it really hit the spot. I kept worrying and trying to think what I was going to say when they interrogated me and asked for my name. I also tried finding a way to support my weight on the table to relieve the pain.

Suddenly, the basement door opened and a man was led in. I immediately recognized Lt. Batchelor, our navigator. He was wounded in the right leg, but he hobbled over to the table and gripped my hand.

"By God! Am I glad to see you, Colonel Greening."

The sight of Batchelor and the mention of my name brought my memory flooding back to me. I suddenly remembered our plane being hit, the crash, and the terrifying parachute drop.

"What happened to the rest of the crew?" I asked. "I think I saw five chutes."

"I can't remember how many chutes I saw, exactly, but I think I saw six," he replied.

While our cuts and wounds were being cleaned, the soldiers, whom I now recognized as Italians, took off our clothes and searched us from head to foot. I was offered another bottle of beer, but refused it because I felt so bad. Our captors stood around saying things that were meaningless to us, but some comments apparently were extremely insulting, judging from the gestures that went with them.

A crowd of civilians had gathered outside of the building where we were being held. Those who could see us through the windows were shaking fists and shouting. I don't recommend being captured near a target still being bombed. Infuriated civilians had killed many hundreds of our boys. They would have torn us to pieces in their futile rage over the bombing if they could have.

A military guard came in a car and held off the crowd. Batchelor was able to help me into the vehicle despite his leg wound. We barely avoided rocks thrown by the mob. We relaxed a little when the soldiers finally got the old car started, and then rattled off to some unknown location. Bombs still were crashing down on Naples. I glanced back at Mt. Vesuvius, awed by the sight of the massive smoking volcano standing there impervious to human affairs.

Our guards were privates, but they acted like members of the Italian high command who had custody of the most important war booty to ever enter the country. The driver hurled the old buggy along at wide-open speed through the streets. It couldn't do much over 30 mph, but its cornering on the narrow streets was breathtaking.

In a little village not far from Naples, we slithered to a stop in front of a jail. Here we were met by another maddened mob. My legs and ankles were useless, but the guards stood back and indicated I had to walk to the building. I could only crawl, which delighted the crowd. They spit at us, threw stones, and laughed uproariously at my feeble attempts to try to walk. Batchelor helped as much as he could and we finally entered the jail where we were temporarily safe.

The heavy, stone jail was old and dirty. With Batchelor's help, I crept up a high flight of rickety stairs. They seated us in an office at the top. My ankles were so swollen that I had to remove my shoes. My body screamed in protest whenever anything came in contact with my legs. I wanted to lie on the floor, fall asleep, and wake to find it was a bad dream.

I lifted myself up from the chair with my hands to relieve my leg pains, while taking in the surroundings. The walls were old and cracked, and flyspecks covered everything except the highly polished desk in front of us. Through the barred windows, the crowd screamed their hatred at us. A majestic portrait of Benito Mussolini scowled down at us. When the door opened, the guard snapped to attention and motioned for us to stand. A handsome and self-important looking Italian officer entered.

I couldn't rise, so I pushed myself up as high from the chair as I could with my hands. The officer sat down and drew a large manila envelope from a shabby briefcase. As he emptied the envelope, my cigar, two letters, insignia, handkerchief, and cigarette lighter spilled out on the table. The Italians spotted the cigar the same time I did. If you knew about the rarity of good cigars in Italy at that time, you can understand why it was never seen again.

After the officer studied the contents of the envelope, he snapped a command at the guard, who nearly knocked himself out scrambling through the door. The guard brought back a meek looking interpreter whose efforts were pitiful and only succeeded in infuriating our interrogator. I couldn't understand the interpreter, nor could he understand me. The officer screamed at us as if I'd understand Italian if he'd just shout loud enough. He waved a pistol under my nose, while making gestures that surely would have made his comments quite imperative if I'd known what he was saying. The interrogation was a miserable flop, at least from the Italian point of view.

The frustrated officer left the room, holding his head in his hands. Our guards were ordered to take us back to the car. I recalled the crowd's cruel laughter when I had painfully crawled into the jail. I decided not to let them see me crawl again. Somehow I made it downstairs using the banister, but I wouldn't have made it to the car without Batchelor's help.

The screaming mob had grown quite large by then. The guards made a solid line on either side of us as I inched my way toward the car. Little kids—just little fellers—wormed their way through the guards' legs and let us have it with clubs, and they could really hit. I felt like I deserved some sympathy for my injuries, so the crowd's anger made the blows hurt even more. The adults kicked, spat, and struck at us with more venom and hate than I'd ever seen before. I was determined to walk to the car. Stones hit the wall all around us. We crawled into the car and quickly rolled up the

windows to stop the crowd from grabbing at us. In the midst of all this, to my surprise I saw a couple of sympathetic faces in the mob.

It was hard for me to believe that I could be the object of such hate. I always had tried to be a friendly guy. At that point, I didn't comprehend that I appeared to be a demon to this crowd. Our bombers had just obliterated part of Naples and killed hundreds of people, but I didn't comprehend this. From 10,000 feet up, an airman just sees a target; a railroad marshalling area, a bridge, or an airfield.

The car proceeded through the streets toward an ominous glow that lit up the darkening sky. Shattering explosions and bright flashes disturbed the dusk. This was my first introduction to concentrated mass destruction on the ground, seen close-up on a terrible scale. As we drove further into Naples, I began to face up to what made the mobs react the way they did. As we passed by each stricken city block, I also realized what a tough job a ground soldier has.

In the distance, smoke billowed from the area that my B-26s had bombed. The sight was awesome and sickening. The whole city appeared afire, with flames reaching thousands of feet into the sky. Riding on, we passed within a few hundred feet of the railroad marshalling yard that had been targeted. Trains and boxcars were piled up or smashed into unrecognizable piles of junk. Some boxcars still were exploding. Ships were sunk in the harbor, and everywhere we looked there was chaos, ruin, and death.

Nothing ever impressed me more than this did! Up to then, I'd bombed targets in Japan, North Africa, Sardinia, Sicily, Pantelleria, and the Italian mainland. I'd been on the ground in Africa when Jerry bombs had come down around me, but this was my first exposure to the results of a large-scale bombing raid. Grimy faced men rushed about fighting fires and pulling battered bodies from the wreckage. I saw a dead horse and driver stretched out on the sidewalks. I saw dead and wounded people with no one to attend to them.

Then, I saw a group of three or four children. They must have been clinging together in terror. A bomb had splattered their little bodies all over a wall. I couldn't look anymore. I was sick at heart and mind to think that this was my doing. I thanked God this wasn't happening in America and hoped it never would. I hated the whole miserable mess. The full impact of mass death pressed deeply into my brain. I had to close my eyes. I felt no satisfaction in our successful bombing mission. I wanted to believe it hadn't happened. Our guards watched us to see if we were proud of what we'd done, but there was no sign of pride on either of our faces. Finally, I understood why the crowd hated us so much.

We arrived at another jail and were interrogated again. The interpreter spoke English fairly well, but he couldn't understand us. We used this to our advantage and pretended not to understand him. The officer in charge, apparently of high rank and quite impressed with himself, was easily aggravated. He became deeply enraged. The interpreter sweated as much as we did.

The Italian fascist emblem was displayed on everything in sight—uniforms, stationery, walls, and doors.[1] I wouldn't be surprised if it was on their underwear. The guards were courteous and soldierly in the officer's presence, but when he left the room they swaggered about and tried to look tough. The enormous quantity of stars, braid, ornaments, and other decorative items on their uniforms seemed to make them feel quite superior to American officers in plain khaki uniforms. Our insignia, consisting of a pair of wings and two collar ornaments, were taken away at the previous police station, but later returned.

After the unsuccessful interrogation, they seemed to be trying to decide where to take us next. I hoped they'd get us out of Naples because I knew that the bombing would start up again that night. From the mission planning that I'd attended before the flight, I knew the British were due to attack at any time. My legs ached and Batchelor suffered from his leg wound, and sitting in hard straight chairs made it worse for us. We wanted to lie down on the floor, but we wouldn't give the guards the satisfaction of seeing us do it.

Suddenly, air-raid sirens began wailing. This quickly took our thoughts off of our aches and pains, and even improved our speed in creeping to an air-raid shelter. The guards weren't eager to take us to a protected area, but they had to if they wanted to get under cover themselves. The trip into the basement was long and painful. Batchelor helped again, even though he should have had assistance himself. British bombs plastered the area all around us. The door on the cell next to us was blown off.

After the raid, we were taken to a truck that had a very small cab. By this time, I felt like screaming every time I touched anything or anyone bumped into me. We squeezed in with the driver and two guards. Every movement the vehicle made brought pain. My head ached fiercely and each heartbeat caused a horrible pounding in my befuddled brain. The truck couldn't go any faster than a crawl. Gas fumes filled the cab each time the gears were shifted, which made my headache worse.

A few miles north of Naples, we eventually arrived at a little hospital and seaplane base on a small island. We crept miserably to the third floor of a military barracks and into a room with double-deck bunks and dirty blankets. The beds looked inviting, even though consisting of flea-ridden burlap. Unfortunately, after I dropped onto one, there wasn't a part of my body that I could lie on without hurting even more.

What a night! My throat was swollen, my head throbbed, and my sprained ankles ached, but the worse part was coming to the realization that I was a prisoner of war. This was the most frustrating feeling I'd ever had. I thought about Dot and my mother, and what they might go through before learning about what had happened to me. I hadn't been in command of my group for long and I was heart broken by my fate. I'd never figured something like this would happen to me. The only consolation was that I felt confident that I wouldn't be a prisoner for long. I was certain the war was almost over. After all, this was July 17, 1943, and we had been in the war for over 1 1/2 years. I thought we had the Axis on their heels.

I thought back to the Tokyo raid, a little over a year before. Maj. Davy Jones, who participated in that attack, now was a prisoner of war too. Maybe I would run into him. Lt. Tom Griffin and Lt. Griff Williams, also on the Doolittle raid, had been downed in Sicily a couple of weeks before and were supposed to be prisoners.[2] I'd heard that the Japanese had captured and executed some of our unfortunate boys in China. I told myself that I was a lot luckier than they were.[3]

Suddenly, I remembered a recent rumor that the Germans had promised to turn any Tokyo raiders falling into their hands over to the Japanese. I sure hoped they wouldn't connect me with the raid. It gave me plenty to think about.

My thoughts ended abruptly when an air raid siren wailed. Guards burst into the room and motioned for us to go to the shelter. The walk, or I should say my crawl, down to the shelter was something to remember. I couldn't get them to help me and I had to inch along very slowly, until I finally made it to the ground floor and outside to a hillside cave. The air-raid shelter was dirty and wet, with one bench sloping toward the floor at just enough of an angle to be impossible to sit on.

It seemed liked hours before the attack ended. During the raid, we saw five RAF planes overhead. I didn't see a single aircraft go down, but we were told the next morning that thirteen were destroyed. From that point on, I took all Axis information with a grain of salt.

We endured three trips to the air raid shelter that night. I'd have preferred remaining in bed and taking my chances. On each trip, we pleaded with the guards to take us to a hospital. Once, they actually intended to do so, but while getting us into an ambulance, some bombs fell within a mile or two, which scared them enough to forget the idea.

I spent a sleepless night. In the morning, we were taken to a flooded bathroom with a toilet that had been plugged up ever since Julius Caesar left the place. From a window in the washroom, we looked out over the Bay of Naples to the city in the distance. Fires still burned and the rising smoke obscured Mt. Vesuvius. From a window on the other side of the building, we saw four or five seaplanes riding at anchor within a few yards of the shore. If we'd been able to climb into one of them, it might have been an opportunity to escape. It's probably a good thing we didn't try, because we observed later that it required four or five expert mechanics to start the engines. Of course, if we had tried to fly one of the planes back, our own aircraft probably would have shot us down.

Later in the day, about nine bedraggled Americans were brought in to keep us company. Two from my group had landed in the water after the raid and were taken prisoner by one of the seaplanes. One fellow had spent considerable time in the ocean and suffered from exposure. His face was parchment colored, his eyes yellow, and he couldn't keep anything in his stomach. He was extremely uncomfortable. Later, I learned he had jaundice.

Another prisoner, also from my group, had been in a plane knocked down by a fragment from another one of our aircraft that accidentally had been struck and blown up by one of our own bombs. The latter unfortunate aircraft must have been the incredible flaming mass that I'd seen falling from the sky the day before, which I'd thought might be a new German weapon.

The other men were from another group and they didn't know us. On our first attempt to converse with them, they gave us cold stares. They'd been well trained to not divulge any military information to planted spies, which we might have been. In my state of mind at the time, however, this was almost the last straw. Our own countrymen wouldn't even speak to us! After I calmed down, I was glad they'd acted that

way. On more than one occasion, information was gleaned from prisoners in just such a fashion.

Shortly after noon, we were taken to a dressing station to be patched up. Unfortunately, it meant going down three flights of steps again. I figured a few more of these trips would be enough to transform me into a permanent casualty. In the courtyard, we saw German troops loading ammunition and equipment into small boats that were similar to our landing barges. Their equipment looked shabby in contrast to the fine equipment we'd been receiving from the States while stationed in Africa.

I noticed that the officers strutted in stiff military fashion when giving orders to the enlisted men. They looked at us with bored expressions, apparently trying to show contempt for Americans. They seemed to take great pride in how well dressed they were, and how much braid and ribbons they wore. In fact, they looked as if they were ready for a full-dress parade. This was my first experience with German officers and it didn't impress me much. We didn't treat our enlisted men like dirt the way those officers did.

I realized the equipment they were loading probably would be used to kill our men. I felt I should do something to try and destroy it. I suppose it was fortunate I was injured because it gave me an excuse not to attempt such a foolhardy thing.

We were examined at a small dispensary and our cuts and wounds were cleaned and bandaged. For some peculiar reason they applied iodine to every black and blue spot on my body. I was "iodined" from head to foot, making my skin sore for four days.

When we returned and passed the Germans loading equipment, the officer in charge noticed us. He shouted and gestured as only a German officer can, creating panic in the ranks. Apparently, he was protesting to our guards for allowing us to observe what was going on. We were roughly hustled up the barracks stairway and not allowed to peek outside.

After another miserable night, we were notified to make preparations to move out at 10:30 AM. We went downstairs for the last time and boarded an open-bed truck that looked like the first motor vehicle ever built in Europe. Its top speed was about 10 or 15 mph, downhill with a tail wind. When idling, the contraption shook from stem to stern. There were so many guards that there scarcely was room for the eleven of us who were prisoners. The truck took off with a jerk that almost left everybody behind, then jolted its way along the road to Naples.

Thousands of people were busy in the streets. When we arrived in the middle of the city, air raid sirens started wailing. People began jabbering and running wildly in all directions. One woman went full tilt down the street, screaming as loudly as she could and dragging her youngster behind, bouncing and dangling like a doll. Other small children without parents blindly ran everywhere, crying at the top of their lungs. The air raid shelters were jammed to capacity. Streetcars were abandoned and people disappeared as if by magic.

One elderly man, apparently too old to do much running, just sat in a streetcar with an expression on his face that said, "To hell with them! A bomb probably won't fall here and, besides, I've lived long enough anyway."

The truck made it to the top of a hill with steam pouring from the radiator. Getting further from the center of town, we started to relax, until we came to an airdrome. We knew this was an ideal target. The field was covered with planes of all types. Some were taking off and others were being left to their fate. A large, six-engine ME-323 lifted off just as we came into view of the field. The ground personnel were in the air raid shelters. Now and then, we saw a face peering anxiously from a shelter entrance. Leaving town, we heard the all-clear signal. A raid hadn't materialized and all of the excitement was in vain. It made me realize the value to our side of false alarms, which hurt Axis morale and caused losses in time and labor.

The old truck wheezed along the road north of Naples for hours and hours. We saw little German or Italian military equipment and never were delayed by military convoys or vehicles. This was quite a contrast to Africa, where the roads were jammed day and night with Allied men and equipment moving forward.

About 2 PM, the truck coughed to a stop by a farmhouse, where the guards demanded water from a farmer. The guards sat down and had a meal of grapes, bread, canned meat, and wine. We thought the food looked pretty bad, which turned out to be irrelevant since they didn't give us any. After finishing the meal, they broke open cartons of some kind of hardtack biscuits. These were about the size of a teller mine and just as hard. We tried eating them, but were corrected by the guards who had us dunk the biscuits in a five-gallon pail of water.

After soaking for 15 or 20 minutes, the biscuits grew to about twice their original size and were soft enough to eat, but tasteless. We received one small can of meat to divide among us to add flavor to the meal. By now, we realized the Italian guards had eaten royally compared to us. We consumed all of the biscuits, since we hadn't had a meal since we were in the air raid shelter, two days before. It soon got to where we'd eat anything even resembling food.

About dusk, we came to the outskirts of Rome. Long columns of Italian civilians were leaving the city, most of them carrying bundles of belongings or pushing carts. They seemed angry and scared. When we approached an airfield, we discovered the reason for the congested highways. The airdrome was in shambles and numerous aircraft were afire on the field. Some of the smoldering wreckage indicated that the fires had been burning for several hours. A large-scale attack had occurred in the area, which explained why we had heard air raid sirens in Naples. Our formations going north to bomb Rome had passed by Naples. The hangars had been blasted into a mere skeleton framework, and some stray

bombs had landed squarely in the roadbed, causing disruptions. Civilian traffic became heavier as we neared Rome.

Though we kept grim and expressionless faces, we couldn't help but be proud of the successful Allied raid, but soon our human instincts overrode our pride. We pitied these poor people, most of whom probably wanted to end the war immediately. We hated seeing children so helpless and bewildered, even though we realized this was part of the brutal methods required in conducting a winning campaign. I thought, perhaps, it was best that our military forces were clearly showing our superiority, because the fascist elements would see the handwriting on the wall and give up. As prisoners, we realized the Allies had greater strength, since we had observed the military forces and situation on both sides.

The horror of Naples was repeated in Rome. Railroad yards were ablaze and there were fires all over the city. People scurried about in every direction, most of them wide-eyed, frightened, and panicky. If they had recognized us they would have killed us in revenge. Our guards, however, seemed determined to get us to our destination.

Some bombs had missed the targets, hitting churches and homes, and many civilians had died. For the most part, however, the accuracy and military effectiveness of the bombing was excellent. The targets had been carefully selected, and the railroad yards, oil and gas storage facilities, and airfields were thoroughly neutralized. Naturally, the civilians took note of the bombed-out churches a thousand times more than they did the military targets. We were delayed by traffic jams several times, but fortunately it was dark enough that the angry crowds couldn't identify us.

Our driver apparently was confused. He stopped at every sentry box to ask for directions, but didn't seem to get much help. We drove on into the countryside north of Rome for what seemed like an eternity. It grew bitterly cold, and our bruised arms and legs ached and cramped up even more. Our only consolation was that the guards had to endure it too.

The wheezy truck finally stopped alongside an old, walled monastery high in the mountains, about thirty miles north of Rome. I later learned this town was Poggio. A quarantine camp was located here. I couldn't move on my own accord and had to be lifted out of the truck. The lads helped me to a seat in an office, where an Italian "Maresciallo," or sergeant major, confronted us. It seemed at a glance that he was a hard-bitten customer with little love for anyone, much less American prisoners.

We were told in no uncertain terms that we were to conduct ourselves as prisoners of war. We were to stand at attention and salute the Maresciallo whenever in his presence. We would be interrogated and were expected to answer all questions.

It was plain he was using all the bluff he could muster. In fact, he bluffed so much to get our respect that he lost it. I never did salute him and only on a few occasions did anyone stand when in his presence. He screamed and yelled at us, but that was about as far as it went.

Our names and serial numbers were taken and we were assigned quarters. When the Maresciallo noticed my rank, he bubbled over with joy.

"This is the first time we've had such a high ranking officer in our camp. I have a special room I have been saving for just such an officer."

I said, "I would rather be with the other fellows if you don't mind. It will give me someone to talk to."

"Meester Lt. Colonel, you take your orders from me, see! When I feexa you up in a room you take it and like it, see!" I moved into the room.

The bed was the first thing that met my eye. It had a mattress and pillow, and even springs. I lost no time in easing my bundle of aches and pains down on it. Unfortunately, I quickly discovered that an iron rod had been welded across the middle, eliminating any comfort the bed might have provided. I am sure that the rod was placed there just for that purpose. It was a steel bed and the rod couldn't be removed.

The next day, prisoners were taken one at a time to the commandant's office to be interrogated. Of course, we knew the Geneva Convention rules stipulating that a POW is required to provide nothing more than name, rank, and serial number. This was all we intended to give. The commandant was a polite, smooth operator. He spoke English fairly well and acted as if we were just having a companionable chat. He claimed nothing we said would be taken down or used for military intelligence. This was laughable and put us on guard even more.

He said to me, "You see, we have enough data on you and what you are, to fill out all the information we want. We know from our records on your group that you are a group commander."

"Where did you get that?" I asked, actually a little perplexed. He was right about me being a group commander, but that position is supposed to be filled by a full colonel, whereas I was a lieutenant colonel.

He pulled out a folder, showing the organization of a U.S. Army Air Force group. It was completely erroneous. I suspected it was intentionally wrong to get us to correct it. It indicated there were 9 to 12 bombers, 15 to 20 fighters, 4 or 5 observation airplanes, and a couple of rescue planes in our group. It also listed the number and rank of pilots supposedly in a group. It was wrong, but I acted amazed that they had such accurate information. He let me go.

The next few days were boring. My room was clean, but empty. I stared at the brown, plaster walls. I had no idea about how POWs were treated and assumed that this was what we could expect for the duration of our imprisonment.

MAKING SURE OF IT *"Lt. Col. Mark E. Hubbard, of St. Paul, Minnesota, singled out this 'Stuka' [JU-87] from twenty-four which were dive-bombing at Sened, North Africa. The colonel's squadron broke up the German attack and the Stukas scattered and ran for home. Col. Hubbard followed this one and shot him down in a side deflection burst. The 87 tried to land after being hit and crashed in the attempt. This was Col. Hubbard's fourth of six victories. From this attack, five 87s were downed and one FW-190."* Not as Briefed

I was glad to be alive and have this much, but I had a hard time overcoming a feeling of hopelessness. ✪

NOTES

1. The emblem of the Italian *Fascisti* included a bundle of rods encasing an ax, copied from an ancient Roman magistrate's symbol *(fasces)*.

2. Capt. David Jones was shot down over Bizerte, North Africa, on December 2, 1942. Lt. Thomas Griffen and Lt. Griffith Williams were captured on July 3–4, 1943. All three men spent the rest of the war as POWs.

3. The Japanese captured eight Doolittle raiders in China. After the war, it was revealed that Sgt. Harold Spatz, Lt. Dean Hallmark, and Lt. William Farrow were shot by a Japanese firing squad, October 15, 1942. Lt. Robert Meder died on December 1, 1943, due to beri-beri and dysentery. Four other men survived nearly 3 1/2 years of brutal treatment as prisoners of war.

THE VET'S RETURN *"A Marauder, on the approach, at Telergma, Africa, February 1943." This ship in the 95th Bombardment Squadron was part of the 17th Bombardment Group from which came all of the volunteers for the Tokyo raid. Not as Briefed*

CHAPTER SEVEN

IMPRISONED IN ITALY

There was a small slot in my cell door, just the right size for a pair of eyes to peer in and see what was going on. Every few minutes, a guard clattered up and peeked in. The eyes were distracting. I imagined them peering at me all of the time. I woke up at night, imagining viewing slots all over the room and each with a pair of eyes staring at me. I wanted to chuck something or poke fingers into the eyes whenever they appeared.

To visit the dirty latrine at the end of the hall, I had to knock on the door and wait for the guard to let me out. As I passed the other cells, more eyes peered out at me. After the first few days, I took to hiding against the wall by the cell door to make the guards think I'd escaped.

By the fifth day, I couldn't stand the solitude any longer. I jumped to my feet the best I could on my sore legs and ankles, and pounded on the door for the guard.

I shouted, "Comandante! Comandante!" until the guard understood that I wanted to see the boss.

He shuffled off to deliver my request. In about twenty minutes, he led me to an office where the commandant was waiting.

I said, "I know I am a prisoner of war and shouldn't expect favors. Nevertheless, I would like to ask a few things if you don't mind."

Then without waiting for a reply, I added, "Do we have to stay here in solitary confinement for the duration of our imprisonment? Don't we ever get anything more than a bowl of spaghetti soup a day? Can't we get anything more to eat? Are we ever allowed outside of the room?"

The commandant acted surprised, replying, "Aren't you getting your Red Cross parcel? Haven't you been given any books to read? Are you able to walk if you did go outside? What would you like to do to pass your time?"

He then called for the Maresciallo.

While we waited, I found out for the first time that we should be receiving parcels shipped by the Red Cross. I told him that I liked to draw and wanted to get some paper and pencils.

To my amazement, the commandant said he'd provide these materials that afternoon. I decided to polish the apple a bit to see what else I could get, so I replied that I'd like to draw his portrait, if he wouldn't mind. I didn't realize what I was starting.

The Maresciallo, whose name was Domenico Cuccaro, arrived and took me off to get my first Red Cross parcel. It was a British Christmas package left over from the last year. I was so overjoyed, I nearly forgot my sore legs and other worries. When I examined the parcel's contents in my room, I wept with joy. The chocolate was old and bleached, but tasted better than anything I'd ever eaten. I noticed the other boys were being issued parcels too. I felt relieved it wasn't just a favor being extended to me. I also was issued a book and a

TAXIING AT TELERGMA *"B-26 Marauders taxiing out from dispersal area at Telergma, Algeria, to take off for a mission in April 1943. At that time the Fox, Herr Rommel, had his tail between his legs and was hot-footing for Europe via Cape Bon, leaving the remnants of his vaunted Afrika Corps to fight a delaying action."* Not as Briefed

deck of cards. I never in my life enjoyed receiving anything quite so much.

Among other items in the parcel, there were five packages of English cigarettes. I'd only smoked an occasional cigar up to this time, but decided I'd try smoking cigarettes if it helped pass the time. I became a confirmed smoker, but wish I hadn't ever taken it up. An American Red Cross parcel was supposed to be issued weekly and included in it were a small amount of macaroni, a few potatoes, some cheese, and a slice of bread. I think it saved my sanity.

With the sketching materials I'd received, I began peeking out of the eyehole and drawing caricatures of the guards. The guards liked the pictures.

The next day, as I'd promised, I was taken to the commandant and made a portrait of him. I doctored it up to be as flattering as was reasonable, which pleased him to no end.

As I was leaving, the Maresciallo came in and immediately was attracted to the portrait. He lingered around my cell afterward, until finally I suggested that I do one of him. He promised he'd take me to the garden for a proper background for the portrait.

The Maresciallo also told me what he thought about the Allied raid on Rome, where supposedly the Americans had intentionally bombed churches and schools.

I replied that I'd been in Rome right after the attack and hadn't seen any schools or churches deliberately bombed, but the railroad yards and airport were thoroughly destroyed. Perhaps a few bombs had strayed and hit churches, because Rome's churches were so numerous that I don't know how we could bomb the city without hitting one. I told him not to believe the newspaper propaganda, but to go and see Rome for himself. (In fact, he visited Rome later. When he returned, he acknowledged that only a few churches and schools had been bombed. He was a bit chagrined about this.)

The next afternoon just before going to the garden, the commandant came to my room and gave me a box of German pastels and some decent paper in appreciation for the sketch that I'd made of him. The pastels were good ones. I used them to draw the Maresciallo in the garden. We selected a spot with a fish pond and decorative stone grotto as a background. Previously, he always wore a shabby uniform, but today he was in full dress with all of his fancy ribbons. He struck a pose such as I'd never seen before, holding it without batting an eye for several hours. I had a good easel and everything I needed to make a full-length portrait on a fine, large sheet of pastel paper. While drawing the portrait, he informed me that this place was a Catholic monastery, over 400 years old.

I knocked myself out making him one of the handsomest fascists in all of Italy, with just enough of his obvious features in the portrait so that he'd recognize himself. I think I made a fairly presentable portrait of him. I must have, because afterwards he never came on duty in anything other than a full dress uniform. He came to my room frequently asking questions about art and, incidentally, revealing much of his frustrated life history to me.

The second evening after I drew the Maresciallo's portrait, he came into my cell and told me to follow him. As I started leaving the room, he dashed back and picked up the pastels and paper. Something obviously was up. When I questioned him, he told me to keep quiet since he might get into trouble if we were caught.

My legs were still bad and I could barely walk; however, I wasn't going to miss this for anything. He

TAG—YOU'RE IT! *"P-38 Lightning and Messerschmit 109. Capt. Art Smedley, on a mission near Gabes, Tunisia, tangled with a formation of ME-109s. Smedley shot the first one down from a near vertical dive firing position. In his pull-out he encountered another ME on the tail of a squadron mate. This he also nailed, but was caught himself by a third 109. He parachuted to safety and was taken P.O.W. At a German base hospital he met both his victims of the dog fight!"* Not as Briefed

led me through the garden about fifty yards to the back wall. I noticed a walkway and old iron door in the wall. Nightfall was coming, and I felt like I was in a medieval setting. He pulled a large key from a pocket and inserted it into the lock. After a short struggle, he managed to get the rusty lock to work and opened the door, which protested noisily. I don't believe it had been used in years. Dirt piled up against both sides made opening it even more difficult. When we were outside, he closed and locked it carefully, then motioned me on. This promised to be an interesting evening.

We walked quietly down a road to a small but well kept villa. It stood among a group of houses with its own wall around it. I was glad we didn't go any farther or I couldn't

have made it. He slipped up to the back door and told me to wait until the coast was clear. He knocked quietly on the door. Soon, a large, jolly looking Italian lady, apparently the woman of the household, came and let us in. I was escorted into a well built and nicely kept house, which was more modern and a finer accommodation than I thought existed in this locality.

The first thing that caught my eye was a festive table full of cold fried chicken, salami, bread, salads, wines, brandies, and coffee. Then I took note of the occupants. The gentleman of the house was a congenial looking fellow who had

two daughters with him. They obviously took delight in my expression when I saw the bountiful table.

After introductions in Italian, which I didn't understand, it only took but one invitation for me to sit at the table and go to it. I believe I ate as much as all the rest of the people in the house put together. It was superb. The farmer's older daughter, stout like her mother, obviously was the Maresciallo's sweetheart. Her sister was a little honey about twelve years old. I'd been brought here to draw portraits.

After I'd eaten so much that I could scarcely see, I started the portrait of the older sister. I made her appear slimmer and beautiful, but also made sure it was a proper resemblance. It turned out pretty good in my estimation. She immediately produced just the right sized frame and glass, so we mounted it and hung it on the wall over the buffet.

FILL HER UP *"Lt. John A. Lanehart's Mitchell being re-serviced on a field in the desert at Hergla, Tunisia… [F]lying tactical support of the desert army was a full-time job."* Not as Briefed

The little sister took a seat as soon as I'd finished, ready for me to start on her. I told the Maresciallo that doing two portraits in one night was too much if they wanted me to do a good job. (I was hoping for another visit to this place, so I could get another dinner.) I was able to bring back some milk that night for the lad with jaundice, since it was one of the few things that he could keep in his stomach. I also brought onions and several bottles of wine for the other lads.

As I'd hoped, the procedure was repeated the next night. There was the same fine dinner and the portrait sitting was easier since the younger daughter was quite cute and posed

well. After finishing the portrait, more wine was brought out and, as a congenial guest, I accepted refills often. The Maresciallo did the same, but at more frequent intervals. In fact, he accepted more than I considered advisable. I still was leery of him because of the harsh way he had treated us when we first arrived at the monastery.

Around midnight, he suggested that we go back, which I welcomed. I'd become bored listening to the conversation in Italian, which I didn't understand. We bid our hosts goodnight and left by the back door. It was dark and only the stars were shining.

When approaching the back gate of the prison, my inebriated companion said, "Are you going to escape tonight?"

The question came suddenly and was a shock to me. I replied, "What did you say?"

"I said, do you plan to escape tonight?"

At first, I thought the other fellows might have been talking about such plans and were overheard by the guards.

I replied, "Why do you ask me such a question?"

"I want to know because if you are going to escape, I want to be able to go with you and get out of Italy," he explained.

"If I were able to walk," I said, "I'd be a poor soldier if I didn't try to escape and get back to my lines. If I told you I was planning to escape you would probably shoot me and get yourself some credit for catching me outside of the grounds."

MAKING IT ROUGH FOR JERRY *"P-40 Warhawks and ME-323 six-engine German transports off the Cape Bon Peninsula. There 'Gigants,' attempting to evacuate personnel from the Tunisia area in May 1943, found how expendable they were. Seventy-four were victims... in one long, running battle."* Not as Briefed

"No, I am serious. I am not drunk and if you feel you could walk, I would leave with you and assist you to get back to your lines. I am sick and tired of the war and know that Italy is going to lose in a couple more months."

I decided I'd better try to make use of this opportunity and lay some plans for the future. It would've been futile for me to escape then, because I spoke no Italian and couldn't run or even walk over 150 yards.

I told him, "If you will see me later about this and I am any better, I would be game to make a try."

He agreed and we went into the building. I lay awake most of the night thinking about the possibilities. It really sounded good. I felt even more positive about the plan when I turned over and banged my hip against the iron bar welded in the middle of the bed. The last thing I remembered that

night was a pair of guard's eyes peering through the peek hole.

The next morning, I grabbed a pencil and paper, drew a realistic set of bloodshot eyes, and stuck them over the inside of the peephole. I heard the guard's footsteps approaching. He stopped at the door and looked in—right into a pair of eyes looking back at him from a half inch away. He uttered something in Italian, which must have been bad. In fact, he was so angry that he could hardly fit the key into the lock. He open the door and tore down the picture. He gave me a thorough lecturing on something or other while gesturing wildly.

Presently, he calmed down and took a look at some of my drawings. Changing his expression somewhat, he said "buono." Using hand signs, I asked if he would like his

portrait drawn. Catching on, he beamed from ear to ear and struck a handsome pose right there in the middle of my cell. I made a pretty fair pencil sketch of him. Afterward, he actually left my door open so I could look out in the hallway. This made me realize just how much freedom meant. I couldn't have gone five steps out that door, but just seeing it open relieved some of the boredom in my existence. Of course, I felt worse than ever when he closed it again.

Afterward, all of the guards and cooks stopped by and I drew pictures of them. The cook put a little more spaghetti in my bowl and sneaked in a couple glasses of wine. In fact, my art activity caused something of a traffic problem in my room. The guards even showed me some respect. If I could have spoken Italian, I might have been able to ask for more from them. I decided that if this kept up, prison life wouldn't be so bad.

I also drew some pastels of beautiful women and made a self-portrait, which came out fair. I stuck them on the wall. During a quiet moment one day, the door suddenly opened and a half-dozen high-ranking Italian officers entered the room. I couldn't believe that they wanted their pictures done too. They looked me over as if I were some kind of freak, then admired the pictures on the wall without saying a word. They had more braid and medals than any six officers I'd seen up to that time. Presently, the commandant came in and told me that they were visiting officers, checking on camp conditions. These officers hadn't had an American officer of my rank in this camp before. They wanted to see what sort of a joker they had in the bag. I don't think I impressed them much, but it was mutual.

The Maresciallo came every night, taking me to other farmhouses outside of the camp to make portraits. I tired of it, since this wasn't helping my sprained ankles any. My greatest problem was that he marched us around and around each house before entering, to ensure there wasn't anybody there besides the family we intended to visit. None of these homes were as nice as the first villa we had visited, however. A real kicker came when he offered to take me boar hunting in the mountains. I definitely refused. I was certain that word would get out and both of us would be in a lot of trouble.

After about two weeks, my ankles were much better and I could walk fairly well. My left leg bothered me, however, and it seemed to swell up at odd intervals. Also, the wound in my knee was infected. Nevertheless, I figured I'd be able to make an escape attempt soon if the Maresciallo made an offer again. I was to the point of asking him sometime during the following day. I didn't know it, but my chance had passed.

ROCKET ATTACK
"B-24 Liberators undergoing a rocket attack by ME-110s twenty miles off the east coast of Italy near Pescara. The entire element of four ships shown here was shot down by additional German fighters after being crippled by this attack." Not as Briefed

We pulled away from Poggio with a terrifying jolt and careened downhill at an ever-increasing speed. The engine, of course, wasn't in gear—it would've completely jumped out of its mounts had it tried to keep up with the speed we were going. When we reached a level stretch, the gears finally were engaged and the bus putted along at about 10 to 15 mph. We prisoners weren't in any hurry, however. We still had a war to wait out when we arrived at wherever it was that we were going.

In about two hours, we entered Rome again. The Maresciallo was with us and he pointed out the sights. As we came to the business section, I realized the reason for the curtains. They were pulled closed to keep the Italian people from looking in and identifying us as the enemy. They still were angry about the recent bombing.

We approached a well-guarded building and passed through three sets of double barbwire. Each barbwire set had a passageway down the middle, providing a walkway for a guard. The guards were posted at least every seventy-five feet and there were more of them than prisoners in the place. In effect, the guards were about as much confined as the POWs. We didn't see one looking the least bit friendly.

We were told that this was a brand new senior officers' compound, but it wasn't occupied yet except for a few British lads acting as caretakers. We were brought here to await transportation to the next camp, which would be our permanent one. The Maresciallo told us that the permanent facility would issue Red Cross parcels every week and there would be a musical band, movies, a theater, educational facilities, and sporting activities. Our officers also would be allowed to internally manage the camp, controlling all

Fairly early the next morning, I was called into the courtyard along with the other lads who had been brought here with me. We were briefed about leaving and we settled our accounts for purchases of Italian cigarettes and toilet articles. Incidentally, these items were plentiful in Italy at the time, and our having access to them constituted a privilege that I didn't appreciate until some time later. We were ordered to get our things and board a bus-like vehicle, similar to one that I'd already ridden earlier in my captivity. This was a regular passenger model, with fancy but dirty curtains.

A sardine would have felt alone in its can compared to the way we were jammed into the bus. Every moving part of the bus opposed every other moving object, each with its individual squeak or groan. I figured the gasoline, or turpentine, or whatever they were burning flowed into every place in the bus except the carburetor. Somehow, the vehicle started out under its own power.

Ross Greening being shot down over Naples, Italy, in plane #42–2907. Washington State Historical Society, Tacoma, Washington

put in there and after two hours we were given one blanket each. We received no food. A large bucket was tossed in during the night to be used for a toilet. A few edible items remained from our Red Cross parcels. I used a meat can for a pillow and the floor wasn't the softest cement I'd ever slept on.

By morning, my hips were as sore as if I'd ridden all night in a crowded subway car. We weren't released from the room until the afternoon. It had been boring, but not unbearable, and the worst thing was the smell of the toilet bucket. We had nothing left to eat except the cans of meat, but unfortunately we didn't have a can opener and couldn't open the tins. We weren't

activity as long as it conformed to the regulations established by the Italian government. I figured our next stop would be so bad that they had to say this to prevent us from trying to escape en route.

After the lecture, the Poggio guards left us for good and we were escorted to a basement. Though the structure was well built, there was absolutely no furniture. It was totally empty. We were placed in two different rooms. The one I was in consisted entirely of cement, had a small window, and was as escape proof as any cell I'd ever seen. Five of us were

desperate, however, and decided we could wait until we had a chance to ask for a can opener.

When the guards finally came, we were taken to the front porch and each of us was given a small bowl and rusty spoon. Soon, a vat of spaghetti soup and a few slices of bread were lugged into the compound. The lukewarm soup tasted like dishwater. As a matter of fact, I would have preferred dishwater as it might have had more nutritional value. This soup had so little spaghetti in it that it was a toss-up between a couple of men to see who got a piece. We liked the bread and found an opener for the Red Cross cans.

I decided I'd better see what I could do to get better accommodations for us. When back in our cell, I pounded on the door and shouted for the guard, who came out after about an hour to see what the noise was all about. I told him I wanted to see the commandant and was led out.

I met Captain Bali, an extremely arrogant Italian officer, who wasn't the most receptive man in the world. He looked at me as if he were positive I was a private in disguise.

"Capt. Bali," I said boldly, "I think our boys are getting sick from sleeping on cement floors." In fact, one lad did have jaundice.

"I'm not an old hand at being a prisoner of war, but to me this entire house seems to be empty. We could make out much better on the wooden floors upstairs. One of our boys looks to be ill enough to be put into a hospital. Can you do anything for us?"

He said yes, and told me that he'd take care of the requests.

I felt like a real hero, getting what we wanted with so little fuss. I was taken back downstairs to wait. Towards dark, a guard came to the door and beckoned me outside. I followed, anticipating that I would receive instructions for the whole gang. Instead, the guard showed me to a room in the upper part of the house that was the best equipped one I'd seen since leaving the USA. There was a steel cot with a fairly thick mattress, and a wash stand and towels. Next to it was a real bathroom with all the fixtures, including a huge, tile bathtub. I couldn't believe such a place existed here. It was really swell that we were to be treated so nicely.

I turned to thank the guard and ask him if I could see the other rooms, but he was gone. I started down the stairs, but was stopped by another guard. I yelled for the commandant again. An interpreter came and informed me that the room was for me, but the others would have to stay where they were.

He said, "For you it is all right to sleep in these rooms because you are a senior officer and this place is built for senior officers, but the others are not, so they will have to stay where they are."

He added, "You may stay out in the yard as late as nine o'clock, but after that time you must be in your room."

I said, "If you please, I'd like to see the commandant again. I think this is a dirty deal and if the others can't stay in rooms, I'd like to be put back in the basement with them. In our country, we take the same treatment that we expect the others to take and I don't intend to be an exception here!"

"The commandant is gone for the night and will not be back until tomorrow. Goodnight," he replied.

I was frustrated and humiliated. I had a fine room with a bed while the other men sat on a cement floor, even the fellow who was sick. I remembered the remark about being allowed outside until nine, so I strolled out. Fortunately, I could access one of the basement windows to the room where the jaundiced boy was located. I heard him vomiting into a bucket. I called to them through the window and told them the story. Of course, none of them believed me, which cut to the quick.

I slipped back upstairs and grabbed all of the blankets from my room and a few more that I found in an adjacent room. I included a can of milk that I'd been saving from my parcel. I brought the load down to the window and slipped the works to them. The milk was for the sick lad. At nine o'clock, I went to bed trying not to be too comfortable, but I couldn't help sleeping like a log.

In the morning, I was down at the entrance waiting for the commandant, who didn't arrive until 10 AM. I started talking before he was through the gate and didn't stop until the boy with jaundice had been moved to a cot in an upper room. He received no other attention. During the time when the men were allowed outside of their cells, I left my room open to all. It was aggravating. I had a swell place to stay, but couldn't change a thing to save my soul. There even was

The best view of Vesuvius is right over it in a parachute. I landed ⅓ the distance from the top— Sure thought my goose was cooked!

an orderly who wanted to clean up after me, but I refused to let him in.

I was sorry I'd taken up smoking because I began to crave cigarettes after we could no longer get them. I begged and bummed a cigarette now and then from the guards, and shared them with the boys in the basement. We only got about one puff apiece, but it helped. We became very hun-gry during the five days at this compound, and we could only talk the guards into adding one extra ration of bread for each serving. It was just a slice, but it helped fill up the stomach cavity a little better.

Over the fence in back, we could see the Vatican about 400 yards away. We had learned that you supposedly could be free if you got inside the Vatican, so we inspected it closely. However, I felt freedom would be coming along soon enough for us anyway.

We were called out on the morning of the sixth day and told to get ready to leave for our permanent camp. The boy with jaundice was required to come along. He was extremely sick and shouldn't have been out of bed, but he didn't com-plain.

An Italian officer and at least ten guards would accom-pany us. The officer had learned just one English statement. "If you make an attempt to escape, you will be shot dead," was his constant reminder.

He didn't look like he could shoot the side of a boxcar from the inside, but his men seemed pretty tough. No doubt, it was inadvisable to ignore the threat. I, for one, had decided to move along when they told me to, but if I saw a chance to get away, I was determined to do so. However, it would have to be a situation that was more "sure" than "risky."

Since Rome's main rail yards were demolished, we were taken by truck to another station northeast of the city. From there, we would take a train for Chieti, the location of another POW camp. We passed by Rome's main rail facili-ties, which hadn't been straightened out and still were a mess.

When the truck reached the station, we boarded a train that soon was filled to capacity with Italian civilians who oc-cupied all of the available space. Several compartments were cleared out so we could sit down and be watched by our guards. The train soon pulled out to cross Italy eastward, toward the Adriatic Sea.

It was interesting watching the civilians getting on the train. Many of them carried their bundles of goods wrapped in blankets or cloths. It was a scene of total awkwardness, with people jostling each other, their bundles coming undone, and the train leaving some behind in a general mix-up. Some well-dressed people boarded too, but they didn't receive any better accommodations than the others. Some noticed us and scowled. Others appeared to be friendly. We smiled at them all.

As soon as our guards noticed us smiling at people, they pulled the curtains in the compartment. Just before the curtains were drawn, however, we saw a rather good-looking young woman in the crowded aisle who appeared to want to be friendly. She apparently recognized us as Americans. After the curtains were pulled, one of the lads slid his hand out and gave her hand a squeeze. About a minute later, her hand slid back in with a couple of cigarettes. We lit up immediately. A little later, her hand came in again with grapes, which we ate right away. A whole pack of cigarettes followed, giving us the chance to light up again and even offer the guards some. They were dumbfounded by our sudden acquisition of cigarettes, but I noticed they didn't question the source and smoked them as heartily as we did.

We succeeded in becoming a little more informal with the guards as we squirmed amongst ourselves trying to get more comfortable. Our girl friend in the hall gradually pushed her way into the compartment, seemingly as if the

MAKING HISTORY AT PLOESTI *"The Mitchells made history at Tokyo, the Libs made history at Ploesti. In July 1943, Col. 'Killer' Kane led one hundred and thirty hand-picked, long-rehearsed Liberator crews on a low-level, 500-foot bombing attack against the German-held oil fields at Ploesti, Rumania. Incendiaries and 1,000 pound demos with 45 second fuses raised Cain with the oil stores. Twelve-hour delayed-fuse bombs dropped by the first wave added to the havoc long after the Libs had headed home to their bases in far-off Africa. But the price was a high one: of the 130 ships engaged on the mission 92 got home!"* Not as Briefed

crowd forced her to. It wasn't long until she was sitting on the corner of a seat, with the curtain forced back to where we could see her better. She opened her lunch box and shared food with us. Luckily for us, she found lots more cigarettes and passed them out freely. We soon had ten apiece. The party was becoming a grand success until the officer of the guard made his rounds and found her there. I don't know what he said to her, but she left and wasn't seen again.

The train made good time and soon came to our destination, Chieti, which was located not far from the Adriatic

ATTACK BY MAC *"Lt. Col. L.G. McCollom (Ritzville, Wash.), flying a P-47 Thunderbolt, caught this luckless ME-109 trying to attack the bomber formations on August 19, 1943, above the coast of France. Col. Mac returned safely from this mission but a visit to Adolf's 'Festung' on November 25, 1943, became a prolonged stay at Stalag One."* Not as Briefed

Sea. We formed three lines with the guards in a square around us, and then were marched about a mile to a high-walled compound.

When we entered the gate, we saw POWs playing ball and sunbathing in an open square in the middle of stucco barracks. They immediately stopped to observe us. We were searched and then turned loose to report to the senior camp officer for assignment to quarters. Mostly English officers were held at Chieti. Only about 200 Americans out of a total of 1,500 prisoners were incarcerated there.

The compound's high walls blocked any view of the outside world, except for a couple of hilltops near the town of Chieti itself. Guards were stationed at intervals around the walls in guard boxes and machine gun posts. It didn't appear possible for a bird to escape alive from this place. I looked at the crowd gathering to meet us and saw a tall blonde fellow. I recognized Capt. Frank Walsh from my old group. He'd been shot down exactly five months prior to my graduation

day to POW status. I was glad to see him alive and well. His co-pilot also was here and in good shape.

I noticed nobody said, "I'm glad to see you." They avoided any mention of a welcome. Mostly, greetings amounted to, "Sorry to see you here."

We were taken to report to the senior American officer, Lt. Col. Max Gooler of the Infantry Corps, who had been a prisoner for many months. After such a long period, however, he didn't appear to have grown to like the place any better. Frankly, I was flabbergasted to see that anyone who'd been a prisoner for a long time could be as sane and good-natured as he was. I soon learned lessons about patience and self control from Col. Gooler. He was an all around fine gentleman and would have made the war tougher for the Germans had they not caught him when they did.

While introducing my lads, I caught a glimpse of an officer that I was certain had been killed. Lt. Col. Sam Agee had been the commander of a neighboring group to mine, and a good friend from the days before the war. Later, I moved into the same room with him and Col. Gooler. I noticed how much better off the three of us seemed to be than most of the other fellows who were jammed together in larger rooms. My roommates, however, pointed out the benefit of a room crowded with men in the colder months. No heat whatsoever was provided to any of the barracks.

One by one, we were interrogated by the Allied personnel to get the latest news from the outside world. The most asked question was, "When do you think the war will be over?" or "How soon will the Allies get up this far?"

I recalled the Maresciallo at Poggio saying I was a lucky man, because the war would be over for Italy in a couple of months. Consequently, when asked for my opinion, I

TWO FOR THE SHOW *"Trying to knock out the leader of a formation with a head-on mass attack was a favorite maneuver of the Luftwaffe. Sometimes they succeeded, but not in this instance. Col. J.R. Byerly was leading his Group of Forts over Athens, Greece, in December 1943. Attacked by enemy fighters over the target, his crew accounted for three of them, but Jerry knocked out No. 2 and No. 4 engines. With full boost on No. 1 and No. 3, the Colonel limped home to his base. No. 3 cut out on the final approach, but a safe landing was made with No. 1."* Not as Briefed

thing, more from homesickness than anything else. We ate at a central mess. There was a band and orchestra, as well as a glee club and theater troupe. The international YMCA supplied the band instruments and equipment. The men displayed amazing ingenuity and originality.

For the theater, the POWs had constructed a stage with props and lights from little more than tin cans, old clothes, and other scrap materials. They used every piece of wood and cardboard in the Red Cross boxes and crates. Most of the men were British and they seemed especially enthusiastic about the theater. I'd never been a playgoer, but I learned to appreciate good acting here, especially because I realized how difficult it was to

PROVING A POINT *"From a B-26 cockpit, Pantelleria dead ahead. In the early summer of 1943 this island, Italian-owned, off the coast of Tunisia in the Mediterranean Sea, was subjected to continuous aerial bombardment until the garrison surrendered. Then American troops landed on the island."* Not as Briefed

answered that the war would be finished "two months from now." I didn't realize at the time how this statement would haunt me for a long time to come. This was only early August 1943.

Sam Agee showed me around the camp and explained its organization and how it worked. Conditions were surprisingly pleasant although everyone complained about every-

pull off these productions. We saw Italian movies occasionally and there was a fairly complete library containing all sorts of books from Wild West stories to Shakespeare. It was almost beyond belief to me that such things were allowed in a prison camp.

The talent of the men was amazing. POWs who were scholars, teachers, or experts in various fields taught regularly scheduled classes in arts and crafts, foreign languages, mathematics, business, law, dramatics, music, fishing, politics, cooking, mechanics, English, and other subjects. Some fellows had learned to play musical instruments from scratch and now were members of an excellent camp orchestra.

A small dispensary attended to minor ailments. We could do just about anything we wanted inside the camp. Every week or so, we also were allowed to leave the camp in escorted parties to go swimming in a nearby river, if we promised not to attempt to escape while outside. Athletics predominated—baseball mostly. With better food, we'd have been as physically fit a group of men as any in the world. A central reporting service posted daily news, so everyone had a good idea about what was going on in the outside world. This was the most important thing for morale.

The Chieti compound probably was as escape-proof as any camp that I ever was in, nevertheless there were well-organized plans to escape and many attempts were made. I still wasn't able to walk well, so I wasn't in any condition to try to leave. However, I did participate in some of the plans. Three escape tunnels were being secretly constructed. The Italians discovered none of them. I didn't know anything about tunnel #1 and never saw it.

Regarding tunnel #2, the entrance was located in a fire pit where water was boiled for the camp. A grate under the hot coals covered the opening. It was taken out whenever men went into the tunnel. The tunnel extended to a large storm sewer and continued down it to a point where noxious sewer gases caused difficulties. The fellows could only work there for a few minutes, and then withdrew for rest and better air in a room underneath the fire pit. Meanwhile, another shift continued the work—there were about three shifts of three men each. It was a fine project because the incriminating tunnel dirt was left in the sewer to be secretly washed away by storm water.

Tunnel #3, the one that I worked in, was started in a fire room off from the heating plant. Near a large furnace

there was a cement-lined pit with large steps leading down into it. The pit probably provided access to the furnace's firebox. For the tunnel's entrance, the boys cleverly had removed one of the marble slabs in the steps and inserted a box filled with dirt. The box fit perfectly under the step, giving it support. The marble slab and box were removed to provide access to the tunnel and then immediately put back in place.

All of the tunnels were cleverly constructed, particularly #3. Hand-operated bellows circulated the air in fine style. Candles made from rancid margarine indicated when the oxygen was running out. If the flame of a candle became smaller and smaller at the far end of the tunnel, it indicated that oxygen was getting low and they'd call for more air. The guys back near the entrance cranked a bit harder on the blower, and fresh air would come through. To keep the walls from caving in, the tunnels were lined with pieces of wood secretly scavenged from bunks, chairs, the barracks, and other sources.

A man entering tunnel #3 went in feet first, then turned over and slid down on his stomach to a little compartment. There was a radio set, electric lights, and, in fact, everything needed to keep the work going. Little ore carts on small wooden rails hauled out the dirt. When plays were about to be performed, men carried empty pillowcases with them to the theater. It appeared to the guards that the POWs simply were going to the theater with their pillows to sit on. The pillowcases then were secretly filled with dirt.

When walking back, the men surreptitiously dropped the dirt in a well. The prisoners had constructed the well in such a manner that it appeared to occasionally cave-in around the sides. This provided an excuse for the amount of dirt found in the bottom of the well. This worked for a long time, and several people escaped through the tunnels.

Acquiring items needed on the outside if we escaped was quite a trick. When captured, most men had compasses, maps, money, and other things that they wanted to hide from the guards. I was no exception. I too had maps, and money obtained by various means from the Maresciallo, plus a compass saved since the bailout. When stripped down for a search, I found that the easiest way to secretly hide these items was to hold them in my fists. Guards never looked in my hands. Another method that worked, though not quite as well, was to hide things in our clothing and other possessions that were stacked outside of a room when it was being searched. The whole time I was a POW, I hid cigarettes, matches, a compass, money, and other items in my hands, which never were found.

The biggest problem wasn't escaping from the compound, but evading recapture on the outside. Roll call was taken twice a day. If someone was missing, the guards immediately started a search and alerted the authorities in surrounding localities. Escapees had an awful time of it. It was particularly difficult to pass through railroad stations and roadblocks.

Consequently, our men contrived a plan to get the Italians to start a search and get it over with before a man actually escaped. During every roll call over a period of three months, this "escapee" secretly hid in one of the tunnels to keep from being counted. The Italians thought he was missing, and blocked the roads and searched the railway stations.

This subterfuge was kept up until the Italians ceased their search. Then it was time for the lad to go. He had little trouble on the outside and actually made it all the way to the Swiss border, where, unfortunately, he was picked up.

Less fortunate were two other boys who got out and tried to steal an airplane. They were shot dead in their tracks.

When I arrived, the Italian food rations were sparse, the distribution of Red Cross parcels was low, and there wasn't a local black market to tap into. I realized I needed to act quickly or go hungry. I fell back on my art and went to work. At first, I drew portraits of my roommates for display. Later, I made sketches for a British padre, who proved to be a good advertising agent.

It wasn't long until another Englishman came along who wanted a portrait done, and he traded a pair of shorts that I badly needed. Someone else had extra cigarettes that he wanted to exchange for a portrait and thus I began accumulating a reserve of cigarettes. I acquired and traded jam, canned milk, cheese, laundry work, and chocolate by drawing about twenty-five portraits.

A number of people were engaged in forging passports, which introduced me to a technique that I later used. Little hand-done sketches that looked like photographs were made for the identification cards. A fairly good depiction of a guy's face could be made with a pencil. By shellacking a sketch a number of times, you'd be surprised how much it looks like a photograph. The fellow getting as far as the Swiss border used one of these identification cards. Though he eventually was captured, his fake passport worked every time he showed it.

One morning, a delegation of British lads came to my room and asked me to attend an art club meeting. They said I was a good artist, and feeling flattered, I accepted. I was the only American attending. Well, the first thing they did was elect me president of the art society and I had to give an inauguration speech right then and there. I never felt very comfortable speaking in public. I'd had little contact with the English before and wasn't really acquainted with their customs and habits. They're not as boisterous as Americans, so I felt ill at ease making a speech to these boys.

After getting to know them better, I found them easy to get along with and as congenial as anyone else. I strongly suspected that they also wanted me in their club for my rank, which carried some weight in the compound, particularly for keeping a room for a workshop. As newly arrived groups of POWs crowded into the camp, some clubs and organizations had to give up their spaces. The highest-ranking club presidents were the ones who kept a room the longest for club activities.

Some of the artwork being done in the compound was quite good and my first action as club president was to organize an arts and crafts exhibit. We took over an unused latrine for a display hall, and with some boards and blankets made display booths in the stalls. We exhibited anything the fellows could dig up and it proved to be an interesting and worthwhile show. For example, one lad exhibited his collection of butterflies. Some boys had made model airplanes, and quite a few exhibited their paintings. Many objects were made from makeshift materials, but the work was outstanding. They hadn't really been noticed before because there hadn't been a place to display them.

We invited the Italian commandant of the camp to the exhibit. It ran about two weeks due to popular demand and created some interest among the Italians. They notified other officers from the surrounding area to come and see the exhibit.

Because of the recent disastrous defeats suffered by the Italian army in North Africa and Sicily, Mussolini had been forced by his own government to resign as *Il Duce* on July 24, 1943. Due to this turn of events, we hoped that our forces soon would be advancing rapidly up the Italian mainland and rescue us.

When sitting with the art society one evening discussing the merits of letting the show run for a few more days, a special broadcast came over the camp's YMCA-provided

loudspeaker system. Marshall Badoglio, the new head of the Italian government following Mussolini's overthrow, openly declared the war at an end for Italy on September 8, 1943. We were delighted to hear that the Italian government had abandoned their German ally and capitulated. What followed was nothing short of riotous. We used up our stored, emergency food in a big dinner celebration. Naturally, we figured we were going home.

Having been a prisoner for close to two months, I considered myself a veteran POW and was sick and tired of it. Our British senior camp commander, however, told us to remain calm and quiet because the Germans still were in control in our area. Like most of the fellows, I thought we'd be returned to our own lines because we were under Italian control, and not German. The Allied intelligence services sent a message to us that nobody was to leave and walk out until definite orders came.

Our Italian guards began deserting over the walls. Meanwhile, we heard about a camp up north where POWs broke down the gates after the Italians left, but then were mowed down by German machine guns stationed outside of the compound. We stood by, following orders, except for three men. They left and eventually made it back to our lines. Soon, all of our Italian guards were gone except for a few Carabiniere policemen who remained stationed at visible points whenever the Germans were near. We conferred with the Italian commander, who turned control of the camp over to us. We actually were required to guard ourselves in one of the more unusual circumstances of the war.

Passing German troops were becoming more evident each day, and we requested that the Italian police remain in the towers. The Allies had invaded southern Italy and we thought our boys were well on their way. As far as we were concerned, they would arrive in only a matter of days. Little did we realize how difficult it would be for our troops fighting against the Germans—the slow moving Italian campaign

would last until the end of the war. Also, some die-hard Italian fascists were remaining loyal to the Axis cause.

We still believed, however, that the Jerries couldn't hold us. Unfortunately, we miscalculated and our camp was occupied on September 23, 1943, by a detachment of German soldiers. The Italian guards had long since gone over the hill to avoid being drafted into the German army. We felt pretty foolish when the Krauts suddenly took over—lock, stock, and barrel!

We still didn't think that the Germans would keep us, until we were notified on the same day to prepare to move southwest to Sulmona, which was to be an embarkation point for taking POWs by train to Germany. Now, it was every man for himself, and nearly everyone planned to attempt to escape and feverishly made up packs for carrying blankets and water for a getaway.

Trucks arrived and 214 Americans, including myself, were loaded and taken to Sulmona. Ironically, the original POWs at Sulmona had been freed after the Italian capitulation on September 8 and before the camp was taken over by the Germans. When we arrived, only a portion of the camp's original prisoners were still there—mostly hospital cases, and a number of escapees who had been recaptured or who had returned due to starvation and thirst when in the mountains.

Our guards were German paratroopers, who were unfamiliar with the clever schemes and shadowy trickery of the POWs. The guards were improperly placed and the fences had been breached in quite a few places. We hardly arrived before lads started going through the wire. Up to this point, some were still of the opinion that we weren't being sent to Germany. However, the German lieutenant in charge didn't leave any doubt in our minds when he called our senior officers together for a short lecture.

He said, "Why should I leave you fellows here and have you try and kill us later!"

When this word got out, it caused the greatest mass preparation for escape that I ever saw. It spread like a plague through the camp, as men made up escape bundles and scouted the wire for exits. We briefly had an advantage, since these front line Germans troops had little or no experience as prison guards. Unfortunately, they learned fast.

Most recaptured escapees were put in solitary confinement for punishment. However, we had ways of smuggling food and other items to the guys in the cells. In fact, it was a pleasure to be in solitary confinement and there was a waiting list. The Germans didn't realize why the line-up got so long.

There was evidence all around the camp indicating the hasty evacuation by the former inmates. They had gone to the hills as soon as the Italian guards abandoned the compound. Italian civilians, suffering from the economic deprivations of the war, immediately came into the camp and lifted everything they could find. Hospital personnel remaining with the sick and wounded were unable to stop the pillage. Consequently, they called on nearby German detachments to save what little food and supplies were left.

A few days after the Italian capitulation, some of Sulmona's escaped POWs had begun returning to find food and drink. The fare in the hills was poor and at this time of the year the streams were dry. The fellows suffered mostly from the lack of water. Most of the men had fled to a mountain range, almost bare of trees, located immediately to the rear of the camp. The Germans had anticipated their difficulties and posted guards at all of the water sources. Many boys in search of water were picked up by the soldiers and returned to the camp. Soon after our arrival, hundreds of the former inmates were back in. All were of the opinion that the walls and wire could easily be breached and the Germans wouldn't be able to guard the place well enough to hold us.

As soon as we located a place to bunk, Sam Agee and I walked around the compound, selecting some choice spots to go through the wire that night. At each corner of the camp, the guards had set up machine gun positions, covering the full length of the wire fence. However, there were

blind spots. Perhaps at least half of the men were fixing up their traveling kits. Sam and I each had made packs from old coats and loaded them up for a move after dark.

About two hours before dusk, two men approached a low spot under the fence on the camp's south side. They went through, but were stopped by an alert guard not ten feet away. The guard admonished them and returned them to the compound. They immediately attempted to escape at another spot. This time they were caught in the wire by another guard and returned. Again, they tried to escape and were detected. We figured that the guards must have been stupid not to put them in confinement cells. On a fourth attempt, they got away and I never heard from them again.

The whole camp was abuzz about the guards' laxity and how the boys hadn't been punished or threatened, so the run began. Men from all of the barracks hit the fence. Frank Walsh actually grabbed a top wire with his hands and put his foot on a bottom wire, then pulled and tore the fence down to get through. The sound could be heard a hundred yards away, but the guards made no attempt to stop him. I later learned he was free for a month before being caught.

Some guys put on German uniforms and marched through the gate. They saluted and the guard opened the gate to let them pass. German guards were on duty within the compound and barracks, so this trick wasn't too difficult. Only one of the POWs could speak German, however.

About a mile from camp, when they were trying not to attract attention but acting cocky as you please, a German non-commissioned officer passed by them going in the other direction. Unlike the regulations in our military forces, German privates must salute all non-coms. Our boys in private's uniforms didn't know this. The non-com stopped and arrested these "troops" for failing to salute.

They were brought back to a guardhouse, where their true identity soon was discovered. A German noticed the pistol holster that one of the men was wearing. When he learned they were Americans, he made a frantic dive for it.

When the cover of a Luger holster is lifted, the gun is raised to a better gripping position. When the German grabbed at this holster, however, a chocolate bar popped out instead of a Luger, much to the guard's amazement.

The men were tossed into confinement, but later that evening broke out and escaped through the wire. I never found out what happened to them afterward. The escape attempts soon grew to ridiculous proportions, and fellows were being hauled back about as fast as they were getting out.

Sam and I had found a likely spot to try and escape, and we were in the barracks making a few final preparations when we heard two shots. There was a flurry and stampeding of feet down the hallway. We stopped someone going past the room and asked what had happened.

"Somebody was just shot out there!" was the reply.

"Where is he?"

"Oh, he's lying out there in the compound."

We started for the door just as the man was brought into our barracks. Blood gushed from his right leg. He was laid on the floor of the room next to ours and a couple of our doctors came to attend to him. He was a British captain with a prominent reddish mustache, who had been standing by the hole in the fence that Sam and I had selected for our exit. He wasn't attempting to escape, but merely watching others going through the wire. The shots came out of the dark, about thirty yards outside of the camp. The guard had fired right into a crowd, hitting this fellow.

"Where did they hit me?" was his first question.

"Only in the right leg," answered the Doc.

"Thank God! I was afraid it might have been in the stomach and that would have been curtains for me," he sighed.

Suffering from shock, he was unable to determine where he'd been hit. When the Doc tore his pant leg away, we could see that the wound was nothing to take lightly. A bullet had squarely entered his thigh about six inches below the hip. On the back of his leg, a chunk of flesh nearly the size of a fist was gone. It made me feel faint. Blood flowed all over. I left, not being of much use and not wanting to observe.

Our doctors tried to stop the bleeding, then took him to the Germans for further treatment. The Jerries sent him to a field hospital about a mile from the camp, where he was put on a cot and the medics were sent away. He lay there for a week unattended and then died from a blood clot. His wound could have been mended with little trouble. No reason was given for the refusal of treatment.

Needless to say, this incident dampened our spirits and no more escape attempts were made that night. In the dark, the guards fixed the fence and put tin cans on the wire to act as sound alarms. Thirty-seven Americans and twelve Brits made good their escapes that night, but nobody got away during the succeeding seven days.

The commandant informed us that we'd be sent to Germany as soon as transportation was available. He said the front lines were getting closer and the move would have to be made soon. It was tantalizing to know freedom was so close and yet so far away.

During the daytime, we saw fighter sweeps over our area. They included American P-40s which looked mighty good to us. It was ironic to look up at them cruising overhead free as birds and realize that the pilots soon would be back at their bases. We never saw opposition against them at any time. Jerry definitely was on the run. If only the Germans couldn't find transportation in time, we might be overrun by our own troops. We hoped that this would happen, but it didn't. ❂

CHAPTER EIGHT

POW TRAIN

Sam and I decided to find a hiding place to try and stay behind when the Jerries moved everyone out. The only difficulty was that there were hundreds of other fellows with the same idea, but we figured we'd be the smartest and find the ideal hideout. We began looking around. That afternoon, we found a place in the barracks ceiling where there was a somewhat hidden hole in the plaster where we could get through. We planned to create a sleeping place in the attic, store some food and water up there, crawl in just before we were to be shipped out, and stay up to two weeks if necessary. We went to work.

The room was a flea trap. Fleas and bedbugs were everywhere. Just outside of our door, two other POWs were digging like moles under the cement steps. They planned to bore a couple of breathing holes through the walls and, when it came time to hide, have someone cover up the entrance. It seemed like a good idea, but ours was just as good.

We needed to put supports in the rafters to keep our weight off the weak plaster in the ceiling. We smuggled a large plank and some small boards through the secret hole, and slid them along the rafters to the far end of the building. We thought we were the craftiest individuals alive. While searching about in the attic, we found nine unopened Red Cross food parcels that someone had hidden, but left behind when they departed. This was a break, since we had no Red Cross and little Italian provisions left.

The worst shortage at the time was the lack of tobacco. We were saving all cigarette butts. Colonels, majors, privates, and all would run like the wind if a "snipe" were seen that might have a shred of tobacco in it. Col. Gooler had saved a few cigarette packs for just such an emergency. Now, he graciously shared them with us. I had saved a few packs myself from my portrait fees. It was rather funny butting all cigarettes, then butting the butts, and again butting those butts until the remaining bits of soggy tobacco were so strong that they knocked the top off your head with one drag. We'd run out of papers and had nothing but toilet paper for rolling cigarettes. We found that the various brands of toilet paper had different flavors, which provided a topic for discussion and argument.

While preparing our hiding place, we ran into some obstacles. The first was in regard to our water supply. Within a few hours of stashing it in the rafters, mice started drinking it and consequently we soon found drowned rodents in the water. Capt. Picket, who was privy to our plan, volunteered to stay up there one night to see what it would be like. We pushed him up and closed the hole. All was quiet for about an hour, then we heard a frantic rapping to get out. Picket spilled out alive with bed bugs. He said as soon as things had quieted down, the bugs had set out looking for blood and found him. It was more than a person could stand.

The next day while we were up in the attic trying to combat the bug problem, we heard a noise. Before long, a head poked up through another hole in the plaster, about two rooms down from ours. Somebody else had decided to hide up here too. We called them into our room and pointed out the foolishness of so many of us trying the same thing. Just then, we heard another noise above us. We looked up at the cover of our hole, saw it slide away, and a Jerry's red face peered down with a big smirking grin. Needless to say, this turned the tide. We gave up on the attic—mice, bed bugs, roommates, and all.

When walking through the compound, very discouraged, I saw a sight I'll never forget. The place looked like an anthill with men secretly digging holes, boring through cement walls, and making hideouts in every conceivable spot that could be found.

Sam and I decided not to be discouraged and kept looking for the perfect hiding place. We figured we could outsmart the Germans if we used our heads. There was an abandoned guard tower that the Germans didn't use in the middle of the camp. We climbed up it to look over the compound. We spotted a wall that shored up the bank next to the foundation of one of the barracks. It consisted of large stones that looked like they

could be removed. We remembered that an Englishman, who had been moved out, told us about a hole he had started in this bank.

We dashed down and searched carefully until we found where he'd been working. A small hole had been started and the stones covered the hole perfectly. Inside, the ceiling had been cleverly reinforced just under the surface of the ground behind the wall. The only disadvantage was that Germans outside of the camp manning machine guns would be able to see us when we walked away from the area. It was going to be difficult to haul out dirt without them noticing. When I look back at it now, we could have used a bulldozer and it wouldn't have mattered. We found out later why the Jerries didn't pay much attention to any of this.

Sam and I worked for a couple of days, trying to make the hole big enough to hide in before the Germans moved us out. We planned to make it the size of a double bed, put supplies and blankets in there, and stay a week if necessary. We worked like beavers filling cardboard boxes with dirt and secretly carrying it out to the flowerbeds and shrubs around the camp. Of course, about a hundred other guys carried dirt to the same places. Before we were finished, the flowers were almost completely cov-

BLOWING HER TOP *"Mt. Vesuvius, south of Naples, was a comforting check-point for Italy-based fliers. But not on April 25, 1944. A mild eruption that day scared the daylights out of everyone in the vicinity. Before it subsided, hot lava and ashes had destroyed numerous American aircraft based on the fields nearby."* Not as Briefed

ered. Two fellows dug "graves" right underneath the tower in the middle of the compound, where they intended to be buried alive, with only small air holes to the outside.

We decided our best hope would be to make such a well-camouflaged hideout that ours would be overlooked while the guards were finding the others. We learned that the Germans were sending search details around the compound, eliminating all of the tunnels and hiding places that they could find. We carefully replaced the stones, certain that they'd be unable to find our cleverly camouflaged spot.

When the guards arrived at the stone wall, to our amazement they walked almost directly to our hole, poked a long crowbar into it, and pulled it to pieces. It was a wreck when they left. Sam and I, feeling low, watched this from our window. We decided we'd have to make our getaway after they put us on the train.

Meanwhile, a new menace began tormenting the camp. Bed bugs! They were eating everyone alive. They were in every bed and wall, the ceilings crawled with them, and it was impossible to go into the attics. We commenced a campaign against them. I think the bugs realized that we were after them and they were determined to multiply even faster and overwhelm us. They appeared everywhere. All of the bunks were pulled out into the yard and torn apart in order to get at the cracks and holes in the wood. Fire, insect powder, boiling water, and lye routed them out. They were big, fat, and full of blood. Some boards literally dripped with blood from the bugs that we killed.

For three days, the campaign continued; however, there wasn't a noticeable decrease in the number of bugs. Almost every bunk had been burned and soaked with powder. The bed boards were burned only enough to kill the bugs, then reused because there wasn't any new lumber to build new beds. The charcoal from the burned pieces blackened everything, making us look like coal miners. Many men slept in their blankets outside on the ground to avoid the insects. At this time, food was getting scarcer, cigarette butts disap-

peared altogether, and the bed bugs kept multiplying. We definitely weren't a happy bunch.

Suddenly it was over. The Germans began loading prisoners aboard trains and shipping them north. The bulk of the British lads were moved a few days before our turn came. It seemed impossible to avoid our fate, but we were still trying. The first day that they began moving Americans, many still sought good hiding places. Sam and I were sitting in our room bemoaning our fate, when we heard a burst of machine gun fire raking over the roof. Scurrying outside, we saw a couple of our boys hurrying down from the abandoned guard tower in the middle of the compound.

Lt. Amin, a boy from my group in Africa, had been standing in the tower when a guard outside of the wall opened up with a machine gun, trying to kill him. Amin was shot cleanly through the forearm, suffering only a flesh wound. When he heard the shots, he ducked and then scrambled down the tower. Seeing blood dripping down onto the steps below, he thought someone above him was hit. Not until he realized there wasn't any one above him did he know that he'd been shot.

Col. Gooler demanded an explanation. The German commandant explained that he'd instructed the guards not to permit any prisoners on the abandoned tower. If anyone climbed the tower, they were to be fired upon. Then he grinned, said he'd neglected to send the order to us, and apologized for the mistake. What a morbid sense of humor! We stayed out of the tower after that.

The first trainload of Americans went out the day before Sam and I were scheduled to go. We'd requested to be taken on the last train, hoping something might come up allowing us to escape or hide until the Germans left. During the loading of an earlier train, two Englishmen had made a break for freedom and one succeeded. The other was shot at point blank range with a full clip from a guard's sub-machine gun. The burst blew his head off. Strangely enough, he was

the best friend of the poor fellow who had been shot through the leg that first night. They died on the same day.

The last of us to leave held a double funeral for these two friends. Stanley Brach, an American Catholic priest, conducted the service. For some reason, the Germans permitted us to bury only one of the men. We placed his body at the head of the compound and marched by in formation. It was a touching scene. Around the world, this kind of thing probably occurred a hundred times each day because of the war, but our ceremony made an indelible impression on our minds.

Finally, our turn came to be dispatched to Rome, and then north to Germany. The "compound ghosts" also were rounded up. These were men who'd been scheduled to go the day before, but had succeeded in temporarily hiding out. Most of the men who hid were found. A few actually did succeed in staying, but at a terrific cost in pain and suffering.

About 800 of us were herded onto the athletic field and lined up for counting. Most of the men had baggage. I carried my hard-to-get pastels and art materials in addition to my blankets and toilet articles. We remained on the parade ground all day. It was hot, and the men were really miserable because they wanted to take all of the clothing they could with them, and the best way to do so was to wear it. I saw one fellow with a sun chair made of scrap lumber and bits of old cloth. I don't suppose it got very far. Most of the men's clothing was dirty and full of lice. The prospect of being a POW in Germany was serious enough without these other discomforts. Some of the English boys had been in the bag for over two years by then, and they were destined for more. It was hard for all of us to face up to it.

Some of the German guards said, "What are you worrying for? We are the ones who should worry. Soon you will be in charge of us because we are losing the war."

Others were a little more confident in "Der Fuhrer" and told us, "Just wait another month, you'll see. We'll have the English and Americans kicked out of Italy by that time."

One of the guards said something I'd heard before and was destined to hear again and again. When I asked him how long he thought the war was going to last, he answered, "I think it will be over in two more months."

Two months! I'd heard this same comment two months ago when I was first taken prisoner.

By 5 PM, about half of the lads had boarded the train. Five of us, including Col. Gooler, Sam Agee, and I, were allowed to go back to the barracks and check for anything that might have been overlooked. There was nobody around except some German guards poking through the items that were left. I saw one of my portraits that somebody had paid for with a good can of jam lying on the floor with a big footprint on it. This made me angry.

Earlier, I'd burned close to $40,000 in various types of currency because we didn't want the Germans to have it. It was money that the Italians had taken from the lads during interrogation, but returned after the capitulation. When checking the ashes to be sure it was all gone, I thought about how little money really meant at a time like this. I had burned $40,000 and it had impressed me no more than burning a newspaper.

In one room, we found a bottle of wine. Everyone in our small detachment was called in for a toast to a quick Allied victory. During my rummaging, I found some beautiful art pencils that I couldn't resist taking. I stuffed them into my already full pockets. Finally it was time for us to return to the athletic field.

On the way back, we saw groups of German soldiers heading for different buildings. Shortly after they entered a building, sub-machine gunfire erupted. They shot bursts into the ceilings and the attics. I knew of only one attic where some of our boys were hiding, but there must have been more elsewhere. We had been warned that this would happen, which discouraged most of us from hiding in the attics, but unfortunately not everyone had received the word.

As we arrived back at the athletic field, the hospital cases were leaving the camp. Some were in no shape to travel, but they were given no alternative. The Jerries trucked us to the station. To our surprise, the Germans issued Red Cross parcels that they had found in a supply room. Each man was given one for the trip to Germany. This turned out to be a good thing since the Germans issued no other rations whatsoever. Most of us carried water in homemade canteens.

I was in the last truck to leave and the Red Cross parcels were given to us just as we boarded. It was difficult to keep from opening them and eating all we could. The parcels were intended for invalids and contained mostly milk foods, oatmeal, and drinks, but they were really welcome. The truck had only two German guards—the driver, and another who watched the eight of us. This was a contrast to the Italians, who'd assign at least six guards besides the driver. Little did I know at the time, but this was to be my last ride in a motor vehicle for nineteen months.

The effects of a bombing raid were very evident at the railroad station. Huge craters pock-marked the streets and railroad yards, smashed machinery was lying about where it had been dragged out of the way by repair crews, and twisted rails were mixed up with burned and battered rail cars. We hoped the bombers wouldn't come again until we were out of the way. Guards stood around the yard covering all avenues of escape. It would have been suicide to make a break for freedom. The guards didn't look too friendly either. No doubt, they'd been thoroughly reprimanded by the German commander for allowing so many POWs to escape from the camp.

The senior officers, myself included, were put in second-class passenger cars attached behind a line of cattle cars. The whole train hauled 800 men, including 176 American officers. Each cattle car was loaded with forty POWs. These men were destined to remain closed in for several days, and were seldom allowed to get out to walk about or relieve themselves.

Six men were assigned to each compartment in our passenger car. An aisle extended along one side of the car and the compartments were on the other. We weren't required to remain in the compartments at first. Of course, each of us walked about looking for the best way to make an escape if the opportunity came up. It should've been easy for the guards to see what our intentions were, but they seemed to give no indication that they knew such thoughts were in our minds. That was all right with us. The guards were quartered

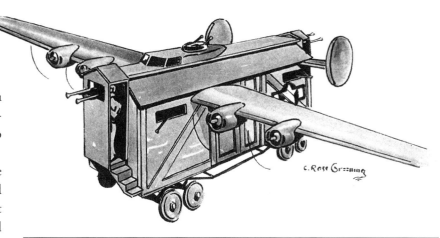

THE FLYING BOXCAR [B-26] *"Square, solid, capable of a heavy bomb load and called slow—the Consolidated Liberator four-engine bomber was jokingly called the Flying Boxcar. Enemy pilots preferred attacking it than the Boeing Fortress, very often to their regret and sudden death."* Not as Briefed

in two compartments at the end of our car. It didn't seem possible that there were only nine guards for the trains, but that was all we counted when they got on.

The cattle cars, on the other hand, were locked shut just before the train pulled out. I was aware that many of the fellows secretly carried iron bars and other tools with them to pry up the floorboards after the train started out. We sort of wished the Germans had put us in those cars. Our disadvantage was that guards were in the carriage with us.

We had to wait for about two hours before the train started to move. It was just about dusk, which would be ideal

for traveling to Rome free of the threat of an Allied air attack. After reaching Rome, we were to proceed north. We left Sulmona full of anticipation. Every man felt tense and excited. Each did his best to appear calm, but we weren't very good at it, because when we tried to make casual conversation our comments made no sense.

My head was bursting. This just couldn't be happening! They couldn't be taking us to Germany where we'd have to sweat out many more months, or maybe even years, of this war! The guards told us that their prison camps provided better accommodations than the Italian ones, but frankly we didn't believe them. It wasn't much of an inducement to want to stick around.

Lt. Col. Max Gooler, the oldest American prisoner, had been a POW for fourteen months. He'd been captured at Tobruck in North Africa along with 30,000 British soldiers. He was on pins and needles. It was easy to see that he was going to jump to freedom or be killed in the attempt. From the minute the train started, it was all we could do to keep him from trying to escape, which would have been fatal. It wasn't night yet and the guards still were fresh and alert. We figured it would be best to wait until dark and when the guards had grown tired. The train chugged slowly through the mountains toward Rome.

When the train slowed down to stop several times, we observed the actions of the guards as they got off. We wanted to know where they went, what they did, and how they reboarded the train when it moved out again. The guards did their duty well. They carried oil lanterns, jumped down off the train shortly before it stopped, and waited until the cars started rolling again before getting on. We planned to jump when the train was still moving slowly, so we'd avoid breaking a leg or spraining an ankle.

Sam and I observed the guards at about three stops, then decided on a plan. At the next stop, we'd walk to the end of the car where the fewest guards were located. We would jump out the door just as the train started moving out. That might give us a chance of getting down behind a railway bank. Meanwhile, the guards would be unable to leave the train for fear of being left behind. Also, the jerking of the moving train might throw the guards' aim off if they shot at us.

Soon, the train came to a stop just as our car passed a building on the left. There was about a three-foot-deep ditch on that side, with thick brush above. It was dark enough outside that someone couldn't be seen unless they were in the lamplight. Sam and I walked to the end of the aisle, trying to act as calm as possible. We both leaned out of a window and engaged in conversation. I don't know what we talked about. My knees were shaking and Sam might have been a little frightened too. A guard stood near us on the car steps waiting for the train to pull out. We planned to wait until he came in and started down the aisle to his compartment. Then we'd leap out the door while the train was going slow enough to keep from hurting ourselves.

Giving a warning toot, the engine started to move out. My heart seemed to pound louder than the chugging locomotive. The guard on the steps turned, stepped into the door, and started to pass around us. Just as we raised up from our leaning positions in the window to let him by, we heard a shot on the other side of the train, right by our compartment. I think my heart stopped beating, because there could be no other answer to why shots were being fired. Col. Max Gooler was an old-time infantry officer with twenty-four years of service. He wasn't as spry as he once was, but he could fool you. Max wore thick eyeglasses and he might have thought the train was rolling. In fact, the train hadn't moved out yet when he jumped.

We were panic stricken, thinking he'd been hit. We didn't see movement in the brush and figured that was the end of him. At the sound of gunfire, the guard at our end of the train stopped and quickly stepped back to the doorway. The train was moving by now, so the guard couldn't get off a shot. He came back jabbering and motioning for all of us to return to our compartments. Gooler was gone, just as we'd guessed. Looking out the window, we could see nothing. The train was moving fairly fast by now and we had no way of knowing his fate.

I felt sick at my stomach, fearing the worst. I had seen lots of men get killed, but it's always hard to take, especially when it's someone you know well. Of course, our chance of escaping was gone. I think I suddenly developed a fever, and Sam too. We remained quiet, sitting in our seats. One of our men, Lt. Krebs, was an interpreter for us. He was as quiet as we were.

I finally asked, knowing it was probably a foolish question, "Was that Col. Gooler who jumped?"

"It sure was," Krebs replied. "He was standing there with one foot up on the seat and had his glasses off. I didn't know he was going out, but it was obvious he was up to something."

I asked, "Do you think they hit him?"

"It's hard to tell, the train started moving and he jumped. It was hard to see in the dark just what he did, but it looked like he lit in that ditch then started crawling up into the brush right away. You could hear him plain as could be. I heard the guards shouting, then one of them fired right into the place where it looked like he had gone. I didn't hear him cry out, so I don't think he was hit."

SPITS OVER FRANCE *"On January 22, 1943, over Bordeaux, France, twenty-two Spitfires escorting Douglas-Boston Havocs were jumped by sixty Focke-Wulf 190s. In the dog fight which followed, three Focke-Wulfs were shot down for the loss of one Spit. Captain D.H. 'Barney' Ross of Huntington Park, California, flying a Spit that day had a big time with the Jerries. A few missions later Barney was shot down and did a long time with the Jerries."* Not as Briefed

Three German guards started up the aisle, looking into the compartments to determine who was missing. They poked lanterns into the face of each man as they shuffled along the aisle. When they came to our compartment, they started counting and deduced that one of the four men in our compartment was gone. To make sure their figures jibed, they counted the rest of the fellows before they came back. None could speak English, so they asked me in German where the missing man was. I asked Krebs to translate.

"They are demanding to know where the other man is," Krebs interpreted.

"Tell them he must have gone to the dining car," I wisecracked.

When Krebs told them my reply, it was obvious from their guttural yaps and spitting that they didn't have a sense of humor. They shoved their red faces close to mine, and gave me a sound bawling out with as many grimaces and threats as they could conjure up. In fact, they screamed so loud that my ears rang—but of course, I couldn't understand a word they said.

Krebs then did a bit of shouting in German himself. He told them they were not very good soldiers, because a good soldier would never shout and scream at a Lt. Colonel even if he was one of the enemy. If there is anything that offends

a German, it is being told he isn't a good soldier. They fancied themselves as the best in the world. After hearing Krebs' remarks, they stopped shouting and left, but not before warning us that we'd be shot if we left our compartments or opened a window. I felt they weren't kidding.

(We later learned that the guards' bullets had missed Col. Gooler and he'd played possum. After about a month of freedom, however, he was picked up and had a very rough time of it in a German prison camp.)

They posted two guards in the aisle at our end of the car and looked into each compartment every few minutes. It didn't appear that we'd be able to get up and walk about again during the trip. However, the guards were tiring and losing their alertness, and it was only a question of how long we had to wait for another chance. Unfortunately, we were getting weary also. I tried to relax and get some rest before our next break came.

The train clicked along through Italy's central mountains, making only a few stops during the next couple of hours. We must have crossed over the main pass and begun the downward slope when we came to a section of damaged railway. The area apparently had been bombed a few days before. Stops became frequent and the traveling slowed. Up ahead in the boxcars, the boys were feverishly working with their secret tools to create exits. Some cars had ventilation windows. In those cars men merely had to slide back the windows, wait until the train stopped, then climb out and drop to the ground. The Germans couldn't watch all sections of the long train. From the agitation exhibited by the guards, it was obvious prisoners were getting out.

Krebs overheard the guards saying that they admired certain types of escape attempts. After Max Gooler jumped, they had said, "That's the way a real soldier does it."

When somebody cut a hole in a boxcar floor and dropped out, they didn't approve. They liked a bold, brave attempt at escape. This gave us a clue as to how to act if we escaped and were recaptured. Stand up straight, act like a soldier, and give them your name, rank, and serial number, and nothing more. When one guy cried, they considered him a lousy soldier.

On one occasion, Krebs listened as they talked outside of our compartment. When they found a man missing, they confiscated the supplies he'd left behind. Not many escapees left much, but some in their haste didn't take the Red Cross parcels. After every stop, guards came back to our car with their arms full of supplies and eating better than they had in months. The Germans hadn't had real coffee in years, so the Red Cross coffee was a prize. Our only satisfaction was that this must have made the guards realize how much better supplied our men were than the Axis armies. I hid Gooler's things under the seat. When they came looking for his parcel, we told them he'd taken it with him.

About 2 AM, I was almost entirely relaxed when I felt a hand grip my forearm, startling me from drowsiness. It was Krebs, who was impatient to attempt a getaway. He whispered in my ear, "Colonel, the guards have left the aisle! I think we could slide the window open and drop out quietly when the train slows down."

It was true! Most of the guards were sleeping, except when the train stopped.

I suggested that we watch and see what happened during the stops. When the train was standing, the guards seemed to be only getting up from their seats and poking their sleepy faces out of the windows.

Krebs opened the window and stuck his head as far out as he could to check on the guards. Suddenly, he left the window and opened the compartment door. I had no idea what he was up to, but heard him call for the guard, apparently asking for permission to go to the restroom. He called out rather softly. When no guards answered, he boldly walked to the latrine at the end of the car. As fortune would have it, the train stopped. He climbed out unnoticed. The guards didn't check on us at this stop, so all was well.

I poked Agee in the ribs, saying, "Sam, if we want to get away, now is our best chance. Krebs is gone and they haven't noticed it yet. When they do notice his absence, they'll watch us all more closely and we'll have had it."

"OK," replied Sam. "Let's get going."

We stood up and slid the compartment door open. Sam stuck his head into the aisle and softly called for the guard, "Postern! Postern!" but got no response.

We walked boldly down the aisle in the direction that Krebs had gone and opened the door at the end, which wasn't visible from the aisle. We both scrambled out onto the car couplings. Sam went left and I went to the right. It was blacker than pitch with light rain falling. Italian railcars had a coupling arrangement consisting of a bumper on each car with a connecting center link. I hung on astride the bumper on the right, waiting for the train to slow down. Unfortunately, the train seemed to be picking up speed instead. The swaying and jolting became severe. Sparks from the carriage wheels flew all around.

I looked in a window on my side, which provided a view down the aisle to the other end of our car. A guard's lantern sat not far from our compartment, illuminating the interior with a weird glow. The wind and rain whipping my hair in my eyes added to the tension. I crawled down onto a step to the car's right door, but decided I'd be too easily seen by a guard looking out of a window on that side. I decided to crawl into the boxcar in front of our car.

I knew the boxcars had a small compartment for a sentry box at each end. This might provide a place to hide until the train slowed for a stop. I didn't pay much attention to Sam, but I assumed he was scrambling around much the same as I was. Just as I was crawling into the little end compartment, my hands came in contact with something on the floor. I lightly felt it and realized that it must be the cape of a guard who had fallen asleep on the floor from sheer exhaustion. I thought, it's a miracle I didn't wake him. I almost

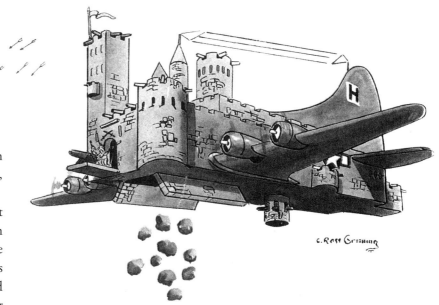

THE FORTRESS *"The Boeing B-17, Flying Fortress, the most famous ship of the Air Force. It [had a] capacity to repel enemy attacks and still do heavy damage to his war machine and production centers."* Not as Briefed

jumped off right there, as a hot flash of fright prickled over my skin. I expected a blast from a gun. Fortunately, I thought I hadn't touched him hard enough to awaken him. I crawled away, apparently unnoticed. (After the war, Krebs told me that he was hiding there, just as frightened as I was. He thought it was a guard grabbing him and he kept quiet. Krebs eventually made his escape.)

I slipped back to my spot on the bumper and watched through the window in case the guards inspected the compartments. Suddenly, a guard sleepily stepped out of a compartment and walked slowly down the aisle, looking into each room. He paused momentarily, holding the light high, to count the number of men in each compartment. Coming to ours, he looked in and then started on. He suddenly realized no one was there, and took a double take. He slid the door open and disappeared into our compartment. In a second, he came out on the run for his own compartment where he had left his rifle. He came back, loading a shell into the chamber on the way.

What a situation! The guard might shoot first and ask questions later.

Sam said, "Let's jump!" but the train was going too fast.

I said, "No, I'm going to grab that guard." I yelled to Sam to stay down and I ducked through the door.

I hesitated a moment in the end hall, then calmly walked around into the aisle, hoping the guard would think I'd been to the latrine. This didn't fool him and he ran up and put his rifle muzzle in my stomach. I'd always imagined that in situations like this you could summon additional strength, but it isn't true. I lost strength. Just as the muzzle touched me, I grabbed the barrel and hoisted it up with all of my might. Luckily, I was bigger than he was. The gun didn't go off, but we fell to the floor with me hanging onto the gun barrel for dear life.

Meanwhile, the train was slowing down, which was swell for Sam who made his getaway, but not so good for me. I thought sooner or later the guard would get his gun back and might want to take his spite out on me. He had other ideas, however. When he wrung the gun from my grasp, he lunged toward the end of the car sensing that there was someone else back there because I'd just come from that direction and our compartment was empty.

Other guards came to see what the racket was about and they whacked me a couple of times with their gun butts. Padre Brach came out and got involved. In the confusion and darkness, I slipped into a compartment and joined a small gang of friends, hoping the guards couldn't identify me. They suspected I was the one, however, and the commander of the guard pushed me back into the empty compartment. He was incensed that he'd lost another POW.

Brach could understand some German and told me that the guard said he was going to shoot me. Shaking his gun in my face, I really thought he was going to do it. I didn't know what to do. I thought that only a miracle could get me out of this. Fortunately, he wasn't sure if I was the one that had started the ruckus. I was left there with a guard pointing a gun not more than two inches from my face. It was an uncomfortable spot to be in!

I heard a shot and worried about Sam. I was certain he'd been found. Brach came back to get Doc Gallo. When he saw the guard holding a gun in my face, he knocked it down, saying, "Get this out of that boy's face. This is ridiculous," and bawled the guard out in good fashion.

I'd never seen a man so brave in the face of danger as Padre Brach. I think he figured he had religious immunity and could get away with more things than the rest of us. I'd come to admire him at Chieti, and now had even more reason to do so. (After the war, I recommended him for a decoration for his outstanding courage.)

The train momentarily stopped, then started up and moved about fifty yards, before halting again. All of the guards were outside by then and I heard gunfire. They couldn't be shooting at just one man, I thought. But if they were, they sure were making it tough for him. It was useless for me to get up, since I was being watched. I was befuddled by the turn of events. When I was finally alone for a minute, I shoved the Red Cross food under the seats, leaving empty boxes for the Jerries to confiscate when they came back to see who was gone.

Soon, it became obvious that something was happening further up the train. I heard several more shots and lots of shouting. The guards walked back and forth with their lanterns across the fields, looking along the fences and hedgerows. Presently, five wet, muddy, and bedraggled POWs were herded into my compartment. The guard left them and charged away. The boys explained that they'd escaped through a hole in the floor of their boxcar, but were caught lying on their faces in a field. A bullet had grazed the forehead of one of them, leaving him bleeding and dazed, but conscious enough to be thoroughly frightened. They said that many had bolted and quite a few had been shot. Our five POW doctors on the train weren't allowed to tend to the injured men.

We remained here for about an hour while the guards canvassed the train, seeing which cars had been sabotaged by the prisoners and couldn't be used for holding them anymore. The men were moved into the secure boxcars. Some cars were overcrowded with up to sixty men, which didn't allow them to sit down. My new companions soon were taken to another boxcar and a guard was posted at my compartment door. The train started up again.

I now was the senior POW officer on the train and the Germans gave every indication that they weren't going to lose me. The guard shouted and screamed at me in German, expecting me to understand. I decided it was best to remain silent, rather than trying to make myself understood without an interpreter. This seemed to aggravate the guard even more. I was so weary and tense that I didn't much care.

Brach was in the compartment next to mine. The Germans knew he was a padre and probably felt a little different about shooting at him than at one of us. Brach had decided he was going to help our men regardless of the consequences. He came to my room first and pushed right past the guard, who objected but didn't stop him. He asked me what had happened, but I didn't have much to tell him. I said some of the boys were hurt and needed help. I had no way of talking or pleading with the guards, and if I had, they probably wouldn't have paid attention to me anyway. I was excited to the point of being sick after struggling with the guard in the aisle. I worried about Sam too, but worst of all, I still was a captive.

Brach couldn't speak German or Italian, but he did know some words of each. Mixing English, German, and Italian, he somehow got the guards to figure out what he was saying. I was feeling very low, but when I heard the padre talking in his peculiar dialect, I couldn't help but burst out laughing. He walked about wherever he pleased. The guards protested, but they didn't stop or harm him.

Whenever we halted, Brach boldly stepped off the train and saw to the needs of the lads in the boxcars. Guards poked guns into his ribs, but he ignored them or told them to shoot if they wanted to.

He had grown a little goatee while a prisoner. He said, "I might want to escape and I want to look like one of the padres in the hills with their little cloaks and skull caps."

Because of his brashness, he could have gotten away many times, but he didn't take advantage of any chances to

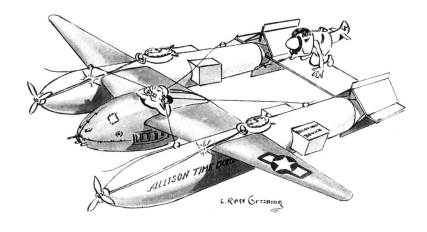

THE TIME BOMB *"The Lockheed Lightning, P-38, is often called the Allison Time Bomb in jest. Engine trouble in one was never serious if a pilot kept his head; if he didn't, the Lightning made him feel he was dangling on the wrong end of a bolt from the blue."* Not as Briefed

escape. By staying, he succeeded in keeping the guards off my neck and helped restore order on the train.

After about an hour, two majors in the next compartment decided they'd try escaping by jumping from the train while it was moving. Maj. Ferguson was a bomber pilot and Maj. Parson, a tank man. They planned to ease open the window while others in the compartment watched the guards, then crawl outside and hang from the windowsill. When the train slowed, they'd drop off. Parson would go first, then Ferguson.

While they were making their plans, the train was passing over some rugged stretches of track, resulting in a rough

ride. Unfortunately, when Parson climbed out of the window, the train came to a smooth section of right-of-way. This apparently gave Parson the feeling that the train was slowing down, because the jolting had eased off. He decided it was slow enough that he could jump. Actually, the train must have been doing at least 40 mph. The sound of him hitting the ground could be heard throughout our car. He rolled and tumbled through gravel and then must have crashed through a fence or two. I can't imagine that he survived the fall without injury. Ferguson didn't follow and I can't say I blame him.

We still were in the mountains and in the darkness it wasn't possible to see if we were passing by flat terrain, steep slopes, or drop-offs. The guards heard Parson's fall, and, of course, started a rumpus again. The sergeant in charge looked seriously worried because so many prisoners were escaping. It was a tough job for only nine men to guard a trainload of POWs. The guards' chances of getting any sleep were almost nil. They tried putting guards up ahead in the little end compartments on the boxcars, but it was too wet and dirty. They gave up this plan at the next stop.

I finally fell asleep from sheer exhaustion and didn't waken until we came to the Rome rail yards. Though it still was dark, I could determine that the bombed station now was in surprisingly good shape. The yard lights purposely were barely visible, but quite a number of guards could be seen roaming about the area. Additional guards boarded our train at this point. After about an hour's wait, the train pulled out and headed north. I slept through the rest of the night.

I awoke at dawn. My head ached, my eyes burned, and my skin felt hot and dry. The events of the previous twenty-four hours had taken a toll on me. I thought that if I could sleep during the day, I'd be in better shape to make an escape attempt in the night. Between periods of fitful slumber, I faintly remember peeking through sleepy eyelids at the passing landscape from time to time. With each mile northward, however, my spirit and morale sank lower. With addi-tional guards, the Germans were able to better watch the train and they could get some sleep. Our prospects didn't look good.

At each stop, Brach headed up to one of the boxcars and arranged to have the men get out to stretch and relieve themselves. Of course, the guards protested, but he didn't stop. They confined him, however, to tending to only one car at a time at each stop. If the padre could do this, I thought maybe I could too. On my first attempt, I was rudely shoved back into my seat and a gun was shoved in my ribs. I didn't try again.

Since we were traveling north, our chances of getting back to our lines should we escape were growing slimmer. We soon were winding through the Apennines and stopped just outside of Florence on our way toward Bologna. By now, the guards had slackened their vigilance and we were free to walk around in the car once again.

Capt. Gallo, an American doctor born in Sicily, told me he had an easy escape plan for when we arrived in Florence. When the train slowed down, we would simply step off the back and just stand there, like we were taking in fresh air. He thought we could just stand there and let the train pull away. If the guards came after us, it would only be because they'd noticed we hadn't boarded when the train started to move. This plan seemed ridiculous to me, but as it turned out, he was the smart one.

When the train stopped, we stepped off the end of the car. The guards were looking and pointing at the scenery. When the train started to roll again, one of the guards yelled and stuck his gun down at me. I still figured Gallo's plan was ridiculous. I jumped back on the train, but Gallo didn't move a muscle and for some reason they left him. They might have mistaken him for someone working on the tracks. He just stood there with his hands in his pockets, waved at us once, and walked off into the station. (He later was recaptured at an Italian wedding, full of wine and having a good time.)

The train passed out of the mountains and entered northern Italy's Po Valley just before dusk. The Po Valley is flat as a tabletop and we fairly flew along the straight tracks for hours in the dark. It was impossible to jump off at that speed.

I wanted company, so I moved into another compartment occupied by Padre Chutter, a South African, and Lt. Col. Kouns, a paratrooper captured in Sicily. Kouns had a severe case of jaundice when at the POW camp. He had tried to remain in the hospital because he was so ill, but the Germans moved him anyway. For the past couple of days, Kouns had been eating and storing up as much energy as he could in preparation for jumping off the train. He told me that he was going to make an escape attempt that night. I didn't think he was in any condition to be jumping off a train, but he was determined to give it a try. He had a box of Benzedrine tablets that he was going to take in the night so he could stay awake and jump when the chances were good.

He said, "I don't smoke, do you want these cigarettes?" He gave me all of them and I lit one.

Then he said, "I've got this thing figured out. Those guards all leave their posts as soon as the train gets going at a certain speed. These other fellows have been jumping a bit too soon. You can jump if this thing is going pretty fast if you roll with it. Come with me and we'll get off this train."

I'd grown so weary that I couldn't work up much enthusiasm. Such an effort seemed futile this far north.

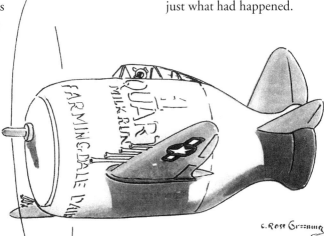

THE FLYING MILKBOTTLE
"The Republic Thunderbolt, P-47, caricatured [with] undeserved derision. At the beginning of the air war in Europe, the Thunderbolt range was very limited and escorted bombers to relatively 'easy' targets— 'milk runs' in Air Corps jargon. Later its range was greatly increased with the addition of belly tanks and it was in this ship that the great aces—Zemke, Gabreski, Gentile, and Johnson—hung up their amazing records." Not as Briefed

Kouns continued, "I'll tap you when it's time to go. Leave your seat and we'll jump off the train, all in one motion."

We stayed awake most of the night, watching the guards. However, they mixed up their routine, making it difficult for us. About halfway through the night at one of the stops, there was lots of noise and shooting. Some of the boys up ahead had managed to break out and make a run for it. The guards saw them and fired at them. I heard that one man was killed, but I had no way of knowing for sure just what had happened.

Dawn was just breaking when Kouns touched me on the arm and said, "Come on, lets go."

Being very sleepy and foggy minded, I thought he had exclaimed, "Good-by."

I replied, "Good-by," having completely forgotten about what he had in mind.

He walked to the end of the car and jumped out before any of the guards had a chance to even notice him. I watched through the window and saw him make a neatly executed somersault into the brush. I still was sort of stupidly dazed, with sleep blocking up my brain. Seeing him go seemed like a dream. His escape wasn't noticed by anyone and I'd really missed a good bet.

By now, our train was in the mountains in the far north of Italy proceeding toward Brenner Pass and Austria, which

Hitler had annexed to Germany. I didn't have a map, however, and couldn't tell for sure where we were. German troops were bivouacked in the fields on either side of the tracks. Evasion would be next to impossible in this locality. When the train stopped early in the morning, we talked to a Belgian gal dispensing Red Cross pea soup and grapes to anyone that wanted to partake.

"What's the matter? Are you fellows prisoners?" she asked in English.

"Why don't you just walk off the train here. There is a lot of confusion. Lots of people are running around. Come on, just walk off the train."

One fellow started to speak to her in Italian and she panicked, saying, "Don't be stupid! Talk in English. They understand Italian around here."

We stepped off the train and walked over to her to get some grapes. The guards were running all around and I don't know why they didn't get angry with us. They had threatened to shoot us before, but by this time I'd learned that you could act dumb and get away with quite a bit. She gave us grapes and wine. Then, the guards began motioning for everyone to board the train.

I walked right on by them and stepped into a small room in the station. The train started chugging down the tracks. I was excited. I thought I'd really escaped and would be going south on the next rattler.

The train already was moving at a fair clip when a guard stepped into the little room, indicating that I had better get on the train.

I had to run hard and grab for the compartment door handle. I was very frustrated.

By now, my morale had hit a new low. I was thoroughly tired and beaten, and felt dizzy and silly. I could have broken down and cried, or struck my best friend in the face for no reason at all. My mind became completely blank except for one thought—we were just about to enter Germany where I'd be a prisoner for months or even years. It was a helpless feeling. There was nobody to provide help, and the prospects for the future held no hope, only despair. We didn't know how the Germans treated POWs, but I thought they'd be pretty tough.

It suddenly struck me that this war was the most mixed up mess that the world had ever seen. Hundreds of years of conflicts may have seasoned the Europeans to warfare. Nevertheless, I couldn't help but believe that only a few individuals in modern times had experienced anything like this. It had never really meant much to me when I read about these kinds of events in history books. But now, I was living a part of the next story that historians would write about. I thought that young people, reading about this war in the future, probably wouldn't have any clearer idea about what it "really" was like than I had before it all started.

War struck me as an unexplainable phenomenon, despite the fact that it had happened a thousand times in the past. Why did it have to occur at all? Why did men chase each other through the hills with guns, trying to blast the brains out of someone they didn't know? Why herd men around, cooping them up in barbed wire pens to waste away precious years? True, we had our reasons to fight for our country, but at this point the trials we were experiencing seemed useless and unnecessary to me.

Fortunately, I wasn't suffering too much, although the men in the boxcars weren't having it so good. But they were making it, and we were all still alive. Nevertheless, it made no sense to me. ✹

CHAPTER NINE

ESCAPE

I wanted to lie down and never wake up again. I didn't want to eat, even though I'd only had a little hardtack, cheese, and grapes the day before. I still had some of the precious Red Cross food and my canteen. There was a knot in my throat the size of a grapefruit. From the way they looked, the rest of the fellows must have felt the same way. Conversation seemed pointless; besides, talking to someone only irritated our already bad dispositions.

The train stopped at a small station to pick up another engine to assist with the pull up the grade. As the spare engine passed us, the engineer called out to us in Italian, suggesting that we jump in the next few miles because he'd be deliberately going slow.

Larry Allen, who was a newspaper correspondent before his capture, heard this. The guards were becoming so weary that they didn't think straight, but, unfortunately, neither did we. Allen didn't wait long. He jumped along with Major Ferguson into a vineyard alongside the tracks. Ferguson rolled off into the ditch and out of the line of sight, but Allen fell over backwards, disappearing under the train. I thought surely he must have lost a limb, or worse![1]

At the time I saw them jump, I had located some water and was using a cupful to shave. I cleaned the soap from my face and decided I'd jump too. At least I could have a few days of freedom in the mountains, even though we were so far north that it seemed impossible to get back to our lines.

By now, however, the train was going too fast for me to jump off. I was so tired I couldn't figure out what I wanted to do.

The train continued up the Adige River valley and entered a narrow gorge with high mountains on either side. Here, after crossing near the mouth of a tributary river flowing at the base of a cliff, we entered a railroad marshaling yard. A sign above the stationhouse identified this town as "Bolzano." It sounded to me like it might be an Austrian name and the people didn't look Italian, except for a few railroad workers. I didn't know my geography or I would have known that we still were in northern Italy, approximately fifty miles south of Brenner Pass and the Austrian border. It wasn't until later that I learned that a local German-speaking population was the majority in this far corner of Italy.

The fellows in our compartment talked it over and figured that this marshaling yard would be a good target for our bombers. Destroying the bridge would stop traffic on a main route from Germany and repairing it would be difficult.

The train stopped in the middle of the station, the engine was unhooked, and we were left standing. A hospital train, full of wounded Axis soldiers, pulled up alongside of us. After about fifteen minutes, Padre Brach started to leave the car to make his usual rounds. Just as his foot touched the ground, a rising crescendo of air raid sirens pierced the air.

Major Howe (a fighter pilot) and I met in the aisle at a window, looking into the sky for planes. We knew they were after the marshaling yards and bridge, and here we sat, right on target!

"There they are," he shouted, "right over our heads. This is it!"

The German hospital train hurriedly pulled out. We all saw the bombers at about the same time. The tiny silver specks in V formation were coming straight toward us and the raid was going to be a big one. We ran to the door and gestured to a guard to let us out. We wanted off because the train was a juicy target for the flock of "Forts" coming at us. The guard unslung his rifle and forced us back into the car. I heard the AA guns begin firing and looked up to see the sky full of American four-engine bombers directly overhead.

The first bombs hit with an unreal suddenness. The thundering blasts made me drop and hug the floor, trying to squeeze into the grain of the wood. The other men in the car were doing the same. Out of the corner of my eye I saw Padre Brach out in the yard, standing up straight with his hands folded under his chin and his face pointed to the sky. I could no more have stood up at that time than jump into a blast furnace. Frankly, I was powerless to do anything. Our car

I would rather fly on 50 missions than go thru this again — We were 800 prisoners located on the target at Bolzano, Italy when the forts came!

A Wartime Log

was only 150 feet from the bridge. One moment I was lying on the floor, and the next I was outside on the ground—blown right out of the car!

The awful closeness of the ear-splitting blasts made me as rigid as stone. I believed the next bomb would land squarely in my back. I wondered if I'd be able to feel it when it struck. The bombs were falling in patterns. Strings of explosions could be heard starting some distance away and then thundering closer and closer, until the noise grew so loud that it didn't seem possible that we weren't getting hit. The train disappeared in clouds of smoke and dust. Railroad cars went sky high.

I don't remember how long the bombs came down, but I thought about more things in that short period than I normally did in weeks. I wanted to see my wife again more than ever. What would she do if I were killed? How would my mother react to the telegram that so many thousands of mothers in the US had been receiving? Those concerns meant so much more to me now.

Lying prone next to the wall of a loading platform, I heard blast fragments splattering against the wheels. The shards made a peculiar smack when hitting the wall above my head. Chunks of brick flew about. When a bomb hit close, the blast raised our bodies totally off the ground.

Suddenly, I felt ashamed. I could jump up and run if I wanted, but the poor lads in the boxcars were helpless. A guard firing a bullet at me would be nothing compared to the impact of a 500-pound bomb. They were trapped and their fear must be indescribable. What a mess if one of the bombs connected directly with a boxcar!

There was a momentary pause, then the bombs came again. This time, I huddled up next to the tracks, trying to get my body lower than the rails. Suddenly, I saw a pair of legs hurrying along the line of boxcars, pausing momentarily at each door. After that, I saw more legs going in all directions. Someone had pried himself out of a boxcar and was opening the doors to let the men out. I felt ashamed that I

hadn't done this. I admit that my mind wasn't capable of getting me to do anything. The crashing bombs lifted me off the ground again and I dropped down as the earth cracked and sagged. Every piece of shrapnel and each shrieking bomb seemed to be heading right for me.

When the bombing stopped, I still was in one piece. POWs were running everywhere. Some had dropped to the ground when the bombs hit, while others blindly ran in spite of the explosions. The thick dust and smoke was suffocating, and all but a couple of guards were gone. I gave those that stayed credit for having the guts to stick it out, but when they started shooting at the running men, I was gripped with cold fury.

I don't know what got into me. I jumped to my feet and started toward a guard to knock the rifle from his hands. He was trying to force men back into the boxcars and didn't see me coming. I don't know if he'd shot anyone, but he'd stopped firing when I reached him. I kicked the gun out of his hands just as he leveled it on one of the boys. The other guards killed five boys that I know about.

Since so many men were lying face down on the ground because of the bombs, it was hard to tell whether they were hurt or not. At the other end of the train, guards were herding lads in the direction of air raid shelters. We moved toward a gate, now realizing that our guards wanted to leave the rail yard just as much as we did. Suddenly, we made a break for the town, running in all directions.

With some other prisoners, I ran almost a block but suddenly found myself in a blind alley in a courtyard. We were trapped. Some German soldiers caught us and said we had to go back. Just as we were about to board the train, we heard planes overhead and the fireworks started again. Bombers were making another pass at the yard and a few bombs hit some distance away.

Then the familiar pattern of bombs began rolling toward us again. Suddenly, a few guards with guns couldn't hold us; nothing could! I took off like a scared rabbit.

Everyone ran for every possible kind of shelter. I ran into the town as fast as my legs could carry me. I faintly heard rifle shots, but couldn't tell if it was our guards firing. The AA guns and the bombs drowned the sounds out. Getting shot by the Germans was unimportant to me at that particular moment; I was more worried about being bombed by Americans.

Not looking right or left, I ran up the first street in town, struggling through dust and smoke. A string of bombs came toward me and I hugged the sidewalk next to a stone building. I think I hit the dirt again seven or eight times. One salvo hit in the middle of the street and everyone was knocked down. Someone landed right on top of me sobbing and crying in mortal terror. It was a young German soldier, who couldn't have been over seventeen years old, if he was that much.

I said something silly in German, like, "This is nichts goot, isn't it!"

He didn't hear me and I didn't much care. I actually had to force him off me so I could get up and run.

As I got to my feet, a one-armed Italian fellow motioned for me to get back down, but he didn't know what I had in mind. This was my best chance to get away and I wanted to run. I raced on as fast as I could and saw an incredible sight as a bomb hit a building. The window casings jumped out and remained suspended for a moment, then the whole building disappeared in a cloud of dust. The shock wave hit me and I landed in the dirt.

I ran down the street and found myself in another blind alley. It ended in a little courtyard that had a revetment of sandbags in the middle. This looked like it would offer some protection, so I vaulted over the sandbags and landed smack in the middle of a manned German 88-mm gun emplacement!

The gun fired just as I realized where I was. The roar of the cannon nearly floored me. At first, I thought a bomb had landed in the revetment. I must have swallowed my heart a dozen times. It was full of soldiers, who were loading and firing the gun as fast as they could. They were working like mad and I was in the way. They were tripping over me and shells were flying here and there.

I thought the best thing that I could do would be to get out of the way. I tried to act natural, dusted off my trousers (I had on a British battledress outfit), and started out the revetment exit, dodging the ammunition carriers. The Germans took no

SHORTY GETS ONE *"'Shorty' Klaiser [was] a Bombardier. He flew in a B-24. When he got behind a twin-fifty nose turret he felt he was the equal of any six Luftwaffe pilots. He proved it when he knocked down this FW-190 when it jumped Shorty's Lib during a raid on Bremen, 1943."*
Not as Briefed

notice of me, so I raced out of the courtyard and back down the street. At the first turn, I headed uphill to the higher part of the town.

More bombs hit and a shower of window glass came down on me from a nearby building. I had a quick glimpse of an attractive young woman standing with a bicycle at her side, close to a brick wall. She was crying in terror, but I was in no mood to console anybody and kept running. Rounding a slight turn, I ran squarely into two Italian men who seemed to know at a glance that I was an Allied soldier.

I pointed at myself, saying, "Americano, Escape!" I knew no Italian, but assumed that this word might pass in lieu of something better. It did! They caught on immediately and grabbed me and all three of us raced off together.

Soon, we came to an inn and I was steered into it and down to the wine cellar. The cellar was being used as an air raid shelter and was full of Germans and Italians, both military and civilian. My Italian friends gave me a green sweater and an apple, and left me to stand there alone. If I was caught, they didn't want to be nabbed too. For our mutual security, we said nothing. The good-sized cellar was filled with old casks and it really was a beautiful old room. I went over and sat in a corner, making myself as inconspicuous as possible. The men came over and talked loudly in Italian every time a German came near.

Soon, it was apparent that the raid was over and the occupants, including some German officers, drifted away, as did my newfound friends. I couldn't tell if they wanted me to follow, so I stayed until I was just about the last one left. Then I went down to the next level, which apparently was a basement drinking cellar. It was deserted, so I looked for a hiding place. A hallway led to three doors, but they were locked.

Then I found a box and barrel in a small, dead-end hallway. There was a burlap sack behind the barrel. I grabbed the sack and crawled into the barrel. By pulling the sack over my head, I figured I'd be fairly well concealed. I thought that if I could just hold out until dark, I'd be fine. Then I could hide in the nearby mountains and make further plans.

I tried settling down, but found that my cramped position wasn't doing my bad leg any good. Also, it wasn't too long until I needed to urinate. This indeed was a problem. On several occasions, a German had come for a bicycle parked against the barrel. If I got up to go, I might be discovered, and I didn't want to be captured for such a foolish reason. Finally in desperation, I peeked over the top of the barrel and spotted a potted plant not far down the hallway. I popped out of the barrel and deftly stepped to the potted plant to relieve myself. It was too bad, because it was a very beautiful plant.

My stay in the barrel must have lasted about six hours. Darkness came with agonizing slowness. Occasionally, people came into the basement to retrieve things, and one time there was a fair sized crowd discussing the events of the day. It sounded like they spoke in German, which made me think I was in Austria. I thought this meant that evasion would be extremely difficult for me just to get back to Italy, where I still would have a tough time getting back to our lines.

When all was quiet, I painfully crawled from the barrel. My muscles were so stiff that I almost fell on my face. I took the sack to help disguise myself as a worker. With the sack on my shoulder, I hobbled unnoticed to the inn's doorway. The front door was locked, so I unlocked it and

left, hoping no one would get in and steal anything because of me.

The moon was shining in the warm air. I headed west and uphill through the town. I passed a number of people, none of whom paid the slightest attention to me. I decided I could relax. After 2 1/2 months, I finally was free. The feeling was exhilarating and I could have screamed at the top of my lungs with sheer joy. If I'd been recaptured the next morning, it still would've been worth it just for these few hours of freedom.

I walked through a maze of streets to the outskirts of town and found a trail winding up the mountainside. I was free and just couldn't believe it! I was full of life and energy, and wanted to run up the steep trail. Most of the village was blacked out, but a few lights twinkled. There also were some lights in the rail yards, where it looked like preparations were beginning for repair work after the raid. Some fires still burned. I stopped at a small stream and took a drink, and it tasted just like the cool, clear water from the mountain creeks back home—like ice-cold champagne, only better.

It was October 3, 1943, and I had been shot down on July 17. It really wasn't a long time, but it had felt like years. I realized that in the future when I talked about our "fight for freedom," it would mean a lot more to me than it had in the past.

As I approached some houses, I heard radios playing inside. When the occupants heard the nails in my army shoes clicking on the rocks, the radios were turned off. Lights also were extinguished in some of the houses. I heard no voices, but I felt eyes peering from the darkened windows. I sensed their tenseness about someone approaching and causing difficulties for them.

I picked a likely looking house and knocked on the door, hoping I'd meet a friendly occupant. I was certain someone was home, but nobody answered the door. I tried several other places with the same result. At a couple of homes, dogs barked and growled at me. I thought it was

pointless to try and find help here, and decided not to make contact with people until I had walked far enough south to be sure I was in Italy. I plodded on up the mountain in the moonlight and the warm, night air.

Freedom tingled in every nerve; it was good to be alive.

At intervals, I looked back down at the town, which seemed so home-like. The mountain was bigger than it had seemed at first. The trail was steep with switchbacks. It seemed as if I could've jumped off the mountainside and landed on the rooftops below. It wasn't long until the moon went down and walking became more difficult. I located the Big Dipper and the North Star to see what direction I was traveling. I was going west. Maybe, I thought, I'd see the Alps when I made it to the top of the mountain. Maybe, I'd eventually get to Switzerland.

I don't know how long I walked, but the effort began to take a toll. I lit one of the cigarettes that Kouns had given me. Fortunately, I had two boxes of Italian matches with me. When nearing the crest, I decided to sit down and rest. It wasn't until then that I realized how tired I was. I crawled about four feet off the trail, found some moss for a fair mattress, and was asleep in no time.

In an hour or two, I awoke trembling from head to foot in the night air, which now was cold. I jumped to my feet and thrashed my arms to warm up. I pulled the sack over me, but it didn't do much good. I scraped together a few sticks and made a small fire, then curled my body around the flames as close as I could. I didn't want a big fire attracting attention. After warming up a bit, I fell asleep again.

I woke up not long afterwards and found myself lying in the ashes. I started the fire again and tried the same procedure. Suddenly, I heard voices from people on the trail, so I quickly stomped the fire out.

Two figures approached silhouetted against the stars. They spoke German and were wearing boots as nearly as I could judge from the sound of their steps. Their backpacks clanked and clicked as they walked along. I assumed they were soldiers. I lay still where I was. I think I could've touched them as they plodded by. I resisted a strange temptation to jump up and frighten them.

After they'd gone, I decided against restarting a fire because it could be seen for miles. I tried to sleep, but it was futile. By now, dew was falling and my clothes became damp. I was bitterly cold and miserable. I pulled the sack around my shoulders and walked on up the hill. I heard the first blasts back in Bolzano, indicating that the Germans were trying to clear the wreckage from the previous day's bombing.

Near the top, I came to a farmhouse and decided to raise someone if possible. I knocked on all of the doors and windows to no avail. The farmhouse was quiet as a church and tightly locked. The barn was dirty and muddy, and the hay was wet. I couldn't find a place to rest or get warm. I shook from my chattering teeth. The Big Dipper had slowly turned, but no streaks of dawn were showing in the east. I did chin-ups on a branch of a tree until I had no strength left, but I still couldn't get warm. I finally concluded that I hadn't had enough to eat in the past three days for my body to create warmth.

I walked back to where I'd stayed by the trail and tried to sleep, but it was no use. I was so tired and weary that I felt I could sleep a week, but my trembling from the cold kept me awake. I thought about all of the bad beds I'd slept in during my life and now they all seemed good.

After what seemed like an eternity, dawn began creeping up in the eastern sky with tantalizing slowness. When I went back up the trail, the sight before me took my breath away. My climb last night in the dark had taken me right to the edge of a cliff, higher than any I'd seen before. Scattered below me in seemingly inaccessible places wherever there was room to grow anything, were little farms.

I started walking along the mountainside, trying to decide what my plan of action would be for the day. Soon, farmers would be coming out to chop wood and do chores. I decided I'd approach the first one I came to and try to get something to eat. Church bells began ringing far down in the valley. I'd read about how sounds travel over vast distances in the Alps and now I realized it was true.

The trail that I followed led to a farmhouse that must have been built generations ago. An old man was at the back, chopping wood. I climbed over a fence and asked him in English for something to eat. He didn't pay much attention to me, but I could tell his curiosity was intense. I asked for food in Spanish, which also had no effect. I reverted to gestures and hand signs, and started stacking wood for him. Without saying a word, he stopped chopping and walked into the house.

In about ten minutes, just as I finished stacking the wood and sat down on a log, he returned with a cup of terrible tasting ersatz coffee. It did have cream in it, however. I drank the coffee, and waited about a half-hour before deciding I wasn't going to get anything else. I knocked on the door and returned the cup. A family was inside, sitting in a primitive room, and they all wore wooden shoes. It was hard to tell what their nationality was, but they almost certainly weren't ethnic Italians. I caught a few words sounding like German, so I decided to leave.

I followed the trail until I was out of sight, then turned off and headed downhill. If they were German, I thought they might notify the authorities, so I decided not to use trails in the daytime. About a hundred yards from the trail, I found a carbine that an Italian soldier evidently had discarded after leaving the army. I didn't want it nor need it, so I left it there.

I experienced some rough traveling off the trail when following a sort of spur leading off the mountain. It seemed to me that nobody could be living here. However, after crashing through the underbrush for a mile or so, to my amazement I broke out into an immense clearing, which contained a beautiful farm. The clearing was surrounded on three sides by steep, cliff-like mountain slopes. It was as inaccessible a spot for a home as any I'd ever seen. I sat down

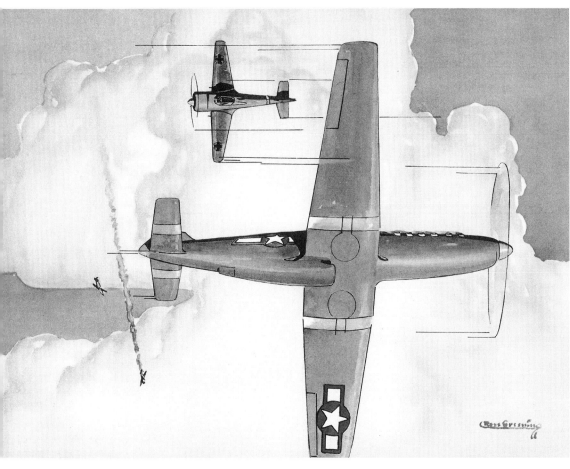

LUFBERRY IN EARNEST *"A P-51 Mustang and a Focke-Wulf 190 in a dog fight, engaged in a Lufberry Circle. The Lufberry, named after its originator, Raoul Lufberry, World War I ace, is a simple fighter tactic. It will pay off for the man whose plane can turn inside his opponent's without stalling out. The first to falter will be the victim."* Not as Briefed

Finally, I said "Italia?" and pointed in different directions, trying to get her to guide me. I then pointed straight down at the ground and asked "Germania?" and got a definite nod. So I must be in Germany! I thought.

I pointed south and repeated "Italia?" and got another nod. I then pointed north and asked "Italia?" just to see if she nodded at everything. She shook her head and pointed south, correcting me by saying "Italia," followed by other words that were meaningless to me. I was sure I needed to go south some distance to reach Italy.

I went on past the farm and came to an overlook above a vast valley. To the west stood some high, snow covered mountains that I figured must be the Swiss Alps. Suddenly, on a cliff about a mile ahead, I saw a beautiful castle that commanded a view of the entire valley. I headed for it, hoping to find a vantage point where I could spot a way to get down the mountainside

on some rocks just above the clearing and watched to see who might be coming or going. I fell asleep in the sun for an hour or two.

When I awoke, the warm sun had dried out my clothes. I took off my British battle jacket and cut off the pockets and shoulder straps to make it look more like a civilian coat. Then I approached the house. An elderly lady answered my knock and, of course, she couldn't understand me. She looked decidedly German and her words sounded like German too. I got nowhere with my hand gestures requesting food.

and, perhaps, also select a route south through the broad valley. I came across an apple tree and picked two partially ripe apples. They tasted mighty good, but weren't enough to satisfy my hunger.

In about a half-hour, I arrived at the fascinating old castle, which was deserted. The masonry had gone to pot and the site was overgrown. I walked cautiously up the trail to the entrance, then made my way around to the top wall on the valley side to take a look below. The castle seemed to stand 3,000 or 4,000 feet above the valley floor. The view, as beautiful as any I'd ever seen, took my breath away. I heard village bells—dozens of them chiming all at once up and down the valley. To the west jutted the Swiss Alps; and to the south and east were smaller mountains and valleys.

I felt transported into a completely different world as I took in this scene. From where I sat, the entire landscape appeared to be at peace. The military vehicles on the highway far below me didn't look any different from civilian vehicles. Later, I learned that this was the Adige River valley, which converged with its Isarco tributary immediately below Bolzano.

I observed this scene for a couple of hours, and decided that I could proceed down the valley by a series of roads visible from my lofty perch. I identified the towns, prominent houses, and a bridge that would guide me to the south. Once down there, it would only be a matter of proceeding undetected toward the south to the Po Valley, where I could make future plans.

Traversing northwest over the Alps, on the other hand, was almost an impossibility, especially at this time of year as snow began accumulating in the higher elevations. I also had heard that the mountain passes were well guarded.

I slowly started down the steep mountainside by a series of switchbacks. I planned to take my time because I wanted to enter the valley at dusk. Just as I started out, the elderly woman whom I'd met at the last farmhouse came plodding along the trail behind me, carrying an empty basket on her back. The basket was large enough to climb into. I couldn't believe that she intended to carry it all the way down the mountainside and then bring it back up full.

When passing by, she gave me a suspicious look and pointed to the south saying "Italia?" and then to my feet.

I nodded.

She shook her head disapprovingly.

It must be a long way to Italia, I figured. She left in a flurry, making her way down the trail like a mountain goat. She looked at least sixty-five years old.

I "moseyed" along, watching the sun and trying to estimate when it would be best to reach the foot of the moun-

tain. As I went on, I felt a few hunger pangs under my belt line. I'd seen some fine looking vineyards near the base of the mountain and I anticipated feasting on grapes. I stopped to rest for a moment on a large rock, but fell asleep.

I'd slept about a half-hour, when I was awakened by the approach of an elderly man coming up the trail. He carried a huge load on his back that made my eyes bulge with wonder. He appeared to be even older than the woman. The elderly seemed to be the only ones left in these parts to do the work. Of course, the young people probably were off to war.

I heard some fine yodeling coming from a hillside. When I replied with an American yodel, it stopped the concert.

When lower down, I spotted the vineyard and cut across to it. Like a sly fox creeping up on its unsuspecting victim, I reached up to the vines and grabbed as many grapes as I could carry. Then I scrambled back to a hiding place to eat them. They tasted sweet and good. After gorging myself, I stretched out on the ground to sleep a bit more and wait for sunset. Just as I began to get comfortable, however, my stomach began protesting. Within a few seconds, I'd chucked up everything and felt miserable. I'd eaten too many grapes too fast.

I finally dozed off to horrible dreams. I was at home and under a constant bombing attack. I ran and dove into shelters not quite big enough to offer protection. I'd almost reach my house, when I'd have to run back again to avoid detection by German guards patrolling the yard. At times, I could see my mother and wife in the living room, but I couldn't get their attention. Darkness came and the town was in flames. People ran in all directions. I hid in a clump of brush by a roadside, taking it all in. Finally, the brush caught fire and I had to run some more.

I awoke to find I was sliding down the hillside. I rose to my feet and walked on down the trail a little further to some back lots behind the first houses. The sun had gone down, but it wasn't dark enough to go any further. Then the mosquitoes came out; hordes of them zinging and stinging for

all they were worth. They must have been Nazi mosquitoes because they really had it in for me. I took to counting them and slapped nearly a hundred off a knee before they drove me away.

As I rose to leave, I saw the elderly lady that I'd met before, trudging back up the trail with her basket filled to the brim. She staggered from the load and was just starting the real climb. It didn't seem possible for her to proceed on up the mountain. When seeing me, she said nothing and looked guilty, which immediately made me suspicious. I thought she had reported me.

I immediately started out for the river in the gathering darkness. I found that my estimates of distance were wrong. I walked and walked toward the river, but I passed my checkpoints with agonizing slowness. Finally, I went off course and wound up at the river, about a mile from the bridge. By now it was fairly dark.

I didn't want to retrace my steps around a farmyard, so I cut across, which led squarely into a chicken yard. In the dark, I tripped on a feed pan and went sprawling into a fence, creating a barnyard riot. Chickens squawked and dogs barked louder than they probably ever had before. Of course, the owner ran out to see what the racket was about and found me calmly walking out of the yard, kicking loose wire from around my feet and brushing dirt off my clothes. I said nothing and he said nothing, so everything was fine.

Soon, I crossed the bridge and entered a large apple orchard on the other side. Four apples went to the Allied cause. I wanted more, but remembered the episode with the grapes.

The further I went into the orchard, the more difficult walking became and soon I was ankle deep in mud and water. The moon was bright, but the trees cast shadows and I couldn't see where I was stepping. Shortly, however, I was back at the river, so I climbed a dike and walked along it towards a town.

When entering the town, I'd intended asking someone for help. By now, I was ravenously hungry, but the people all looked German so I kept quiet. It seemed that my only chance to escape this region would be to head back to the Bolzano area and then proceed down toward the plains. I came to a small bridge guarded by sentries, but luckily they took no notice of me as I shuffled across.

On the other side, I saw a sign indicating "Bolzano 6k," which I took to mean six kilometers or about four miles. My hips were sore and my legs ached from the long walk, but I continued on. Soon, as I got nearer to Bolzano, I had doubts about my plan. Here I was, in my third day of freedom, and I was heading right back to the place I'd just escaped from. I felt there was no rhyme or reason to my plan.

By the time I reached the town limits, I'd passed a numbers of soldiers and civilians. None paid the slightest attention to me. ✿

NOTE

1. Larry Allen of the Associated Press escaped, but later was recaptured and eventually repatriated by the Germans. See, David Westheimer, *Sitting It Out: A World War II POW Memoir* (Houston, TX: Rice University Press, 1992), 214.

CHAPTER TEN

HIDING OUT

When passing a barracks, I saw a number of German soldiers going in and out. They all seemed to be having a good time. Closer to the center of town, I came to an inn and stepped into the doorway. The place was full of soldiers, drinking and enjoying themselves, and some were eating sandwiches and cold cuts. My mouth watered at the sight, but I figured I'd better move on.

I began to see the results of the bombing. Barricades and red lights screened off huge craters in the road, and a roadway bridge was blown-up from a direct hit. Coming closer to where I'd run frantically through the streets, I saw that the rail yard was the biggest mess of all. The Germans had the place lit up at night to allow for the cleanup to proceed. Tracks were twisted and tossed about like playthings. I wandered through the yard and towards the railroad bridge.

Mrs. Rita Pavoni of Pescantina, Italy, gave Ross a corduroy suit that had belonged to her son. Ross probably had this photo taken at Verona in late November 1943 and used it in a forged identification card. *A Wartime Log*

People all around me were working and making repairs. Smashed and piled-up rail cars lay indiscriminately around the yard. The main damage had been done to the bridge itself. It had received a couple of direct hits and had fallen into the river, making it difficult to repair. Rail traffic in the yard had stopped, looking like it was going to remain that way for a week. Our boys had done a good job.

A throng of civilian and soldier passengers came walking across a footbridge next to the destroyed railroad bridge. From all appearances, they had just stepped off a train on the other side. This was what I was looking for. Walking against the pedestrian traffic, I crossed the footbridge and approached a train that was unloading and getting ready to head back south. Perfect, I thought! I could jump aboard.

To complicate matters, however, a middle-aged lady with five or six bags stood where she had been let off the train. Evidently looking for someone to carry her things, she spotted me. I tried to ignore her, but she came up to me speaking in a demanding way.

I didn't understand her words, of course, though I could easily assume that she wanted me to carry her bags. I pretended not to understand, which wasn't hard to do, but then she started speaking in different languages. I thought I recognized German, Italian, Spanish, and French. I'm glad she didn't try English. I held my hands to the sides of my head, trying to indicate that I was deaf and dumb. When I started to step away, she grabbed my arm and pulled me towards the bags. I saw the train pulling out, so I wrenched myself away and ran for the engine.

The engine was pushing the cars out of the station. I reached the steps leading to the cab and climbed up. An Italian met me at the top and blocked my entrance. I said one word, "Americano!" and tried to push further into the cab.

At this, the Italian pointed at the man handling the throttle and said "Tedesco!" (German) and tried to push me off, but I didn't know what the name "Tedesco" meant and didn't much care. I pointed to the coal car and was about to force my way further in, when he grabbed the hand rails on either side of the doorway and kicked me squarely in the stomach, knocking me off the engine to the ground.

The train wasn't moving fast, so I jumped to my feet and ran forward to the baggage car. The door was open and I jumped aboard before the Italian baggage man could stop me. Again I pointed to myself, shouting "Americano."

He immediately slid the door closed and put me in a seat by the mail compartment. I was weak and tired, and didn't much care what happened. This fellow, however, looked as if he was going to help me. He rattled off words I didn't know, but with hand signs and gestures, we began to understand each other.

He was eating his supper of bread, apples, grapes, and wine, and offered to share with me. The grapes and apples were good, but the bread was as old as shoe leather and tasted the same. The wine was bitter and full of sediment. My stomach began churning from long-term neglect and the excitement, and I almost chucked up the food. By pointing to a stack of parcels and baggage at the opposite end of the car, I indicated that I should find a place to hide.

At this, my new friend jumped to his feet and led me to the first-class carriage next to the baggage car. He put me in a fine compartment, where I took down the window curtains to use as bedcovers and plopped down, falling asleep in seconds.

The next morning, the ground outside was white with frost and I awoke shivering from the cold. The train was standing still on a siding. A couple of apples stood on the window ledge, which the baggage man must have left for me. I ate them and "imagined" that they were something a little more nourishing.

My legs were stiff and sore from the previous day's walk, and I was bruised from the fall from the engine. My left leg was swollen to an alarming size and ached something terrific. I tied my shoelaces as loosely as possible, but I didn't want to take the shoe off fearing I wouldn't get it back on.

I rose to my feet and tried walking back and forth in the aisle to warm up, but being stiff and sore, I had to give it up. Soon, the train started moving—but it was heading north! I looked out of the window and saw that I still was in the valley that led up to Bolzano. My Italian friend was nowhere to be seen and the train was going too fast for me to jump off. I sat in my seat hoping things would turn out all right.

We eventually pulled up to a German airfield and stopped. To my alarm, it was exactly the same place where I'd boarded the train the night before. The train had returned to pick up more soldiers and civilians for a trip south. There was considerable activity on the field. JU-52 transports were groaning in and out at close intervals. Supplies were stacked about in piles and a tremendous crowd was gathering to board the train. They had worked themselves into a sort of frenzy to get a seat on the train.

German officers began pouring into the first-class coach. I sat next to the window and pretended to be asleep. Soon, they filled the compartment. Figuring that detection was inevitable if I stayed here, I got up and walked as calmly as I could toward the end of the car where I saw my friend from the previous night. A number of Germans eyed me suspiciously, but no one questioned me. I still wore a uniform, which should have tipped them off even with my pockets

Abandoned castle overlooking the Adige River valley. A Wartime Log

and shoulder straps removed. My beard was three days old and I couldn't have looked more like an escaped prisoner if I'd tried.

When the baggage man saw me, he looked as if he might faint. I'm certain that he forgot I was on the car. His reaction should have made the German officers realize something was suspicious, but again I was lucky. The baggage man motioned toward the rear of the train, then held up three fingers to me and said something about vegetables. His words were more than I could fathom, but I did figure out his intent to send me off to some safer place. I stepped out of the first-class car and walked toward the end of the train.

Once, I looked back to see if the baggage man was still watching me. He was, and he motioned toward a car on the siding not connected to the train. The car looked like a good place to hide, so I climbed aboard. Inside, I found military gear, packs, and weapons for a whole carload of soldiers, but nobody was there. I pushed some of the stuff off a seat and made myself comfortable. I was afraid that if I suddenly turned and left the car, it would attract attention. As a matter of fact, I felt like everybody was watching me, but no one said a thing.

In a few moments, a German conductor stomped into the car and walked right into my compartment, sputtering unintelligible words. My only answer was a shrug of the shoulders and a helpless gesture with my hands. It must have meant something as he took hold of my arm and started me outdoors. I felt I was being taken in for sure. The conductor marched me out of the car and along the train to the third class carriages, growling and grumbling as we went. He pushed me into a compartment where there was an empty seat next to the windows.

The Germans and Italians in the compartment eyed me as I entered, but made no attempt to talk to me. I pulled my sack over my lap and tried to act sick, which wasn't hard to do. Some people were digging into their lunches while waiting for the train to start. The sight of bread and grapes made

On the third night after escaping I walked back thru the target- It was flat and the train bridge down - I crossed the river on a foot bridge and spent the night on this train in the background- In the morning it took me south as far as Verona- It was crowded with soldiers + civilians none of whom recognized me or my uniform

Bolzano rail yard. A Wartime Log

my mouth water. I sat back in my seat and feigned sleep. If I could appear to be asleep for the whole time at least nobody would talk to me. My biggest concern was that I'd be asked for my ticket and passport. The train was soon so overcrowded, however, that it didn't appear that a conductor could get through to me.

After loading the train—even filling the restrooms with passengers—we started south. My heart thumped with each chug of the engine. Every mile south would be one less mile I'd have to walk to get back to our lines. The faster the train went, the higher my spirit soared. Whenever the train slowed down, my optimism dropped, as vivid scenes came to mind of soldiers catching me and sticking me behind barbed wire. The trip went smoothly, however, and nobody tried to converse with me. It was hard to feign sleep for so long, because I was so excited.

The train stopped at numerous stations going south and most had the names posted. This didn't help me, however, because I didn't know the towns in this area. I did a better job of judging how far south we were by observing changes in the terrain.

At each stop, boarders shuffled for the empty seats. The compartment I was in had a door to the outside, which was opened each time we stopped. Sometimes, a station agent or conductor peeked in, apparently seeking extra space for passengers, but they never bothered me.

By late afternoon, we were nearing the Po Valley. I figured I'd better get off the train soon before my amazing luck ran out. I'd heard people mention "Verona" a few times, so I thought that we were close to this large Italian city, which was located about 150 miles south of Bolzano. When the POW train went through here on the way north, I remembered Verona as being on the northern edge of the vast Po Valley plain.

When the train stopped at a small station on the city's outskirts, I decided this was the place to get off. (It was a good thing too, as I later learned. In Verona, all of the passengers were checked for tickets and passes.) I stepped out of the compartment door and headed for the stationhouse. Near the exit, I noticed German guards checking people's passes as they went through the door. I'd get caught if I went there. I quickly looked for another exit and saw a doorway leading into another part of the station that might have a window or exit.

I ducked in and, to my utter dismay, found I was in a blind alley. It was a power control room of some sort, probably for an electrical system, since many of Italy's trains ran on electricity. I didn't want to go back out immediately, which would make it obvious that I'd made a mistake and thus attract attention. I stood still and waited, hoping for more good luck.

Shortly, a German guard came into the room and said some unpleasant sounding words to me. I did my customary shrug of the shoulders, and he took me by the arm and escorted me to the main doorway. He was aggravated and wasted no time in shoving me out of the station and into the street. I was past the German checkpoint and free to go wherever I wanted! Would wonders never cease? How long would this luck last?

I saw a load of Italian prisoners being hauled away from the station by this same exit. Some of them looked at me and I gave them the high sign as I walked down the street to a road leading out to the countryside. (I later learned I was in the vicinity of Pescantina, about seven or eight miles north of Verona.)

I walked about a mile before sitting down to rest. I was weak from hunger. I proceeded on to a farmhouse that didn't look particularly prosperous. Could I get lucky again? I watched the house and road for a long time to see if any Germans were near, but none came by. As it grew dark, I went around and crossed into the field behind the house. Luscious grapes grew on the vines, but I needed something more substantial. At the side entrance, I knocked and waited.

The Bustaggi house. "Every meal—it was the same—always 'Polenta' (corn meal). The men never took off their hats even to eat. We ate some poison mushrooms once." A Wartime Log

"I spent some time cleaning wine vats here as well as making lots of wine. Incidentally I drank some too." A Wartime Log

I'd heard talking inside, but it ceased. Soon, a pleasant looking middle-age woman came to the door.

"I'm an American escaped prisoner of war," I said boldly, hoping that she understood English.

She didn't, so I pointed to myself, saying, "Americano!"

At first the word didn't register, but then her eyes widened and she started trembling. She called another woman to the door, who must have been her mother. They conversed excitedly, until they suddenly realized that I was standing outdoors in plain view. They grabbed me by the arm, pulled me inside, and took me to a back room, where they asked all kinds of questions, which I couldn't interpret. A young daughter with a baby girl also was there. They repeated themselves again and again, then began shouting, probably thinking my hearing was poor.

I finally shushed them up by holding a finger to my mouth. They immediately caught on and quieted down. Then I pointed to my mouth and made eating motions. They sat me down at a table and gave me a meal I'll never forget. First came the wine—I had one glass before they set a bowl of rather coarse spaghetti and chicken soup before me. I had two helpings. Next, came cold cuts, which I cleaned up with no trouble. After this, cold fried chicken. I ate until I thought I'd pop. More wine was offered, but I was feverish and only wanted water. I drank five glasses of water, which perplexed them no end. They figured water only was for washing hands and clothes.

Someone brought in an English-Italian dictionary, but it was so mixed up that I couldn't find the words I was looking for. Soon, a man came to the house and shook my hand, but he looked very worried about my being there.

The lady who first answered the door had kept her eyes on me most of the time. Her name was Rita Pavoni and her daughter was Elsa. She brought out a corduroy suit that fit me perfectly. (Later, I learned that Mrs. Pavoni's son, who was about my same size and age, recently had been killed while serving in the Italian army.) I gave them my uniform, which they took away. Later, they brought me a razor for a much-needed shave. Just as I finished shaving, two bicyclists, a man and a young woman, came into the yard.

The man stepped up to me, saying in fair English, "My name is Toni and this is my daughter Nellie. We live in America for seventeen year. We will help you if you would like us to."

I shook hands with Toni and Nellie and was as glad to see them as anyone in my whole life. Their formal names were Antonio and Nela Peduzzi. Antonio was middle-aged and owned a restaurant, and his daughter Nellie was in her mid twenties. They had been summoned to come meet me.

I told them briefly about what had happened to me in the past few days, and how I'd come to be here. I explained that I wanted to go south and try to get back to Allied lines. When I told them about my last train ride, they were astounded. They thought it was impossible for anyone to come as far as I had, especially while wearing a British uniform.

Toni said, "You don't want to go south. It's not safe. You will be caught soon if you do. Stay here and soon the Americans will be here. In fact, if you will wait here just two months you will be freed by them when they come through."

I remembered all of the other times I'd heard "just two months," and answered, "I don't think they'll be here that soon. My leg is pretty swollen and I need to eat for a few days. I would like to stay for a while to get back into shape if you have a place for me."

Nellie replied, "My father has a good place for you to stay in the mountains nearby. We will come by in the morning and pick you up to take you there. You must be very tired so you'd better try and get some sleep."

I was taken to a haystack in a shed, where a luscious bed had been prepared with big thick comforters. I dove in and was asleep in minutes. I'd been cleaned up, fed, and given clean clothes. It was a wonderful feeling.

I awoke early in the morning to the sight of the family's small son peering up at me over the edge of the haystack.

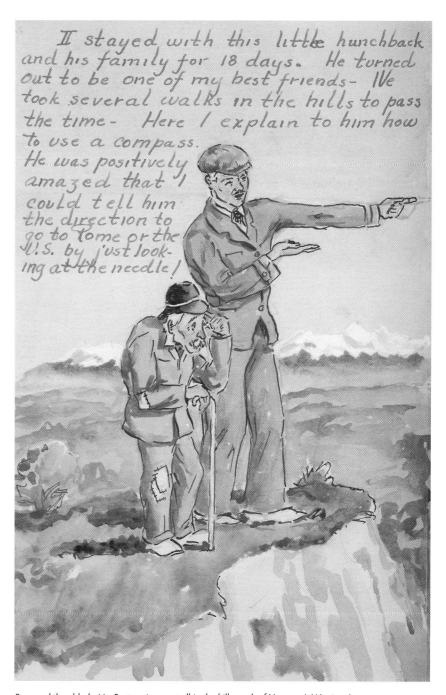

I stayed with this little hunchback and his family for 18 days. He turned out to be one of my best friends—We took several walks in the hills to pass the time—Here I explain to him how to use a compass. He was positively amazed that I could tell him the direction to go to Rome or the U.S. by just looking at the needle!

Ross and the elderly Mr. Bustaggi on a stroll in the hills north of Verona. A Wartime Log

He brought me bread and ersatz coffee for breakfast, which was delicious.

Toni was waiting to take me by bicycle to a hideout. I wore my GI shoes because the Geneva Convention rules proscribed that a soldier must wear at least one article of an official uniform to keep from being shot as a spy if captured. I kept my insignia and wings in an inside pocket. I felt more conspicuous in civilian clothes, however, than in a uniform because I'd worn nothing but uniforms for so many years. Nevertheless, the civilian clothes felt good to wear.

We peddled our bicycles into Pescantina, where Toni owned the "Ristorante California." Germans were in the town, but they paid no attention whatsoever to me. We cycled to the restaurant and took the bikes into the kitchen. I met Toni's wife and looked over the restaurant. Toni offered me a glass of wine before we started out again. For the next two months, I drank only wine. Drinking water here was considered as much out of line as drinking wine all of the time would be in America.

After downing the wine, we started for the hideout. Toni peddled about fifty yards ahead of me. A friend of his, coming along just for the ride, escorted us. We passed through several small settlements on our way to the mountains. After biking about eight or ten miles, we reached the little town of San Peretto and stopped at a restaurant that looked at least two centuries old. It was clean inside, though. We now were well into a valley next to the mountains.

Toni told me he'd been born near here and he was taking me to relatives. I found out that the Italians seemed to have relatives everywhere. Toni ordered a fine meal for us and more wine. Toni kept up with the best of them when it came to downing wine.

After eating, I met Mr. Quirino Righetti and his family, who occupied the house and ran the restaurant. The woman of the house was Mrs. Angelina Righetti, and there were three daughters, Edda, Anna, and Danila, and two sons. One of the sons, Rinaldo, was about my age and had escaped from

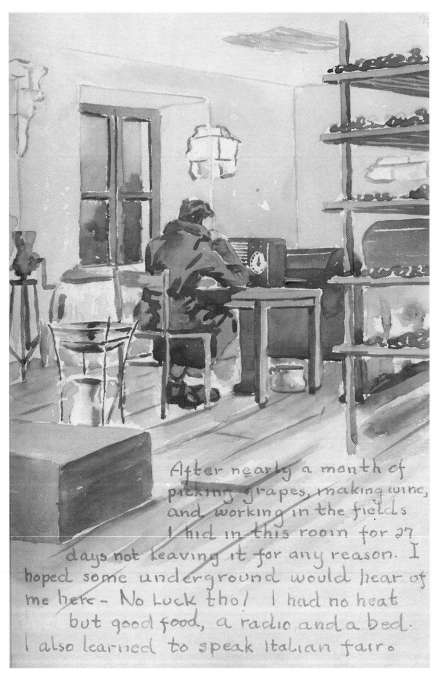

After nearly a month of picking grapes, making wine, and working in the fields I hid in this room for 27 days not leaving it for any reason. I hoped some underground would hear of me here – No Luck tho! I had no heat but good food, a radio and a bed. I also learned to speak Italian fairo

The third-story room at the Righetti residence. A Wartime Log

the Germans in northern Italy when sent north for military service. He had no love for the Germans. The other son, Italo, was a youngster.

We were trying so hard to understand each other that we took no notice of two German soldiers who had entered the restaurant. When she saw them, Mrs. Righetti just about fainted. Rinaldo wanted me to dash into the backyard and up the hill. If I'd done that, of course, I'd be caught in a flash. I indicated to them to keep right on talking in Italian in a normal tone. The Germans sat down and waited for service from the older sisters.

Soon, I rose to my feet and walked slowly to the door. I paused, then strolled outside into the backyard. The Jerries

paid no attention to me. After walking back a bit further, Toni and Rinaldo joined me. Toni said that this was the first time that Germans had entered the place. That was why they became so excited. They couldn't help but believe that the Germans were looking for me.

Toni said he had to leave, but would send some things from time to time. He also would see that I was sent somewhere else for a while to keep me hidden. He left as Rinaldo and I, waiting for the Germans to leave, took a walk up the hillside and brought back a load of firewood.

It was dark when we returned and saw that the Jerries had set up a tent about a block from the restaurant. This caused a long family discussion about my welfare during the evening meal. They felt none too easy about me being there. Things were complicated because I couldn't speak Italian, but I was beginning to pick up a word here and there.

Just as we finished eating, in walked two German officers covered with ribbons and medals. They were stiff and formal, and demanded food from Mrs. Righetti. She grew excited again and looked very scared. The Germans sat down at the table behind me.

"About Dec. 1st, 1943, I boarded the train at Verona, Italy, to go to Yugoslavia. It took me to Venice where I spent the night in the station. Cividale and Udine were next—I walked from Cividale on." A Wartime Log

Rinaldo, who was sitting with me, kept on talking in a low tone. Although I didn't understand a word he was saying, I nodded my head and took a sip of wine at intervals to appear to be interested. We made no attempt to move and the Germans paid no attention to us. We all were growing bolder as time went on.

Soon, the officers finished and got up to leave. Mrs. Righetti saw them to the door and just before they left asked for cigarettes. They obliged with a whole pack, which she immediately brought to Rinaldo and me. We had a good laugh, finishing our meal smoking German cigarettes.

I was shown to a bedroom that I was to share with Rinaldo. The comfortable third-story room had two beds and I was given the best one, which actually had a soft mattress and white sheets. I slept well at first, but in the middle of the night I became sick to my stomach due to the wonderful meals of the day before. I spent the rest of the night throwing up a lot of good food. When morning came around, I was weak and ill. Mrs. Righetti gave me some sort of brandy or syrup with a high alcoholic content. It helped a little.

She also noticed my bad leg and decided to dress it. She indicated that I wasn't keeping it warm enough, so she wrapped it in some wool scraps. My leg was swollen and extremely sore, and getting worse. Of course, I wasn't doing it any good with all of the walking I'd done. I started learning Italian in earnest because I knew I'd need to know some of the language if I ever hoped to get back to our lines. Angelina Righetti was my teacher and I began developing a deep friendship with her.

I stayed there for three days, hardly knowing what they were saying to me. I couldn't see how they intended to keep my presence a secret, because everyone in the neighborhood was talking about me being there. I could tell it worried the family a great deal. They did everything they could to make me comfortable and apologized for every little thing that

Rinaldo Righetti. A Wartime Log

wasn't just right. There always was a full decanter of wine on my table. They also had a radio, which I really welcomed.

On the evening of the third day, we were sitting in my room listening to the radio. The Germans forbade this, so we had to keep the volume low. I'd just located an American broadcast when Rinaldo reached up and turned the radio off. I looked at him questioningly and saw tears welling up in his eyes. I looked at Angelina and she was crying too. This was confusing. Maybe I'd done something wrong or somebody was coming to recapture me. With my very limited language skills, I couldn't find out what was the matter. Before long, the rest of the family arrived and they were all crying. I looked at myself in a mirror to see if maybe I was dying, but I looked okay!

After the tears, many bottles of wine, and drawing sketches, I learned that I was going to have to move and they didn't want me to go. The peculiar thing was that I had to leave that night. It already was quite late and I was ready for a good night's sleep, but I gathered up my coat and hat when told to go.

As I left the house, all members of the family, including Mr. Righetti and the sons, soundly kissed me. We started up the hill in the darkness and passed the sentry tent with no trouble. Rinaldo kept nervously "shushing" me all the way past the sentry tent, which was far more noticeable than just acting normal. I was being sent to the home of Angelina's parents.

We climbed a trail up a rocky mountainside for about 1 1/2 miles, until coming to a cluster of farm buildings that stood considerably separated from the majority of farmsteads in the hills. Rinaldo had me wait outside while he entered the house to see if all was clear.

Before long, he returned and brought me in, introducing me to his relative Guiseppe Bustaggi, also known as Beppi. I tried out my newly learned Italian phrases. We decided that they'd claim I was Sicilian, because the people of this area couldn't understand the Sicilian dialect. I personally decided that I wouldn't talk to anybody except the family I was staying with.

I went into the house and met Mr. Bustaggi and his wife, both in their seventies, another son, Angelo, and a daughter, Nela. The elderly man had suffered from infantile paralysis and consequently was deformed and very small. What he lacked in stature, however, he more than made up for in good heartedness. They were all in the kitchen by a smoldering fireplace. The ceiling was low and the ever-present wine bottle was on the table.

When making a toast to a quick Allied victory, I tasted the best wine I'd ever had in my life. The brothers, Angelo and Beppi, were expert winemakers. Their theory was that water was to be used for washing only, and then as little as possible. If you didn't drink wine on every possible occasion, then you were considered a bit insane.

After talking late into the night, Rinaldo left and I was shown to a spare room where I was to sleep. The bed consisted of a rather high table covered with a feather mattress. The sheets had been repeatedly patched until it was difficult to tell which parts were original. It was clean and comfortable, though, which was all I wanted. I felt that I was among genuine friends, but I couldn't help marveling at the strangeness of my circumstances.

In the morning, I was fed bread and ersatz coffee. I never got used to the coffee, but it filled you up and that was all that was necessary. Beppi asked if I wanted to help pick

grapes in the vineyard. I thought this was wonderful. I was glad to have something to do to keep me occupied and I also could eat my fill of grapes.

I picked and carried baskets of grapes until I thought I'd drop. The noon meal of corn meal, or "polenta," tasted even better because of my keen appetite from work-

The Righetti family of San Peretto, Italy. A Wartime Log

ing. I worked as hard as I could and the time passed with remarkable speed. It would've been wonderful if only this could have lasted.

That night we had polenta again, but this time with some sort of sauce that varied the taste. Wine made all the meals quite palatable, especially this wine. Angelo had two varieties, a red table wine and a red sweet wine. He made his own barrels and kegs, and grew his own grapes. He stored wine in the cellar, and in odd barrels stored in the attic and extra rooms around the farm.

Some days later, when the time came to squeeze the grapes, I got in the vat and stomped my feet to my heart's content. We poured the grape juice into kegs and carried them around the place, putting some in one barrel and some in another. I'd have a glass of wine every time I felt I could hold another. It was a really interesting experience.

As the days passed, the chestnuts ripened and we picked hundreds of pounds of them. They were much better tasting than the ones I'd eaten in the States. They brought a good price at market too, selling at 10 lire a kilo. The sight of people gathering chestnuts was picturesque. Men used long poles, reaching as high as they could, to knock nuts from the trees. They also climbed the trees to reach the elusive nuts beyond the range of the poles. Some trees were enormously big, making the task of handpicking quite dangerous. A

neighbor fell and was killed, putting a damper on the festive season.

We returned to the vineyards after the end of the chestnut, or "marrone," season. The best grapes had been saved for making the sweet red wine. They were allowed to ripen a bit more on the vines, then picked and placed inside on drying racks for two or three months. When about fifty percent of the moisture was gone, the grapes were smashed into juice. It made a delicious, sweet, after-dinner wine that tasted for all the world as if sugar was added, but none was used. Of course, sugar was unavailable because of the war, as were many other commodities.

When we finished the wine making, there wasn't much to do. It was necessary for me to keep out of sight as much as possible to keep the neighbors from talking, so I took walks in the mountains and woods. My little hunchback friend, Mr. Bustaggi, went with me on some of these excursions, teaching me a little grammar. I was catching on well, though it took me about ten times as long to tell a story. When my hosts related their stories, the words came too fast for me, but I'd act as if I understood just the same.

Angelo was a carpenter by trade and considered one of the better-educated persons in these hills. He'd had five years of schooling, compared to the two or three years for most of the others. People came to him for advice because of this. When I told these people that I'd been schooled for seventeen years, they couldn't believe it. I tried to tell them about some of the things that I'd learned. However, it was hard for them to understand some basic concepts and facts that we'd always taken for granted in America.

My small compass was a source of amazement to the old man, who couldn't understand how I could tell the direction to a town by looking at the little needle. It proved hopeless when I tried to explain to them how we navigated by the stars. This did help pass the time, however, and I found that they began to show respect for me because of my education.

The Bustaggis had skills, however, that astounded me. With no training, they accomplished some feats that would've been very difficult for an engineer to compute. The terracing of their land was a superhuman accomplishment, and the stone walls were as solid as the earth itself and neat as could be.

Making a barrel with seasoned wood was one of the most amazing feats I ever watched. For days, Beppi sawed out the planks and Angelo planed and singed pieces of wood. Then one day, Beppi started assembling the planks, creating a fine-oak barrel with about a hundred-gallon capacity. It was as finely finished as if done by machine.

I did some woodcarving and other activities in the carpenter shop to pass the time. One day, while working on a carving, I had a meal of polenta with fresh mushrooms just picked from the field. After a while, Rinaldo Righetti dropped by to visit. When I looked at him, however, my sight was hazy and he seemed far away. I remember shaking hands with Rinaldo and having a glass of wine. My arms felt light and it seemed as if I were going to float right off the face of the earth.

I went outdoors and walked around, trying to figure out what was wrong. I couldn't even feel my feet touching the ground. What a strange sensation—I thought maybe I was going crazy. I decided that if I lay down, maybe it would go away. I headed back for the house and then my mind went blank.

When I opened my eyes, it was dark and Angelo was leaning over my bed holding a candle in my face. He was trying to feed me pickled cherries from a jar. They tasted good and I ate several.

"How do you feel?" he asked.

"Fine," I answered.

"You have eaten poison mushrooms!" he informed me. "Mamma passed out in the field and the dog found her. We didn't know you were sick until just a few minutes ago when we found you in your room."

"Am I going to die?" I asked.

"No, you will be OK soon. If you were going to die you would have been dead before this."

Cherries and Russian vodka seemed to be his antidote for the poison. Mrs. Bustaggi and I were the only ones affected by the bad mushrooms, but it was too close to suit me. Mrs. Bustaggi had passed out when she was looking for firewood and the rest of the family didn't miss her until suppertime. They started searching and found her in the field with the little dog sleeping beside her. It took me several days to completely recover from this peculiar experience.

One afternoon, I heard a babble of voices coming from below. I went to the window to see an elderly lady coming like the wind up to the house. Her eyes were wide with fear when she came inside.

"The Tedeschi is coming," she shouted. "Go somewhere and hide!"

I felt my chances of being caught were greater if I ran into the hills, but since these people were so excited, I thought it best to go away. I hid in the woods all that afternoon, only returning when the old man came up the trail to get me. It was obvious that they'd been badly frightened because the Germans hadn't come up here before. The Bustaggi family couldn't think of any reasons for this other than that the Jerries were looking for me. We decided I needed to hide someplace else for a while.

I approached Angelo, proposing that we form a partisan band here in the hills. The local young men were hiding out in the mountains, just like me. They'd left the Italian army after the capitulation, but had to evade the Germans to keep from being drafted into the Axis forces. The hills had

many hiding places and we'd know all of the farms and people that could be trusted. Angelo and Beppi seemed in favor of the idea. Angelo said I'd be in charge and he'd be my lieutenant. There was an old barn he knew about high on a hill and there were at least forty men he could ask to join. Angelo and Beppi left that night to talk to the other men. They wouldn't let me go along, fearing that I'd be caught.

After their return, they informed me that they couldn't get more than eight or nine men to join us. The other men disapproved of the proposition, mainly because any trouble we might cause would bring the Germans into the hills in force. The local population would suffer, losing their farms and homes as a result. The fact that I couldn't speak Italian well was a big obstacle too; it appeared the plan just wouldn't work. Even those men who were agreeable wanted to wait a while longer to see how fast the Allied forces advanced up the Italian peninsula. The idea was abandoned for the time being.

Toni Peduzzi and Angelina Righetti came to visit on one occasion, bringing flour and fresh meat for a big feed. It was a welcome change from polenta. Cigarettes were difficult to find. Angelo and Beppi provided an occasional cigarette, but most of the time they only had the "makings" and I didn't

ROSS'S PRIMARY ITALIAN FRIENDS

Verona Area
From Pescantina—
Rita Pavoni, daughter Elsa, and a young son [older son KIA, Italian army].
Mr. and Mrs. Antonio (Toni) Peduzzi, daughter Nela (Nellie), and son Italo [Ristorante California].

From San Peretto di Negrar—
Angelina and Quirino Righetti, sons Rinaldo and Italo, and daughters Emiliana, Edda, and Danila [restaurant operators].
Mr. and Mrs. Bustaggi, sons Angelo and Guiseppe (Beppi), and daughter Nela [hill residents].

Cividale Area
From Masarolis—
Mr. and Mrs. Pietro (Pete) Comugnero [farmer].
Herma Zamparutti [schoolteacher].
Padre Don Amelio Pinzano [Catholic priest]

From Valle—
Elio and Elena Borgnolo, son Claudio, and daughter Renata [Elena: schoolteacher].

From the four villages of Pedrosa, Reant, Masarolis, and Valle—
Lilia [of Pedrosa], Amabile, and the other "little sweethearts" and mountain children.

know how to roll a "fag." I took an old newspaper and cut some cigarette papers for practice. After two or three days, I could make a fair "roll-your-own." During the times when tobacco was unavailable, we rolled grapevine bark and dried leaves. One puff usually was strong enough to hold a person for quite a while!

After I'd been with the Bustaggis for eighteen days, Beppi took me back to the Righettis' restaurant in San Peretto. From there, I would be sent to another hideout. Arriving at the Righettis' place late in the evening, I immediately was taken up to the bedroom where I'd been quartered before. I didn't know it, but I was destined to remain here for twenty-seven days.

For several days, Rinaldo looked for another place higher in the hills where I might be able to stay, but with no luck. I hung on, hoping that maybe they could get word to the underground for assistance and eventually sneak me through the lines.

I remained in the bedroom throughout most of November, waiting and waiting, but with no results. If I'd left the room and was seen in town, or even in the restaurant, people would know I was there and start talking. Sooner or later, word would get to the Germans. ✿

CHAPTER ELEVEN

NURSED BACK TO HEALTH

One day in my bedroom hideout, I turned the radio dial to a BBC broadcast and heard the announcer interviewing a fellow who'd recently escaped from an Italian POW camp. His name was Claude Weaver and his companion was Lt. Harold Rideout—both had been in the Chieti camp with me! Weaver described how they'd made their way back and came through the lines without too much trouble. Hearing this, I was impatient to get going.

Toni and Nellie Peduzzi came to see me a couple of times and brought cigarettes and some books. I read the books many times over. I rationed the cigarettes for as long as temptation would allow. Time and again, however, I'd just sit with my head in my hands, staring into space with an empty mind. Meanwhile, I recorded in a diary all of the things that had happened to me since being shot down.

At night, Angelina Righetti came up to the room after finishing her restaurant chores to tell me about the day's happenings as well as stories about her family. On one occasion, she told me how faith had brought her son Rinaldo back to her. She believed miracles really happened.

She explained, "Rinaldo was in the Italian army and I was afraid he'd be killed. I made a trip to Marstar, the mission in the mountains, and took his photograph to lay at the feet of St. Mary and I prayed for his safety. Lo and behold, he was assigned to a home unit and never had to go to the front. Later when Italy capitulated, I was afraid that the Germans would take Rinaldo north or force him to fight for them, so I went back to the mission in the hills where I again prayed for him. I came home after three days of traveling to see if my prayers would be answered. That night, Rinaldo walked into the house, worn-out after escaping from the Germans in north Italy."[1]

Angelina insisted on tucking me into bed each night and saying prayers over me. The night that she told the story about Rinaldo, she pinned a cross on my undershirt, stating that as long as I wore it, I wouldn't be hurt. Her sincerity and faith regarding miracles were about enough to make me a believer in them, too. She treated me like a son. I realized there were some fine people in this war-torn country.

In the mornings, I listened to the 8:30 broadcast on the radio. The news was depressing. The Jerries were holding on and making the Italian campaign something for our boys to remember. I felt sorry for the frontline soldiers, who lived day in and day out in the snow and mud. Although the news reports didn't say anything about the deplorable conditions, I knew our boys were out there suffering more than anyone could possibly imagine unless they'd been through it themselves. There wasn't much said about our lines, which indicated to me that major difficulties were being encountered.

On warm days, bees buzzed into the room, attracted by grapes drying on the racks. With scissors, I clipped off the ends of their wings to give them a faster flying speed. I then

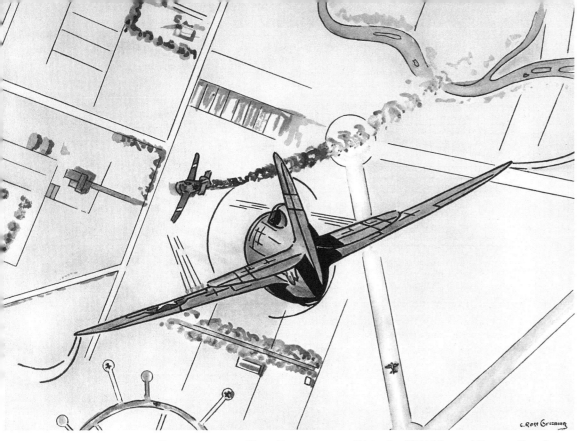

CHALKING UP ANOTHER *"Major Gerald W. Johnson of Owenton, Kentucky, getting number fourteen of eighteen victories on February 25, 1944. Light flak on March 27 stopped a string of victories which threatened the great records of 'Gabby' Gabreski and Colonel Hubert Zemke... Eighteen airborne victories [was] a phenomenal feat in the E.T.O. where air-to-ground victories fattened many of the best records. On an escort mission, coming home from Bordeaux, light flak from an AA outfit in Normandy jinxed Gerry's luck. March 27, 1944, was that black letter day; the Luftwaffe probably breathed a lot easier after that."* Not as Briefed

checked to see how many of the clipped-wing bees came back during the following days.

I studied the Italian language as much as I could, but sitting day in and day out was about to drive me crazy. I watched the leaves on the trees turn from green, to brown and red, and then they fell off and winter was at the door. Windstorms shook my third-story room until I thought the roof would fall down.

Sometimes, Angelina brought green tobacco for me to cut and season for her. I saved some and cut papers out of a dress pattern for rolling cigarettes. A puff of this strong tobacco was kind of like taking a swig of carbolic acid. I tried making cigars, but couldn't get air to pass through them.

Angelina also brought corn for me to grind and I made ersatz coffee out of grape seeds and wheat.

A large marmalade bucket served my lavatory needs. I was very embarrassed about this because Angelina's daughters had to carry it out to empty it, since I had to stay hidden.

As time dragged by, I'd go back in my mind to all of the things that had happened to me in the past. I remembered how I'd had poor marks at the start of flying school, but later was fortunate to earn one of the best grades given out at graduation. I'd had several forced landings and many close calls without being hurt. I recalled events in the minutest detail. Sometimes, I'd become so engrossed in my memories that I'd go to sleep and dream out the rest of it. Sometimes my dreams provided entertaining variations. I eventually looked forward to the nighttime because I'd encounter things in my sleep that were new and interesting.

Almost every night, Germans visited the restaurant and drank wine, making enough noise to wake the dead. On Sundays and holidays, Italians played games at the restaurant. One involved matching fingers and shouting out numbers, which I could clearly hear. Through the shutters of my room, I also watched people in the backyard playing some sort of game with wooden balls. It must have been interesting based on the racket they made.

The Germans occasionally came through the local villages confiscating food and livestock for their troops. I urged the Righetti family to hide as much food as possible, because soon the Germans would take just about everything.

Angelina brought me some huge jars that could hold about a hundred pounds of grain. I filled them up with ground corn and the jars were buried in the backyard.

My routine was so regulated that I knew what time it was within a few minutes at any point in the day. I didn't have a watch, but a church bell rang at the top of each hour. I awoke exactly at 8:10 AM and dressed by 8:30 to listen to the morning news broadcast. Breakfast arrived at about 8:45, and my growing appetite would tell me if it was late. At noon, my stomach again told me just when lunch would arrive. I stretched at the same times each day and dialed to radio programs just a minute or two before they went on the air. When darkness fell, I became sleepy at exactly the same moment and would fall asleep at 9:30 PM in my chair, if I wasn't already in bed.

Sometimes on the radio, I heard President Roosevelt giving words of encouragement to the boys overseas. Occasionally, when he had a special message for POWs, I couldn't stop my tears. I thought a lot about Dot, mother, and the people I knew back home. I was concerned about whether or not they knew what had happened to me. I was determined to notify them somehow. (Not long afterward, I was able to get a note to a priest and it was wired to the US.[2])

My thoughts kept returning to the current reality. I was in as impossible of a spot as I'd ever been in my life. I was deep in enemy territory during mid-winter and I had an injured leg.

Toni Peduzzi and his daughter, Nellie, came to visit again. I was so pleased that I hugged them both when they came into the room. Nellie wasn't a bad hug either. Toni said I could go to Verona if I wanted to and I might find a contact there who could help me. I thought, if nothing else, at least I'd be doing something and could escape this infernal confinement.

I decided to bury my diary in the courtyard and asked Nellie to try and send it back to the United States after the war if I didn't survive. I included a letter to Dot and my mother with the diary:

In the event I am caught or am killed without reaching home it is my hope this notebook will get to you thru these friends sending it. You will have to get their names and addresses from them as it is not safe for me to mention them here. I have promised them they will be repaid for their troubles in protecting me, as they did so at the risk of their lives. Their kindness and aid have been of the best. I have never experienced an equal before. I hope my things get home to you. I had $1,000 in cash I left with [Maj. June] Hanford before I was shot down. I would have tried to continue further in getting back to my own lines except my leg would swell up and ache so bad I could not make over one or two miles a day. I don't know what is the matter with it—probably some small [foot] bone broken.

I have a great respect for the Italian people altho some of their guards treated us badly when we were first captured. I guess that was to be expected.

All the time I have been a prisoner my worst suffering was longing for all of you and home. I believe I've reviewed every moment of my life as the only thing I had to do was think during those long hours of waiting. Actually this experience has been thrilling and most exciting. I wouldn't take a million dollars for it nor would I go thru it again for ten million if I could prevent it. The main thing I have learned is that America is certainly worth dying for if it becomes the least bit necessary. I feel whether I die in the attempt or not I've earned more than money can possibly mean as this effort of mine should make me a good shareholder in pride for our country along with the millions of others who have done likewise. I wouldn't take my share of the Lincoln Park Gulch in Tacoma, Washington, for all the other countries I have seen. Don't let any American lose appreciation for what they have. Even during our worst depressions, times are better in America than anywhere else I have seen during their boom times. If there is anyone who doesn't believe it let them try it away for a year or so, to live with the people—not the tourists.

The main thing our country can learn is generosity—not the rich man who isn't giving up something personal but the person who gives more than he is getting himself. That can be learned from these people who if they have three cigarettes and none promised for the future will give you two of them. I can now eat corn meal and spaghetti three times a day, week after week, and really thank God for it. I can sleep anywhere and live closer to nature than I ever believed possible. I have also learned to really thank God for it. I have learned how to pray and not only on Sunday… I believe if I am permitted to live thru this experience I can never forget God for an instant and will be a much better man for it. I believe others in the same situation are of the same opinion. I hope there are others who can benefit from our experiences by our word for it and not have to experience them. I hope the whole United States will be better for it all. My main subject to God is thanks for you, Mom, and for our family. I couldn't have been blessed better, Dot. It's been during these times I most deeply appreciate you and our life together. You mean everything to me and all I am working for. I have had the best of everything I know. I have the best wife, mother, dad, sisters, friends and country on this earth, I know. I've seen others and feel I can compare. If I don't get back I am grateful for what I've had and am looking forward to meeting all somewhere again. If my diaries can be worked into anything that might sell by someone who can write, I'd like you to have them written into a book which might bring some ready cash to help you and I really want something to come to these people who have helped me here if it can possibly be done.

All the love in the world. Ross

I was given a cardboard valise and Angelina fixed me up with extra underwear. I was going to the city in style, but they told me I had to wait a few more days. A few more days! Lord, how long they took! I thought Toni would never come. My injured and swollen leg frustrated me, since it was impossible for me to walk very far. Angelina had regularly offered prayers and one night she said that my leg would be

well in the morning and I wouldn't have to worry about it anymore. I didn't think much about this at the time.

The next morning while I was listening to the radio, the door burst open and Angelina excitedly entered in her stocking feet. She talked so fast in Italian that I couldn't understand what she was saying. She tried to put my coat on my back and hide my things at the same time. She wrapped up some tobacco on a shelf and hid it under the bed in great haste, muttering "Contrabando, contrabando!" Then I heard her say something about "Fascisti," and that someone downstairs was about to search the house for contraband. If they did, they'd find me and all would be over. The fascists would kill the entire family for harboring me. Angelina wanted me to run downstairs and out the door as fast as I could go.

I asked Angelina to contain herself, and told her that it would be unwise for me to run. I would walk out of the house as calmly as possible. I'll admit, I was extremely excited and nervous.

I put on my coat and cap, then walked casually downstairs to the second floor, where the fascist officer in charge and his assistants were searching the rooms. I didn't leave immediately, but stood around quietly for a few moments. I tried to make it appear that I just happened to be in the house and didn't know a thing about the search. The fascist officer was a tall, scowling, dark looking villain. His black cape was slung in dramatic fashion over him in great folds. He wore black boots—a storybook character if I'd ever seen one.

When he caught my eye, I said "Buon Giorno" in my best Italian as I passed by him.

He returned the greeting and let me pass. I walked to the door and out into the street. No one paid attention to me as I walked away. I quickened my pace up the street and headed for the hills. I went to Angelo and Beppi Bustaggi's farmhouse, since I didn't know where else to go.

When I arrived, the kind old man kissed me when I walked in the door. I was so scared that it wasn't until I reached the house that I thought about my bad leg. To my amazement, the pain and swelling were gone! This was unbelievable! I began to think that maybe Angelina knew more about miracles than I realized.

I told Angelo and Beppi about the search at the restaurant and they laughed. They thought it was a big joke to put something over on one of the fascists around here, but I knew how serious it really was. I'd been told that a family nearby had just been machine gunned by the fascists for harboring an escaped prisoner. Five members of the family were killed, including a babe in arms.

Before long, Rinaldo arrived and said he'd be taking me back to his house tonight. Toni would come for me the following day and we'd go to the city. I told Angelo that if I returned to Allied lines, I'd come back with a planeload of weapons and supplies if I could. We walked out on the hill and arranged signals for dropping equipment. While waiting for darkness, we paused in a small cabin in the mountains where we cut wood and stacked it for future use.

When arriving back at the Righettis' place, I learned that the fascists had left without causing any trouble. I slept well that night, full of anticipation for the following day. Toni Peduzzi arrived in the morning with an extra bicycle. I packed my things on the carrier and departed for Verona. Before I left, the family shed tears and kissed me good-bye. They had been amazingly kind to me. I knew I'd never forget them.

We traveled about seven or eight miles, passing many tanks, trucks, and soldiers. I noticed much more of a German presence than before. We left the bicycles in a parking lot on the edge of the city and walked the rest of the way. In Verona, I saw German soldiers acting much the same way as our troops did. However, there was a big difference regarding their relationship with the civilians. They didn't seem friendly to them, and I saw no sympathy expressed by the Italians for the Germans.

When passing a market place, I bought a map of northern Italy. We finally came to a small, one-room tailor shop in a back street. Here I met Toni's cousin, who would look after me while I was in the city. There wasn't any sign on his place, but he had all the business he could handle. It seemed to be a black market shop, but I was told nothing about it. Toni's cousin told me to come back later and he would find a place for me to stay.

Toni guided me around Verona, showing off some of the sights. We stopped and had a drink at a number of wine shops. A man and wife who had lived in California for a time owned one place. After making enough money to live well in the old country, they had returned. Toni left me there and went to his home. I sat in the cafe, sipping wine and waiting for night, when I'd return to the tailor shop.

While I waited, the wine merchant introduced me to an Italian fellow who said he could contact other Americans and possibly get me to their hideout. He'd be back in about three days. About dusk, a German soldier came into the shop and sat down next to me, ordering a glass of wine. He looked as if he wanted to strike up a conversation, so I left. I feared his Italian language skills would be better than mine.

When I got back to Toni's cousin's place he took me to a boardinghouse, telling the proprietor that I was a Hungarian and needed a place to sleep. I was given a nice bed in a frigid room. People seemed curious and tried to question me after Toni's cousin left. I told them I was tired and wanted to sleep, so they left me alone.

In the morning, I awoke at my usual hour to find everyone gone except one of the proprietor's sons. He was waiting for me to leave so he could lock the door. After wandering about the town, I concluded that there were Germans everywhere, and they frequently checked identification passes on the streets. On one occasion, I passed a German guard who I thought was going to ask to see my pass. To distract him, I quickly asked him for a cigarette and received

a whole pack. He let me walk by without asking any questions. I enjoyed the smokes.

I returned to the tailor shop at noon and Toni's cousin took me out to a restaurant. Ration tickets were required to receive food, thus I needed to be with my new friend to get anything to eat. All of the restaurants were half filled with soldiers and I had to eat sitting next to Germans. It was nerve wracking, sitting there trying to act relaxed. The food wasn't too good either.

For three days, I wandered in the freezing streets. I couldn't find a place to relax and keep warm. I tried staying at the tailor shop, but I felt uneasy about the stream of soldiers going in and out of the place to have their uniforms fixed. During those three days, Toni's cousin told me that 125 soldiers had approached him trying to acquire a set of civilian clothes in order to desert from the German army. He could accommodate only a few.

A German officer entered one afternoon while I sat on a bench in the shop. I knew it was harder to fool the officers than the enlisted men. He looked at me suspiciously, which made me nervous. I pulled out my cigarette makings and tried to roll one. Tobacco spilled on the floor because my hands shook so badly. Noticing this, the German officer came over to me. To my astonishment, he handed me a ready-made cigarette. I took it, accepted his light, and walked out. I went back to the wine shop to meet the man who was contacting the Americans hiding in the hills. He had bad news. The Americans didn't want me because conditions were difficult and there wasn't enough food or space for me.

That evening, some Germans on a motorcycle stopped me. They asked for directions, which I gave them without hesitation. Of course, I didn't have a clue as to where it was they wanted to go, but they took off, following my instructions without the least suspicion. I decided I needed to get out of this city.

The next morning, I walked eight miles north to Toni's restaurant in Pescantina. I don't know how I found it, but I did. Toni had rooms for rent and he put me up in one of them. Nellie contacted a friend of theirs, who came to visit me. He promised to try and get me to Yugoslavia; however, I'd need an identification card to board a train. In Yugoslavia, I hoped to find an airstrip used by the Allies to supply the patriot forces. Perhaps, I could board a plane back to our lines. It all seemed so simple.

The next day, I bicycled to a photo studio in Verona and stood in line with soldiers and civilians to have a picture taken. I waited about 1 1/2 hours and nobody questioned me. The photos were ready in two days. We falsified an identification card that looked quite authentic and I purchased a little holder for it.

I had to wait a few days at Toni's restaurant until arrangements could be made for taking a train. Meanwhile, I asked Nellie if she could provide me with drawing materials, so I could sketch to pass the time. She had some papers that had been taken from an English-owned villa in the city. The occupants had left books and other items when evacuating the place before the outbreak of the war. Nellie showed me an old, leather-bound portfolio, from which some sketches and paintings had been removed, leaving the background paper available for use. When I asked to see the pictures, I discovered they included century-old paintings that looked almost priceless to me. We immediately wrapped them up to preserve them.

That same afternoon, Nellie brought in a reward poster that had been nailed in front of the restaurant. It notified civilians that 1,800 lire would be paid to them for bringing in escaped POWs, dead or alive. After reading it, I showed her a handbill dropped by one of our planes, notifying the Italians that they'd be given 5,000 lire for assisting Americans or Brits in escaping.

The next morning, final preparations were made before leaving for the train. My destination would be Udine, located about 150 miles to the east. Nellie and a friend, Dr. Roberto Pavoncelli, would travel on the train as far as Udine, but they'd be in another passenger car. From Udine, I'd proceed without them to the Yugoslavian border, about 20 or 25 miles away.

Toni brought two bottles of champagne up from the cellar for a departing toast. He filled two large glasses for us. For the others, he poured small champagne glasses. Frankly, I think it was too much champagne for me at the start of a trip. When I mounted the bicycle to go to the station, I could hardly stay on. I think Toni was having trouble too. We weaved and bobbed down the street, fortunately in the right direction. When we arrived, we found out that the four o'clock train wasn't leaving until eight that night.

Toni needed to return to the restaurant, so he kissed me good-bye and left. I told Nellie that I'd meet her at the train, thirty minutes before departure. Then I went to a movie theater and saw a show I couldn't understand. It was old fashioned and very melodramatic; however, it was a good way to pass the time.

By 7:30 PM, I returned to the station and found Nellie. We got our tickets and found seats with no trouble. The train was very crowded; about half of the passengers were soldiers. Nellie and Dr. Pavoncelli boarded the car ahead of me, so if I was caught they wouldn't be implicated. It was dark and foggy when we left. I immediately fell asleep and didn't wake up until a few miles from Venice.

On arriving at Venice, we learned that we'd have to stay there until the morning to make connections with the next train. The station was full of soldiers and each person was being carefully checked at the exits. We decided that we'd spend the rest of the night right where we were—I found an empty compartment with upholstered seats, which made for a good bed, while Nellie and Dr. Pavoncelli slept in another nearby car.

In the morning, we caught the train to Udine. About an hour into the trip, I rose up to stretch and bumped into a man coming into my compartment. He said something about checking my card, so I immediately pulled it out. He looked at it and passed on. I was asked for my identification card a second time before we arrived and again I had no problem. Things were working out; if the Italian fascists couldn't see through my disguise, I thought I certainly could fool any German.

About noon, we arrived at Udine and walked to the center of town. We ate at a restaurant, and then tried to find the fellow who was supposed to be able to help me. This took all afternoon, but we finally located him in a cellar during an air raid. He took charge of me, allowing Nellie and Dr. Pavoncelli to return to Verona.

He took me to a small shop near the center of town and showed me to a bed at the back. He had studied English from a book, but couldn't understand my spoken English very well. Consequently, I communicated to him in Italian, and he spoke to me in English.

"Tomorrow you will be in Yugoslavia. The next day you will be at an airdrome, and the next day you will be back in Naples," he informed me.

This was too much! I couldn't believe it would be that easy. Nevertheless, I wanted to take his word for it, since he sounded so convincing. He said he'd be back at 8 AM and tell me what to do next. I went to sleep with high hopes.

It was raining in the morning. At eight o'clock, my friend and two other men showed up to take me to the railroad station. I'd be given instructions and would make my way through Yugoslavia by myself. He seemed confident and I felt there wasn't any need to worry about the future. I finally was in the hands of the underground. What a laugh this turned out to be!

I was given the names of people and places where I was supposed to go and make contact. They also gave me a light overcoat to wear in the rain. The two others led the way to the railroad station, purchased my ticket, walked me to the train, and then left. This train was a small local rattler. The

engine pulled out hissing and puffing as if each belch would be its last.

I'd been told to get off at Cividale, about twelve miles away. When the train entered the station, it was still pouring down rain. I set out for a nearby village and the mountains. I arrived in time to see a funeral procession, which lent a weird atmosphere to my situation. The hearse was hand drawn by people all dressed in black, carrying candles and chanting as they made their way down the street. I didn't know how to get to the next village on my itinerary, so I pulled out a small sign saying I was deaf and dumb and needed directions.

I showed the sign to a young fellow, who was watching the funeral procession passing by his house. At first he gave information by word of mouth, but then he realized I was deaf and dumb and he tried to continue with signs. I almost burst out laughing at his antics and the funny noises he made. However, I found out where to go and started walking. Soon, I began to feel sick and weak, but didn't know what was the matter. I trudged on a little over four miles to my goal at the foot of a valley. By this time, I felt so tired and ill that I stopped at a small restaurant to get something to eat, but they wouldn't serve me anything except wine.

I bought a glass and took a seat at a table with a young Italian lad. We soon struck up a conversation and I identified myself. When I told him about my escape plan, he told me it wasn't possible any longer. I'd been so convinced by my contact in Udine, however, that I just couldn't believe this boy. I told him I was going on in spite of what he said. He insisted on buying me another glass of wine and then said

"A housewife of Valle, Italy, near the Yugoslavian border, resting with a load of hay being carried home to the cow." Greening 1955

he would go with me. His father was living in New York and the lad wanted to go to America after the war.

"Come up and stay in my house until the war is over. It will be only two months," he said.

We started up the valley and ran into an elderly civilian dressed in an Italian army uniform with no leggings, a fur cap, and heavy hobnailed shoes. When I was introduced, the man spoke to me in English.

"I live in America four year. You can spik English to me alla time an I undersan perfect!"

His name was Pietro "Pete" Comugnero. He said he'd take me to his house and I could go on later if I wanted, but it wasn't possible to get through to Yugoslavia anymore. Being so close to the Yugoslavian border, I didn't want to believe this. I had to find a patriot band that would see me through! I wasn't going to give up just because these fellows told me it couldn't be done. As we reached the end of the valley, the trail steepened and the rain didn't let up one bit.

As we started climbing, I realized I had no strength. I could scarcely proceed. Pete saw that I wasn't looking well and offered to carry my bag. My other friend had left us at a fork in the trail. We came to a steep cliff where the road was blown up and almost impassable. Pete said this was the work of patriots, who'd dynamited the road so the Germans couldn't get their vehicles up the hill.

About dark, we arrived in Pete's village, which was called Masarolis. In the heavy rain, the village looked ancient and dingy. The houses were jammed together and smoke hung heavy in the air, creating a depressing scene. The cobblestone

"After a short rest, she picked it up as easily as one would a shopping bag, then she walked briskly on to her home." Greening 1955

polenta. The walls of the room were black and greasy from years of exposure to smoke. The town did have electricity and there was a light on in the room, but its output was diminished by the smoke and gloom. Off to one side stood an old wooden table with a few crude kitchen utensils and a mangy cat lying on it staring at the fire. Chicken droppings covered the floor and other debris was scattered around. A bowl lay in the corner where chickens had been feeding. I heard a cow bawl in an adjoining room.

I was feeling very sick at this point and went outside where I threw up. Pete came out and brought me back in. I kept my head down to within several feet of the floor to keep out of the smoke. I found a stool and squatted down on it. I felt terrible and my new surroundings didn't look promising. I was handed hot polenta and a glass of sour wine, but I had to pass up supper this night.

I told Pete I was sick and needed to go to bed. I figured that Pete's wife must be bothered with ulcers from her appearance. She was as goodhearted as Pete and, when she learned that I was sick, she disappeared and returned with some special wine that she stirred in a pan along with a gold wedding ring and a spoonful of sugar. This concoction was boiled and given to me in a bowl. It must have been better wine or the sugar made it taste good, because it went down smoothly. It was supposed to cure me.

Pete took me to my sleeping quarters, which was a loft above the cow, and I was given a blanket and pillow. Just as I curled up to go to sleep, Pete came back and told me there was a patriot meeting at the padre's house. I could see them if I went over right away.

We stumbled along the wet, cobbled streets to the padre's house, which was surrounded by a wall. This house unquestionably was the best domicile around.

A crowd of rough looking individuals was gathered in the kitchen, which had a stove that kept the small room warm enough for comfort. Most of the men appeared too young to be away from home. They gave me dirty looks as I

streets were so rough that it was hard to make your way along.

The entrance to Pete's house was nearly blocked by a huge pile of cow dung. The door was open and smoke poured out. At first, I thought the house was on fire, but on entering I saw that instead of a fireplace or stove, the household hearth was on a stone block in the middle of the room. The smoke was allowed to seek its own exit. An elderly woman stood over the fire stirring a huge pot of smoky

entered with Pete. Don Amelio Pinzano, the vicar of Masarolis, was a youthful, handsome fellow. Across the table from him sat an attractive young woman, who, I later learned, was the village schoolteacher, Herma Zamparutti. She was very intelligent and had taught herself English from a book. Near the padre was a tough looking character who looked as if he'd pick a fight with the first man that spoke up.

The schoolteacher was filling out enlistment forms for a patriot band. I told her my story, and said I wanted to join a guerilla band so I could get to one of the airstrips in Yugoslavia where Allied planes landed supplies for Marshal Tito's forces.

The tough looking fellow broke in, saying, "You Americans and English are no good! None of you know how to fight and besides you are all so soft you can't last after you get into the hills. We will not help any of you any more. We tried to help some Americans and all they wanted to do was sleep and eat while we do all the fighting and work. Besides, why should we take you back to your lines where you will go home and have a fine bed to sleep in and good food to eat while we have to stay here and live in misery? We will not do anything for you."

I persisted, "I want to meet the leader of the patriots around here. I have been told by the agent in Udine that he will get me through the lines."

He replied, "Our chief was killed two days ago by a dive bombing attack and now I am the leader. I will not help you. You must stay with our band and fight with us. If I let you go now you probably would turn out to be a spy and get us all shot!"

It is not a star..... just a trifling thing with a great heart

Herma Zamparutti, the schoolteacher of Masarolis, Italy. A Wartime Log

This was very discouraging and I refused to believe it. I argued for an hour or so, and got nowhere. I told them I couldn't fight as well on the ground as I could in the sky—I was a trained airman. I said I'd get through some way even if they didn't help me.

Pete took me back, where I spent a miserable night in the loft. I was extremely sick in the morning, but determined to continue to the patriot chief's village, despite the report about his death. The patriots agreed not to shoot me as I proceeded to the next town if Pete's wife went along. Rain fell heavily and Pete and his wife wanted me to wait another day, but I was determined to go.

Mrs. Comugnero and I left about noon, climbing the trail up the high hill and then down to the village, which stood on a steep slope. The houses seemed to clutch at the mountainside for dear life. I was escorted into one of the smoky rooms to wait until some Englishmen came to talk to me. The people here confirmed that, indeed, the patriot chief had been killed, as previously reported to me.

I waited several hours for the English boys to arrive. Meanwhile one of the farmers brought a note left in his house by a British captain some weeks before. The captain had written to a friend, advising him not to try to get out through Yugoslavia because the conditions were impossible. The intense conflict between the Axis elements and the partisan groups was terrible, widespread, and confusing. The captain said that, instead of going to Yugoslavia, he was heading to the plains and the Po Valley and then south to our lines.

My prospects didn't look so good. I began believing what the local people were telling me, but I thought that I'd get the real story from the four Brits in town.

As I waited for the English boys to show up, my hosts tried to feed me. Everything turned my stomach except for a cupful of milk. They told me that if I didn't eat, I'd die, and they actually looked worried about me. I hadn't eaten anything substantial for two days and was worried about my illness also.

About dusk, a man came and said that the Brits were here and I was to meet them by a fence at the edge of town. I went there but didn't see anybody. As I turned to go back, all four of them appeared from behind trees brandishing clubs. They weren't taking any chances about a German spy in plain clothes being sent up there to catch them. I laughed and gave them a bit of good old American slang. It worked and I was introduced all around.

Three were privates from the desert army and one was a sergeant, who'd been the engineer on a Sunderland flying boat shot down in the Mediterranean Sea by an enemy submarine's deck guns. We went back to the house. The attitude of the local people changed as these boys came in with me. It was plain to see that they'd made a big hit in town and were well liked.

The boys sang and joked with our hosts. They had composed and sang songs with cleverly worded puns that were understandable if someone knew both English and Italian. Much of it wasn't fit to print. Of course, the local people didn't know the double meanings, so nobody was offended and we all had a good time.

I felt so ill, however, that I cut it short and asked the fellows if we could go to their hideout and talk over plans. They agreed, and after bidding everyone adieu, we left for their mountain hideaway. It was raining and miserable, but we soon reached the hideout, which was an old abandoned shed. We tried to start a fire to dry out our clothes and struggled with the wet wood, until we finally just let it smolder.

I learned that these boys had been in the area for two months. They'd been mixed up with the patriots and even participated in some of the raids. In their opinion, the patriots weren't capable of waging war in a way that would be of much benefit to the Allied cause. The guerrillas were mostly young fellows and their activities usually just put the local people in harm's way, resulting in losses of property and livestock. The liaison personnel dropped by the English had found it difficult to organize the resistance groups.

A British major, supposedly dropped into the area to lead guerilla activities, had just been killed in a German dive-bombing attack and two parties of escaped prisoners also had suffered heavy casualties trying to get to Yugoslavia. One party of eighty men had been wiped out almost to the man as they tried to cross a river. Shortly afterwards, a party of forty had been partially wiped out near the same place, just a few days prior to my arrival.

My four English friends were more fortunate because they'd stayed by themselves, except for the time that they joined the raiding parties. They were confused about their future course. They'd been five strong up to three days before my arrival, when one lad was captured by a German patrol.

I listened intently and decided I was on the wrong track. Chances were not good in this area. The weather was getting worse each day, too, which made traveling more difficult.

I asked them, "Why don't you come with me and we will walk south to the Po Valley in hopes of getting to the lines, or over to the west coast of Italy where we might get a boat to take us to Sardinia or Corsica?"

"You have a good suit of clothes and we are in rags," one told me. "It would be impossible for us not to be recognized in our state, whereas you could get away with plenty."

In spite of that, the sergeant said he'd like to go with me regardless of what might happen. He was sick and tired of waiting around. It would be better to go down to the plain, than sit here and freeze to death.

The others chose to remain, hoping that something positive would develop. Toni had provided me with money and I gave some to the boys, so they could buy wine when they had a chance. We crawled off to bed, which was on a pile of leaves near the end of the shed. They only had a couple of blankets and it was a cold night. We also used our coats as blankets. Rain dripped through the roof, falling on the leaves and us. By morning, I was eager to return to Pete's hayloft.

The boys took me to the top of an extremely steep hill, where we washed our faces in a stagnant pool of water. Fog and rain shrouded the view, but village bells could be heard ringing below. After washing, we spent an hour picking lice out of our clothes and tried to warm up by a weak fire that smoked up the shed.

I left by myself to return to the village, where I found Pete's wife waiting to escort me back. Beside her on the trail lay a huge bundle of wood. I wouldn't have tried to lift it, let alone carry it over a mountaintop, as she was going to do. It was incredible that a woman of her size and age could do this, but she accomplished it without complaint or hesitation. I felt embarrassed, walking along while an elderly woman hauled such a load. I carried nothing but a little cardboard valise.

After arriving at the Comugnero house, I proceeded to the loft where I literally "hit the hay." I scarcely had the strength to move my aching bones and fell asleep quickly. I was awakened when Pete's kind wife brought a bowl of food to me. I tried to eat, but only succeeded in losing it all in a few minutes. I was so sick that I decided I'd have to ask for medical help. I'd been unable to keep food down for five days.

I pulled on my wet shoes and plodded over to Padre Pinzano's house, where I assumed I could receive some sort of medical attention. The padre was there with his housekeeper and Herma Zamparutti, who sympathized and offered suggestions about what my ailment might be. The padre said he'd go to a village about nine miles away and ask some doctors there for advice. He'd claim the information would be for an ill cousin.

I suddenly had an idea and asked for a mirror. I'd hardly seen my reflection in a mirror for almost four months. My fears were confirmed. My eyes and face were as yellow as parchment paper; I had jaundice! Recalling the prisoner with jaundice that I'd met earlier, I knew I needed to be kept in bed for at least two or three weeks. This was going to upset my plans for escape, since I couldn't travel. I explained what was wrong and my companions agreed with my diagnosis. I asked the padre if I could stay in his house because it was the only place in the hills where I could possibly get proper treatment.

He said, "Our schoolteacher has the extra room in the house, but if she will agree to stay with the housekeeper, you could stay in her room."

Herma agreed and I was put in a fine bed in the second-story room that overlooked the front courtyard. The room was as cold as ice, but I grew warm under the covers and realized I'd hit a stroke of good fortune. If I'd been deep in Yugoslavia, I would have been helpless and, more than likely, wouldn't have come out alive. Padre Pinzano was able to get some powders that were supposed to help cure jaundice, but they didn't seem to work very well.

My first visitor was the patriot chief. He came into my room, I suppose, to see if I was playing possum. He was belligerent.

"What is the matter with you Americans? You can't seem to do anything but get sick and cause us trouble," he said.

"My Slovakian ally," I replied, "you are just so much baloney to me! If you are man enough to wait until I'm able to get out of bed, I'll give you the greatest thrashing of your life. I think you and your entire band are the biggest bunch of dead beats I've ever seen in my life. Beyond that, you haven't the foresight to see beyond your nose. Get out of this room and stay away from me. If you can't offer some good suggestions, I'll do things myself and I'll show you how one man can get to the places he wants to go without help. Go away!"

Startled, he immediately changed his attitude and became friendly, telling me his life story. He apologized by explaining how they'd been besieged with escaped prisoners for months and had grown tired of trying to help them. Their biggest problem was that they had insufficient military equipment and supplies. Their attitude towards me was the result of many things coming to a head. He told me about his brave exploits as a patriot soldier, which seemed to be the biggest and wildest story I'd ever heard in my life. He waved his gun about, emphasizing the details of his exploits.

The final tall tale was one in which eight German soldiers armed to the teeth had cornered him alone in a wine shop.

"What could I do when they entered?" he said. "I had no choice but to grab the nearest machine gun from the hands of the first soldier and beat his brains out. Then I killed all of the others with the gun and left the store. Outside, I shot my way out of the village leaving many dead German soldiers behind me."

I asked him, "If you are so brave and can do so many impossible things, it surely should be a simple matter for you to get me through to an airdrome where I can be taken back to my own lines. After I get back it is obvious that, as a pilot, I can do a lot more damage against the Germans than I could with you carrying a rifle. Don't you see how much more good you could accomplish by this, and by helping all of the others who are trying to get back where their effort can be put to much better advantage?"

I apparently changed the man's opinion of me a little and he said he might try to help. He left when our conversation was interrupted by the arrival of the English sergeant, who came to discuss escape plans. When the sergeant saw my condition, his face dropped in disappointment. I told him my illness would delay me for at least three weeks. However, I asked him to come back at the end of that time, if he still was in the area and wanted to travel with me.

"OK," he said, "I will leave and see if I can't locate some help for us as well as get myself a pass and some decent clothes. I'll check in now and then to see how you're getting along."

"Incidentally," he added, " as I was entering the village, the people were all stirred up over the approach of a large German patrol on its way up here. I wouldn't worry too much, however, as these people get stirred up over almost anything. I'll just buzz along up the hill to tell the other boys not to come into town. All the village folks seem to be worried about you. They can't help but believe the Germans have heard about you and are on their way up here to pick you up. It seems nothing can be kept a secret around here."

He said good-bye, just as the housekeeper came in telling me about the approaching Germans. I looked out the window and saw the three English lads walking into town. I gave them the high sign from the window and then crawled back into bed.

Padre Pinzano came in at the same time, very excited and red in the face. We quickly cooked up a story that I was his deaf and dumb cousin, and my mother and father had been killed in a bombing raid. I was staying with him because I had no other place to go. I left my identification card on a chair by the bed, in case they came in to look at me. The padre left for the mountainside, I think, with the hope that he'd avoid all contact with the Germans.

In a few minutes, I heard a commotion outside. People were running and I heard gunshots. I glanced out the window occasionally, but saw nothing. Presently, the

housekeeper came into the room with a glass of water and the medicinal powder for treating jaundice. She was so excited that I could scarcely tell what she was saying. She made an attempt to put the powder into the water, but missed the glass completely. I don't think she even noticed as she handed it to me to drink. She also had a raw egg in her pocket intended for me, I think, but she only succeeded in dropping it on the floor where it splattered.

After a few minutes, Herma came into the room and beckoned me to the window. I sat up on the bed and looked out into the courtyard, seeing several soldiers standing by the gate. Another detachment of Germans came into the yard leading the three English lads with their hands in the air. Later, I was told that they'd heard about my illness and were on their way to see me when they stumbled into the patrol. Some Germans with flamethrowers had trapped them. They saw me in the window and put their thumbs up in the familiar "high sign." Regretfully, I learned later that they were led down the hill, stood up against a wall, and shot.

After the British soldiers were taken away, the Germans prepared to search the padre's house. Herma went downstairs to let them in. I heard them stomping around in their heavy hobnailed boots. They seemed to be looking the place over with a fine toothed comb.

Soon, I heard the heavy steps of a soldier coming up the stairs. He first went into the padre's bedroom and spent a few minutes. Next, he came to my door, which was closed and had a latch that was difficult to operate. The upper part of the door had a window and I could see the Kraut's red face as he tried to work the latch. He held a submachine gun of some sort, had a large pack on his back, and carried several potato-masher grenades in his belt.

Just as the door latch opened, I heard Herma approaching on the run. Scarcely had the German entered my room when the shouts of the young Italian schoolteacher stopped him. She told him I wasn't to be bothered; that I'd die if not left alone! I acted like I was unconscious, or practically out

of my mind, which wasn't far from the truth. He saw my yellow complexion and knew I was ill.

To my amazement, the soldier left without coming in, but in about half an hour he returned and again tried to get the latch to work. He noisily jimmied and twisted it, until finally giving it a whack that practically tore the latch off its hinges. He entered and was half way to my bed when Herma came at him again. She acted furious and fairly flew at him. She boldly kicked him in the shins, grabbed his arm, and shoved him towards the door, shouting words that I didn't know existed in the Italian language. She was crying by this time, but remained brave.

In uncertain Italian, the soldier demanded to know if I was wounded or really sick. Somehow she convinced him that I was ill because he left and didn't return. If he'd checked and seen the old bullet wound in my leg, he would've thought I'd been fighting on the side of the patriots. This would've had disastrous consequences for all of us.

The entire German patrol took up quarters in the house. When the padre returned, he found that the commanding officer had taken his bedroom. The commandant quizzed the padre about me and apparently was satisfied by the story we'd cooked up. I learned that the local patriot band was completely routed and unable to reorganize. I wondered about what might've happened to their "brave" leader who talked such a good fight. The patrol remained in the house for two days. Meanwhile, the padre slept on the floor in my room. I offered to give him the bed, but he refused.

The Germans rounded up the village's able-bodied males and marched them down the hill to repair the road, which had been dynamited some weeks earlier by the patriots. The soldiers didn't bother me again, but I had some anxious moments wondering if my luck could hold out. The Germans didn't know it, but the padre's house was the headquarters for the patriot band in that area headed by a Russian-trained Serb named Grunta, whom I met later.

I couldn't eat for five more days. On several occasions, I tried to consume milk or soup, but threw it up almost immediately. I lost weight and thought I wasn't going to pull through. Padre Pinzano tried to cheer me up. He told me that if I died, it would be difficult for him to explain why there was a dead man in his house. He often went across the street to the church and said prayers for me.

I grew so weak that I was unable to rise up. Many villagers came to see me, including Pete and his wife. Finally, at the end of the tenth day, I held down the first food, a glass of milk.

I was consumed with weird thoughts and nightmares. In my dreams, Germans entered the room and ran me through with bayonets. The pains in the nightmares generally were due to my stomach cramps. At times, I awoke not knowing where I was or what had happened. I remembered experiencing this same strange feeling at Randolph Field during my flight training. I awoke one evening in the hospital and was told that I'd been in an accident. At first, I refused to believe it, but later realized that I really had cracked up.

That was the time that I dove my Seversky BT-8 into the ground in the middle of the airfield. The plane smashed into the sod, wheels and nose together, and flipped, scattering parts all over the place. I was knocked cold. My instructor, Lt. Tom Darcy, told me all of the details. I figured I'd be washed out and sent home for lack of good judgment.

When I sadly told Lt. Darcy that I had enjoyed my short stint in flying school, he said, "You're not going home now. You have just lived through a serious crash and you'll be a better flyer for it. You'll never lose respect for an airplane, and you'll appreciate everything you do much more than if you never had an accident."

Here I was again—thinking things were at an end for me—and Lt. Darcy's words came back to me. I knew that if I survived this illness, I'd be a better man for it. I'd never pass a hospital again without appreciating the doctors and nurses who try to help others pull through. Villagers did pray for

me, but I don't think many cared all that much for me personally. I often felt alone and had difficulty keeping my mental strength up.

The days went by and the room always was cold. When I improved somewhat, I grew very bored. Finally, Herma located a deck of cards for me and I played endless games of solitaire. After two weeks, the Germans returned to the area again looking for patriots and escaped prisoners. Each time they came near, the town's residents became agitated. At least a dozen different people gave me advice, but there wasn't a practical suggestion in the whole lot. It was hard for them to understand that acting excited was the worst thing to do. The Germans became deeply suspicious if any townspeople appeared frantic.

Late one night, the housekeeper came and said two dark-faced visitors wished to talk to me. She wanted to know if I dare see them because they might be German spies. I told her that if they were spies, they'd find out about me anyway, so send them up. They were a distressing sight when they entered the room. The two men were South Africans who had been surviving in miserable conditions. Their clothes were old, cast-off Italian uniforms, torn and tattered. Sport caps pulled down over their ears provided some warmth, and their feet, wrists, and necks were wrapped in rags to protect them from the cold. It was easy to see that their spirits were at rock bottom.

When I asked them to tell their story, I learned that they were escaped POWs. They had been in the British army and were captured a couple of years ago. They were released during the Italian capitulation and came to the mountains to join the patriots. Because of their dark skin, however, they were having all kinds of difficulty avoiding detection. They only left their hideouts at night to seek food. Fortunately, they had some Italian money, but they were unable to buy much with it. Most of the local people thought they were spies. They didn't know where to go or how to get along, and both were sick with colds due to the winter weather. They

stayed about an hour and left. I commiserated over their plight and realized I was fortunate for getting good breaks.

The weather improved a few days before Christmas and the sun began to shine, but, of course, that meant the German patrolling would increase. I was able to get out of bed now and I tried taking a walk every day to gain strength. When passing along the rough cobblestone streets one afternoon, I unexpectedly walked right into a German patrol coming through the town. I just stared at them, as the local people did, and stepped aside to let them pass. Not one soldier paid the slightest attention to me, even through they were searching homes.

I spent the whole time sitting on a stone block in front of a house and wasn't interrogated. Several local residents frantically waved and motioned to me, as if I didn't know these were German soldiers. It would've been a dead giveaway if I'd done anything other than what I did.

After they left, I returned to the padre's house. Pete Comugnero was there and told me it was too risky for me to remain in the village any longer. I'd have to take up residence in a cave about a half mile away. (Pete and his wife were treating me like a son and I was growing very attached to them.)

Pete's wife took me to the small cavern and helped me fill it with leaves for warmth. It was located above a cliff and about a hundred feet back on a grassy slope. The entrance was at the foot of a large bush. To enter, you squeezed into a small hole feet first, then dropped down into the complete darkness of a larger chamber. This part of the cave was about 8 feet long, 6 feet high, and 4 feet wide, and had small sta-

One of the family homes in Reant, Italy—located in an area culturally influenced by the Slovenes of neighboring Yugoslavia. Greening 1955

lagmites and stalactites. At the back was another tunnel leading off further into the mountain. There didn't seem to be any reason to go deeper into the mountain, so I made my abode in the front chamber.

Mrs. Comugnero provided me with a blanket and other essentials, and I spent a week there. During the good weather, I sat outside in the daytime and relaxed a little.

I had an olive oil lamp with a string for a wick. The first night, I heard rustling in the leaves. When I struck a match to see what it was, I discovered that the lamp wick was gone. In a few days, I got a replacement, but this wick disappeared too. Finally, I put the lamp on a high shelf where it couldn't be reached and waited. I discovered that the cave's other occupant was a field mouse.

When you're alone for long periods of time living in the damp darkness, company of any sort is highly desired. I'd been talking to myself, so I was delighted with my new friend. One night while he was rustling through the leaves, I made no movements whatsoever. He crawled up on my chest and sat there, looking at me with little eyes barely visible in the faint lamp light. By feeding him tiny bits of string soaked in oil, he became quite tame.

Pete came early one morning and told me that the Germans had posted a notice forbidding any residents to leave town for the next few days. If anyone violated this rule, they'd be shot without warning. This meant I'd have to stay hidden in the cave and Pete would bring me food after dark. The patriots had shot two soldiers the day before and this crackdown was the Germans' response. It grew tiresome being in the cave day and night. Rains made the cave damp, and I planned to move out. I assume my little roommate did so also.

I decided I'd be better off if I tried to go south, even though I still was weak. I returned to town and told Pete my plans, which met with considerable opposition. Pete's wife cried and carried on something fierce—she was sure I'd get killed. Pete told me to stick it out just "two more months," because by then the war was sure to be over.

Padre Don Amelio Pinzano on a mountain slope near the village of Reant. Greening 1955

Nevertheless, my mind was made up. I'd head directly south for the Adriatic coast where I'd try and find a place to rest, then continue through the Po Valley to the west coast of Italy, and then attempt taking a boat to Corsica or Sardinia. If this couldn't be accomplished, I'd walk south to our lines or wait until our forces advanced to where I was.

I went to see Padre Pinzano and bid him good-by. I left a letter to be delivered to my wife after the war was over, just in case anything should happen to me and I didn't get home.

I also wanted to retrieve my map, which Herma had hidden when the Germans first came to the house. I learned that the map couldn't be found, since she was on vacation at her home in the valley. I'd have to proceed without the map, which would be difficult.

Just as I was leaving the padre's house, I met one of the South African fellows. He looked more bewildered and lonesome than ever. His sick partner had been put to bed in a village about nine miles away. He said we were the last escaped POWs still in these parts, with the exception of two New Zealanders who were hiding somewhere nearby in a cave. He was trying to find them in order to have companionship. We went to a wine shop, and over a glass of wine we talked about the possibilities of going south. Regretfully, I didn't want to travel with this man because he was so readily identifiable. We bid each other good-bye and good luck, and then departed.

Many of the village residents had heard of my plans and advised against it. I suppose they were correct, but at the time I just couldn't stay put. I spent my last night in the cave and departed early in the morning. The kind padre met me on the trail and walked down to the village, where he left me. About a mile further, I came upon a German patrol, but wasn't stopped or questioned. I walked slowly, until I'd covered the eight miles to the little railroad station, where I caught a train to Udine.

On arriving at the Udine station, I passed through inspection with my pass. I'd been told about a ball-bearing merchant and I proceeded to his place. He ran a black

market business in flour at the back of his shop. I hoped he might offer some alternate escape plan.

It was December 30, 1943, and the townspeople were in a festive mood, preparing for the New Year holiday season. The ball-bearing merchant's place was locked up tight. He evidently was away. Many Germans were about and it didn't seem at all advisable for me to make my identity known to anyone. I came to a wine shop where a crowd was playing card games. I noticed a sign stating that rooms were available. I approached the innkeeper and put on my deaf and dumb act, writing my request out on a slip of paper. He asked me in writing where I was from, and if I had an identification card. I produced my card and he gave me a room.

Being in this room was like heaven. I cleaned up and went downstairs to the card room and watched the men playing games. I walked around the streets a bit, trying to find a place to eat without a ration card, but I was unsuccessful. I bought wine and went to bed. I only had 250 lire, so I wouldn't be able to enjoy such comfort as this for many nights.

I paid my bill the next morning and started out for the west coast. Not knowing the towns along the rail lines, however, I chose not to go by train. If I had my map, I could've traveled in style. I thought of stealing a bicycle, but couldn't find one unattended or unlocked. Finally, near the edge of the town, I saw a man leave a bicycle on his front step. The walkway passed close by, so I eased up to the bike with the intention of taking it. When I was about three feet away, the door opened and the man stepped out to bring the bicycle into the house. He frowned at me, as if knowing my intentions. I must have been red in the face.

I continued walking slowly, so as not to tire out too quickly. ❈

NOTES

1. "When I visited northern Italy in 1955, Angelina again told me more about her belief in miracles. Since his youth, Rinaldo had one eye that never was quite right. When he was still a small boy, Angelina had walked to Marstar, a three-day round trip. She placed Rinaldo's picture at the shrine and prayed for his eyesight to be cured. She never could understand why a miracle wasn't granted. Years later when Rinaldo was drafted into the Italian army, his poor eyesight prevented him from being assigned to combat. At that time, Angelina believed her prayer finally was answered, but in an unexpected way."

2. "Later, with the assistance of a friend from Viscontina, a town near Verona, we determined that a message might get through to the US if sent by the Vatican. In Verona, we talked to a Catholic priest. We'd rehearsed for the meeting. When my friend explained that I was deaf and dumb, I presented a note indicating that I wanted to contact my mother. I then wrote a short message to 'Mrs. C. Grini,' which was reasonably close to the American pronunciation of our family name, while still sounding Italian enough to not arouse suspicion. I said I was doing well and hoped to return to America after the war. I signed it 'Carlo Grini.' I assumed that if my mother received the message, she'd understand that I'd sent it. The priest assured me that the message would be dispatched to the Vatican as soon as possible.

"Following the war, I learned that the message was delivered, but it nearly scared my mother out of her wits. After the Vatican wired the note to the US, a priest approached my mother's house. He knocked on the door and his arms were folded in a prayerful attitude. With a serious, low voice, he said, 'Are you Mrs. Grini?' Mother immediately replied, 'Yes, I'm Mrs. Greening, what is it that you want?' He continued, 'I want to be sure. I have a very serious message and I want to be certain that you are Mrs. Grini.' At this, my mother nearly screamed, fearing the worst kind of news. The priest stepped into the house and said, 'Everything is all right. I've a message from your son that he's alive and well, and he will come back to America after the war.'"

CHAPTER TWELVE

THE NEW ZEALANDERS

After about two hours, I came to a small town where I tried to get something to eat, but finding food was a problem. Most of the men were out celebrating and the women at home wouldn't help me since they needed their husbands' permission to do so. I told some that I was a patriot, which frightened them because they thought I might harm them. I told others I was an escaped prisoner, and I tried the deaf and dumb routine without success. Finally, I was given a piece of bread tasting like angel food cake.

I walked on, arriving at a German airfield where a few Focke Wulf 190 fighters were parked. I entertained the idea of trying to steal one. I sat at the edge of the field, trying to figure out a plan that might work, but couldn't come up with one that didn't have holes in it. The field wasn't well guarded, but the distance to the planes was too far for me to cross and still avoid detection. Even if I made it to a plane, I couldn't read German and wouldn't understand the various instruments. And, if I managed to take off, our fighters or anti-aircraft guns at the front lines probably would shoot me down.

After about 1 1/2 hours, I saw a young, handsome Italian fellow approaching on a bicycle. I walked along beside

Renata Borgnolo, April 1947. A Wartime Log

him and told him my story. He seemed somewhat afraid, but agreed to take me to an inn about a mile away where I might be able to get something to eat. At the inn, he introduced me to a young man who must have been the proprietor. When he discovered that I was an American, he almost grew panicky, saying the town was full of Germans. He told me I should get out of the area right away. This was very discouraging to me.

I left and wandered aimlessly on, becoming tired and hungry while my legs and feet ached. I realized I shouldn't have attempted to make this trip so soon after my illness. My mind grew blank as darkness fell and it became cold. I stopped and asked for directions to a train station. I was told that it was about three miles away at a place called Palmanova. I walked painfully into town and came to a wine shop full of Italians celebrating New Year's Eve. I entered unnoticed and bought a large glass of wine. This gave me a little courage to try more desperate measures, so I called the nearest Italian to my table and told him about my situation.

His eyes widened. "You must get out of this town right away," he said. "There are over 2,000 Germans here and they are sure to find you. Only two days ago an American bomber fell near here and one of the crewmen still hasn't been found. The Germans are looking for him."

"I am not going to leave unless someone gives me some help!" I answered, raising my voice a little. "I haven't had anything to eat for two days and I can't go until I at least get some food. If you don't help me, I will make enough noise to bring the Germans here and they will catch me with you. We'll all get into trouble then."

This little speech brought several more Italians to my table, who sympathized with me, but they weren't much help. Most were evading the Germans themselves, having left military service after the Italian capitulation. None, however, offered me a place to stay or anything to eat. I was given wine, which I didn't want to drink on an empty stomach.

Finally, the man I'd first approached agreed to let me stay in his barn for just one night. He also promised to bring me something to eat if I wouldn't leave the barn. By now, I figured I needed to return to the mountains if I was going to find provisions and evade detection. I told this fellow I'd stay in his barn and leave the next morning on the train. We left the wine shop.

The barn was a large, low-ceiling structure holding seven cows. My host said he'd come back with food. I rummaged around trying to find a place to sleep. I finally pulled some hay down from the loft and put it in the feed trough, where I would stay warmer being nearer the cows. The promised food never came, and, unfortunately, the cow in my stall drooled over me half the night and tried to eat the hay underneath me.

I stayed fairly warm, but my spirits were as low as they ever were in my life. It was New Year's Eve and I was nearly starving. The cows were the friendliest thing I'd seen for two days. I kept thinking about the people at home having their holiday dinners, and I tried to comfort myself by being thankful for being alive. A small light in the barn allowed me to see Bessie's large orbs staring down at me from time to time. At midnight, I rose up and walked about a bit to warm up. Just before climbing back into the hay, I gave Bessie a big hug and wished her a Happy New Year.

On the morning of January 1, 1944, I awoke with stiff and sore limbs. My bad leg was so weak I could scarcely stand on it and I trembled from the cold. A farmhand came to take care of the cows. I asked him for the time and learned that the train was due to leave in about fifteen minutes. I left for the station, walking dizzily like a drunken man. I wasn't noticed because lots of people were staggering about from the previous night's drinking. I purchased a ticket to Udine. I was so sore that I found it difficult to sit upright in the waiting room, but I made it to my feet when I heard the engine approaching.

The train was completely full, but it stopped anyway to pick up the few people waiting at the station. When attempting to board, I didn't have the strength to make it up the first step. I grabbed at the handrail to keep from falling and was close to passing out. Suddenly, a strong hand grasped my arm and pulled me into the car. I was amazed to see a kindly looking German officer giving me assistance. He'd seen me and came down to help. He even went so far as to find a space in a compartment where I could sit down. It made me realize that some Germans have a heart, although I couldn't help thinking what my treatment would be if he knew that I was an escaped POW.

The trip back was uneventful, but also depressing when I thought about how long it had taken me to walk this same distance. At Udine, I passed through the gate without suspicion and walked to the ball bearing merchant's place in hopes of finding him. Again I was disappointed.

The townspeople were celebrating New Year's Day and my mouth watered at the sight of various people carrying food about. I passed a restaurant where I saw some customers drinking hot chocolate. I lingered by the window, seeing if ration cards were required. To my delight, they weren't. I entered and ordered a cup of hot chocolate and a wafer. The chocolate was a substitute type without sugar. I wolfed down the first cupful in two gulps, and ordered and drank another. To avoid suspicion, I stopped there and left.

Outside, I found a street vendor selling dirty, cheap looking, bread sticks with a small dab of saccharin sweetened jam. I bought three to complete my New Year's dinner.

At the station, I boarded the shuttle train for the mountains. After the shuttle dropped me off at Cividale, I'd have to walk eight miles to Masarolis, which would be difficult in my condition. I left the train and started walking. The town was barricaded against patriot attacks, but I wasn't stopped or questioned at any of the guard posts. It was hard to keep my legs moving and I had to rest every few hundred yards. At the foot of the mountains, I stopped to rest on a boulder in a dry riverbed, and either fell asleep or passed out because it was nearly dark when I awoke.

That climb up the hill was the most difficult I'd yet experienced, but I finally came to Masarolis where Pete and his wife lived. I was so exhausted that I opened the door without even knocking. They were eating dinner, but when they saw me, they jumped to their feet and hugged me. Pete's wife cried and said she'd prayed for my safe return.

It was almost like walking into my own home. Pete was overjoyed. He dashed out to the storeroom and broke out a bottle of his best wine. His wife fixed boiled chicken and white bread. I forced myself to eat slowly and chew thoroughly, knowing I could easily hurt myself if I ate too much or too fast. That meal tasted as good as anything I'd ever had in my life. News about my return spread through the village and many came to welcome me back. I returned to the cave that night and decided it wasn't so bad after all.

A few days later, I offered to help Pete in a little plot on the side of the hill, which overlooked the road below. I needed to do something to gain my strength back and Pete was glad to have the assistance. We planted grapevines. We dug and picked rocks out of the ground for several days.

After making a long deep trench, we filled it in with fertilizer and good dirt.

"Just think," Pete said. "In only four years this little line of vines will produce enough grapes to make fifty liters of wine."

Our tools were old and primitive, and the plot of ground was situated right at the end of a switchback in the trail. It was such a small area that it hardly seemed worth the bother. We worked from sunup till sundown, however, and at noon Mrs. Comugnero brought us hot soup and cornmeal. I grew so engrossed in the work that I forgot to watch the trail for patrols. Suddenly, while setting a pole, I looked up to see German soldiers surrounding us.

The officer in charge came up to me, asking in very poor Italian, "I am in the mountains looking for patriots. I am also looking for an American Lt. Colonel who is supposed to be hiding up here. Have you seen anybody who doesn't live here?"

I was so surprised that I didn't have a chance to be scared. I said " No" in Italian, but suggested he talk to the padre who might be able to answer his questions. I don't know why I recommended the padre, but I couldn't think of any one else.

They moved on and I quickly left in the other direction to wait on a hilltop, just in case they grew suspicious and came back. I arranged with Pete to signal with a small fire when the patrol had left the area. When Pete thought the Germans were gone, he tried to light some brush piled up at the end of his field. He was having difficulty getting his only match to strike when the patrol showed up around the bend. The leader lent Pete a match to light the fire!

I spent the next few days doing little except traveling over to the padre's place in Masarolis to listen to news broadcasts about the war's progress. At the house, I often encountered a small, well-dressed, middle-aged man. He seemed to be out of place for those parts, but I asked no questions. I learned that he spoke seven different languages, but his

"Amabile helped us a lot getting food. I made more than 100 of these portraits while staying in my cave. (Drawn from life)." A Wartime Log

Italian wasn't too fluent, so I assumed he wasn't a native of these hills. I met him several times and we played cards together. He was friendly but quiet.

Each day as I was recuperating by walking in the hills, I'd see him standing on the hilltop someplace. Being near Yugoslavia, there were many people of Serbian ancestry in this locality who had light colored hair like mine. His hair was fair, too, and his hands were not those of a farmer. We were suspicious of each other. Sometimes we took walks together, but nothing was said between us about his reason for being here.

Early one evening when I'd arrived at the padre's house to listen to the radio, this little man came into the house very excited. He called me into a separate room and asked me who I was. I told him I didn't care to tell him.

He said, "Well, you are hiding around here someplace and I would like to know where you are hiding. It's very important."

I told him, "I don't want to tell you where I'm hiding."

He replied, "Well, maybe if you understood we are surrounded by the Germans it would make a difference. They are here to get you and they are here to get me."

He produced extensive identification cards indicating that he was a communist commissar trying to recruit Italians. He ran the whole show in a wide area, he said, and now he was in great danger. He didn't know how to get out of the village and thought I might know a secret escape route.

I said, "I've been told by patriots that you want nothing to do with us, and that you don't like the Americans or English because we have caused you so much trouble. Why is it you think I can help you now?"

"You must help me," he said. "They are searching the village very thoroughly and if we are caught, we both will be killed. If we get out of this, I promise I'll help to get you out of the country and back to your own lines."

At that point, I decided to accept his story at face value. I went to the door and motioned for him to follow. We crept outside to the wall and then along a street through the middle of the village. We came to the only latrine I'd seen in the town, went in, and crawled down into the sewer and out a culvert. It was a pretty gruesome trip, but we got outside the village. In the dark, we heard a guard's footsteps as he walked his beat across a little wooden bridge.

We followed a little creek bed on our hands and knees until reaching the foot of the cliff where my cave was located. We climbed up and entered the cavern, where we covered ourselves with leaves. The little man, whose name was Mr. Grunta, clapped me on the back, saying "Bravo!" whereupon he produced a bottle of "Grappa" or brandy. We celebrated our escape with a toast.

Grunta was an older man and the next day he was ill from exposure, dampness, and the sewer filth. He became a little delirious and I was afraid he might die. I spent the next few days trying to rustle up food and medicine for him. I'd been able to find another blanket so he could stay in bed most of the time and keep warm.

From my hilltop lookout about a half-mile from the cave, I observed a German patrol that came into the hills and occupied a small stone barn. I counted how many soldiers went in, and when the same number left in a little while without their packs, I went down and relieved them of some supplies. I couldn't read the German labels, but I grabbed what I thought was quinine, plus saccharin, baking powder, biscuit dough, a bottle of brandy, butter, blankets, a pup tent, clothing, sugar, salt, and other things I thought I could use.

I took the stuff back to our hideout. I gave Grunta the pills on the best schedule I could figure out. I even fixed up hot packs to get him sweating. As luck would have it, either because of me or in spite of me, he recovered. I brought in food as often as I could until he was able to get about for himself.

Naturally, Grunta began feeling quite secure around me and confided in me. He described his efforts to organize partisan bands throughout this part of the country. He explained that his primary purpose, however, was to preach communist doctrine. He was a Serb and had been trained almost all of his life in Russia. We had many discussions about communism. I told him that I couldn't reconcile what he was telling me with what I knew about communism. I said we'd been taught that it was a lot of propaganda and not to be trusted. He couldn't believe this.

Sometimes, we became a little "huffy" with each other. I told him I was willing to try and prove my points. For example, he believed that the Russians were flying in supplies for the patriots. However, I knew that Allied equipment, not Soviet, had been dropped along with a British major—I'd seen some of the radios and the "Irving Company" labels on the parachutes. I offered to go and recover one to prove that it was American made.

That night, I went to see Herma and together we brought a section of chute back to the cave. She could read English and told him that it was indeed American made, and the tins of Spam that had been dropped were clearly part of an American food parcel. Grunta had thought these labels were some sort of Russian script that he was unfamiliar with. I think this conclusive evidence shook him up.

In other discussions, he'd say that Americans were "bloated capitalists." I hadn't heard this phrase before and for the first time began to suspect that the Russians were deliberately spreading negative propaganda about the United States.

Grunta claimed that a minority of Americans ran the country and they drove Cadillacs on some streets in Washington, D.C., that actually were paved with gold. He said that the privileged Americans lived high and mighty in comparison to the rest of the world, but that workers in America were in poor straits with little to eat, inadequate housing, and poor clothing. He was surprised when I claimed that I was an "average" American and had been raised under "typical" conditions.

He maintained, "You are the exception—by far the exception."

He'd never seen Americans and his perceptions about them came only from the Russians.

I said, "You should believe a few more things that you see, and not just what you're told." I added that I was willing to provide more proof, but in the meantime we shouldn't waste time in idle chatter trying to convert each other.

I told him that I thought the local patriot band wasn't worth the powder to blow itself up. If they had any sense, they wouldn't try to keep me here to fight with a gun when I was trained for combat in the air. I could come back in a plane and shoot up as many German soldiers in fifteen minutes as his band of 2,000 men could in months, and with a lot less expense and loss of life.

I also exclaimed that I didn't have confidence in their operations. Fighting only with light weapons such as rifles and mortars wasn't enough, and their scouting systems were poor. On one occasion when I was deployed with a patriot band to fight off a German patrol, the leader issued a rifle to each man and about three rounds of ammunition. By the

time the Germans were in sight, all of the members of the band were gone except me. I decided I wasn't going to hold off a German patrol by myself. I returned the rifle to the cache and left.

Finally Grunta said, "I believe your story and I'm going to get you back to Naples."

He informed me that he was leaving, but he'd make arrangements for me to escape through Yugoslavia. He knew I'd been wounded in the knee and had problems walking, which would be compounded by wintry conditions. He figured I should be able to walk out after the winter, and besides, it would take him about that long to put a plan in place.

"I will be gone a long time," he said, "but I guarantee I'll be back in three months, and by the time the snow is gone all the arrangements will be made for you to go right through."

Three months doesn't sound like a long time, unless you're living under leaves in a tiny cave in the cold mountains. I took it all as a good joke, saying, "Sure, I'll be here in three months."

That night, we visited the padre's house to listen to the radio. While trying to dial in a station, there was a knock at the door. We both peeked out of the kitchen window and saw what looked like two men in German uniforms standing at the front door. There wasn't any way to leave the house, so we hurried to the outhouse and locked ourselves in.

The housekeeper admitted the two men. Instead of being Jerries, they were the two New Zealanders I'd heard about from the South African. They came into the kitchen and the housekeeper called us back in. I was introduced to Bob Smith and Jack Lang, who'd been prisoners in a small camp not far from Cividale. They'd escaped from the Germans and had gone to Yugoslavia.

Their story was fantastic. For two months, they'd been with the patriot forces and suffered from exposure and hard-

"This is Bob Smith one of my cave mates. First captured by Germans on the desert. He made 5 unsuccessful escapes (10 Samoa St., Wellington, N. Zealand)." A Wartime Log

ship. Their appearance gave testimony to their tale. Both were thin and haggard, with unshaven faces. They wore tattered civilian clothes and parts of German uniforms stolen from a patrol cabin in the mountains. Earlier in the war, Bob Smith was captured in the desert and had escaped on five occasions, only to be recaptured each time.

Jack Lang, on the other hand, had been assigned in Greece as part of a rear guard action. He evaded the Germans for sixteen months before being seized. Both were bewildered and tired. They were visiting the padre's house to listen to the radio just like Grunta and I.

I liked these fellows the minute I set eyes on them. Both were enlisted men, but one was passing himself off as a

"This is Jack Lang one of my cave mates. He was captured in Greece after evading for 16 months. (British Army—Albert St., Thames, N. Zealand)."
A Wartime Log

major and the other as a captain, because they received better treatment if people thought they were officers. Actually, Bob was a sergeant major and Jack a private. They spent that night with Mr. Grunta and me in our cave. They told me they were living in a better cave and invited me to come and stay with them for a while if I wanted.

Soon, my cave began filling with water, so I moved into the New Zealanders' cavern located high on a mountain about four miles away. Their cave was located at an elevation of about 2,500 feet in the face of a cliff overlooking the Po Valley. Being near the upper end of a kind of blind valley, it proved to be an excellent hiding place because it couldn't be seen from either side, nor from above or below. The approach to the cave along the face of the cliff was extremely

difficult. The first part of the trail was over loose dirt, and then it led into rocks and the face of the cliff. The cave opening was an oblong slit. It was fairly spacious inside, with a dirt floor and stalactites on the ceiling.

During my first week there, I learned that the unfortunate South African I'd talked to was shot by the patriots who took him for a spy. He was picked up on the trail below our cave with a head wound. He died in a German hospital in Cividale. I never learned what had happened to his companion.

We set about improving the cave for our comfort. We had no tools or materials, so we began searching through the hills. At an old farmhouse, we found a broken pick blade, a rusty shovel without a handle, and bottles, newspapers, and boards. We packed this assortment of junk back to our cave, some three miles away over precipitous trails.

With a small machete used for cutting firewood, we carved handles for the pick and shovel, then dug out the excess dirt in the cave to make the floor level. We built a small platform immediately in front of the cave and put the dirt there. This platform provided a level place to stand or sit outside. Next, we built a mud fireplace, a stairway into the cave, and a bed, chairs, table, and shelves.

We also constructed an entryway, placing a German pup tent over the opening. The remainder of the cave mouth was filled in with mud and sticks and covered over with sod. We cut brush and trees to camouflage the outside platform. The trail to the cave needed a few footholds, so we dug those into the rock and cliffside. All of our work was camouflaged as carefully as possible.

The fireplace and chimney drew nicely once it got going. Smoke went out up the cliffside next to some whitish rocks and couldn't be seen from any angle. By the time it dissipated at the top of the cliff, it no longer was visible.

We set about making arrangements for food in the nearby small towns of Valle, Reant, Masarolis, and Pedrosa. The cave gave us a feeling of refreshing independence,

"The inside of our cave included a fireplace, a cupboard, a table, a chair, a bench, a bed, a stairway, a clothes rack and a wood box— all of which we built ourselves with practically no tools."
A Wartime Log

because we didn't have to impose on people who risked being executed if the Italian fascists or Germans caught us hiding in a village. We visited each of the four towns on alternating nights so we wouldn't be a burden and because the villagers could better provide for us when we did visit.

As the crow flies, these four mountain villages only stood about five miles in a northerly direction from Cividale, which was located down on the edge of the plain. The steep, winding trails, of course, made for longer walking distances between places.

We selected certain families in each village to visit and had a "Mom" in each town. We took particular pains to know what was going on in the communities, so that we could converse intelligently with the people when we visited. The children became our pets and we made a big fuss over them, which made a hit with the parents.

We grew so interested in some of the kids that we worried and fretted over their welfare, wondering whether they'd get a decent break in life. It pained us to see the way some of them had to live in these hard times. We just couldn't help comparing their lives to our own childhood years, when we'd been given every opportunity while growing up. These little kids had no advantages whatsoever and seemed destined to live in poverty. Their bodies were covered with sores and rashes, and they barely had sufficient clothing. Many died before reaching the age of five or six. As soon as they were able to walk, they had to work.

The average child in this area went to school for only two years, while the more fortunate attended three to five years. In this particular region, centuries of conflict had changed the borders many times and things had remained unsettled for generations. A Slovene minority lived here, separated by the Italian border from their brethren in nearby northern Yugoslavia (this boundary had been established after World War I). Many local residents didn't even learn the official national language, (Tuscan) Italian, until they started attending school.

A schoolteacher discussing the war with me said, "The Italians invaded Ethiopia to civilize the Ethiopians, when they hadn't yet civilized the Italians."

Large families lived in small houses with no heat other than what came from the kitchen fire when meals were prepared. The eternal kitchen smoke was enough to drive a person mad. All of their clothes were homemade, even the footwear. They usually wore a pair of wooden shoes for working in wet weather, and cloth slippers during dry weather.

Our worst hardship was acquiring food. The main diet was cornmeal, which was boiled down into a cake each night, making "polenta." It was good, but grew tiresome as a steady diet. We stopped at our selected houses, asking for a small contribution of food. Sometimes we received potatoes, but mostly we were given cornmeal. We tried to time our visits for when special items or a few meat scraps might be available.

Tobacco was scarce and we made our own. When finding green tobacco, we'd dry it out, cut it up into fine pieces, and then soak it in water for a few hours. When dried out and smoked, it practically knocked us for a loop because it was so strong. We used newspaper for papers. Matches were another scarce item. We kept a bed of coals going in the fireplace when we didn't have them.

Day after day we watched Allied bombers flying over northern Italy, blasting targets in the Po Valley. After the major raids, people became elated because it indicated the war would be over that much sooner. They expressed their joy by slapping us on the back and giving us cigarettes and wine. After big raids, we made it a point to visit the villages so we could join in the celebrations.

We also became proficient at making bird and rabbit traps. We borrowed a net from the villagers, who'd evolved a system for trapping birds over many generations. We caught small birds, a number of rabbits, and several quail. Unfortunately, predatory animals ate many before we got to them. All we'd find would be a small pile of fur or feathers. Wild game wasn't plentiful—besides, we had competition from the local people who also were foraging for food. (Bob said his sympathies were with the hunted.) Once, we presented a rabbit to a village woman to prepare for us. She did so most graciously, but when we sat down to eat I was given what was considered the choicest part—the head complete with teeth and eyes. It was a gruesome sight, and I had to excuse myself and go outside. Bob and Jack covered for me and made sure it was removed before I came back.

Green vegetables were unavailable in the wintertime; however, we did get a few beans and some onions once in a while. The lack of salt was a big hardship and sugar could hardly be found. Of course, those things must have been more common in peacetime, but the villagers told us they were difficult to come by even then. After a while, we finally acquired about four tablespoons of sugar and poured half of it in a large bowl of cornmeal. We actually thought we'd used too much sugar since it tasted so sweet. Milk originally was plentiful in the hills, but the patriots and Germans confiscated so many of the cows that it eventually became scarce.

The trips in and out of the cave at night were frightening. We had to feel along the trail with our feet and the going was slow. More often than not, one of us lost his footing and slid halfway down the cliff to a fringe of trees. We also had some difficulty in getting water. The nearest source was a spring over the crest of the hill and we only had two rusty, half-gallon pails to carry it in. Half of the time, we spilled it trying to get back to the cave. I gained a real appreciation for the water taps back in the USA. Each day, one of us would do both the cooking and the water carrying.

The mountain hideaway. A Wartime Log

Our shoes soon began to wear out from rough use in the hills. We tried to devise slippers made of rags and sacks, but even these materials were hard to find. We stayed in bed nearly all day long on the cold days to keep warm.

A schoolteacher in one of the little villages helped provide us with a few things to help pass the time. Of course, I asked for pencils and paper. I began making portraits of the little children in the hills and drew well over a hundred of them before we left. I also made sketches of our cave and the towns around us. We also cut, seasoned, and whittled softwood to make model airplanes and I did some wood sculpturing to help pass the time.

The people in these hills hadn't seen an artist of any type before, consequently I made quite an impression, though my work was average enough in circles back home. This allowed us to get cigarettes and even eggs at times in exchange for my sketches. We even held an exhibition of our woodwork and drawings at our hideout.

Our cave started looking like a packrat's nest after the first weeks. We dragged in every bit of dry wood, scrap tin, nails, cloth, or anything ever manufactured by human hands that we could find. We aired our blankets every other day and tried our best to keep the lice count down. Socks wore

out rapidly and we patched and re-patched them with cloth scraps until it was difficult to tell which parts were original.

Our efforts at developing good will among the villagers paid dividends after a while and they invited us into their houses when it was safe to do so. People grew so goodhearted that it made us feel ashamed to take the things they offered. The residents of one town called us their "brothers." We were always referred to that way when we entered the village.

When partisan bands from other regions swept through our area, which was quite often, we'd hide from them. Their activities brought reprisals by German planes and soldiers. For weeks, hardly a day passed that we didn't hear fighting of some sort nearby.

One day, two Germans in a car were driving toward a mountain village about two miles from us. They were intercepted by patriots and killed. The patriots then mutilated the bodies by poking out the eyes and cutting open the stomachs, and the corpses were put back in the vehicle and burned. This brought on attack after attack from the Germans in reprisal. Dive-bombers and fighters attacked the villages, whether the partisans were there or not. Several times, we watched large numbers of Germans patrolling below our cave, searching the hills all around us. They didn't come up the face of the cliff so we figured we were safe.

The weather held up fine until the end of January when winter came with a vengeance. Drifting snow could prevent us from leaving the cave and one time forced us to remain inside for about a week. We had enough wood to hold

The view south toward the plain from the mountain hideaway. A Wartime Log

"Reant, Italy—This town called us her 'brothers' and supplied us on many occasions with food and sometimes wine. (Drawn from actual location)." A Wartime Log

out for that period and slept through the snowstorm like bears in hibernation. We forced ourselves to bathe in the bitterly cold water from a tin bucket and we tried to keep our clothes clean. Hygiene was important to prevent illness and we knew we couldn't get help once we became sick.

During one snowy period, we learned that a village was holding a three-day dance and we decided to go. We spruced up the best we could, then used old socks for mittens and rags for scarves, and headed out for the dance at a wine shop. The floor consisted of rough-hewn logs that could surrender up large splinters to a dancer's foot. We made it a point

to dance with the old folks, as well as the young ones. We drank wine until it practically ran out of our ears. A concertina and piccolo played sour harmony, but to us it was the best music we'd heard for many moons.

An amazing feature about these festivities was that the men danced with each other as much as with the women. Some town dignitaries danced with us, and one patriot member with his red scarf grabbed me and swirled me around like I'd never been swirled before. He held me as affectionately as he would a girl. I actually think I blushed. Bob, Jack, and I danced together and tried a few American steps that created some attention from the rest of the crowd.

We'd been practicing a trio song arrangement by using our combs and pieces of paper to make bazookas. Our musical harmony stopped the dance. We had to do two encores.

After three days of dancing, we were content to remain in our cave for a week to rest up. The dance was lots of fun and a godsend after the monotony we'd been enduring. We spent time studying a first-grade Italian primer and practicing Italian by translating newspapers word for word. However, our greatest difficulty in learning to speak the language was that few people in this Slovene-influenced border area spoke proper Italian.

Our ability to travel in the black of night always amazed me. When I first moved in, Bob and Jack told me that we'd have to feel along the trails with our feet, because we wouldn't be able to see the ground. I thought it was a joke. Later, I learned that feeling along a path by foot was the only way to get around in the dark. Of course, moonlit nights were exceptions and made for good visibility, but each moonless night was an adventure.

We'd leave the cave knowing just how many steps were necessary to pass along the frightening cliff to reach the ridge. From the ridge, we'd navigate to the different villages by the bends and rocks in the trails. It amazed me how soon I got to know these paths intimately. This skill gave us an advantage when patrols caught us in a village. We knew the

ground so well that it wasn't a problem to feel our way silently through the back streets and get away to the mountain tops.

A daylight trip, however, was necessary to reach our water hole, which was fairly near one of the villages. We generally kept to a brushy, tree-filled draw to avoid detection by patrols.

One morning when making a trip for water, I had just arrived at the spring when I heard a horse whinny. I dropped to the ground behind a bush and looked up the trail. Just then, a mounted German came over the ridge followed by about fifty others. They passed within a few yards of the water hole and entered the village. I watched them search the houses. There was no trouble and the patrol left by a trail leading out from the other side of the village. When telling the villagers about this a few hours later, they were amazed that I was brazen enough to stay and watch the Germans.

On another foraging expedition, we chose to enter a village just before dark. The townspeople were growing very excited because the Germans were on the way. Many of the young men who were evading the draft were taking off to hide in the hills and we were told to get out ourselves. We must have felt particularly bold, because we didn't leave until we filled our food bag. We left the town from one end just as the Germans entered at the other. This

"Claudio Borgnolo—This young Italian boy helped us most of all. When the weather was bad and we were snowed in he got in to us with food. (Drawn from life)." A Wartime Log

added to our prestige as bold adventurers and I noted greater respect from the people on later visits. We got a little too cocky for our own good.

On one occasion, we left the cave early and sat on a hill waiting for darkness before entering a village. For lack of anything better to do, Bob, Jack, and I started a mock battle among the rocks. Each of us carried a homemade cane, which served as a make believe firearm. Maybe the long hours of waiting and the inactivity made us feel coltish, but we started a sham battle this evening. Up one side of the hill and down the other, we fired and shot at each other making sounds of explosions and bangs with our mouths. Now and then one of us crumpled to the ground in a good imitation of a death struggle. Of course, we always revived and continued the battle.

Our canes changed to stick horses and we galloped back and forth shooting with our fingers like pistols. Our horses were shot from under us and death ran wild. We laughed and yelled like crazy men until suddenly I saw one of the villagers, an old man, watching our antics from a viewpoint not a hundred yards away. He must have figured we were absolutely mad. We tried to ignore him and galloped off out of sight. I don't think that incident helped our standing any.

Bob and Jack wandered into a village one afternoon carrying their food

"Valle, Italy—We got food here many times and attended some of their dances. An ME-109 strafed this place several times. We eluded a military squad when they encircled us one night." A Wartime Log

packs. Unknown to them, two Germans who had detached themselves from a patrol had entered the town to inspect the place. Of course, the food packs would identify Bob and Jack as patriots. They came upon these Jerries so unexpectedly that they had no time to break and run.

They were too close, so they tried to unconcernedly walk right up to them and continue on past. The Germans eyed them suspiciously, but didn't try to stop them.

When they were a couple of hundred yards away, the Germans must have decided to investigate and called for them to halt. Both boys broke and ran for dear life down the hillside, heedless of the bullets whizzing by them. They were chased from this village to another, where they dove underneath some hay in a barn and hid until the Jerries left. It was a close call.

We usually stuck close to our cave when the Italian patriot activity picked up. I never saw them attempt very many really bold stunts. Most of the action that we observed was when the Germans were chasing them. Sometimes, mortar explosions and machine gun fire could be heard in the hills. Then aircraft would begin dive-bombing and strafing. I was at the water hole one time when an ME-109 came screaming straight at me. I hit the dirt as he fired, but to my relief he didn't start shooting until he was right over my head. He was attacking the nearby village of Valle. The heavy stone walls of the houses prevented much damage from occurring, though one little girl was killed.

From our position on the side of the cliff, we saw a party of patriots do an excellent job of blowing up a large enemy munitions dump. The smoke and debris sailed thousands of feet into the air and the shock wave from the explosion was tremendous. After two months, the Germans re-established the munitions dump, probably figuring the patriots wouldn't think of trying to blow it up again. They figured wrong. We observed this explosion, too. The second blast was even greater than the first and rocked the whole countryside. The Germans didn't try to reestablish the dump again.

One pleasant Sunday afternoon, when many of the Italians from the plains were taking strolls in the mountains, I was sitting alone beside a trail enjoying the view and dreaming of home. I watched two men approaching from below. Soon, they came up to me and stopped to rest. I exchanged salutations, but the younger man remained quiet. My greeting led to a conversation with the older man. He was curious about me, asking why I was in the mountains. He said he knew I didn't belong here and suspected I was an escaped prisoner.

I told him that he was right, and he became intensely interested.

He then told me that my friends and I were welcome to come to his house on the plain just below for food and wine whenever we wanted to. He also claimed he knew of another American and two New Zealanders who were hiding out not far from his home.

I strongly suspected that this actually was us and asked him if he could be mistaken. No! He'd seen them and they were a different trio. Based on this, I felt we'd be smart if we went down and tried to find these fellows. They might tell us something about how they planned to get back to Allied lines.

While the conversation went on, I noticed that the young man didn't say a word. I asked the old fellow about

this and he replied that his companion was deaf and dumb. I immediately showed my identification card that indicated I was deaf and dumb. I learned that the young man was injured in a plane crash while training in the Italian Air Force. He'd been left stone deaf and unable to utter a sound.

After they left, I went to find Jack and Bob to tell them this story. We agreed to try and find the escaped POWs at the base of the mountain and also visit the elderly man for food and wine. We went down a few days later. From our viewpoint on the hill, we could see his house from far away. Our estimate of the distance was way off, however, because we walked and walked for what seemed liked hours before we came to the place.

When we arrived late at night, the old man was in the kitchen with his wife and daughters. We were warmly greeted and they set about preparing a meal for us. Eggs, cheese, and wine provided the main fare, which suited us fine. We ate and drank until we were full to the top. As a matter of fact, we were treated so warmly that we almost drank too much wine that night.

At about the time we figured we couldn't hold another drop, the deaf and dumb fellow walked in. This called for another drink, which we should have refused, but didn't. Again, we figured we'd had enough and suggested that we'd better be leaving, when another family friend stopped by and was introduced to us. This called for another glass of wine all around.

This happened a couple more times, and then it became imperative that we leave to get some fresh air. We'd found out that we wouldn't be able to find the escaped POWs we were looking for, but this seemed rather unimportant in our present state. We were given some cheese to take with us and we staggered out.

The night was beautiful with a full moon and it wasn't the least bit cold. The wine emboldened us to prowl around and ask for more food to take back with us. We picked the most prosperous looking house we could find and gave it a

try. It wasn't wise to approach wealthier appearing places because usually they were the homes of fascists—other families couldn't live in such high style at that time. However, good luck was with us again and we were invited into the home.

We were taken to the living room where we presented our hard luck story and requested a little food to take with us. The mother of the family immediately dashed to the back of the house to get a bundle of things fixed up for us. While we were waiting, the eldest son went off in another direction and returned with a large bottle of wine. For good manners, we felt compelled to have two more glasses of wine each. It was a sweeter and more potent variety. We almost requested a place to sleep, because it was apparent we soon would pass out at the rate we were going. I hardly remember leaving the place.

When we got outside, we could scarcely stand on our feet. We also didn't have much of a sense of direction and ended up in a large courtyard. Dogs started barking and a nearby door opened. In order to avoid embarrassment, we acted as if we were just about to knock and had been surprised when the door suddenly opened. We again told our hard luck story and asked for food to take back with us. This time we were given a bottle of milk and some cornmeal, but before leaving we were invited to share another bottle of wine. We didn't know if we could get it down, but each of us drank another large glass just to be polite. We looked like clowns as we stumbled out the door.

The cave was only six miles away, but we had to climb 2,500 feet in that distance. The incline was something to remember. From the bottom looking up, the mountain looked like a sheer wall. We staggered and stumbled along so full of wine that we would've thumbed our noses at any Germans if we had met them. Bob carried the milk and, during a moment of playfulness, he fell and broke the bottle. In checking to see if he had cut himself, Bob found that both of his coat pockets were full of eggs. Jack and I inspected our pockets and found eggs also. It was going to be tough getting them to the cave over the last bit of trail without breaking them.

We climbed and climbed, pausing to rest every few hundred feet. Each time we stopped, we fell asleep. When one of us happened to wake up, he'd arouse the others and we'd struggle on. It seemed as if we'd never get to the cave. Several times we slipped and fell on the rocks, but didn't break any eggs. At last, we had only about 500 feet to go and we went in different directions. Bob started up the middle, Jack to the left, and I went right.

Bob's section was the shortest, but the steepest and most difficult. I saw him in the moonlight hanging on the side of the cliff trying to make his way straight up, and then he lost his footing and fell with a crash. He rolled over rocks and brush for at least seventy-five feet. All I could think of was that he must have crushed the eggs in his pockets. I proceeded carefully for the last few feet, thinking I'd be the only one to arrive with unbroken eggs.

I sat waiting on the front platform. When Bob appeared, his clothes were torn and dirty and he was completely exhausted, but he had come through the fall without breaking any eggs! His shinbones were scratched and his face was bruised, but he had the glow of victory in his eyes! Jack was equally successful. It was a miracle that all we lost was the bottle of milk. We spent the next three days resting up from our ordeal and never went down to the plains again.

The snows left at the end of February, which was a great relief. We'd come home with wet feet so many times and our shoes were getting so worn that the prospect of warmer days was a godsend. As the weather improved, children from the towns began visiting us. Every day, some of these little fellows stopped in at the cave. We appreciated these visits, but we also feared that they'd be followed or the main pathways would get beaten down enough to be observed by German patrols. At the villages, we asked the parents to try and keep the children home both for their safety and ours.

Nearby to the east of the cave, there was a vantage point that we occasionally visited to observe the surrounding countryside and all of the approaching trails. The position was a precarious one, because it was on a large rock that hung out over a nearly perpendicular cliff. One day, I climbed out to the lookout's furthest point, with Jack close behind. Far below, we saw three figures approaching by way of the lower trail. They were at least two miles away and could barely be seen. I watched until they were close enough to the cliff that I could tell they were young girls. We shouted and waved to them.

They waved back and proceeded to the base of the cliff and then began to pick their way up. Each had a package slung over a shoulder.

We yelled at them to go back, but they continued on up the dangerous slope. Deeply concerned for their safety, I involuntarily gripped and clung at the rocks and crevices in an effort to help them out. I even made grunting and straining sounds. I just couldn't believe these three little girls would be capable of climbing a slope that would challenge an experienced mountain climber. Jack and I started to go down as far as we dared, but they shouted for us to go back because we might fall! We went back up as told and waited for them to arrive.

Soon, the three had ascended to a point about fifty feet below us, where they could stop and rest. They pointed to their bags indicating that they had something for us. We shouted at them to forget the bags and come on up, but they merely waved and picked up the bags. The only assistance they allowed us to give them was a hand at the top. Even here, the slope was steep enough to make walking somewhat precarious, but it was nothing compared to what they had just climbed.

At this point, we offered to carry their bags, but they emphatically refused, saying there were "Eggs!" in the bags and we might break them if we tried to carry them.

The pretty little girls were about nine to eleven years old and from the nearby village of Valle. Earlier, we had complimented them about their good looks and presented them with portraits. They had managed to get eggs and cigarettes from their families to give to us. When we asked them why they took such a long and precarious route, they said it was because of our warning to the village parents about children being noticed if they continued to visit us by the regular route. We were simply amazed by this. Later, when eating the eggs we remarked

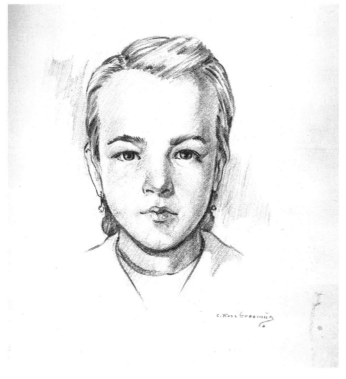

"This is Lilia one of our little sweethearts who brought us food and sometimes a few cigarettes. (Drawn from life)." A Wartime Log

When they presented the socks to us, we were completely overcome and humbled by the consideration and favors of these kind people. They were doing what they could to help us in our difficult circumstances. I realized that a gift means so much more when it comes from someone who has so little to begin with. The villagers were suffering very hard times during these war years.

Late one afternoon in March 1944, one of the young girls who had climbed the mountain to give us cigarettes and eggs came to our cave in a state of excitement. She

about how much better they tasted because of the little girls' incredible determination and efforts.

As time went on, we made several attempts to improve our footwear. Of course, acquiring good shoes was virtually impossible, but we were able to get some rags, which by a stretch of the imagination, we converted into something resembling socks. The young children noticed our plight in this regard. Unbeknownst to us, they brought the matter up with a schoolteacher, Mrs. Elena Magini Borgnolo. By taking up a collection from all of the pupils, they were able to buy wool yarn from a village at the foot of the mountains.

Three families knitted up some beautiful socks and some of the children brought them to the cave. They casually mentioned that they had something for each of us.

told us that two patriots had learned where we were hiding from one of the villagers, and they were on the way to find us. She explained that the informant had been given considerable wine to loosen his tongue, otherwise he wouldn't have said a thing. We told her to head back to the village and we would meet the patriots somewhere on the trail.

After she left, we climbed to the mountaintop and waited on the trail for their arrival. Soon, we saw the two patriots walking along the track assisting a very drunk villager who was guiding them to us. Before they reached the cave, we stopped them and asked what they wanted.

"Your friend, the patriot commissar, is here and wants to see you in the village tonight! We are his bodyguards and have brought him back from Yugoslavia."

In the event that this might be some kind of trick, we decided that it would be best if only two of us went. One of us should stay and watch the cave. Consequently, Bob and I went to Valle, while Jack remained at the cave. If Bob and I walked into a trap, Jack might be able to escape and later tell of our fate.

We approached the village with caution, coming in from a side approach after watching the town for nearly thirty minutes. We proceeded to the wine shop and entered one at a time. It wasn't a trap. My friend, Mr. Grunta, who I hadn't seen for some three months, was there buying wine for everyone. He jumped up and threw his arms about us and shook our hands vigorously. Then he took us to a table at the back of the shop and filled up a large glass of wine. His men had been attacking German airfields.

"I've made all the arrangements as I promised. You'll be able to leave within three weeks to go to an airdrome where you will be flown back to your own lines. I have checked all along the line and have made preparations for you to get through. You have to wait three weeks because the weather will be bad for that much longer, but you will be able to travel after that time. It will take you about two weeks of walking to get to where you need to go."

Bob spoke up, "But Jack and I were in Yugoslavia for two months and were with patriots who wouldn't help us. Why will they help us now?"

Grunta replied, "That was because many Germans disguised themselves as escaping prisoners last winter and made lots of trouble for the patriots. Now I have made arrangements for you and they will trust you and know you are coming. They would like to help all escaped prisoners, but they

Elio Borgnolo of Valle. A Wartime Log

lost a lot of men last winter trying to get too many through. Now there are very few who are trying to get through and it is much easier."

"Bob and I will go back to our cave and talk it over with Jack. If you are around in the next few days, we will see you and let you know if we want to try it again," I told him.

We stayed awhile longer and had more wine. After we left the inn, we visited the Borgnolo's house. Again over wine, we were discussing the possibilities of leaving the region when a young woman broke into the room shouting, "The Germans are in town and have surrounded the entire place!"

We quickly walked into the cobbled streets and headed out a back way to our favorite creek bed, which was half full of water. We left the area without being seen.

Back at the cave, we told Jack about the plan, but he wasn't in favor of it, having tried that route before only to be disappointed. I was for making a try when the three weeks were up. Finally, we agreed we'd attempt it, but if we met too much difficulty at first, we'd change course and head south across the Po Valley and see if we could make it to our lines in that direction. At least by then the weather would be better and we'd be able to sleep out in the open without much discomfort.

Early the next morning, the schoolteacher's husband, Elio Borgnolo, arrived at the cave's entrance. He was concerned about the fact that the patriots knew where our cave was located. He thought we'd be foolish if we didn't leave the cave for another place.

Elio took us downhill about two miles and showed us another cave that had been used by some escaped prisoners

for 11 months during World War I. It was well concealed, but much damper and less comfortable than ours. It also was quite far from the nearest village, which would make our trips for food more difficult.

We didn't think the danger was great enough for us to move. We believed the patriots wouldn't bother us and that our cave was more secure than the other one. Our friend left a little discouraged because he hadn't convinced us to move. We appreciated his concern, though.

The weather was bright and warm the next day. Early in the morning, air raid sirens could be heard moaning in the plains below. Bob and I decided to climb to the top of the hill to watch any action that might be coming our way. As we left the cave, we saw Jerry fighters scurrying up from their airstrips. From the numbers of Focke Wulf 190s that were taking to the air, it was easy to see that they expected something big coming.

Just as Bob and I reached the top of a peak overlooking the entire countryside, we heard the distant rumble of approaching bombers. The sound came from the direction of Yugoslavia and the German fighter planes were heading out in that direction. Soon, the Allied bombers came into sight. They were tiny specks high in the sky, flying in elements of three and closely bunched in flights of nine planes. The different flights were closely staggered to provide mutual protection. I counted over 150 before a tremendous air battle broke out right over our heads.

The Jerry fighters had aligned themselves in string formations, with two strings simultaneously attacking either side of the bomber formation. The Germans opened fire with their 20-mm cannons at great range. The thunderous reply of the bombers' machine guns particularly impressed me. Thousands of .50 caliber slugs were being fired at the attacking Jerries. From a distance of about two miles behind the formations, we saw incendiary and tracer bullets hitting the ground in a large pattern, kicking up dirt and starting small fires as the incendiaries exploded on impact.

I'd never seen such a spectacle. The bullets had spent themselves as they came down and whistled through the air like angry hornets. Their numbers were unbelievable, and it alarmed us that they were coming right at us.

Bob and I hit the dirt in between some rocks while spent slugs smacked and plopped on the ground all around us. The incendiaries started several fires within a quarter mile. Peering from the rocks, we saw a bomber losing altitude fast with a thin trail of smoke behind it. Then almost over our heads, four chutes appeared—tiny specks hanging motionless thousand of feet above us. At first, it appeared they might land on our mountain, but as they dropped lower it was apparent that the wind was blowing them toward the valley.

The bomber flew straight for about a mile, started a dive, and then crashed squarely into a German military compound near Udine. An ugly column of black smoke marked the spot. Just beyond, the first bomb blasts began blossoming in the railroad station, and then airdromes on the far side of town disappeared in huge clouds of smoke and dust. Five columns of smoke showed where German fighters paid the price of braving the wall of fire from the formation's murderous machine guns.

We'd seen many air raids from our mountain retreat, but this was the biggest yet. Axis planes burned where they stood on the airfields. Flak gunners blasted back at our bombers, but with no effect that could be seen. The gun blasts could be heard almost as clearly as the exploding bombs. After the bombers departed, the straggling remnants of the fighter formations landed back at the fields.

Bob and I headed downhill in an attempt to intercept the parachuting crew members, if possible, and have them hide out with us. Unfortunately, the Germans captured all of them except one man who escaped into the hills. We set out to find him.

In the first village we went to, we learned that the fellow had been seen heading up the mountain and was reported to be carrying 2,000 lire with him. The next party who saw him claimed he had 77,000 lire. The next morning, we heard he carried 77,000,000 lire on his person. It didn't take long for a story to grow in these hills.

Our efforts to find this man were fruitless because we entered communities where the local residents didn't know us. They thought we might be German spies. We never did locate him, though on one occasion I'm sure we were in the same town as he was.[1]

After the big air raid, we learned that Grunta and his two bodyguards were staying in the little cavern where I first hid out. We decided to visit him and tell him that we would accept his invitation to escape through Yugoslavia. At the same time, we wanted to hear the latest radio broadcast from America at the padre's house.

We started the four-mile walk early. On arriving in Masarolis, I went to the padre's house while Bob and Jack stood guard at the edge of town to watch for enemy patrols. The news was most discouraging. Since the time of my escape six months earlier, the Allies had advanced only a short distance up the Italian peninsula and still were south of Rome.

All along we'd been hoping that an Allied seaborne invasion would land somewhere on the northern Adriatic Coast near where we were. I'd even pictured in my mind how I'd make my way to safety when our front lines were established at nearby Trieste or Venice. I'd also struggled in my imagination over how I'd get through the German lines, but I'd pictured it all happening right in this vicinity. I suppose wishful thinking had convinced me it couldn't happen any place else. Now it was certain that our lines weren't going to advance toward us any time soon. We'd have to make it back on our own.

I met Bob and Jack at the edge of the village where I relayed the bad news to them, and then we went to Grunta's hideout. The two bodyguards, with their machine guns, rifles, and hand grenades, had turned the cave into a small fort. We missed the little commissar, who was out on the prowl for food. We visited for a while and told them we would see them later, nearer the time for our departure to Yugoslavia. Then, we'd meet to learn the details about what we were to do and where we were to go. We returned to our cave for the night. ✤

NOTE

1. "Later when I was a POW in Stalag Luft 1, I met the pilot of the B-17 that was shot down. He informed me that the man we'd been following through the villages was the flight engineer and he was successful in contacting the underground and returning to our lines."

*"Bob at work—The bed in our cave
in the mountains. We spent 3 months
in it. (Drawn in the cave)."*
A Wartime Log

CHAPTER THIRTEEN

Recapture

Early in the morning on March 23, 1944, I awoke to the sound of machine gun fire down the cliff from our cave. I didn't pay much attention to it, since we'd been hearing this kind of thing for so long.

I dozed off again and must have been asleep for about 30 minutes. Suddenly, an ear splitting crash awakened me! I thought the cave ceiling was falling in. A couple of small boulders had dropped down, and dust and smoke filled the cave. I jumped to the fireplace where it was safest from falling rock. Bob and Jack were sitting upright in bed with a look of disbelief in their eyes. Then I looked up at the ground sheet covering the cave entrance and saw that it was full of holes. I realized we'd been fired upon from the outside.

"Jerries!" I exclaimed. "It looks like we have had it." I could hear shouting outside and it wasn't in Italian.

Then we all started yelling back. "Cut it out, you stupid bastards, you're going to hurt someone!"

Suddenly, Bob dashed for the door, shouting, "They'll chuck a hand grenade next if we don't come out!" He was an old infantryman and was pretty wise to these things.

"Wave something white, Bob!" I warned. "They might shoot you as you go out the door."

Bob grabbed an old dirty towel and stuck it out first, then followed. Outside he confronted a man in full battle gear holding a submachine gun in one hand and a hand grenade in the other.

"You are American," he said. "How many are there?"

"I'm the only one," answered Bob.

The soldier refused to believe this and demanded that the others come out immediately.

Bob called down to us and we came out.

The German patrol took a quick look in the cave, then the leader turned to us, saying, " I'm a doctor, are you hurt?"

We were so frightened that we didn't have the presence of mind to even notice if we'd been hit. We said "No." Later, Bob noticed he'd been grazed by a bullet along the top of his scalp.

The doctor smiled at us and said, "You're all very lucky as I was about to throw this grenade into the cave when you didn't come out right away, but since I can speak English, I understood your shouting and didn't want to kill any Americans. I'm not German, I'm an Austrian. I'm sorry I caught you, because I was looking for patriots. Since I'm with German soldiers, I am sorry, but you're now my prisoners."

My knees shook so badly that I could scarcely stand. I looked at Bob and Jack. They were in about the same shape. We'd come about as close as you could to getting killed. The doctor complimented our arrangements in the cave. He gave us cigarettes and let us eat up our food. They also let me keep some of my pictures. We were told to take our blankets and a few things and then we were marched away. As we rested at the top of the cliff, I took a long look at the trail leading to the hideout.

"How'd you find the cave?" I asked the doctor.

He explained, "We'd been looking for patriots all morning and had come up the valley you see below us. We shot two patriots just below your cave, and were climbing on up the cliff when we stopped to rest at the top. I noticed one footprint in the loose dirt and couldn't figure out why it would be there, so I went down to investigate. I then saw another print and discovered a place where you had covered up some other prints. This led me to the cave, where I shot into the entrance."

We well knew the brutal, no-quarter-given type of warfare that was going on between the Germans and partisans in this border area of Italy, Yugoslavia, and Austria. We were indeed lucky that he recognized us as "Americans," since Austrian and German soldiers generally adhered to the Geneva Convention regarding Americans and Brits, but not so with captured patriots who they normally shot on the spot.

We joined the main German column and marched into nearby Valle. The villagers knew what had happened by the time we arrived. Many were in tears as we walked through. This was humiliating because these people thought we were

"Looking south—The Adriatic Sea and the town [Cividale] where we were first taken after recapture. Our cave was in the hill from which this picture was drawn." A Wartime Log

invincible. We saw the schoolteacher, Elena Borgnolo, standing on her upstairs porch crying hard. We felt we'd let these people down after all their efforts to help us.

We continued on a long trek with the large column as they patrolled for patriots, but none were found. We reached the base of the mountains late in the afternoon and then began a march I'll never forget. The German commander wanted to show us how tough his troops were and we walked for about ten miles without stopping. Of course, we were just as determined to show him that we were as tough as his men. We kept up the pace as best we could. Carrying our personal gear and blankets was our biggest problem. We shifted loads from one to another as we walked along to keep from getting too tired.

About 1 AM, we arrived in Cividale at the garrison courtyard. Several of the younger soldiers passed out when we stopped, which indicates the difficulty of the long hike. My head was swimming and my leg was so sore that I could scarcely stand on my feet, but I was determined to show the Germans that I could take it.

We were kept at the garrison for three days and interrogated. I was sent to the intelligence officer, who told me I'd face serious charges for being caught behind the lines in civilian clothes. I pointed out that I did have some articles of my uniform on my person, and carried insignia for my rank and branch of service. I pointed out, too, that if I were a spy I wouldn't be hiding out in a cave in isolation where I'd be ineffective. I also mentioned that German soldiers, despite many opportunities, never recognized me as an escaped Allied soldier. The officer angrily sent me back to my cell.

On our way north by train, we stopped at a camp in Spital, Austria, located about 125 miles north of Cividale. As we marched down the streets of the town, the column passed close to a horse and wagon. When I stepped alongside the wagon, the horse suddenly swung his head out and bit me viciously on the left arm just below the shoulder. I was so angry I wanted to go back and kick the horse, but the

guard prodded me on with his gun. At Spittal, our blankets were taken from us and we were left with nothing but the clothes we had on. The night wasn't very cold, however, so we slept fairly well.

When leaving the next day, we approached the same horse. We tried to steer a guard close enough to the brute that he'd get bit. The horse lunged at him, but the guard must have known the ways of horses, as he eluded the attack with ease.

We boarded another train heading west and were given Red Cross parcels. We ate until we nearly burst and smoked cigarettes until we just about "spun in." The chocolate disappeared and we ate powdered milk like it was candy. Soon our mouths were all stuck up with powdered milk, butter, and sugar all mixed together. We became quite woozy after the first hour of this "bash."

We learned from other prisoners riding the train that we were being taken to a punishment camp at Landeck, Austria, only a few miles northeast of the Swiss border and right amongst the high Alps. The snows were so deep that it would be impossible for anyone to go far if he managed to escape from the camp.

Two men guarded us, with the ranking soldier appearing to be a corporal. The soldier of lower rank always was saluting the corporal and seemed quite afraid of him. We waited until the German corporal left the car, then we gave the other guard some cigarettes. He allowed us to linger and talk to the other prisoners at their seats for a few minutes as we went to the restroom.

The other POWs were mostly South Africans who also were escapees. Like us, they'd been recaptured and now were being sent to Landeck for punishment. One, in fact, had escaped from Landeck and told us about it. From the description, it was a grim place. He told us that at first we'd be put in solitary confinement for thirty days and then put to work in the mines for another thirty days, and all the time on short rations. The British and Americans, he said, were treated

somewhat fairly, but the Russians were afforded terrible treatment.

Another prisoner, who was a Russian and a fine looking lad, but appearing very haggard, said we were in for a very bad time. He'd been in this camp before and was the only survivor from forty men taken in with him. He'd been taken out of the camp and sent to a medical facility for an examination to see why he'd survived.

He said we'd be pushing carts by hand in the mines with no mechanical assistance. We'd be required to load ore into the carts at a stiff pace, and it was rare when the carts didn't come back hauling a body or two. It was nearly impossible for a man to get adequate sustenance from the one ladle of rutabaga soup provided each day. He'd stolen a few items of food here and there and thought that was one reason why he'd survived. Also, he clearly was a sturdy individual who'd led a rugged life. It appeared he wasn't the type to complain about extreme hardships, but he was in tears as he told us this story.

I can assure you that this made a big impression on the three of us. The Russian lad was being taken back to Landeck because he'd escaped from the medical center! He'd had a miserable time running in the hills for about three months, not really knowing where to go, and he'd frozen his feet before being recaptured. He mentioned that he'd never heard of officers being brought to Landeck before.

That afternoon, the train approached the mines, which lined the hillsides. We could see men busily working small ore trucks several hundred feet above us. The snow was even deeper and the mountains were higher as we approached Landeck. Escape seemed to be an impossibility in this area.

After debarking at the station, we were escorted into the camp. Barracks covered the big flat at the base of the valley. It seemed as if mile after mile of barbed wire surrounded the place. Sentry boxes were few, but probably were unnecessary because all of the POWs were either locked up in cells or out on work details.

At just about dark, Landeck's guards relieved the train's sentries and we were taken to a German officer for cell assignments. The new guards shoved us and shouted fiercely, but we couldn't understand what they wanted. A guard coming up silently from behind knocked Jack to the ground because Jack couldn't get out of his way in time. Inside the cell block, we were searched and relieved of all cigarettes and pocket articles. Then, our shoes were taken from us and we were separated.

I was rudely shoved through a small, thick oak door into a damp cell. The door slammed shut with a crash and was secured by at least three bolts. It was so dark inside that I was dizzy at first. With nine feet of snow on the ground outside, it was easy to know why the cell felt like a freezer. I searched around in the darkness and found a table and a dirty, smelly bucket. There was absolutely nothing else in the room. My feet were wet from walking on the floor, and the table top was the only dry spot in the cell.

I sat on the oak "bed" hardly believing this really was happening to me. I thought a guard would return with some sort of bedding or they'd provide some heat. I was shivering within a few minutes, and I shouted and beat on the door, but got no response. All I heard was the yelling of other prisoners doing the same thing. I resigned myself to the inevitable, but couldn't find any way to get comfortable enough to sleep because I was shaking so much. I tried curling up on the table and holding my feet in my hands, but my back became cold. I tried jumping up and down on my "bed" to warm up, and then lying down to see if I could drop off to sleep, but it didn't work. I tried curling up under my suit coat, but it was too small.

It was a nightmare! I kept moving all night to keep from freezing to death. It was hard to tell when morning came, because barely any light came through the cell's small window located near the ceiling. The source of the outside light was another window situated thirty or forty feet down a long passageway. I was utterly exhausted by morning, but still couldn't fall asleep.

I pounded on the door until a guard came. He shoved the door open and pushed a bowl of watery soup in on the floor. It was dirty and foul, but hot, which was what I needed most. A short while later, a guard came with my shoes and motioned for me to go with him to see an officer, who recorded my name, rank, and serial number. The clerk gave a surprised look when I told him I was a Lt. Colonel. I was sent back to the cell to continue slowly freezing.

The next night, I pounded on the door until my knuckles were sore. When a guard finally came, I tried to tell him what I needed. He left for about fifteen minutes, and then returned and plopped something on the floor in my cell. I felt around in the dark and found a wet, frigid blanket that had been deliberately soaked in water. I wrung it out the best I could and pulled it over me. The night was torture, but I managed to get a few hours of sleep.

The next morning, I was taken to the camp commandant's office to be interrogated and told what would be expected of me. Two officers, covered with the usual braid and medals, were waiting in the room looking very impressed with themselves.

They looked up, expecting me to salute them, but I just stood there. The younger officer looked at me scornfully, saying in English, "Don't you know you are supposed to salute your superior officers?"

"I don't know your ranks and can't tell if you are senior officers or not," I answered.

"Surely you can tell we are officers. That should be enough."

"I am an American officer," I said. "A Lieutenant Colonel."

Both officers looked startled and the younger one said, "If you are a Lieutenant Colonel, what are you doing here? This camp is for enlisted men only. You wouldn't have been sent here if you were an officer!"

I presented my insignia of rank, saying, "I don't know how I can prove I am an officer, but I am. If your intelligence system is as good as you say it is, you should be able to tell me my rank rather than having me tell you. The other two men who came in with me also are officers."

The older man, apparently the commandant, replied in broken English, "There must be some mistake. I suggest you go back to your room until we call for you again."

"Do you call that refrigerator a room?" I declared. "If the treatment I am getting here is an example of the character of the German people, then I understand even better why we're fighting you."

"What do you expect as a prisoner of war!" they snapped back.

"Nothing much more than what I am getting now, but I just can't help think what suckers we were to give Germans the things we did when we captured so many of them in our combat zone. We, at least, treated them better than dogs."

I was taken away for a couple of hours. When I returned, both officers stood up and saluted me as I came in the door. It was obvious something had changed since my last visit. They asked me to be seated and the younger officer proceeded to lecture me on the history of the German Reich and why they were fighting the war. He used all the eloquence he could muster to impress me about their cause and how wrong we were to have entered the war against them.

"You Americans seem to have come into the war just for the fun of it. We recently shot down some of your airmen who'd formed a club called 'Murder Incorporated.' You do nothing but bomb our homes and villages where there are no military objectives. We have lost hundreds of thousands of civilians whose deaths couldn't possibly help you win the war. We also know you employ gangsters and pay them for every flight they make over our country to kill civilians. Can you answer any of these statements?"

I replied, "I've seen quite a difference between the German soldiers and ourselves, and I am convinced more than

ever that we're fighting for a better cause than you ever could be. You are victims of your own propaganda. Do I look like a gangster? Do I look like a person who'd get pleasure out of killing innocent people? I'm a typical American flyer and if I am guilty of the things you claim of the others, you'd better kill me now because I'm just the same as them.

"I have one interest and that is to end this war as soon as possible with no other outcome than complete victory for us. I'm not prepared to discuss the political aspects of the war with you at length because I'm forbidden to do so by my government, and because you are a trained interrogation officer. I have no intention of giving you information of any type. I suggest you put me back in my cell, or put me to work in the mines, or do whatever you'd planned for me because I'm not going to talk any further."

He said, "But you must know that we didn't intend that you or the other two be sent here. It was a mistake for officers to be brought here. You will be taken away just as soon as we can get orders directing us where to send you."

I answered, "It's your mistake to send any man to a place like this! It gives each and every one a better reason to see just what we are fighting against, and what we want to prevent from happening in our own countries!" I went on to tell him about how I'd been treated.

"We shall move you to another room right away," he said apologetically.

I was taken away and led to a cell block where Jack, Bob, and I soon were reunited in a room with a window. It was cold, but we slept close together and each of us had a blanket, so we kept fairly warm. We received one meal a day and the remaining food from our Red Cross parcels was returned. After six days, we were sent on.

Two guards escorted us to a train. We boarded, and the train continued in the direction of Germany, but the first evening we were left waiting at a station, where we'd apparently missed a connection. The guards turned us over to the local Gestapo for safe keeping that evening. This turned out to be the worst night of all. We were taken into a guard room, and were pushed and searched by guards who constantly screamed at us. They seemed infuriated because we couldn't understand German. Then we were led into a damp, stinking cell block. The doors in the long row of barred cells were bolted shut, with the exception of the three that we were to occupy.

A Gestapo guard, who was blind in one eye, pointed to a small door. I took one look inside and hesitated just inside the doorway, while stooping low so my head would miss the door top. The guard shouted and kicked me in the back, sending me sprawling inside. He slammed the heavy door shut and shoved home the bolts with a vengeance. It was so cold inside that I couldn't believe it. I heard sounds emanating from other inmates down the cell block; they must have been civilian offenders of the Reich. Their loud moans and violent coughing were evidence that they were in terrible pain or close to death.

I felt around in my pockets and found my matches and a book that hadn't been taken from me. I lit a match and looked around. The bed consisted of the customary plank with a board for a pillow. Unless I could do something, I'd freeze to death. I pounded on the door and shouted, but got no response. Then with the light from another match, I tried to find something to burn. I only saw the board and table. I tried lying down, but was soon back on my feet trying to keep warm.

I pulled the book from my pocket, and began tearing out the pages to line my clothes with them. The book's title, *His Hour* by Eleanor Gwinn, seemed to fit my predicament at this critical moment in time and I couldn't get it out of my head. I removed my clothes and began lining my cold torso with the pages. First, I covered my feet and pulled my socks over the small paper sheets to keep them in place. Fortunately, I had on long underwear, which held the pages securely over the rest of my body. I wrapped my head with more of the small paper sheets and pulled my hat down over my ears.[1]

Doing this warmed me up and I actually felt comfortable for a few minutes. I lay down, but soon was shivering and growing numb from the cold. I got up and paced the floor, swinging my arms, but I soon grew tired of this.

This was worse than the first night in the cell at Landeck. I pounded the door again and again. I bunched up some of the leftover pages from the book and lit a fire on the stone floor. This warmed me slightly for a few seconds. I lit several more pages, but at this rate I'd soon be out of paper. I took the board that was supposed to be used for a pillow and broke it up into small pieces and built a fire, which I practically smothered with my body while trying to absorb all of the heat from it.

Much to my dismay, the smoke filled the cell so completely that I had to lie on the floor to breathe. When the embers went out, the residue smoke was so bad I choked. For the rest of the night, I thrashed about at ten minute intervals to keep from freezing to death.

I swore I'd return to the jail someday and kill the guard who escorted me to this cell. Then I'd dynamite this place and erase it from the face of the earth. I'd never had an urge to kill a man before, but that night I had murder in my heart. It was a feeling that I never before thought I'd have. When the jailer brought soup in the morning, I intended to throw it squarely back in his face. I didn't get that satisfaction, however, because they didn't feed us.

When our escort, fresh from a good night's sleep, came to get us in the morning, he had the nerve to ask, "Schlafen gut?" It was fortunate for me that this soldier couldn't understand English because I used every cuss word in my vocabulary and invented a few new ones. We marched through sleet and rain to the train, arriving soaking wet and numb with cold. My feet were frostbitten and giving me pain.

That evening, I was sick and miserable when we arrived at a New Zealand POW camp at a place called Eichstadt,

KRIEGSGEFANGENENLAGER;

Capt. George R. Bennett (New Zealand), a POW in Oflag VIIB, Germany, to Mrs. C.W. Greening, April 24, 1944—"In case you have not had news of your son Charles (0-22443) I saw him early this month with two New Zealand boys in Germany. I asked the Red Cross to cable which you may have read by now. He appeared to be fit and well & we managed to supply him with Red Cross food and clothes & cigs. He may not be able to write until he reaches his proper camp but this may serve you to expect mail from him soon."

where we again were tossed into the cooler. I was getting mighty sick of coolers by this time. We tried to get a glimpse around the camp and Bob succeeded in seeing a fellow he knew from home. This man saw us enter the cooler and it wasn't too many days before a message was delivered to us. He wanted to know our home addresses and how we were doing so he could notify our folks. We got the information out to him.

We spent a number of days at Eichstadt. Our civilian clothes were exchanged for proper uniforms and we were issued a food parcel, all furnished by the Red Cross. On the second day, I met an English speaking guard and I asked him some questions.

He retorted, "You are a prisoner of war! You are to do as you are told and not ask questions!"

He looked like a fairly regular guy, however, so I continued to talk to him. "You must have some terrible grudge against Americans to treat us the way you do. How much good do you think it will do?"

He told me that he'd been held as a prisoner in America during Word War I and had a tough time there. After talking to him for awhile, I realized his problems hadn't been so bad. It was only because it took so long to get to a prison camp that it had been hard for him.

I told him, "I believe the reason you Germans are fighting this war is because you are such poor losers that you couldn't take the whipping you got in the last one. You're trying to make up for it this time. I've actually met lots of good Germans, but they are American citizens. It's hard to find a good soldier inside Germany. It's easy to tell who the ones are that haven't been on the front lines. They're the ones who take advantage of the helpless."

The guard looked hurt when I mentioned the good soldier bit and he said nothing more. That night, he smuggled in three chocolate bars. Of course, our country's Red Cross originally sent them, but still he did me a favor by getting them to me. I gave one each to Bob and Jack in the adjoining cells.

I had an overcoat and blanket in my cell and could rest fairly well. I couldn't shake the cold, but I slept as much as possible. I looked forward to sleeping because I had wonderful dreams about home and traveling all over the world as free as a bird. Sometimes, Jack, Bob, and I would sing to each other through the peek holes in the doors. We even tried harmonizing, until the guards objected and made us stop.

The Red Cross parcels weren't issued until after our interviews with the commandant. When we asked him why we were being kept here for so long, he said it was to properly identify us and to arrange permanent assignments to POW camps. The German food consisted of black bread, thin horse meat soup, and sometimes a small piece of cheese. Other meals consisted of raw fish. After receiving a Red Cross parcel, we thought we were eating like kings. The parcels actually contained only about $2 worth of provisions, but under the circumstances it seemed to be the best food in the world.

A New Zealand sergeant, who'd been arrested for violating German regulations and was being held for a court martial, was in the same cell block with us. At first, he had some freedom of movement and was able to talk to us through the peek holes in our doors. When we spoke to him, an air raid alarm sounded and the distant drone of planes could be heard. I asked him if he'd seen many air attacks while at this camp. He said there'd been only a few.

However, during the last raid, which occurred not too many days prior to our arrival, Allied planes had passed fairly close to the camp. Of course, the boys in the compound shouted and cheered, not realizing how the Germans might react. The guards opened fire on the crowd and killed two boys outright. After that, directives were announced that POWs were not allowed to go outside or look out of windows during an air raid. It was a hard way to learn the rules.

Notification finally came that we were being transferred to permanent camps. We traveled together by train to a fairly large city in Germany, where we were split up. Bob and Jack were scheduled to go to a camp in East Sudetenland in southeast Germany while I was assigned to an American compound on the Baltic. Somehow, the guards mixed us up and they mistook Bob for me. Consequently, Jack and I were taken to Prague, Czechoslovakia, while Bob was sent toward Berlin.

After we were well on our separate ways, the guards discovered the error. They frantically sent telegrams and switched trains to get us back together again. Jack and I were being held in a station when Bob finally was brought back and exchanged for me. My guards were angry and blamed us for the mishap. However, one of the guards who picked me up was a fairly good natured sort and, judging from his ribbons, had seen quite a lot of action. He indicated that he was tired of the war and knew the Nazis were losing.

As we passed through the larger cities in Germany, I saw the terrible impact of our bombing. The industrial areas were battered and smashed. Repairs had been made to the factories that hadn't been damaged too badly, but others were beyond salvage. Many people were without homes and had constructed flimsy shelters out of salvaged sheet metal and wood scraps, creating shanty towns. Many other families lived in the air raid shelters.

At one station, several soldiers entered my compartment and became quite friendly. One could speak a little Italian, so we were able to carry on a conversation. He told me that Germany was finished and it was only a question of time until he'd be a prisoner and I'd be the guard. He described how the population was suffering and, in so many words, said Hitler was a bum. Most Germans had been led to believe that the United States would remain neutral. When America entered the world conflict, most Germans became convinced that the Nazis would lose the war, but they dared not say so for fear of imprisonment or death. This accommodating soldier pointed out sites of interest as we traveled along. Finally, I grew tired and dozed off.

STAND BY FOR CRASH LANDING *"Lt. G.S. Zebrowski was first pilot on a Flying Fort. On February 21, 1944, during a mission against an airdrome at Gotha, Germany, enemy fighters inflicted heavy damage. Forced to leave the formation, 'Zeb' hit the deck, undergoing constant, fierce attack by fifteen ME-109s and FW-190s. All rear guns and turrets out of action made the Fort an easy target. A crash landing ended the episode but the engineer and co-pilot were already dead."* Not as Briefed

I was aroused by a hand on my shoulder and presumed it was a guard, so I sleepily got up and followed him out of the carriage. When I stepped down onto the station platform, the man I was following disappeared into the crowd. I shook the sleepiness from my head, trying to figure out what was happening. I walked along a few steps and suddenly was grabbed by the shoulder from behind. It was one of my guards, who thought I was attempting to escape.

I then realized that I'd accidentally been following the soldier with whom I'd had the friendly talk. As he was preparing to get off the train at the station, he'd given me a

kindly pat on the shoulder. Being sound asleep, I'd presumed that my guard had wakened me to follow him. My guards, however, were dozing too and had been thrown into a panic when they noticed I was gone. They shoved me back into the car as I tried to explain what had happened. I'd almost escaped without even intending to do so.

The train approached Berlin the next morning. When entering the city's outskirts, bomb craters were few at first and scattered rather haphazardly near smaller targets and objectives. As the train proceeded closer to the main parts of the city, however, the bomb damage and rubble became far

more evident. Soon, there wasn't an undamaged building to be seen.

One of the guards gestured to me, cautioning me not to laugh or smile when I looked at the effects of the bombing or it would invite disaster. I didn't need a warning; I knew how I'd feel towards German airmen if they'd bombed my country.

The train stopped at a battered station and my guards took me down into a subway tunnel. I was impressed by the subway system. The stations were well built and artistically designed, and the modern subway cars provided a smooth ride. Green tile covered the tunnel walls and indirect lighting provided illumination. Huge throngs of people were jammed into the subway, but there was little talk and no laughter. The number of well-dressed people that I saw surprised me.

An unusual number of men hobbled about on crutches minus a leg and many other soldiers and civilians were swathed in bandages. Few seemed to notice me because my clothing was similar to the uniforms worn by a branch of the German military. Thank goodness I wasn't conspicuous.

When we reached our destination and went up to street level, we had to climb over fallen beams and timbers. The station was in shambles and workmen were picking about in the ruins, trying to clean up part of the mess. Below ground, however, I didn't see where any damage had been done to the subway tunnels; the bombing attacks affected only the system's surface sites.

I didn't know where we were going and didn't attempt to ask. Apparently my guards were looking for some sort of headquarters. Whole city blocks were flattened or in ruins and we walked around tremendous piles of rubble in the streets. When we arrived at the correct address, the building was just a mass of stones and wreckage. We went back to the subway and the search continued.

Six times we left the subway and walked in the streets. I was tired and my feet were extremely sore. Each step sent spikes of pain shooting through my toes. I appreciated the opportunity of seeing this famous target firsthand, but I also felt uneasy about staying too long. Twice we hurried into subway tunnels at the sound of air raid sirens, but no bombs fell. Buildings were standing at only one of the places where we came out at street level.

Finally, we stopped at a bomb-damaged hotel that had formerly offered fine accommodations, with statues and paintings lining the hallways. All the rooms had been damaged, requiring repairs or refurbishing in some manner to make them usable again. Some rooms consisted of nothing but the original floor with temporary fabricated walls and ceilings. I tried to picture this same scene at the Winthrop Hotel in Tacoma, Washington, or the Waldorf Astoria in New York; and it made me shudder to think what might have happened if the war had gone against us.

We ate in a cafeteria section where the Red Cross provided a bowl of pea soup. One guard left and came back with three mugs of beer for us. I quaffed mine down in short order and gave him a big "Danke." This seemed to please him, so he went out again and returned with another three beers. I said a couple of more "Dankes" and downed my beer in a few gulps.

We proceeded to a formerly elegant dining room in the basement and stretched out on three tables to sleep. The tables must have been made of softer wood than those I'd previously slept on because I immediately fell asleep. In the back of my mind I worried about air raids, but no bombers came during the night.

I awoke about midway through the night. I looked about, trying to figure out where I was. The lights were on and I saw a number of German soldiers lying about on tables and benches. It took me a few minutes to remember that I was a prisoner. My guards were sleeping soundly on benches on either side of me. I needed to locate the rest room and started up the stairs.

FIGHTER'S FINISH *"Lt. Col. Mark E. Hubbard of St. Paul, Minnesota, was on a low altitude strafing mission over France, March 18, 1944. Set afire in Number One engine by light flak he rolled his ship over and bailed out at eight hundred feet and was taken P.O.W. immediately. Col. Hubbard had certainly not been briefed for this event!"* Not as Briefed

About halfway up, I remembered that I should tell the guards because they'd get upset if they awoke and noticed my absence. I didn't feel much like trying to escape. Berliners had no love for Americans and they might want to find one wandering about loose; many of our lads ended up on the end of a rope in Berlin. I went back and shook one of the guards, frightening him out of his wits. He jumped to his feet thinking I had a gun in my hand. When I requested to go to the bathroom, he looked a little ashamed and allowed me to go without a guard. Some soldiers were awake in the rooms above, but most were asleep. Not one so much as raised an eyebrow at me.

In the morning, we continued searching for the headquarters; although unsuccessful, we did see a lot more of Berlin. The guards didn't attempt to make conversation. In places, people were picking around in the ruins looking for victims or articles of value. The rubble was being cleared from the streets, but I saw no efforts being made toward reconstruction. An intact room was visible now and then in a building where people were attempting to rehabilitate it for a living space. Window glass was unavailable and cardboard was used to replace broken panes. In many window frames, extensive repairs had been made by carefully arranging pieces of broken glass.

I didn't see one car or truck, military or civilian, moving about in the wrecked streets. The only operative transportation systems were the railroad and the subway. Around noon, we returned to the railroad yard. The once modern terminal was a mass of shattered wreckage and only the bare metal framework remained from its glass plated dome. Following the bombing attacks, the wreckage had been cleared and piled alongside the railways, and the tracks had been repaired. Burned and smashed railroad cars littered the yards. It was difficult to understand how railway transportation was maintained under these conditions. Thousands of people were jammed into the ruined terminal and everybody carried their own provisions, including water.

When the train stopped to load, a horde of people rushed to get seats, leaving the latecomers to scramble just to find a place to stand. I saw numerous other prisoners being herded through the station, but none were Americans. The Italian POWs looked disheveled and miserable. I spoke to some of them as we passed by, but guards ended the conversations.

I was taken to a compartment and seated with some soldiers. The train slowly pulled out of the station. I was on the last stage of my journey to one of the German air force's prison camps for Allied airmen. ✪

NOTE

1. One of the pages from the book is preserved in Ross Greening's "A Wartime Log," 1944–45.

COUNTING THE HOURS BY BLOCK NINE *"Block Nine was the 'wheel shed'*: all the field grade officers lived there. What they saw as they came out of their block is reproduced in this picture. Sun-bathing Kriegies were numerous—it was one of the few pleasures afforded them during their stay at Stalag. *'Wheel.' POW term for staff officers."* Not as Briefed

CHAPTER FOURTEEN

STALAG LUFT 1

On April 18, 1944, the train left the outskirts of Berlin and traveled fast, arriving at Barth, Germany, in about four hours. Barth stood close to the Baltic Sea, about 125 miles due north of Berlin. It was a small village appearing to be hundreds of years old. As we marched through the streets toward Stalag Luft 1, we passed a church that looked as ancient as time itself. In the months ahead, its tall, red stone spire would become very familiar to me because it was the most prominent object that could be seen outside the camp.

Down the road, I spotted a huge building looking like a dormitory, which I thought was the POW compound. Later, I learned it was a flak gunnery school with all of the modern conveniences and comforts. We passed by it, and then I saw a maze of low, unpainted wooden barracks surrounded by endless barbed wire. The wire was mounted on double fences, with tangle wire between, and a trip wire located on the barracks' side. Guard towers also dotted the camp perimeter and stood at least twice as high as any of the other structures. Gloomy looking guards stood behind immense spotlights and ugly machine guns poking out of the towers.

Within a half mile of the camp, I heard the din of a cheering crowd. It sounded like a baseball game in progress

and I knew that could only mean one thing—Americans! During these times, nobody in Europe except Americans would be shouting like that. I felt elated and wanted to break into a run. I hadn't seen an American in over six months. I spotted a crowd of boys in an open area amongst the dirty looking barracks. They cheered and jumped up and down like they didn't have a care in the world. Disconsolate looking German guards (or "Goons" as I'd soon learn we called them) in their wrinkled, gray overcoats stared at the "crazy" Americans.

I was admitted at the gate, escorted to a barracks, and led into a room and told to strip. My clothing was carefully inspected, but nothing suspicious was found. I was allowed to dress and taken to see a German major named von Miller. I learned later that he was the camp intelligence officer. He was a dapper looking fellow who'd seen better days. His glance at me made me feel that he was terribly impressed with himself.

"I'd like you to answer a few questions," he said rather casually.

I broke in, "My only answers will be that my name is Charles R. Greening, service number 0-22443, and I'm a Lieutenant Colonel. I've been constantly interrogated since entering this country. I've been treated badly and I've seen things that have given me an impression of the Germans that I'll never forget. If you want any other answers you'll have to use third degree methods."

"You seem overly bitter, Colonel," he said. "I'm not going to torture you or try and get military information. All I need to know is what type of aircraft you were flying, as we have to keep a file on all of the men here. Of course, we know already, but I'd have to send away for the information. Now if you please, tell me the type of airplane you were flying?"

"I have nothing more to say. If you already know, I don't need to tell you."

"OK, you may go now!" he said with some irritation.

Tower at Stalag Luft 1. Note the guard in the window.

A guard came and took me away. At last! I was going to be eating food and smoking American cigarettes provided by the Red Cross, and seeing some friends who were bound to be here. I felt like jumping in the air and shouting for joy, but I restrained myself and calmly walked alongside the guard. We stopped at a shower room where he told me to undress and wash up while my clothes were deloused. A shower! This was too much! I hadn't been able to truly bathe in months. My skin was fairly crawling for want of a good washing.

I tore off my clothes and headed for the shower room, but was told to wait for other men who'd be taking a shower too. They wouldn't turn on the hot water for less than twenty men at a time. I took a peek into the shower room, which was about the size of a large clothes closet. There were ten outlets, under which all of us would crowd together and wash for two minutes. In a short while, twenty men came in. All were excited about getting a monthly shower.

I stopped the first man and said, "You're the first American I've seen or spoken to in seven months. How are things in the States and how are you getting along?"

"Yeah?" he answered. "Gee, I dunno, I guess everything is OK—well I gotta go get my shower now." He quickly got under a tap and waited for the water to come on. I'd just completed my first conversation with one of my countrymen in more than half a year!

I went into the shower and soaked up as much water as I could in the allotted two minutes. After the first bunch went through, my clothes weren't ready yet, so I joined the next bunch of men for another shower. It was wonderful. My skin tingled from the unusual experience.

After dressing, I was led away and passed the first set of barracks, which I later learned was the West Compound of Stalag Luft 1. Up the road a bit, we came to North No. 1 Compound, which was separated from the West Compound by the German quarters.

The entry into North No. 1 Compound was through a set of two heavily guarded gates. There was a large rickety building just inside of the entry, which, I was told, was a center for activities in the compound. It served as the mess hall, movie theater, and the place where classes and other camp projects were conducted. It was separated from the rest of the compound by another set of gates that were left open during the day and locked at night.

There were eleven barracks in the compound, one of which wasn't yet completed. As I came in, I was taken to the first barracks on the left. This was barracks no. 8 and the Allied POW headquarters for this compound. I was put in a room with Colonel Russ Spicer of San Antonio, Texas.

Before Russ even had a chance to open his mouth, I told him he was the first American I'd had an opportunity to speak to in seven months, and whether he liked it or not I was going to tell him my tale of woe. I suggested he listen without any discussion and afterward he could do as he wished.

As I discovered later, Russ was a very composed man. Just as I'd asked, he didn't even say hello. He pointed to his empty pipe and then his tobacco pouch and looked at me for approval. I said, "Go ahead," so he fired up his pipe, and then sat down and motioned for me to tell my story. I talked for 2 1/2 hours. After finishing, I'd gotten it all off my chest. I thanked him and said I was ready to listen to whatever instructions he'd give me. Spicer spoke for the first time and introduced himself, and then took me to meet the other men in the barracks.

The first room was occupied by the supply officer, Capt. Raymond Sanford of Alhambra, California, and the adju-

Lt. Col. Loren George McCollom of Ritzville, Washington. U.S. Army Air Force Photo

tant, Capt. M.W. Zahn from Wausau, Wisconsin. Sanford and Zahn proved to be swell fellows. Zahn gave me two packs of Philip Morris cigarettes, which tasted strange, but good. I was so glad to be talking to these men that I must have sounded like a phonograph record set on high speed. Zahn took me to meet the Allied camp commander, Col. J.R. Byerly of Estes Park, Colorado, whom I already knew. We had a good old rag chewing and I caught up on the latest developments in the war.

As evening came on, a bugle sounded for mess call. Men streamed from the barracks and each carried a cup, knife, fork, and spoon. Sanford and Zahn took me in tow to show me the ropes in the mess hall. When I entered, I saw over 500 boys eagerly lined up for a rather plain but adequate meal of boiled potatoes and Spam, with real American coffee and chocolate pudding for desert. There also was salt and sugar for seasoning! I lit in and it tasted fabulous.

The food was supplied by the Red Cross, and every week each man was supposed to be issued a parcel. The Red Cross did an admirable job in sending sufficient food, but the German transportation system was so laden by the demands and hazards of war that the parcels weren't always delivered on schedule. The parcels included tins and packets of such items as jam, cheese, powdered milk, meat, sardines, margarine, raisins, chocolate, coffee, sugar, and crackers.

The men often turned much of the Red Cross provisions over to the mess hall, where it was prepared cafeteria

"GABBY" *"Col. F.S. Gabreski, Oil City, Pennsylvania, was the leading American ace in the E.T.O. when fate caught up with him July 20, 1944. He had twenty-eight victories—tied with Hub Zemke, his old C.O. in England and his C.O. at Stalag 1... no Luftwaffe product was hot enough to get 'Gabby.' He got himself! Strafing a Jerry airdrome he depressed the nose of his ship to fire at an ME-109 taking off. He was so low his props hit the ground! In the resultant crash landing he was unhurt. Evading capture for five days he wound up in a fist fight with a couple of Hitler Jugend and was overpowered by an onslaught of reserves. Sent to Stalag 1, Gabby was made Group C.O. of North Compound 3."* Not as Briefed

style to make it go farther. The mess hall was unique to North No. 1 Compound and the POWs were fortunate to have it. The Red Cross food frequently was combined with the poor quality bread, potatoes, and vegetables provided by the Germans. I heard men complaining about how little they were getting, but it was a larger meal than I'd had for a long time. Of course, the fellows gave me a bit more than the average share, as they did for all new arrivals.

In the middle of this festive fare, I looked up and suddenly saw a familiar face in this crowd of strangers. I was flabbergasted! It was Mac McCollom, my fraternity brother from Washington State College!

"Mac! You old SOB," I screamed. "What in hell are you doing here?"

We climbed over the benches and pounded each other on the back and shoulders. Before going overseas, I'd asked Mac and his wife Kay to look after Dot. I knew he'd been assigned to the European theater a month or two after I left, but I'd heard nothing afterward. We were in the same college class and the best of friends. I later learned that my wife was sharing an apartment with his wife back in Hoquiam, Washington.

We found room at a table so we could sit together. I noticed burn marks on his face and hands, which was com-

"The three of us spent three long, lonesome, cold months of the winter in this cave. It was located on the side of a cliff and had we not been captured we intended to leave in three more weeks for another attempt to return. A German doctor found us here." Painting provided courtesy of Jack Lang

mon for men who'd been shot down or had crash landed. While talking to Mac, I reveled in my first chocolate pudding in over a year. Lt. Col. Loren "Mac" McCollom, a fighter pilot, had been hit by a burst from an 88 mm AA gun just as he started to dive on an objective. His fighter burst into flames and he suffered severe burns before he could bail out. The outline of his helmet could be seen where it had protected the rest of his head from the flames.

We finished desert and walked to Mac's room where he updated me on news about Dot. It wasn't much information, but it was wonderful to hear. Mac had been a POW for five months and had known I was a prisoner, but he'd thought I had escaped and made it out.

All of Mac's roommates currently were in solitary confinement due to a botched escape attempt. They'd tried to fool the guards into letting them through the gates by carrying a man on a stretcher, while one of their number was dressed in a German guard's uniform and acting as an escort. They'd been detected as they attempted to pass the third gate and had all landed in the cooler for two weeks.

Mac and I decided to share a room and we talked Russ Spicer into joining us. I told Mac that I thought Spicer was

"At 'Stalag One' we often whiled away a quiet evening at cards." A Wartime Log

"Or my roommates McCollom and Hubbard would bitterly battle at chess." A Wartime Log

he didn't mind. I think Mac was a little disappointed in me, not the least of which was because I knew how to operate a sailboat. They could use someone with this skill to help get them across the Baltic Sea to neutral Sweden. The Baltic shore was only 1 1/2 miles from the compound. I also was reluctant to go, however, because I knew the greatest difficulty was not getting past the wire, but evading recapture when once free.

About thirty men planned to leave by a tunnel located in another barracks. Each night, the German guards locked the doors and turned the lights out to all of the barracks, and only searchlights from the guard towers danced about in the darkened compound. Consequently, after curfew it was necessary for Mac and the others to hide out in the barracks where the tunnel was located. I was alone and in bed when the lights went out. At that moment, a man at the far end of the tunnel was notified and he pushed away the last few inches of topsoil, opening up the escape route. A signal was sent back that all was clear and the men prepared to pass through the tunnel and exit outside of the camp. After getting out, small groups of men would assemble at assigned points and then pursue various evasion routes, mostly by way of the Baltic.

The lights were off for about 15 or 20 minutes, when suddenly they came on again. Something had gone wrong! As it turned out, a guard was standing at the exit point with a mean looking rifle pointed at the first man to emerge. As each man came out of the tunnel, he promptly was nabbed and escorted to the cooler by the guards. Finally, one of the boys realized there was a problem and signaled back to the others, who elected not to give it a try. Mac was one who stayed back and didn't get caught.

I was unaware of this at the time because I was having my best night's sleep in a month. In the morning, Mac came back tired and discouraged. I learned that he headed the escape committee, which was a board of senior camp officers who approved all plans submitted by prisoners who wanted

one of the finest fellows I'd ever met. This later proved to be a correct evaluation. Mac's room was designated to hold six men. Bedding consisted of burlap sacks filled with wood shavings that served as mattress, top sheet, and pillow, plus one blanket. I still was sick and worn out from the solitary confinement at Landek and the other jails, and by the preceding months of constantly being on the run. Also, I felt I might be having a relapse of the health problems I'd had in Italy. That bunk looked awfully good!

While grabbing a few moments of rest, I saw Mac peek outside the window and door, and then he came up to me with that weird but familiar look I'd seen in the eyes of other POWs who were planning to escape.

He quietly said, "Ross, we have a tunnel that is completed and a group of us are ready to go out. We'd like you to come with us."

This was too much for me! I was sick and needed a few days of rest after my recent ordeal, and I had just about had my fill of trying to escape for awhile. I told Mac I appreciated the invitation, but would have to take a rain check, if

to try to escape. If a plan seemed feasible, the committee gave its approval and lent assistance.

Escape plans had to be controlled for several reasons—it allowed for better overall efficiency and success, it established a priority system for prisoners who'd been in camp the longest, and the escape efforts needed to be coordinated so as not to conflict with local espionage and spy activities outside of the camp. At any particular time, Allied agents working on assignments in the locality might be endangered if the Germans started a search for escapees. Most of the men weren't told about this last reason for security reasons, and this made it hard for them to understand why the committee sometimes withheld approval for an escape attempt.

Our barracks were rough, wood frame structures standing on small foundation posts about 8 to 10 inches off the ground. The Germans had dug a series of shallow trenches underneath the barracks to allow guard dogs to creep along and detect any tunnelers. Occasionally, the German guards themselves crawled into the trenches and listened to the conversations of the prisoners in their rooms.

A Wartime Log

I rested and recuperated during the first few days. We attended roll call twice a day, which was one of the more boring aspects of POW life. We were called out in the morn-ing and again in the afternoon and lined up five deep. The German staff walked around counting the groups of fives, until the number coincided with the roster of POWs assigned to the camp. More often than not, they'd make a mistake and think someone had escaped. That caused an extra roll call that could last hours, and sometimes additional guards and dogs arrived and were turned loose in the barracks seeking out men in hiding places. It was comical watching the frantic guards trying to make their figures balance.

I adjusted to camp routine after the first few weeks. Breakfast came after roll call and consisted of barley, coffee, and sometimes creamed Spam or corned beef. During the rest of the daylight hours, we attended classes, lectures, or whatever the day's schedule provided. At five o'clock, we received our second meal of the day, which usually was German potatoes, and creamed Spam or corned beef, coffee, and prunes or chocolate pudding provided by the Red Cross parcels. Special Red Cross invalid parcels were given to the hospital patients.

After the evening meal, many of the men walked around the compound's perimeter for their daily exercise. If one stopped and listened to the conversations, it could provide an evening's entertainment. Men who hadn't been prisoners for long generally talked about their last mission. They'd often make noises imitating machine gun fire and explosions when telling their tales.

Some boys walked alone, quietly passing the time with their own thoughts. The war's progress at the front lines always was a prime topic of conversation. And, there was the eternal banter and rivalry between the bomber and fighter pilots; heated arguments along these lines could last for days. At one time, it evolved into a bomber versus fighter pilots' quiz contest in the mess hall.

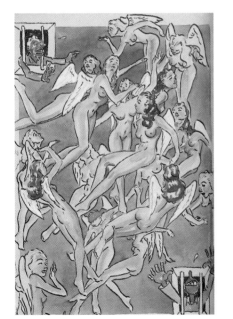

"Why it's hell to be a P.O.W." A Wartime Log

PRISON CAMP *"New arrivals entering the Main Gate of Stalag Luft 1, Barth, Germany. The Nazi flag is riding out a Baltic gale, the wind from the East presaging the great Russian offensive of January 1945. The wagon, left center, is laden with kriegsbrot (German 'war bread'), the P.O.W. staff of life. The new arrivals won't like it—but they'll eat it!"* Not as Briefed

A typical conversation between a newcomer and an old hand from the same outfit went something like this:

"Why, Hello Joe! You old SOB! How did they get you!"

"I was shot down over Schweinfurt—flak and fighters. I was the only one to get out!"

"Well what about the old outfit? Where's old Mike?"

"Mike? He finished his tour and went home!"

"He did? Why that dirty son of a bitch. What happened to the old man?"

"The old man really went to town. He got the DFC and a couple of clusters and then went up to wing!"

"Went to wing! The dirty bastard! I suppose that no good Jim got to go home or got a congressional medal or something! Where's he?"

"Jim did all right. He finished his tour and went home, then got married!"

"Went home and got married! The low down skunk—the dirty rat!"

"Yes, and you remember Lefty. He went home and joined a fighter outfit. Since then he came back and has seventeen victories."

"Lefty did that! He was a no account bum. How'd he ever do that? I suppose he was promoted too! We were in the same class and here I am still a second looey!"

"Whadd'ya mean promoted. That guy's a Lieutenant Colonel."

"Dirty bum! What's Tink doin' now?"

"Tink. He was shot down just last week, three days before I was. I saw him in the hospital in Frankfurt. It was just his second mission too!"

"Ol' Tink got shot down. Gee that's too bad. He was a swell pilot and a swell guy, a real prince of a fellow. They just don't come any better than ol' Tink!"

And so it went. If a guy got shot down, he was all right, but if he didn't, he was just a bum. Of course the fellows didn't mean it that way, but misery loves company. Because of our POW status, we often called ourselves "Kriegies," a name derived from the German word for a prisoner of war, i.e., " Kriegsgefangenen."

After two weeks, McCollom's original roommates were released from the cooler. Lt. Col. Mark Hubbard from St. Paul, Minnesota, Major Dillingham, Lt. Byron Morrill, RAF Squadron Leader Moody, captured American correspondent Lowell Bennett, and a couple of others came in to talk things over and express their spite for the Germans. At the same time, they were jubilant over how they'd put things over on the guards by receiving more food and cigarettes than normally entitled to while in the cooler.

I gradually learned more about the camp's escape projects. Numerous tunnels were being constructed at any one time. The soil at Stalag Luft 1 wasn't particularly good for tunneling. Being near the Baltic Sea, diggers struck groundwater only about six feet down. The soil was sandy with a few clay pockets, so it was easy to excavate, but it needed extensive shoring up. When the Germans discovered a tunnel, they'd make the prisoners cave it in or dig out the top to make it useless. Sometimes guards dynamited tunnels. Due to the numerous caved-in tunnels, a zone radiating out from

COME AND GET YOUR STEW *"This, the communal mess hall of North Compound 1, Stalag Luft 1, Barth, Germany, was the only one of its kind in American prisoner of war camps in Germany. Serving two meals a day from the American Red Cross parcels, the mess staff fed four sittings of five hundred men each—a total of four thousand meals daily. Between meals the mess hall was, on occasion, a lecture auditorium, a play house, a schoolroom, a church—all in all the most indispensable building in camp and, incidentally, the warmest! It later burned to the ground leaving the compound nothing in the way of classrooms or meeting rooms."* Not as Briefed

the barracks to the fences became lumpy and looked like a giant washboard.

Hauling and disposing of the tunnel dirt became a complex art. At first, dirt was flushed down the toilets, but it was simple for the Germans to detect this because the sewers became clogged. The guards then threatened to eliminate the indoor toilets if we didn't desist. Another method involved removing tarpaper from the barracks roofs, spreading about six inches of smoothed out dirt on top, and then putting the tarpaper back. This looked fine from the outside, but the weight of the dirt, especially when wet from rain, could cave in the roof and some did collapse. It wasn't unusual to find that you couldn't open a door because the heavy ceiling was pressing down. This, of course, was a giveaway to the Germans, who'd search and find another tunnel to be eliminated.

Later, we hit on a scheme of dumping dirt on a baseball diamond where we played ball with our YMCA equipment. Naturally, the pitcher's mound needed to be a little higher than the rest of the playing field. The Germans granted us permission to elevate the mound, but they didn't know we'd do it with dirt taken from tunnel excavations. We carried the dirt in our pockets and when we got to the mound, we'd pull a thread releasing the dirt and it would sift down our pant legs onto the ground. It wasn't long before the pitcher's mound was so high that it became obvious something was up and the Germans put a stop to it.

Next, we received permission to develop vegetable gardens and plant seeds provided by the YMCA. Naturally, the

ROLL CALL *"Twice a day this scene was enacted in all the compounds of Stalag 1; in this instance it's North Compound 1. Five deep to facilitate Teutonic higher mathematics, each squadron stood at attention while being counted. Despite the common multiple the procedure was more often SNAFU than not—which necessitated frequent recounts. The latter were tolerable in the warm months, but with the advent of cold weather, bone-chilling gales would roar in from the Baltic in the background. Item II: The byword at Roll Call was a German perversion of our 'Please let zem stands zat ease!'"* Not as Briefed

gardens were an excellent place to deposit dirt. As expected for a garden, each plot appeared to consist of freshly turned up, light, fluffy soil. Unfortunately, during an inspection one evening, two guards walked over a plot and discovered that the soil was as firmly packed as cement. Again, it was obvious to the Germans that we were digging and the guards discovered more tunnels.

By far, our most successful tunneling efforts involved digging a primary tunnel while also excavating one or two decoy tunnels. We'd deposit the dirt under one of the barracks or in another compound. When the Germans finally discovered the dirt, they'd immediately search for a tunnel. If our plan worked, the Germans would find a decoy tunnel and destroy it. Usually our primary tunnel remained

undetected. New decoys would be started to repeat the process again, until the primary tunnel was completed. In all, 140 tunnels were dug at Stalag Luft 1.

Careful surveying and plotting was required to keep the tunnels on track. When the guards discovered a tunnel and caved it in, however, it often was obvious how cockeyed and inaccurate some of our surveying was. This was particularly evident in one tunnel being dug from our compound toward a nearby barracks that was under construction in an unfenced area. It was intended that the tunnel would exit under the new building, thus providing escapees with additional concealment before reaching a wooded area. Unfortunately, the guards discovered this long

SKYROCKET AT SUNDOWN *"Directly east of Stalag 1 at Barth-on-the-Baltic, Germany, was located a German ordnance experimental station. During the early months of Summer 1944, daily at dusk, a trail of white smoke would suddenly appear in the eastern sky, climbing to the north and far west with amazing rapidity. Inmates wondered what projectile or plane had such speed. The Reich left no doubt when it announced in its newspapers that V-2, the new super-rocket bomb, was to replace V-1 in terrorizing the English homeland. But in those early days, stray, unperfected V-2s were dropping anywhere from Sweden to the North Sea."* Not as Briefed

tunnel before it was completed. When it was caved in, the depression showed how it had gone in a large semicircle outside of the wire and then back again, ending up inside the camp!

The POWs devised another simple, but ingenious escape plan at a location where the compound was secured by barbed wire mounted on a double row of eight feet high poles that were about four feet apart. After observing the guards' nightly routine, a carefully timed plan was devised. At a moment when guards couldn't see them, some POWs quietly placed a board across the top rows of barbed wire fencing. Then, a man climbed up over the shoulders of the persons holding the board, crossed over on the board, and dropped down on the other side and dove underneath an empty guards' barracks. The abandoned barracks, eventually intended to be occupied by incoming POWs, wasn't yet enclosed by barbed wire.

It would take about ten seconds for an individual to get out. The men holding the board then would take it back underneath a barracks and wait until a guard passed by again on his routine beat. From my barracks, I watched eight people escape in this way during my second week of internment. This was particularly interesting since Major von Miller, the German intelligence officer, had just told me that no one had been able to get outside of the wire in two years. The coordination was well rehearsed and perfect. Unfortunately, we learned later that these fellows were picked up while trying to get out of Germany.

Some men devised the wildest escape schemes imaginable, but few of them were successful. One officer planned to escape while disguised as a woman. He knitted a dress from helmet liners, and then bleached and dyed it in an attractive color. He also made special padding to give himself a convincing female figure. Every step in the escape scheme was practiced again and again. He planned to put on his clothing and padding at the far end of the tunnel to keep it clean.

Unfortunately, when he punched a hole through the topsoil, he'd failed to allow for the extra dimensions of a feminine figure and became hopelessly ensnared at chest level. It must have looked very peculiar to the guard who walked up and saw a "woman" stuck bust-deep in the tunnel exit. The officer ended up in the cooler for two weeks on short rations.[1]

The notion of being put on "short rations" as punishment was rather peculiar given the fact that we already were on short provisions. Because the Germans sent some of our men in each day to deliver the "short rations" to the fellows in the cooler, we were able to slip in additional food to most of them. Some actually came out of the cooler appearing comparatively "fat." As a matter of fact, a waiting list developed for offenders sentenced to two weeks in the hole— there weren't enough "coolers" available for the Germans to accommodate all of the POWs wanting in.

One very athletic fellow made an escape attempt that almost succeeded, but unfortunately he wasn't able to make advance plans because he had to take advantage of an opportunity on the spur of the moment. A large truck came into the camp and delivered the carcass of a horse that had been killed in a bombing raid. This was to be our ration of one pound of meat per man.

The truck had an empty battery box on the side, which was long enough for a man to hide in, if he was small enough and could compress his body sufficiently. This fellow secretly climbed into the box and the truck left the camp. The vehicle was parked outside of the compound and, in the dark, the lad got out and began making his way toward Allied lines.

Being quite resourceful, he managed to travel about 150 miles during the night. Unfortunately, the next day he was picked up, unshaven and unkempt, worn out, hungry, and completely demoralized. He was brought back to Stalag Luft 1 and put in a cooler that was positioned in such a way that we couldn't provide him with additional rations. Major von

Miller told the lad that unless he revealed how he had escaped, he'd be kept on bread and water for the rest of the war.

Not wanting to reveal how he'd done it, this clever fellow intentionally planned to remain on the bread and water diet for a long time and then pretend that he'd cracked. After two weeks had passed, he finally told a guard that he was ready to talk.

When von Miller came and asked the fellow how he'd escaped, the lad answered, "I jumped over the wire."

In disgust, the major stood up and started out of the interrogation room, saying, "I want the truth. You're going to have to stay here. This is ridiculous. Nobody can jump over the wire."

The lad replied, "I can prove it. I'll show you how I did it. You bring a stopwatch and let me select a spot. But I'd like to have one promise made first. If I do get over the wire, you'll let me return to my barracks?"

Major von Miller thought this sounded fair. He acquired a stopwatch and went with the lad to see him jump over the fence and into the compound. The lad found a fairly secluded spot not far from his barracks. He reached up to the top wire of the outer fence and bar vaulted it neatly. He kept his feet together when landing on the tangle wire between the fences and therefore prevented entangling himself. Without moving his feet, he grabbed the top wire of the second fence and again bar vaulted to the other side. Then he smartly stepped over the trip wire. He gave the German major a jaunty high sign and walked into the barracks.

Von Miller was so amazed that he came to my room and told me about it. He said, "That man told me he could get inside the camp in thirty seconds. By my stop watch, I timed him and it only took ten seconds."

The major continued, "We now know how he got out. This was one of the most remarkable athletic displays I've seen for some time; however, we need to take steps to prevent this from happening again."

Soon, a detail of thirty Germans started placing additional barbed wire strands and tangle wire at the tops of the fences all around the camp. Our escape artist never did reveal how he actually got out.

In another instance, the Germans had discovered a tunnel, and one evening they placed a board over the exit hole outside of the compound just as some POWs were making an escape attempt. By blocking the exit, the Germans planned to capture the men while they were inside the tunnel. Instead, the men burrowed upward and emerged one after another like moles within the compound and fled, thereby avoiding capture.

When an escape was attempted, diversionary tactics often were conducted to draw the guards' attention away. If a man went out a tunnel, for example, a team might cut "obvious" holes in the wire or perhaps let another tunnel be discovered to detract the guards from the actual escape route. An ongoing baseball game could be used to divert the Germans' attention. Sometimes the ball "accidentally" went over the trip wire, which extended around the inside of the compound about six feet from the main fence. We weren't permitted to enter this zone without first obtaining a white flag from the barracks and then getting permission to cross the trip wire and pick up the ball. This proved to be an excellent diversionary tactic.

A number of committees worked together to make the various escape plans more effective. For example, a cartographic committee of no mean ability produced an extremely useful series of maps for this part of Europe. Escapees, of course, needed these to determine directions, mileage, and destinations. Other committee members forged passes and provided money and compasses. Our compasses generally were brought into the camp by the new Kriegies.

PARDON THE INTRUSION *"March, April, and May, 1944, dragged along day after day. It seemed the Invasion would never begin; kriegie morale was low. Then one day at sundown a sudden burst of twenty-millimeter gunfire in the vicinity of the Jerry airport south of the camp brought prisoners pouring out of their beds and through the windows. What had happened is pictured here: two British intruders, Mosquitoes, were 'beating up' the place before heading home to England."*
Not as Briefed

The small compasses could easily be concealed, such as in the mouth or even swallowed and retrieved later. During searches by guards, I'd learned that the most useful place to hide small objects was merely holding them in my hand.

When men were working in the tunnels, a ventilation system frequently was required to provide sufficient oxygen. This was necessary not only for breathing, but also for burning margarine in our lamps. Consequently, blowers were made from tin cans and other materials from Red Cross parcels. Some blowers were operated by a handle and worked on the same principle as a turbine; others were bellows. The Germans thought that the bellows were being used to improve the efficiency of the barracks' stoves, which was true, but they also had a secret secondary purpose. We cut out both ends of butter cans and stuck them together in long tubes to make air ducts. It wasn't uncommon for a "mole" to lose consciousness from lack of oxygen and have to be pulled out of the tunnel.

Wire clippers were necessary for penetrating the wire, but unfortunately they were in short supply. However, some fine ice skates provided by the YMCA had blades that made excellent wire clippers. In fact, after the Germans had captured a pair, they used them to make repairs in the wire fences and claimed the clippers were superior to theirs.

One pair of confiscated clippers remained in German hands for only a short time. After the guards had discovered a tunnel extending under the fence, they set about caving it in, but found it necessary to cut the overhanging wire to proceed. When the Germans severed the wire, however, they made the mistake of leaving the ice skate cutters lying on the ground about a foot from the tunnel exit. They also failed to post a guard at the opposite end of the tunnel underneath the barracks. It wasn't long before we spotted an arm slowly extending out of the exit hole and feeling around for the clippers. The clippers disappeared and weren't found again by the Germans even though they searched for days.

The guards conducted both routine and surprise searches for any evidence of escape projects. The surprise searches, of course, were the most unpleasant for us. A group of Germans would enter the compound for various ostensible reasons. They'd make the appearance of directing their men to various places in the camp, but, when in the vicinity of the barracks they wanted to search, they'd suddenly make a break for it, gather together, and straightaway head into the building. Sometimes they caught our people at their surreptitious work, sometimes they didn't.

To counter these surprise searches, we developed a warning system. Lookouts were posted at each barracks and other special observers were assigned in places where any activity was a concern. A warning consisted of saying, "Goon up." The Germans, of course, suspected that the term "Goon" wasn't particularly complimentary. We were called into the commandant's office one time to explain the meaning of the expression "Goon up." We said it was an abbreviation for "**G**erman **O**fficer, **O**r **N**on-commissioned officer **U**pon **P**remises."

This satisfied the commandant and for a great while thereafter they'd actually announce themselves by saying "Goon up" when in a barracks. This lasted until a guard who had lived in New York City remembered what a "goon" was in the comic strips. Then we were ordered not to use the expression.

In regular military routine, officers normally have a daily roster board indicating whether they are in garrison or out on assignment somewhere. I figured we needed a sign-out board for our room and made one with an arrow for an indicator. When we were "out," the arrow pointed to any one of several activities: daily constitutional, playing baseball, escaping, dinner, not having dinner, etc. The word "escaping" caught the eye of the Germans and it didn't appeal to

HANS GETS STUNG *"When the Mosquitoes shown in the preceding picture shot up the flight line at Barth, a Luftwaffe pilot 'scrambled' into his FW-190. In his anxiety to get a crack at his enemy he forgot to watch his rear. Mosquito Number Two caught him as he was trying to turn inside his intended victim. Onlookers from the Stalag saw the Kraut make a safe—but wet—bail-out from the flaming wreck."* Not as Briefed

their sense of humor. In fact, they couldn't believe our audacity.

Guards accompanied by dogs patrolled the compound nightly. The dogs were poorly fed and vicious. They were trained specifically to prevent anyone from sticking a head or limb out of a window or getting outside of the barracks. One night when the shutter blew open, I raised the window just long enough to reach out and try and close it. One of these canine beasts lunged at me, making every effort to bite my arm off. Fortunately, he wasn't successful.

Lowell Bennett, an American correspondent for the International News Service (INS), was in our camp because he'd been shot down in a night raid over Berlin, December 6, 1943, while flying as an observer in a British bomber. Earlier in the war, the Germans took POWs of senior rank on propaganda tours in Berlin. The prisoners had to agree not to try to escape, and they were given a cultural tour of the great city. As time went on and the bombing assault progressed, of course, the points of interest became fewer and fewer. Finally, the tours ceased.

Bennett went on one of the tours before they were discontinued. When he reached downtown Berlin, he decided he'd rather go someplace else than see the cultural sites. He escaped and made his way to a train, and eventually ended up in Prague, Czechoslovakia. While waiting there for assistance in getting out of German occupied territory, he contrived to dispatch a story to the INS. The story itself wasn't all that remarkable, but his method of dispatching it certainly was. I'm not sure how he did it, but his story describing conditions in Germany and the POW camps appeared in U.S. newspapers.

After his recapture, Bennett referred to this episode as the time he scooped the world. ❁

NOTE

1. This dress currently is on exhibit at the U.S. Air Force Museum in Dayton, Ohio.

CHAPTER FIFTEEN

STARTING ART AGAIN

As already mentioned, I ended up sharing a room with Col. Russ Spicer, Lt. Col. Loren McCollom, and Lt. Col. Mark Hubbard. I roomed with these fellows for a long time and they were as fine a group of men as there was. Spicer had the respect and admiration of every man who knew him. He'd go to any lengths to stand up for the men serving under him. Hubbard was congenial and cooperative, always trying to accomplish his duty in the best manner possible. His knowledge of world events brought on discussions with the other men that constantly kept our room filled with eager debaters and conversationalists. Mac, or "Colonel Mac" as he was affectionately known, was quiet, understanding, efficient, and dedicated to making improvements in the camp.

At first, I felt unable to fit in or contribute much to this housing arrangement. Living and sleeping together day after day brought to light all of a man's faults as well as his good qualities. I couldn't help but be conscious of the other fellows' particular traits. To prevent quarreling and impatience with others, I'd have to learn how to face up to my own character flaws and understand best how to fit into a group.

Occasional arguments, however, did ease the tensions that built up. I had a stubborn streak over which I had little control. When criticized for this by others, my stubbornness in fact compelled me to argue against it, even though I knew it was true. After a period of time, I tried conscientiously to overcome this fault, if for no other reason than to prove to myself that I could do it.

Self-analysis occupied much of my spare time and it got to the point where I thought everything I did was wrong. I felt inferior, which made me extremely moody. I hardly talked to anybody and kept to myself as much as possible. However, it didn't take me long to realize that this wouldn't do, unless the war ended in a few weeks. I was going to have to find something to keep myself occupied.

According to the Geneva Convention of 1929, "officers" in a POW camp were excepted from performing work or labor. The Germans adhered to this policy. In some ways, however, this proved to be a disadvantage, since long inactivity is one of the hardest things to endure.

All of the men were eager to find things to do. Idleness was a serious problem, resulting in some men attempting suicide. Several succeeded. It was the same story in every room—the men were bored and spent much of their time just thinking or sleeping. The YMCA had provided equipment and supplies for recreational and educational activities, and the prisoners considered these things to be a lifeline to maintaining sanity, but something more was needed.

As was the case in Italy, I thought art projects would be of great benefit in a place like this. I visited the supply officer and learned that we had only a few sheets of paper, some rather hard pencils, a few watercolor paints, and pen points with no ink. Art supplies were provided by the YMCA and were quite scarce. I acquired a book of paper, some of the watercolor paints, and a pencil, and then got started.

My first few paintings weren't very good, but it was a beginning. It created interest with some of the fellows and one of them provided me with a box of pastels he had. I started doing portraits, just as I'd done in Italy. I also completed several combat scenes as personally described to me by the participants in these actions and stuck them on the wall for display.

A German major, derisively called "Smiling Jack" Schroeder by us, was among the first to see them. "These are very good," he said. "Will you make me an airplane picture someday?"

"Surely," I answered. "What kind of a German plane would you like to see being shot down?"

This was the wrong approach! The major became red in the face and stomped out of the room while muttering something about German planes never getting shot down by Americans, or by anybody else for that matter.

Another fellow, a guard, was celebrating his twenty-fifth wedding anniversary and wanted a portrait done of himself to send to his wife. We had to do this under cover and sneaked into a small closet in the mess hall where he posed for the portrait. I realized it wasn't quite fair to the rest of the lads in the camp, but I received an egg, a piece of bacon, three slices of white bread, and six onions for the picture. I immediately spirited the food away and hid it in a drawer in my room. Later, I used the food to prepare a special meal for my six roommates.

Although few supplies were available, I organized art classes for the men anyway, and taught about seventy-five students the basic principles of drawing and painting.[1] We scrounged for homemade art materials. Any scrap of paper was utilized, human hair was made into paint brushes, tree twigs were burned to make charcoal pencils for drawing, crepe paper was boiled to glean pigments for paints, can

"My friend Major Steinhower, the German compound commandant, took this photo of me. He didn't know he also got a picture of the 'dog runs' under the barracks. Sometimes the Germans crawled under to listen for information beneath the floors."

labels were soaked to extract the color, and paste was made from boiled potato peelings. Condensed ersatz coffee, in particular, made an excellent rich brown paint, while coal dust created a fairly bright red paint.

By trading cigarettes with the guards, we acquired colored pencils, which were dissolved in water to provide additional colors for painting. Lead pencils were at a premium because the Germans provided us with so few of them, but we were able to supplement

Roll call.

our small supply by bartering with the guards. Pencils were worn down to the point that little holders from tin cans were utilized to save the last particles of lead for our use. When sharpening pencils, we took care not to waste too much lead.

I found it difficult to acquire colors suitable for shadows and the dark rich tones. I did have some black ink, however, that helped somewhat in creating shadows in our paintings. One enterprising lad discovered that the dark brown juice from almost rotten sauerkraut enabled him to paint a camp scene in a beautiful, excellent monochrome.

Our main difficulty, however, was acquiring sufficient quantities of art paper. We used anything we could find, even toilet paper, newsprint, and the backsides of cigarette package wrappers. Sometimes, real art paper could be traded from the guards for cigarettes.

A scene I painted of Stalag Luft One's main entrance, titled "Prison Camp" (page 183), was the result of a perspective technique that I'd worked out for the classes. Perspective drawings normally have vanishing points on either side of the scene and an artist uses a string or something similar to determine these vanishing points. With the technique I worked out, I could make a perspective drawing at any angle

and elevation you cared to choose with a single vanishing point in the center of the picture. This process could be used only when an artist had plenty of time to think about it—and we had lots of that!

For sculpting and carving classes, of course, we needed chisels, hammers, and other tools. The barracks stoves were pulled apart and iron parts were removed and kept hidden from the German search parties. These were heated and pounded into proper shapes, then sharpened to a fine edge on rocks and bricks found around the camp.

YMCA-provided phonograph records, some of which were the latest hit recordings, were played until they were worn out and then broken into workable bits. With a heating tool devised from stove parts, human hairs were set in plastic to make paintbrushes. We found out that brunette hairs worked better than blonde ones for painting. Phonograph records also were melted for use in sculpturing and making model airplanes.

Art classes improved as time went on. Finding new art materials, however, continued to challenge our ingenuity. Some way or another, everybody seemed able to come up with something that could be used in a class. Woodworking

became popular, especially in regard to making model planes. The prisoners' skills and talents usually were insufficient for carving human figures and animals, but they excelled in making models of combat aircraft.

The Germans disliked the fact that Kriegies took up wood carving because we pulled and cut pieces of wood from the walls and ceilings of the buildings. To make picture frames, quarter rounds disappeared from room corners; and to make drawing boards, the bottoms of drawers and the backs of lockers vanished. The Germans searched frantically for these materials and punished offenders with 14 to 30 days in solitary confinement on short rations, but the activity persisted.

Barbed wire was taken from the fence to make nails in spite of German threats to shoot anyone seen touching the wire. Fence posts disappeared, appearing later as mannequins in puppet shows. Modeling clay came from the clay deposits encountered by the men digging escape tunnels. Since so many people became engaged in artistic activities, we decided to put on weekly exhibits in the mess hall.

One man, Lt. Claire Cline from Tacoma, Washington, had a great desire to learn how to play the violin. There were a number of accomplished violinists in camp, but there were too few Red Cross violins to go around. Consequently, Cline couldn't get his hands on one. He decided this wasn't going to stop him and he set about making his own, using wood slats from a bed and the hind leg of a chair for the main body of the instrument.

GERMAN FIELD KITCHEN *"This type of World War I German field kitchen was supplied to the various compounds for heating water. Running hot water was an unknown luxury except in the bi-weekly showers given each 'gefangenen.' The hot water supplied by the field kitchens was used for everything from cooking to bathing. Absent from the picture is the usual long line of Kriegies waiting with empty buckets for a fill-up."* Not as Briefed

The inlay work consisted of coffee soaked pieces from a Red Cross plywood box that was carefully fitted in by a razor blade. Cline scraped the excess amounts of dried glue from the joints of mess tables and boiled it down in a small cheese tin. This provided the necessary glue to hold the violin parts together. Table clamps from a YMCA ping pong net held the pieces in place while the glue dried. Coffee and shoe polish were used to create a stained wood finish. The long hairs in the bow came from the horses towing the "honey" wagons to and from the camp.

He modeled his violin after an Amata that the YMCA had sent to the camp. It took four months for him to make it, working every day until dark. A case was made from KLIM instant milk cans. This violin was so perfectly crafted that the Germans complimented Claire for his efforts. He was able to play reasonably well before long.

An airman named Kuchenbecker built a pair of fine B-26 models. Each was about 15 inches long and a perfect reproduction in every aspect. The ailerons and elevators worked, the cockpit opened and closed, the pilots sat in their seats with maps in their cases, and the radio operator was in his proper place. The wheels, made of rubber from shoe heels, had tread and would drop and retract into their housings. The bomb bay doors also opened and closed in proper fashion. Even the cylinder flanges were perfectly mounted in the engines, which also had removable covers over the engine cowlings. These models were made out of scavenged wood parts and glue scraped from table joints. Kuchenbecker built his models with a broken knife, which he had acquired from a guard and later sharpened to a very fine point.

The men in camp built numerous model airplanes, many of them quite good, but Kuchenbecker's B-26s were the best.[2] Some of the others had a silver finish made from the foil in cigarette packages. They had an amazing amount of detail, even down to showing rivet heads in the wings and fuselages.

A paper mache model made of newspaper and flour depicted the digging of an escape tunnel. It showed how the dirt was removed from underneath a stove, and it included an underground brick wall. Soap figurines depicted how the men worked in the tunnel. The Germans, of course, weren't allowed to see this model.

We made Kriegie versions of *Time* magazine. One copy had the camp commander on the cover and you couldn't tell it from a real issue of *Time*. The inside pages weren't quite as well done, but included worthy news articles, including one about a tour of New York City nightlife written by Frank Leonard. This created considerable attention, resulting in a class titled "How to See New York City," which lasted about four weeks.

One of the navigators was interested in plotting the exact global position of our camp. He made a homemade

Watching a camp sporting event, Ross sits in the front row next to four German officers. Camp commandant von Warnstedt is the second man from the right side of the photo.

The "wire" and a guard tower. The highest tower in camp was last seen in flames on V-E Day.

sextant complete with bubble levels and was able to quite accurately plot the position of the camp.[3]

One day a fellow POW came into my room carrying a package of paper. He said, "This is some very good paper that I've been saving for several months, but I'm not good enough of an artist to use it. I thought you might like it."

I was in no position to refuse. It was beautiful paper—clean, white, and above all suitable for painting watercolors. I practically hugged the guy for his generosity. As soon as he left the room, I started painting. Of course, the first idea that came to mind was to make a picture of a B-26. This presented some problems, however. Just where was the wing located on a B-26? How high was the windshield compared to its width? Exactly where were the gun turrets located, as well as the oil coolers, cowling flaps, and all the minute detail we

had so often seen, but never made the effort to try to remember?

I spoke to a number of B-26 crewmen and we couldn't come to any agreement about the precise locations of these features. Obviously, we couldn't get information like this from the Germans and it was forbidden for us to possess pictures of American planes. I finally completed my painting and it started a series of arguments in camp as to its authenticity. A number of fellows came into my room and talked over the details. Soon, men all over the camp were trying to recall the exact dimensions on other types of planes too.

Since I was the senior allied officer of one of the four compounds in the camp, it was my duty to interrogate new prisoners, insuring that they weren't German spies disguised as Americans. The new men naturally wanted to talk about some of the missions they'd flown and how they'd been shot down and captured. Each time that I listened to a particularly good story, I'd make a little sketch of the battle scene, or whatever it was that had happened. If a sketch appealed to me, I'd try and paint it in watercolors. It was a very interesting process.

When I'd made about fifteen of these, some were put up in the "Display of the Week" section in the mess hall. These paintings were very popular and many of the men wanted me to paint scenes from their combat missions. Soon, I was swamped with requests. Art materials were in short supply, of course, and I had to paint scenes on both sides of a piece of art paper.

As the days went on, more art supplies came in from the YMCA. The art classes progressed nicely and many of the men discovered talents that they didn't know they had. I received more requests to do pictures, but I was able to complete only a small number.

One afternoon in June 1944, a delegation of about six fellows came into the room. "Colonel," the spokesman stated, "I'm a lithographer by trade and a bunch of the fellows mentioned how they'd like to have prints made of some of the combat scenes you're painting. We figure if a couple hundred of us chipped in maybe $10 or $15 a man, we could get 15 or 20 of these reproduced. What do you think?"

"Sure," I answered, "I don't think it would be much trouble, if we can get the pictures home."

We figured that if two hundred men signed up, there'd be enough money to pay for the project. I suggested putting a notice about it on the bulletin board. We typed out an announcement notifying anyone who wanted copies of these paintings to come and sign up in my room and leave a $10 check or IOU written on any kind of paper they had. On the morning that we posted the announcement, I got up and went to roll call. Afterward, I saw that a long line of men had formed at our barracks. I figured that mail or packages from home had arrived. When I entered the barracks, however, I noticed that the line started at my room. All of these men were here to sign up for my paintings!

Before we were through, about five thousand men had contributed to the project, raising $50,000 for it. This many checks and IOUs made for a lot of paper, but we planned to store them away and after the war produce not just a collection of pictures, but a whole book! I had a staff of people type the names on our ancient typewriter. As the typist reached the end of a line, the carriage sometimes flew off and fell on the floor. We packed the checks and IOUs in bundles in a wooden box.

Lt. J.M. Coppinger of Brooklyn, New York, who had a flair for writing, thought up *Not as Briefed* as a fitting title for the book. We collected all of the facts that we could about the actions depicted in the paintings. I continued adding other paintings to the collection, which eventually totaled seventy-five. Meanwhile, Coppinger wrote comprehensive captions for all of them.[4]

Other artistic efforts in the camp included the presentation of plays. One of the productions was "The Man Who Came to Dinner," which already was familiar to most everybody. Male actors, of course, had to fill in for the female characters in the play, "Maggie Cutler" and "Lorraine Sheldon." Special costumes were made for Harold Cook and Frank Sims, who did a fine job playing these roles. Harold's wig was made out of spun glass insulation from the barracks. A slinky evening gown was made out of dyed burlap. The make-up consisted of margarine and red brick dust from our fireplaces. Hats were made out of cardboard, and jackets and dresses were created from tissue paper.

When we first began, the Germans wouldn't allow us to play our YMCA supplied band instruments. They claimed we didn't know what good music was, and they didn't want to see the human race degraded by "cow music," as they called American jazz. We said we'd play only classical music if they'd let us have the instruments, and we agreed to let them hear, and censor if necessary, our first recital.

Our musicians practiced diligently. Mike Spodar, the band leader and a fine trumpet player, made a classical arrangement of the popular song, "Right in der Fuhrer's Face," and we invited the Germans to attend the recital in the mess hall. The room was crowded with Kriegies and you can imagine their response when the first strains of this hit tune were played. The Germans in all their finery were seated in the front row. The cheers, shouting, stomping, and whistling that went on was amazing. The Germans didn't know the tune and thought our enthusiasm was just in appreciation of fine music. They cheered too, so it became our theme song thereafter at each recital.

We also wrote and put on some of our own productions. I wrote a play called "Kriegmalion," as a takeoff on "Pygmalion." Some men composed music. Jim Lashley from South Carolina wrote a song entitled "Low Is the Sun" and Harry Korger composed one titled, "All Through the Night."[5] We also had a fine glee club.

During the performances one evening, the master of ceremonies came out on the stage (which consisted of the mess hall tables pushed together). After parting the burlap curtains, he said to the crowd: "We are interrupting the

program because something very unusual has happened. We just can't believe it ourselves. You'll have to bear with us boys, this is going to be a real treat. The USO had a plane flying into France and the plane was shot down and the Andrew Sisters were aboard. So help me, they are in camp and the German commandant, Colonel Warnstedt, has agreed to let them sing to you."

I knew it was a gag, but I almost felt like believing it myself. The bedlam resulting from this false report about one of America's most popular singing combos was out of this world! The YMCA had sent an electric record player, but the Germans allowed it into the camp only if brought by a guard, because they thought we'd use the tubes to make radios. On this evening, with the guards and the phonograph backstage, the curtains were drawn and out came three crazy guys—one with a gray, hairy chest—dressed up like gals. They lip synched to an Andrew Sisters' record and they did it perfectly. It brought down the house. Harold Cook followed up wearing his fancy female costume (this was the first time we'd seen it) and singing "Oh Johnny." When he winked at us in the front row I almost blushed.

There was another creative endeavor that might not seem like art, but it was—we had competitions in developing a better mousetrap. Some were dillies; the best in the world. There were rolling traps, repeater traps, drowning traps, and lots of other kinds, but the crowning climax came in the latter part of the war when some bright individual decided that the mice ought to have a fighting chance. This philosophy evolved from our particular circumstance of being defenseless prisoners surrounded by well-armed guards. We termed this situation the "rifle pitted against the spoon," since a spoon was the only weapon a POW had.

The most outstanding creation, which gave a rodent a chance to escape, was the 12-way mousetrap. In this tin-can contraption mounted on a large board, six pairs of compart-

ments each had two exits. When a mouse entered one compartment it had two choices—one would exterminate him and the other was a clear exit to the next pair of compartments. Extermination came by such means as a little guillotine, impaling with spikes, drowning, or poisoning. If a mouse made it safely out of the last exit, it crossed over a drawing of a cat's face and went free.

Some mousetraps were set to roll across the floor when a mouse was captured. This rattling alerted the men, who'd rush out, grab the poor old mouse, and flush it down the drain. Mice were a health hazard, but we had an awful time keeping some of the fellows from saving them as pets.

I think some of the men would have eaten them, too, on occasion. ✧

NOTES

1. Greening was trained in Fine Arts and was well qualified to teach painting and drawing. Greening's mentor at Washington State College was the art department chairman, Worth D. Griffin, who specialized in painting portraits of Northwest Indians, pioneers, and early business and political leaders. Greening's own portrait work equaled the fine work of his instructor, with whom he corresponded during the war. For a comparison with Griffin's work, see *Indian Summers: Washington State College and the Nespelem Art Colony, 1937–41* by J.J. Creighton (Pullman: WSU Press, 2000).

2. These models later were placed on exhibit at the Strategic Air Command's Escape and Evasion Museum at Reno, Nevada.

3. His findings eventually were checked and found to be accurate within one mile of the camp.

4. After the war, *Not as Briefed* was printed in a handsome format by the Brown & Bigelow Company at St. Paul, Minnesota, and was widely distributed to the men who had contributed to the project. The volume combined Greening's paintings with Lt. J.M. Coppinger's well-crafted introduction and captions. Brown & Bigelow graciously contributed funding to the expensive project when the collected POW money proved insufficient.

5. Later, the two songs were published and released by RCA on the same record.

CHAPTER SIXTEEN

KRIEGIE KRAFT KARNIVAL

Our "Display of the Week" exhibits in the mess hall had attracted considerable attention; consequently we decided that the whole camp needed a big art blowout. We organized the "Kriegie Kraft Karnival" for July 21–23, 1944, and collected artwork and models from all over the camp for display in the mess hall. The Karnival also would feature gambling games, plays, and music. In general, it was a gala fiesta for all of the men.

When it first opened, there was relatively little enthusiasm in camp except among the fairly sizeable number of men directly involved with the entertainment programs and the arts and crafts exhibits. After the first day, however, interest in the show quickly increased as the lads who'd been inactive realized that men just like themselves had done the artwork and programs. The line-ups to see the exhibits and entertainment programs grew very long indeed.

After the Kriegie Kraft Karnival was well under way, activity in camp increased to the point that the Germans became alarmed. Prisoners were

Pictures from home: sister Shirley's daughter, Karen. "This lil gal 'Karen' promoted me to the title of 'Uncle'—Her Momma and Pappa are the best even tho they are Navy. Oct. 11, 1944."
A Wartime Log

tearing the barracks apart to obtain wood and other materials, while the stoves, toilets, fences, and mess halls were ransacked for metal to be made into tools.

The men who had been bored and perhaps previously thought they had no talent now were developing useful and productive skills and hobbies to fill their time. There seemed to be no end to what the men could do with their hands. For example, they learned that a table knife could be made into an efficient saw and barbed wire converted into nails; consequently, furniture could be constructed for their rooms. Having chairs in a room was a fine convenience.

After the show, some of us got together and discussed the possibility of saving a collection of the art pieces and our daily handiwork, and taking it home for a display after the war. We'd be able to show our families just how we'd survived and spent our time as POWs. The exhibit also could be presented to the American public, where we could express our appreciation to the Red Cross and the YMCA for their aid. For the present time, as an added benefit, such a project would help hundreds of men occupy their idle hours in the camp.

We announced the plan and the entire camp received it with enthusiasm. We went to work, gathering and saving as many objects as we could to help depict all aspects of camp life. As the items were gathered and organized, parts of the collection were shown in a weekly display in the mess hall. We then packed them up and stored them away, hopefully for shipment home after the war.

Tacoma News Tribune—"Lt. Comdr. E. Maxwell Morgan... is shown reading latest letter from his brother-in-law, Lt. Col. Charles Ross Greening, Tacoma air hero, now a prisoner of Germany, to the flier's sisters. Mrs. Morgan, at left, is the former Shirley Greening, and at right is Sea./1c Virginia Greening, now stationed at Washington D.C."

Unfortunately, the Germans thought that a number of the things that we were saving could be used for escape attempts. When the Germans searched our rooms, they often destroyed art objects and models under the pretext of searching for hidden objects. We could see we weren't getting anywhere this way.

Finally, we hit upon the idea of having men in the Red Cross food detail hide these items for us. A party of POWs was sent on a fairly regular schedule to a warehouse outside of the camp to bring our Red Cross food parcels back into the compounds. As the parcels were brought into the camp and emptied of food, Kriegies secretly packaged up artwork and other objects in the crates. After they were sealed up, we told the Germans that we wanted to save some of our Red Cross rations in case of an emergency in the future. The food detail then took the refilled crates back to the German warehouse near the flak school and stored them there. We never

again lost any exhibit materials because the Germans never thought of searching their own warehouse for these things.

As would be expected in our situation, we came to despise a number of the guards, although a few of the Germans were good men. All German soldiers believed that orders had to be carried out explicitly, whether they made sense or not. This made for some rather ridiculous situations at times.

We hardly ever saw the camp commandant, Colonel Warnstedt. He usually delegated duties to his staff and seldom came into the compound.

Major "Smiling Jack" Schroeder, an executive officer, was seen quite frequently. He'd learned to speak English in the United States where he'd been employed by Pan American Airlines. In fact, he still held stock in the company. We called him "Smiling Jack" because he was such a sourpuss. Most of the fellows remembered him for his vigilance in noting when a Kriegie failed to salute him. He put many men into solitary confinement for this violation.

He'd say, "I vill poot you in der coolah if you keep forgetting to salute der sooperior officers! I vill make you respect der Chermans yet!"

The German intelligence officer was Major von Miller, whose main duty was searching the barracks for tunnels and trying to ferret out our escape attempts. He was intensely disliked because of his two-faced attitude. He claimed he owned a home in Santa Barbara, California, and intended to go back there after the war.

BATTLE OVER BIG B *"Boeing Fortresses in a mass bombing flight over Berlin, Germany, under very heavy enemy fighter attack. 'Big B' was one of the hottest targets in Germany during the Spring and Summer of 1944. A large number of inmates at Stalag 1 met their nemesis there. This—and other air battles—were the unique, gruesome novelty of World War II. Viewpoints differed over the relative merits of air power, but the extermination of the Luftwaffe was the great result of the Allied aerial offensive."* Not as Briefed

DESTROY YOUR AIRCRAFT *"Col. E.A. Malmstrom of Indianapolis, Ind., destroying his Thunderbolt in enemy territory after crash landing. 'Destroy your aircraft' were the perennial parting words of the Security Officers before a mission. The occasions for this overt, necessary—but saddening—act were seldom. Not many pilots had the providential luck to be able to land their aircraft in one piece."* Not as Briefed

One day he stopped in the compound and chatted with a group of us. "When the war is over and we can all go back to America, I'd like to see you again," he said with diplomatic politeness.

"Yes, Major," we answered. "Nothing would give us greater pleasure than meeting you in America after the war!"[1]

Major K.H. Steinhower, a fine man, was the commandant of North No. 1 Compound. Each of the compounds had a German commandant who had charge of that section for roll calls and barracks management. Steinhower wasn't in favor of the war, but he had to be careful about this because it was dangerous for a German to appear to be opposed to it. In civilian life, Steinhower had been a professor of languages at a boys' school in Wuppertal, Germany. He had a wife and a son, whom he seemed to have on his mind all of the time.

His face and head were covered with old dueling scars inflicted during his school days when such marks were considered to be in good taste. He must have been an extremely hot headed young man or a poor fencer judging by the number of scars on his face. He was now about 56 or 57 years old and had long since tempered his youthful impetuousness. He didn't become a compound commandant until later in our confinement. We applied all of the pressure that we could on him to secure various benefits for our compound and he responded very conscientiously. Even when circumstances prevented him from doing much, he still tried to help us out the best he could.

We applied nicknames to some of the unsavory characters that we disliked. One old crank was unaffectionately called "The Green Hornet," because of his green uniform. He was the officer in charge of rations.

"Henry the Butcher" and a German guard named "Siemen" were the two most disliked men in the camp. There wasn't an American there who wouldn't have slit their throats if the opportunity presented itself. Henry the Butcher was a former Brooklyn meat shop operator who took delight in insulting every American he encountered. He was only too eager to present a gun to back up his threats.

Siemen was taller, with a dirty-looking mug. He wasn't even liked by the Germans. It was a rare occasion when he didn't pull his gun when screaming at some helpless prisoner.

"Turkey Neck" was the official German interpreter. He was tall, slope-shouldered, skinny, and baldheaded. He characteristically listened to what we wanted interpreted to the German officers, and then he'd relate a totally different message to them in German.

"Alphie" was a buck-toothed interpreter who always was trying to gain favor from both sides. He tried to earn approval from the POWs when he was around them, but acted quite differently, and loyally, when amongst his German comrades. He made the mistake of visiting his home near the Baltic when the Russians were advancing and was cut off. He never returned.

Colonel J.R. Byerly, our senior American officer, was the Allied commander of the entire camp. He performed a superior job in organizing the men into a regular Army Air Force organization. The camp was set up as a Provisional Wing X, with each of the four compounds organized as provisional groups under this wing. The individual barracks served as squadrons under each group. We already were accustomed to this type of organization and it made for simpler coordination of camp activities. The British had their own two groups.

TACTICAL SUPPORT *"British Typhoon knocking out a Jerry Tiger tank during the invasion of Normandy in June 1944. Rendering the Wehrmacht a severe blow to its mobile power, the Typhoons and Thunderbolts played a very important part in the success of the operation."* Not as Briefed

Colonel Hubert Zemke, my old friend from flight school days, arrived in December 1944, replacing Colonel Byerly as camp commander. Included in the letters and pictures I'd previously received from home were a few photos of Zemke's wife "Missy." We'd heard that Zemke had been captured. In anticipation of his arrival, we fixed up a place for him complete with pictures of his wife and a drawing showing his living room at home. He probably was the first POW to find such mementos already mounted on a wall when arriving in a camp.[2] Zemke, a fighter pilot, had collected twenty-eight Nazi pelts before his luck ran out.

The camp was well represented with air heroes. Lt. Col. Francis Gabreski with twenty-eight victories was a rather late arrival. Maj. Duane Beeson, Maj. Gerald Johnson, Col. Russ Spicer, and Lt. Col. Mark Hubbard each were fighter pilots with enviable records. Lt. "Red" Morgan of New York City was a Congressional Medal of Honor winner who was shot down over Berlin. He fell 15,000 feet with a parachute in

AND ONE MAKES TWELVE *"An ME-110 jumped a Fortress formation over Dummer Lake, Germany. It was the pilot's ill luck to have the future ranking American fighter ace spot him. The German dove for the earth from twenty thousand feet. At ten thousand the Thunderbolts caught up with him and he became the twelfth of the twenty-eight victories which were to make 'Gabby' Gabreski surpass the twin records of Joe Foss and Eddie Rickenbacker, and achieve a Colonelcy in the U.S.A.A.F."* Not as Briefed

raid alarm sounded, indicating that our planes were overhead, we were directed to take cover in the barracks. I'd already heard about this rule when being temporarily held at Eichstadt, Germany, with Jack Lang and Bob Smith.

We weren't permitted to dig or use slit trenches, which would've provided far more protection from bombs and bullets than a flimsy, wooden barracks. If a prisoner looked out of a window during an air alert, the guards were instructed to shoot without warning. Also, if a man stepped outside of the barracks, he'd surely be fired upon. Men were shot and killed in prison camps because of this regulation.

We protested to the Germans time and again,

his hands while trying to get it on, finally succeeding just 1,500 feet from the ground.

Another well liked person was Capt. "Pop" Corning who'd fought in World War I. He'd been in a B-25 that was hit and was forced to bail out. Perhaps the sort of life we were living was more difficult for him than for the younger fellows, but he displayed less evidence of it getting him down than any of the rest of us.

The Germans imposed some regulations blatantly intended to break down our morale. For example, when an air

and also brought it to the attention of the international monitoring personnel out of neutral Geneva, Switzerland, but to no avail. For our own protection during an air alert, we posted guards at the exits and strung barbed wire across the doorways to prevent anyone from inadvertently going outside.

On March 18, 1945, in the compound next to ours, Lt. Elroy Wyman didn't hear an air raid warning and walked out of a barracks just as the guard was being changed. He must have noticed that the compound was vacant and realized he'd made a mistake. He turned to run back into the barracks, but was spotted by a guard not 75 feet away. The guard shot Wyman through the head as he was running and killed him. That same day, another fellow was shot through the stomach as he jumped out of a window with laundry in his hands. He was seriously wounded, but didn't die. A couple of days later, Wyman was buried in a small cemetery about a mile from camp, but full funeral services weren't permitted.

Another irritating regulation pertained to our personal Red Cross food. If a man had more than six tins of food in his possession, the cans had to be slit and punctured. The food would spoil if kept for long, so it had to be consumed rather quickly. The Germans wanted to keep us from taking canned food with us during escape attempts. In actuality, it didn't make the slightest difference in regard to a man's escape plans.

With 9,000 men in camp, it was difficult to distribute an adequate weekly ration and abide by this rigid restriction. During Christmas 1944, it took us two weeks to issue one-week's ration of food, which made it practically impossible to save up a reserve of canned food. We knew that tougher times might be coming as the Allies continued their advances

THE HARD WAY *"C-47 Transport and CG-4A Gliders participating in the ill-starred Arnheim aerial assault. First Lt. S.S. Lawler of Tampa, Florida, took over the leadership of this element when the Number One ship was shot down. The target was Nimwegen, but Lt. Lawler's glider was cut loose thirty miles from it. Surrounded on landing, the Lt. and his crew holed up in an old house, fought but were captured, two men being shot after the surrender and two others wounded."* Not as Briefed

and the Nazis became more desperate. We wanted to save as much food as possible. In fact, the German distribution system did start breaking down in the Spring of 1945 and the Jerries also intentionally withheld food for a period, which resulted in "hard times" for us.

Authorization from the Germans was required a week in advance for every written announcement, newsletter, theatrical performance, class, or any other kind of activity that we wanted to do. Unauthorized gatherings were fired upon

in some camps, but never in ours. In one camp, regulations were so restrictive that camp gatherings and educational classes weren't permitted. Despite this, the fellows secretly started classes and completed forty different courses for over a thousand men. They made their own books and some boys actually ended up with frostbitten feet while sitting in unheated rooms listening to instructors. They were fired upon on occasion, but they didn't let that discourage them.

Our hospital was in an ordinary barracks located in the Kraut quarter of the camp. At first, two British doctors who'd been POWs since 1940 staffed the facility. Lt. Col. George T. Hankey was the senior medical officer, with Captain W. Martin Nichols serving as the primary surgeon. Nichols previously was an eminent brain surgeon in England. The job these two doctors performed was nothing short of miraculous. Eventually, other Allied doctors were assigned to the camp.

In the early part of the war, the medical facility had little or no support from the Germans. The doctors had to make their own medical instruments from barbed wire and other scavenged materials. They didn't receive an operating table until the Germans asked Doc Hankey to operate on a wounded German soldier. Up to that time, they'd used a kitchen table. I watched Nichols take out a man's appendix, which in a normal situation is a minor operation, but it required the utmost care and attention when done under the less than satisfactory conditions of our camp.

The medical assistants were picked from the combat airmen having some qualifications to help out. The hospital was terribly overcrowded and the medical staff worked from morning till dusk taking care of men with ailments and injuries. Hundreds of pieces of shrapnel and metal fragments were removed from the bodies of lads who hadn't been properly taken care of by the Germans after being shot down.

Medical dispensaries also were established in the compounds and staffed by the airmen who were most qualified in handling the job. In our compound, Lt. Steve Roper of Lacey, Washington, was in charge. He'd had some training in first aid, but learned a great deal more by handling minor cases every day. There wasn't a dentist in the camp until late in the war, and Roper actually learned how to put fillings in teeth with proficiency. I had some dental work done by him that was excellent.

A handsome, young officer from Chicago named Raymond Brooks came into the camp in late 1944. He'd lost part of his left leg in combat and the Germans had given him rather sloppy care. His leg, which was severed about half way to the knee, had healed over by the time he arrived. He didn't want to stay in the hospital, but chose to share his lot with the other prisoners in one of the crowded barracks. He had a stubborn spirit and strong will, and it was obvious that he longed to get out with the fellows and walk around the compound.

One day, Lt. Byron L. Morrill and Lt. J. Cuthbertson came to me asking for permission to try and make an artificial leg for Brooks. We went to see Brooks and found him more than willing to submit to the experiment. Brooks was taken to the mess hall and placed on one of the tables while the rest of the gang went to work. They measured and figured, then went scrounging for parts and materials, finding pieces of wood, old leather, rivets made from barbed wire, an old shoe, tin cans, and a piece of a phonograph spring.

In about three weeks, the artificial leg was finished. Cuthbertson and I went to the hospital with Brooks to have the artificial leg approved by Doc Hankey. It was a critical moment. Brooks feared it might not fit right, and Cuthbertson and I were worried about being criticized by Hankey for meddling in medical affairs.

The doc fitted the artificial leg to the stump and frowned. He studied it closely and remained quiet. Brooks' eyes were wide with anticipation. The artificial leg was a complex device, intended to carry the weight of Brooks' body along the side of his leg rather than directly on the

MARAUDER'S FINALE *"The B-26 Marauder is famous for its short, fast bomb-run. But Capt. Raymond P. Sanford achieved his fame in a different manner. On December 13, 1943, making a bomb-run on an airport at Amsterdam, Holland, Sandy was hit by heavy flak in Number One engine. His left wing folded; the ship exploded. Sandy awoke, falling free of his ship, still strapped to his bucket seat and armor plate. He unstrapped the seat, opened his 'chute and landed safely. He was taken prisoner immediately!" Sanford was the only crew member to survive.* Not as Briefed

The men in camp watched the Red Cross food distribution more closely than any other activity. The average guy begrudged the men in the ration detail because they felt certain these fellows were putting their fingers on extra food and supplies for themselves. Strict records and distribution figures were kept, however, and posted for all to see. Captain Archie G. Birkner, a paratroop officer from Houston, Texas, was in charge of the detail and he carried out his duty with the utmost efficiency. The only real advantage that the detail got from the job was that they could get out of the camp to the warehouse or the town's railroad station to pick up parcels. It was a break in the monotony of POW life that was envied by everyone else.

stump (the bone in the Lieutenant's stump had been improperly amputated and it was sharp).

After a few more minutes, Hankey looked up with a big smile. "Boys, this is wonderful. This leg is just as good as any expert could make with the materials available. Brooks will have to wear it just a little each day to get used to it, but it should do the trick in the long run."

We were three happy men when returning to our compound that afternoon. Cuthbertson looked extremely proud of his work though he did everything he could to try and keep from showing it.

Guards restricted the number of parcels brought into the camp for distribution because they didn't want Kriegies to store up extra supplies for escape attempts. The unopened parcels were stored in the warehouse near the German flak school about a mile from camp, which gave the Germans an excellent opportunity to steal whatever they wanted. We found out later that they ate Red Cross food almost as much as we did. Even during a period when we weren't allowed to have any of the provisions whatsoever, they were taking items from our parcels.

OVER... AND OUT *"Colonel H.R. Spicer of San Antonio, Texas, bailing out of his Mustang, Tony Boy, off the Cherbourg Peninsula. He had three victories. Hugging the deck, going home to England, Tony Boy was hit in the coolant by light flak. Result: frozen motor over the Channel. Washed ashore after two days and nights in the water Col. Spicer was unable to walk or evade capture. The name* Tony Boy *was given his ship for Col. Spicer's small son who was waiting for his dad at home."* Not as Briefed

same kind of rations as garrison troops, but this didn't happen. We held many meetings with the Jerries on this account, complaining about the inadequate rations that they were issuing to us.

The German black bread, made from wheat stalks and rye, tasted like sawdust unless it was toasted. Our meager meat ration usually came from bloated horses killed in air raids. It took over 3 1/2 weeks for each man to receive one pound of horsemeat, which could include a significant amount of bone. The horsemeat and bones normally were cooked in a stew in large, mess hall kettles. Anything else that was edible also would go into this daily pot.

After the stew was served and consumed, the bones were retrieved and passed around from barracks to barracks according to a priority system. Every barracks received a fair share of horse bones for cooking in a stew for a second, third, or more times. Eventually, the poor old bones were bleached so white and were so devoid of any food value that they were

The Germans also withheld the YMCA's educational, sports, and entertainment equipment if they thought it could possibly be used in escape schemes. For a few cigarettes, however, we usually were able to get the Germans to release some of the confiscated equipment.

In addition to the Red Cross parcels, the Germans provided us with the same kinds of food that were issued to their own civilians holding the lowest level ration tickets. Of course, German civilians had access to unrationed and black market foods to supplement their diet, whereas we didn't. The Geneva Convention stated that POWs must receive the

returned to the kitchen. The Germans retrieved them and gave them to the guard dogs.

Each man received a total of one pound of cheese for every 14 weeks. Some of the fellows wouldn't eat it unless the rations were pretty low, but I figured it was of such an odorous "quality" that, if we were in America, a small slice of it probably would bring a high price. It seemed as if its strong smell practically would let it float away by itself. Potatoes were the staple in camp, and every man received one pound per day, but as much as half of the spuds might be spoiled or damaged by frost during the colder months.

Food shortages lowered morale and sometimes brought out the worst in people, as occurred in the Spring of 1945. I felt badly about some of the things I was seeing and, as one of the camp's senior officers, I released an announcement to the men in my compound on March 16, 1945, titled "Where Do We Fit?"[3]

I began somewhat humorously by telling them that it was certainly becoming easier to like the food because even the "bad" meals now seemed good. Our appetites and tastes were much improved! Two months ago, half of us would have turned up our noses at the meals we were getting—but now, what a difference!

On a more serious note, I urged the men to take a good look at themselves.

What is happening to us? Here are a few things I have seen. The hard workers—the coal detail, have not missed one day of work or delivered one less lump of coal because of the short rations… the kitchen crew, the tin shop detail, the office staff, the camp radio crew, the equipment crew, the maintenance crew, the class instructors, and others have all been doing a superior job.

Let's look at the other side… What kind of pride will let us pick over the garbage pile in order to get more to eat than the next man? What a sense of satisfaction it must give the German private who is guarding us to witness the scene of our men tearing away at the potato peels and rotten cabbage leaves in the garbage pile! How many clever devices have been arranged to steal food from the Mess Hall! It would astound you to know them all… the man taking the food knows he is stealing it from a fellow American who needs it just as bad as he does! No, it's not comfortable to know this is an American camp where we have to guard things and guard each other for lack of trust. Let's look into our rooms where we are crowded 16 - 20 - 40 men to a room and trying to stick it out with no other alternative… Petty grievances, grumblings, disobedience, discontent, [are] goaded further by whining and senseless arguments. Men, who were once willing to die side by side, [are] resorting to fighting and clawing each other senselessly

because neither has the foresight to realize the lack of comfort has to be balanced by an increase in patience and understanding.

We represent a great powerful nation. True enough, but how powerful can we be when we have to resort to a mode of living under our standards? Do we have the fortitude internally to prove to ourselves we are fit to belong to such a nation? Some have proved they can, but those who haven't hold the entire standard low in spite of what the good ones do.

What has happened to all those men who so enthusiastically signed up for the educational classes? Is it a case of "I'll show them—if I can't get enough to eat I'll do nothing to help myself any other way!"?

I hear complaining and bickering amongst our entertainment personnel, the organization most important to morale. Petty differences, lack of cooperation, failure to turn out for practices, postponements, this, that, and the other—all good sound reasoning to give up the ship. Here again, however, some work till they almost drop while others are suddenly becoming temperamental because they haven't just what they need to do their part. Wouldn't a little real spirit help here too? The new band is a good example. They have organized and found time between Mess sittings to practice. We hear them often, and the poor food tastes better. We need more men like this. We need men who have signed up for a job and are sticking it out. We can help each other a lot by forming a will to keep spirit in a project.

Now is a good time to take a reading on yourself. If you're not getting on now, you'll be worse later as there is no doubt times will get tougher. What is happening to us in this process of separating the men from the boys? I am sure we will find mostly men if we just keep reminding ourselves what we are working for.

C.R. Greening
Lt. Colonel
USAAF

A highlight occasion was the arrival of personal packages from home, which often contained things that we'd asked for by letter. One parcel every three months was allowed, but they seldom came on schedule and I received only

two parcels altogether. When the parcels arrived, the Germans opened and investigated the contents, which gave them a chance to take whatever they liked. Seldom did a Kriegie receive a package without something missing and, to antagonize us, the guards left empty candy wrappers in the boxes.

When a shipment of parcels arrived, a list was posted indicating who would be receiving packages. Morale would go up for those getting boxes and down for those who didn't. Most of the fellows were good hearted and shared the coveted contents with their roommates.

Mail call also was eagerly awaited. Since my fateful mission to Naples on July 17, 1943, over a year had passed since I'd received any mail. I'd written home while a POW in Italy and then from Germany, but no return response had come. Finally, on July 27, 1944, I received 26 letters all at once from my mother, Dot, family, and friends! It'd been so long since I'd held mail in my hands that I could hardly believe it. I gathered up the letters and climbed out the window to where I wouldn't be bothered. I found it difficult to read them all. I guess dust got in my eyes.

The letters were postmarked from the last three months of 1943, but it seemed like recent news to me. Included among the letters was one sent in November 1943 by President E.O. Holland of Washington State College. He'd dictated the letter to a secretary while my younger sister, Virginia, who was a student at WSC, sat with him in his office. As with other letters from home, it had gone to one of the POW camps in Italy, then was forwarded to the New Zealand officers' camp (Oflag VIIB) in Germany where Jack, Bob, and I were briefly held, and finally made its way to Stalag Luft 1. The letters and pictures that the Americans and British POWs received gave us proof that our homes and families still existed.

Back home, detailed news about conditions in the POW camps often was restricted or unavailable. Naturally, many of the lads' families, wives, and girlfriends couldn't perceive

or understand what we were going through. This was clearly revealed in a number of the letters received by the fellows. Some of these misunderstandings were humorous, others were not. Following here are some interesting quotes from letters received by the men.[4]

To Lt. G.H.K. from wife

Dear Bill:
I went down to the Red Cross the other day to find out what I should send you. They told me that you could probably send me packages as you have so much food and clothes over there now. They also said you could go to school and learn a trade!

To RAF sergeant from wife in England

Darling:
I have been living with a private since you are gone. Please do not cut off my allotment tho, as he does not make as much money as you.

To British warrant officer from wife

Dear:
I am going to file for a divorce! Mother and I have talked it over and since you have been gone so long (4 years) we decided this was best.

To Lt. P.T. from home

Darling:
I find it difficult to live on your $200.00 allotment…

To Lt. L.B. from home

Son:
We are not sending you any parcels. We hear that you can buy all you need in the stores near your camp.

A POW received a sweater from a woman through the Red Cross. Upon writing her a letter of thanks, he received the following reply:

I am sorry to hear that a prisoner received the sweater I knitted. I made it for a fighting man.

The following is a complete letter received by Lt. L.L.:

Dear Son:
Hello! How are you? We are all well!
With love from all, Dad

To RAF sergeant from fiancee

Sgt.:
You can consider our friendship at an end. I'd rather be engaged to a 1944 hero than a 1943 coward.

To Lt. L.B.P. from aunt

Honey:
I am enclosing a calendar. I thought it might come in handy as it has several years on it.

To Lt. J.A. from wife

Darling:
Sorry I can't send you any money, but I'll send a wallet first chance I get.

To Lt. J.M. from ex-wife

James:
I'll be glad when you get home so I can make our divorce final. I've been living with an infantry captain for some time. He is really swell.

To Lt. B.S. from sister

Dear:
I'm really so worried over Adolph, the cat. I took him to a veterinarian yesterday and he said his diet was insufficient.

To Lt. M.C.L. from wife

My Darling Husband:
Do you get to town very often while a POW?

To Capt. S.W.C. from wife

Dear:
It must be nice to be able to play golf again!

This letter was received by Lt. C.P.N. from a girl he met in Florida over two years before, and after one date never saw her since or ever wrote to her— What a surprise to him!

I am going to spend the summer with your folks. They are fine and all your relations are very kind. All the girls around are worrying about the man shortage and being an old maid, but maybe we can best that when you get home! Your loving fiancee

To Lt. C.B.C. from cousin

Keep 'em flying.

To Flight Officer J.R.C. from wife

Dear John:
I gave your golf clubs to a German Colonel POW here in Canada. I hope you don't mind!

John wrote back and told her to get his golf clubs back and to "Hell" with all German POWs. His country club immediately canceled his membership for not being a gentleman!

With so much idle time, many of the men turned a hand at writing lyrics and other pieces. The American YMCA through offices and printers in Geneva, Switzerland, issued "Wartime Log" books to us, which contained empty pages for keeping a diary or for any other purpose that a Kriegie could think of. [5]

In their searches, the guards often were directed to seize POW poems and writings that were unfavorable to Germans. Also, a censor carefully scrutinized all of the books and other written materials coming into the camp. Later, towards the close of the war, an increase in the arrival of printed materials swamped the censor. Consequently, some things slipped by that contained poetry and writings uncomplimentary to the Nazis. Some of the fellows copied this material into their diaries and logbooks, which in turn were picked up by the German search parties and taken to their intelligence section.

One particular poem contained a parody on "Old Man River," but using "Old Man Hitler" as the subject. Of course, the poem was quite insulting to the Nazis. The Germans pressed court martial charges against a man who'd copied it out of a book. It wasn't until they were shown their own censor's approval stamp, "gepruf," in the book from which the poetry was copied that they dropped the charges. This prompted us to develop a forgery of the German stamp.

Good paper was scarce, so I used my "Wartime Log" for making numerous paintings and sketches, as well as for recording captions, lyrics, and POW writings. I also inserted letters, bulletins, personal documents, family photographs sent from home, drawings from when I was in Italy, labels from Red Cross food parcels, samples of European cigarettes and ersatz coffee (in six little cellophane packets that came with the logbook), and other items and printed materials. (After the war, I added some other pertinent photos and information.) The logbook, in fact, became a complete written and visual account of my POW experience.

Of course, we understood that the life of a POW couldn't be a bed of roses, but the guards' treatment of us often was unduly harsh, unfair, and arbitrary, and the Germans obviously were flouting some of the rules of the Geneva Convention. Incredibly, most of the German guards and officers claimed that they were being fair and just—and

they really believed it! This only made us further despise the Nazi system.

In the latter part of 1944, one of our commanding officers, Col. Russ Spicer, was court marshaled and sentenced to death by a German court. He was allowed to meet his defense counsel only 30 minutes before the trial opened, and an interpreter wasn't present to translate the court proceedings. After about 45 minutes, the court reached a verdict and sentenced Spicer to death. The charges—he'd offended the German Reich by inciting a mutiny and used language derogatory to the character of the German people. The charge and military court was a sham.

It had all originated when some lads in Spicer's section removed a lock bar from the latrine doors and hid it. The guards became angry because they thought this would enable the POWs to dump tunnel dirt into the latrine pit. Of course, they never figured that the lads could deposit the dirt there anyway during the day by simply dropping it down the toilets. Spicer was informed that the bar had to be returned or the compound's coal supply would be shut off. Russ protested on the grounds that this was mass punishment, which was illegal according to the Geneva Convention rules.

Knowing full well that his protest wouldn't have an effect on the Germans, he called the boys together and informed them of the situation. He also told them something about the character of the Nazis by noting how they'd murdered Allied hospital patients during the Arnheim battle in the Autumn of 1944.

"Lads, the Jerries will go to any length to gain an end. We know that by past experience. We know we can't antagonize them without fear of retaliation. But we also know we're winning the war. If we have to sit here for ten years while our soldiers kill every goddamn one of them, then we should be willing to stay and rot if we have to."

For the benefit of the Germans who were standing nearby, he added: "Understand, I'm not trying to incite a mutiny or riot. I'm merely giving facts and information."

A fellow prisoner, Ray Parker, was kind enough to write a poem especially for me and I recorded it in my logbook:

Colonel C. Ross Greening Goes to War

What did I do in the war, Ma'm?
Where did I fight, you say?
Why lady, I've eaten tons of Spam
From Italy to Cathay.

I've flown 'gainst every nation
That dared challenge Uncle Sam,
I've dropped a lot of bombs my dear,
But I ate their weight in Spam.

T'was off the coast of Oregon
This warrior's life began,
My squadron sank a submarine,
The first lost by Japan.

We shipped across in '42
To blast the Nipponese,
Said the enemy, "We've had it!"
Answered we, "So sorry, please!"

We saw the show in Africa
Watched Rommel stomp and curse,
While Allied guns, and planes, and tanks
Put Jerries' armies in reverse.

We journeyed next to Italy
To pave the way for Clark,
While he stole Jerry bases,
We helped bat 'em out the park.

But alas, there came the fateful day
On a special bombing trip,
While I cruised o'er Vesuvius
Kraut flak hit my ship.

I passed some time in prison camp
'Till one day, feeling brave,
I hit the road for liberty
And found it in a cave.

Here, with two New Zealanders
I shared freedom's lark,
We foraged food contentedly
And smoked a heady, grapevine bark.

For six brief months I nestled here
Beneath a wintry sky,
And oft' the days I strayed out doors
To watch the "Forts" go by.

Then, one day, a Kraut discovered us
And gave our cave a leaden squirt,
Said Jerry when he entered
"I'm a doctor, are you hurt?"

Well, they had me bagged for sure now,
No more life so sweetly free,
And I wound up on the Baltic
Spending summer by the sea.

What did I do in the war, Ma'm?
Where did you fight you say?
Why lady, I've eaten tons of Spam
From Italy to Cathay.

I've flown against every nation
That dared challenge Uncle Sam,
I've dropped lots of bombs, my dear,
But I ate their weight in Spam!

Spicer was in jail by that evening and didn't get out again for six, long, weary months. Fortunately, the death sentence wasn't carried out. We assumed Spicer's penalty was commuted in exchange for a similar pardon of a German who'd been sentenced to death in the United States. ✪

NOTES

1. According to Lt. Morris J. Roy's account of Stalag Luft 1, *Behind Barbed Wire* (New York: Richard R. Smith, 1946), the Russian army executed Major von Miller on May 14, 1945.

2. Hub Zemke noted a photograph that included his wife Missy, Dot Greening, and Kay McCollom. *Zemke's Stalag* (Smithsonian Institution Press, 1991), 15.

3. From Ross Greening's "A Wartime Log," 1944–45.

4. Ibid.

5. These 7 1/4 X 9 1/2 inch books contained 151 numbered pages, plus 20 heavier, gray, unnumbered pages in a middle section. A folder at the back contained mounting-corners for photographs sent from home. The light tan, sailcloth covers were inscribed with the title "A WARTIME LOG" above an image of the Liberty Bell, printed in red. The British logs were smaller and had a lion on the cover, whereas the Canadian books displayed a maple leaf. For a comprehensive discussion, see Art and Lee Beltrone, *A Wartime Log* (Charlottesville, VA: Howell Press, 1994).

"When it was all over we tore down the fences and took a walk—home."

CHAPTER SEVENTEEN

LIBERATION BY THE RUSSIANS

After the Normandy landing on June 6, 1944, our morale remained at a high level, though it did suffer somewhat when provisions were critically short or intentionally withheld by the guards. Through our surreptitious sources, we were able to closely follow news about the Allied advances in Europe. By the spring of 1945, it was clear to just about everyone, even the most fanatical Nazis, that Germany was doomed.

In April, with the German military and government in virtual collapse, we learned that the Russian army soon would overrun Barth and Stalag Luft 1. At about the same time, we heard the alarming news that an order had been sent out from Hitler directing that all POWs be taken out of the camps and executed. We knew about this order even before our German commandant heard it, because the camp's German intelligence officers gave us their reports first. They realized that the war was almost over and they wanted to protect themselves by winning our favor.

"Col. Hub Zemke, senior Allied officer, sitting in the former Jerry commandant's office after liberation." A Wartime Log

Col. von Warnstedt had no idea that we knew about the order when he directed all prisoners in Stalag Luft 1 to prepare to move out on foot to a new location. Because we knew this actually was the first step in Hitler's mass execution order, I joined with the camp's other Allied commanders and we went to Col. Warnstedt's office on April 30, 1945, to confront him eye to eye.

Hub Zemke, our senior Allied officer, said, "Colonel Warnstedt, I know what your orders are. We're here to tell you that we don't intend to follow your instructions because to do so would be to our disadvantage. We think it would be better to fight it out with you here. We can assure you that not all of the fatalities will be Americans and Brits."

Warnstedt was shocked by these words and by our knowledge of Hitler's directive. He saw that we were well organized and ready to act.

217

"The control tower on the German airdrome, 2 miles from our camp." A Wartime Log

Being a reasonable man, he replied, "I don't believe in this order myself. As you know, German soldiers carry out orders without question. In this case, however, I think I'd better reconsider."

He continued, "I'd like some reassurance that my guards won't be harmed when they're departing. If you can assure me of that, I'll agree not to carry out this unpleasant directive."

We gave Warnstedt our word that none of our men would leave the camp in pursuit of the guards when the Germans left. As further assurance, we said that armed men from our ranks would be ready to occupy the guard towers and take control of the gates just as soon as the guards exited. With the usual Kriegie ingenuity and energy, by this time we'd secretly acquired hand grenades, ammunition, and nearly 200 weapons. Our ability to act immediately was pretty convincing to him.

A column of about 190 Germans, together with their miserable patrol dogs, left the camp in the night before the first Russians arrived. A few days later, the dogs began coming back alone. We learned that elements of the Russian army caught up with the column and shot it up fairly badly and took prisoners.[1]

Maj. K.H. Steinhower, the German commandant of North No. 1 Compound, remained in the camp. Over the months he had fully cooperated with us within the limits of his authority, as long as he wasn't betraying his own people. He was a good guy and not a rabid Nazi, but quite a good soldier in my estimation.

Shortly before the Russians arrived, Steinhower walked into my barracks, surrendered his pistol and sword, and gave me his camera as a personal gift. After saluting me smartly and saying he'd surrender to the American camp commander, he did an about face to leave the room.

I pulled the gun out of its holster and put it in his back, saying, "Major Steinhower, you are now my prisoner," which I'm sure is exactly what he wanted me to do.

He knew how grim his fate would be if captured by the Russians. I made him change clothes and put on prisoner's garb, and we put him to work incognito in the mess hall.[2]

The Russians were getting quite close by this time. After the Germans left, we sent out advanced details to contact the Soviets as soon as possible, so they wouldn't accidentally bombard our camp. We knew they'd be coming in hordes and laying waste to the German countryside and towns in retaliation for the terrible Nazi atrocities in Russia. Or, at least, that was their excuse as they rampaged

"Major Cooper dispatching the first people from the camp on May 13, 1945." Note the Russian soldiers and trucks. A Wartime Log

across Germany. We felt they'd shoot first and ask questions later, unless we contacted them beforehand.

There were some very experienced infantrymen (paratroopers) in our camp who were experts at reconnaissance and we sent them out to patrol a wide swath of the local countryside. A detachment of our men met the Soviets about 20 miles from Barth and advised the Russian commanders about our situation. The Russians agreed to respect our rights as Allied comrades.

Meanwhile, Lt. Frank M. Leonard (a son-in-law of ex-Governor Hoffman of New Jersey) was dispatched toward our own lines. He would try to contact General Doolittle and see if B-17s could be sent in to haul out our arts and handicrafts collection. By this time, we had 5,000 pounds of stuff packed in 56 crates.

After our patrol had contacted the Soviet army, Gabreski and I decided to go out and meet the Russians. We took up a position near the town, about a mile from the camp. Seeing the approaching column of horseback riders, wagons, and vehicles was a shock. The sight is hard to describe.

The column was bunched together closely and moving as fast as the horses could run. Livestock and wagons obviously had been taken from farms in the countryside. Horses were hitched to the wagons and if one collapsed or couldn't pull anymore, they'd cut it from the traces and put in another. Strings of horses were tied on behind the wagons for replacements. The treatment of horses alone was enough to make a man sick to his stomach. The soldiers seemed to have no regard whatsoever for life, property, or the future. The wagons were filled with loot and the best looking German women the Russians could find. The women were screaming and some horses were bloody.

The residents of Barth were terrified. They'd put Red banners and white surrender flags in the windows, but this didn't spare them. We watched the soldiers pair off and go to each house. As soldiers stood outside with Tommy guns and hand grenades, other men went inside to confront the

inhabitants and bring out whomever they wanted and send them to the column. If an old couple occupied a house, sometimes they were spared from harsh treatment.

Soldiers took anything of value that they wanted, such as antique clocks, kitchen equipment, and bicycles. They had scores of bicycles in the wagons. As the Russians left a house, a soldier on the outside lobbed a hand grenade through the window, regardless of whether or not there were people inside. Quite a number of houses were blown up this way. The carnage was something to behold and we witnessed soldiers raping women right on the spot when they captured them.

As Gabreski and I watched the column pass, a fellow who obviously hadn't ridden a horse before came galloping down the street. The cobblestones were slippery and he was going too fast. The horse went head over heels into the gutter and I thought the Russian would be killed. He wasn't, but he was scratched up, his face was bleeding, and his clothes were torn. He jumped to his feet as quickly as he could, grabbed a club, and beat the horse over the head a couple of times. He walked back to where we were standing and motioned to his foot, indicating for us to assist him in mounting. Gabreski shook his head, "No." The fellow dropped the reins, pointed his Tommy gun, and cocked it. We helped him get on the horse.

Russian vehicles came rumbling up to the gate of our camp and one of the commanders with about a four-day-old beard jumped out. Col. Zemke went out to meet him

"Notice the broad smiles as they march out." A Wartime Log

and was greeted with a full-mouthed Russian kiss reeking of vodka, caviar, and garlic.

The Russians asked us what we wanted the most. When we said steak, they brought in a herd of cattle taken from the local farmers. Nevertheless, we were very hungry and soon had a regular butcher shop set up. By now, we'd discovered that the Germans had kept quite a number of Red Cross parcels from us. We opened these too and had a big feed.

Unfortunately, this proved to be tragic for two men who overate and died as a result. One of them made a cake from a combination of items in a Red Cross parcel and after eating it was immediately seized by cramps. We took him to Doc Hankey, who said the man had the same kind of reaction a baby would if fed harsh food. Hankey did the best he could to save the lad, slicing him open and trying to cut the food out of his intestines, but it had solidified. His stomach was so thoroughly blocked that the fellow passed away before he could be saved.

The British and American high command in Europe had ordered all POWs to remain in the camps until means were provided to get us out of Germany. At Stalag Luft 1, however, the Russians had asked us to tear down the barbed wire fence around the camp. As soon as this was done, many

of our men took off cross-country. It was complete pandemonium.

There were over 1,400 British and 7,700 Americans in the camp at the time. A number of men left because they went berserk at the prospect of freedom. To the best of our knowledge, there were twelve that never were accounted for later. One poor lad was blown to pieces by a land mine. We couldn't identify him; there wasn't enough left. It was difficult trying to talk the lads into staying in camp until some orderly method of evacuation could be implemented. Some men even headed toward Russia. I heard later that one boy was picked up in Moscow while in an amnesia-like state, not knowing where he was. I believe he wanted to be lost.

The morning after the Russians came into town, a Kriegie who was serving as one of our new camp policemen rushed up to me and said several dead persons had been found on the outskirts of the camp. When we arrived, we saw that a German woman apparently had shot her daughter, another young girl, a baby, and herself. A note pinned to a baby carriage stated that they'd rather die than live under Russian domination. This wasn't the only incident of family suicide during this period, of course, but it was the only case

"These Russian trucks carried cripples and baggage." A Wartime Log

"The first day, May 13, 2,500 prisoners were sent home!" A Wartime Log

I personally witnessed. It was appalling, even though death wasn't an unusual sight at the time.

Earlier, we had prevented the evacuating German guards from taking a couple of vehicles with them by simply stuffing potatoes in the exhaust pipes so they couldn't be started. One of these was a small car that I later took out for a drive. When I approached a Russian guard on a bridge, he motioned me over and pulled out a hand grenade after I stopped. I figured he was going to blow up the car, but instead he looked over the side of the bridge, pointed to the water, and threw the grenade into the river.

The blast killed a number of fish and he went down and picked them up. He stripped the skin off with his teeth and began eating the fish raw. He handed me some, but I politely declined. I'd been forced to eat raw fish while in a punishment cell in April 1944 and didn't care to do so again.

The Russians manned a couple of watch posts at our camp and it was interesting seeing them change the guard. They'd face each other with Tommy guns at port arms. The guard being relieved would fire a burst of about five rounds, then

"Thirty men to a Fort—candy bars and 'K' rations were in each ship for the men."
A Wartime Log

the man assuming the post shot a burst in return. The chatter of Tommy guns signaled to all within hearing distance that the guard had changed.

The Russians drank alcohol in copious quantities. When they arrived, they brought vodka and brandy in amounts that staggered the imagination. Our camp's commanding officers were invited to numerous social activities with the Soviet officers, which always were occasions for drinking bouts. Our drinking capacities were definitely not up to Russian standards.

Our camp protocol section told us that the Russians considered it an insult if we didn't consume an offered drink in toto. Obviously, the Russians had sleight of hand methods to disguise and somewhat moderate their intake, while we were caught entirely off balance and consumed far too much liquor in trying to keep up. Many a night we had to relieve one another in shifts to keep pace with the Soviets.

Mark Hubbard served as liaison officer with the Russians, but he soon was in such a red-eyed condition that he had to submit his resignation. The rest of us were then obliged to handle as many of these events as we could. Soon, any American officer who could navigate through one of these gatherings and still be on his feet at the end was appointed to the social detail.

On one memorable occasion, Maj. Gen. V.A. Borisov, the Soviet officer sent to establish martial law in the area, invited Zemke, McCollom, and me to a party at a German estate appropriated by the Russian high command. This party began with toasts to the United States, USSR, and a long list of leaders. In fact, it

seemed as if we would run out of vodka before we toasted everybody.

I asked Maj. General Borisov why the Soviet commanders had allowed the kinds of activities that we'd seen when the soldiers first came into Barth.

"It's obvious that you people haven't fought many wars," he said. "When you allow your soldiers to come into an area and do anything with no holds barred, then the local citizens are very willing to accept my authority when I come to establish martial law."

Martial law had been declared on the same day as this party and the entire situation in the town and countryside indeed had changed.

We were seated according to rank at large festive tables adorned with caviar, raw fish, and bottles of vodka. Both male and female officers of the Russian army sat around the tables in the huge banquet hall, and most of the women were quite attractive in their dress uniforms. Next to me was a tall, good looking female officer who seemed aloof. Our only interaction had been with hand signs, when suddenly, she broke into an operatic rendition of a Russian song. She stood up and threw her arms about while filling the hall with her beautiful voice, commanding complete silence from everyone in the room. She finished to a tremendous applause.

Col. Zemke, not to be outdone, stood up and announced that one of his officers would entertain the group with a song and he called on me. The only song I knew all the way through was "Dear Old Girl." I proceeded to sing in a vodka tenor, which earned not respect but amazement from the audience. It even amazed me. Without the vodka,

"The boys lining up just before loading in the Forts. This jet hanger held concentration camp workers… (note electric wire)." The slave laborers, mostly Greek and French, suffered terribly at the hands of the Nazis. A Wartime Log

I doubt I could've cracked a note. I shattered the notes that I did emit and it almost broke up the party.

Later, I asked General Borisov if the female officer was an entertainer for the troops.

Amazed by my lack of knowledge about the role of women in the Russian army, he said, "These women, every one of them, are military officers. They command platoons, companies, and other units. The one you happened to talk to is one of our more recent heroines."

He produced a Russian newspaper with a picture showing her being carried wounded from a bridge by her own soldiers. She'd led her company in a charge to cross the bridge and was mowed down by machine gun fire, with numerous bullet holes in her body. The soldiers under her command were so incensed that they ran out, picked her up, and wiped out the German opposition on the other side of the bridge.

Borisov said he admired his women officers. They often were more successful leaders than many of the male officers. Soldiers were quite willing to follow orders from a striking woman like her, and particularly one as brave as she was.

As the evening progressed, a Russian band of a "tin horn" variety provided the entertainment. Things remained quite staid until General Borisov enlivened the program with a Russian dance—the familiar deep-knee hopping kind. He was quite a fat little officer, so it was surprising to see how deft he was at performing this difficult dance. This got everyone started and we all tried the dance on our own. Many of our officers ended up flat on the floor. I guess it was from overexertion, but the vodka probably helped. I proceeded to dislocate my knee.

The party petered out rather suddenly when a couple of Russian officers slid under the table. Since Russian protocol demanded that officers not appear drunk in public, aides standing adjacent to the banquet hall rushed into the room, picked them up, and carried them out. I was very glad when the evening was finished. I'm not sure how I made it back to the barracks, but in the morning I was delighted to find myself snuggled in my sack, even though I was considerably the worse for wear.

During the two weeks we remained in the camp after the Russians arrived, the rest of the POWs also obtained an ample supply of alcohol. In a wartime setting, this was quite surprising. It came about in an interesting way. Al Ricci of Keene, New Hampshire, and a number of his compatriots from the camp decided that they'd make a bid for freedom, even though we were nominally free already and just being temporarily detained. Al and his friends planned to row a boat across the Baltic Sea to Sweden, where they hoped to catch a plane home. Al had about $2,000 in checks that he had earned doing laundry in camp.

Unfortunately, the boys weren't sailors. Their boat sank about 200 yards out from the beach and they found themselves swimming back to the German shore. Undaunted, they commandeered another boat and struck out again. They had rowed only about a half-mile when they approached a 3,000-ton tanker, which wasn't flying a flag to indicate its nationality. They assumed it was a German ship and hailed the German captain who lowered a ladder to let them come aboard.

There were German speakers among Ricci's group, so they found out that the vessel had come into the harbor when the captain heard about the Nazi surrender. Now he didn't know what to do or where to go. The cargo consisted of several thousand cases of vodka. This got the immediate attention of Ricci and his fellow Kriegies.

"The second day things went faster and 6,500 were flown out."
A Wartime Log

Ricci informed the captain that he should run up the U.S. flag and then the vessel would be an American ship. This idea pleased the skipper, but he didn't have an American flag. Fortunately, the captain's wife was aboard and she went below to sew one. The boys broke open a case of vodka to insure that the contents were genuine and they sat around a table enjoying themselves, while the captain's wife completed a beautiful American flag. It had the wrong number of stars and stripes, but it generally was the right size and shape. The flag was run up the mast and the captain was informed that no one else should be allowed aboard because the ship now was American property. Then, Ricci's crew appropriated numerous cases of vodka and headed back to the camp.

For several days, their rowboat unloaded cargo from this "American" vessel and the residents of Stalag Luft I became fairly saturated with vodka. Finally, the Russians forbade them from going back to the ship. Strangely, the Russians didn't bother the vessel. When we finally evacuated the camp, the German captain and his ship remained in the harbor, waiting for directions from somebody. We never heard what became of the vessel.

Despite the fact that there was a fine airport adjacent to the camp, the Russians were planning to evacuate us by sending all 9,000 of our men (of which 500 were litter cases) to

"Lt. Col. M.E. Hubbard, C.R. Greening, Col. Russ Spicer, Lt. Col. L.G. McCollom & Lt. Col. Cy Wilson—waiting to take off for home from Stalag Luft 1, May 14 '45." Note the Red Cross crates to the right. A Wartime Log

Odessa on the Black Sea, more than 1,000 miles to the southeast. Word from us had reached 8th Air Force headquarters in Britain on May 7, when Col. Byerly and two British airborne officers flew there and reported on conditions at our camp.

Ex-Senator Harry Cain, who had served as Tacoma's mayor and whom I'd known for a long time, was a colonel in the U.S. Army in Europe. Col. Cain badgered the Russians into sending a message to Moscow to approve our evacuation by Flying Fortresses. Even before Moscow replied, however, Cain dispatched B-17s to get us out as quickly as possible. This was fortunate because Moscow's answer was negative when it finally did come.

The first Fortress to arrive flew in low and buzzed the camp. You can imagine the exhilaration of the POWs. Most of them hadn't seen an Allied aircraft up close for a very long time. The B-17 screamed by, only ten feet from the barracks eaves. In their eagerness to get a closer look, lads climbed up on the roofs. One barracks was so structurally weak from our scavenging for wood and other materials that it collapsed under the men's weight. Soon, scores of B-17s were on the way. Amazingly, 9,000 of us were evacuated in only 2 1/2 days. C-46s took out the hospital cases.

In addition to these B-17s, General Doolittle sent three Forts to haul out our crated arts and crafts materials. First, however, we had to get the freight transported from a warehouse to the airport. Using the capable services of a Russian-speaking American officer from our camp, we stopped a passing Soviet convoy. We commandeered about a dozen or so trucks by telling the Russians that their officers had instructed them to proceed to the Red Cross warehouse and move some items stored there.

The Russians willingly obliged, but when we arrived at the warehouse we encountered a large crowd of civilians trying to break in and get at the Red Cross food parcels. We fended off the mob with javelins and baseball bats from the YMCA sporting equipment. Suddenly, in the midst of the confrontation, everyone was knocked to the ground by an enormous explosion from a nearby ammunition dump. We found out later that it was ignited by a time bomb left by the Germans. All 56 of our crates finally were transported to the airfield and loaded onto the three B-17s sent by Doolittle and flown to Britain.

During the evacuation of the POWs, B-17s were landing at two-minute intervals, and after 30 men piled into each Fortress, they almost immediately began taxiing for take off. General William Gross came from England to take charge of the evacuation, but there really wasn't much for him to do. When he arrived, the Kriegies already were lined up with 30 men in a group and a leader holding a manifest. Gross went to the control tower and watched the operation. The Forts didn't even have to shut their engines off, they just taxied up, loaded the men aboard, and took off.

We were really eager to get out of there. ❀

NOTES

1. "I later learned that Colonel Warnstedt was captured and taken to Russia. Some years later, I received a letter from him after he had returned to Germany with a severe case of tuberculosis."

2. After the war, Steinhower returned to Wuppertal to find his wife and son safe. He resumed his position as an instructor at the boy's academy. When a young man, he'd been one of the early fliers in Germany and had accomplished several gliding exploits in the days when it was a novelty.

CHAPTER EIGHTEEN

POW EXPOSITION

After the airlift out of Stalag Luft I, we were flown to England for some R&R prior to being shipped back to the States. I located General Doolittle, who agreed to transport our art and handicraft materials to the U.S., but unfortunately he was sent to the Pacific before the order could be carried out. The general who next assumed command told us that the shipment would be given "appropriate" priority, which meant about a year's delay. This would completely thwart our plans. We were very discouraged and at a loss as to how to proceed.

Meanwhile, some intelligence officers were interested in talking to me about information I had that would be of value in future war crimes trials. How they found me, I'll never know. An intelligence officer cornered me on the twelfth floor of a London building, where he immediately proceeded with an interrogation. An idea popped into my head and I realized I had the means at hand to get the exposition materials back home, if I played my cards right.

I told the officer that I was the man they were looking for and I had a great deal of information and materials that were of value to intelligence experts. However, I said my directions were that it was to be immediately delivered to a secret installation in Washington D.C. and that no one was to see it before it arrived. Given number one priority, the exposition materials were flown out on three planes in three days. I left London for the USA on June 1, 1945.

I arrived in Washington D.C. to find some extremely puzzled intelligence officers peering through our Red Cross crates full of tin can contraptions, ersatz cigarettes, coffee, and tea, German kriegsbrot (black bread), home-made utensils, model planes, and the other screwball contrivances that came out of prison camp life. After some fast-talking, I was able to get these materials released.

The next task would be to convince the Army public relations staff to approve an exhibition tour, which would showcase POW ingenuity. We felt that most Americans were unaware of this great attribute that their men in uniform possessed.

Now that I finally was back in the United States, my first and foremost priority was to see Dot after two long years of separation. I wired her in Hoquiam, Washington, and told her I was coming home. It turned out that she was visiting old college friends in Missoula, Montana, so I made plans to meet her there.

Mentioning Missoula brought to mind a forgotten promise I'd made with my POW barracks mates a year earlier. We'd agreed to meet after the war at a beautiful, remote guest ranch in the mountains outside of Missoula that Hub Zemke knew about and had described to us. Our plan was to join up one month after the war ended and bring only our wives and a case of whiskey. Longing to escape from our congested living conditions, we wanted to get away to the mountains and the wilderness. I'd forgotten about this plan until Dot's mention of Missoula brought it all back.

With the help of some friends, I boarded a B-26 and left Washington D.C. for Montana. Engine trouble forced us to land in Chicago and then we were grounded by bad weather in North Dakota, so I hopped on a crowded train. Passenger tickets were impossible to purchase, so I just got on the train and told the conductor I wasn't leaving and would stand all the way if necessary. I hunkered down in the club car with a copy of Ted Lawson's *Thirty Seconds over Tokyo*, which I hadn't read before.

TACOMA TIMES—
Lt. Col. Ross Greening in London Broadcast. Another thrill was in store for Mrs. Jewell R. Greening… she heard her famous airman son broadcast from London a radio account of his experiences during almost two years of treatment at the hands of the enemy. A police short-wave set brought his words to her "clear as a bell."

An ex-merchant marine type noticed me and for some reason or the other deduced that I was one of the boys in the Tokyo attack. He was pretty well tanked up and grabbed the book out of my hands. He insisted that I autograph it as a present to him, so he could give it to his son. I didn't get to finish the book and found that this fellow was almost impossible to get out of my hair. He insisted that I take his bunk when he found out that I didn't have one. This was nice of him, but I didn't want to put anyone out. Besides, the lack of a bunk for one night after two years of sleeping just about anywhere I'd lay my head down was the least of my worries.

This fellow insisted on heckling me most of the night. When he learned that I was meeting my wife in Missoula, he made quite a commotion in the car, insisting that all of the passengers witness the scene at the station. This irritated me intensely. About ten minutes from Missoula, I stood up, grabbed the fellow by his coat lapels, and lifted him off his feet.

I said, "Mister, if you so much as stick your nose out of the door of this train when I get off, I'll come back and knock your nose clean off your face." I departed the train without seeing a trace of the fellow.

After what I can only describe as the happiest, most anticipated, most loving reunion of my life, Dot and I went to stay with our friends, Dick and Margaret Hickey, in Missoula. I told them about our planned get-together. I called Hub Zemke's parents in Missoula and found out that his wife was there, but she knew nothing about the plan to go to the mountains. We waited a few days, hoping that Hub would show up and I tried to reach some of the other fellows by phone, but finally decided they'd forgotten about the idea.

Dick thought the place Hub was talking about was Laird's Lodge on Lake Lindbergh in the wild and spectacular Mission Range area north of Missoula. The road there was rough, twisting, slow, and full of long dusty stretches with trees and more trees, but when we finally arrived it didn't seem possible that such a beautiful spot existed. Dick and Margaret left us, and my POW roommates never did show up. Frankly, Dot and I didn't mind.

Lindbergh Lake was deep, narrow, and ringed by rugged, snow-capped mountains. It was named after

Ross pitching in with the enlisted men and officers in setting up the U.S. Army Air Force POW Exposition.

Charles Lindbergh, who had spent some time here after his flight over the Atlantic in 1927. The lodge was a massive building, all hand built with a huge stone fireplace and wonderful log furniture. There was a large dining hall and kitchen, quarters for the staff, and many outbuildings including a barn and corral for horses. It was used primarily by wealthy hunters from the East as a base for pack trips into the wilderness.

"Cap" Laird had run the place with his wife, but unfortunately he had just died and his wife was struggling to manage the lodge on her own. Dot and I fell in love with the place and decided to use my military back pay from my time as a POW to buy it. We went into partnership with

Dick and Margaret Hickey. They'd manage the place and we'd be silent partners. We never regretted our decision.

After a wonderful visit with my mother in Tacoma, Dot and I returned to Washington D.C. I presented the POW exhibition plan to Colonel Hal Bowman and General Rosie O'Donnell. In a few weeks, it was officially approved as the "Army Air Force POW Exposition" with a staff of twenty-two. I would serve as the commanding officer and Maj. Jack Fischer was the executive officer. Lieutenants Byron Morrill, Steve Turner, Frank Leonard, Albert Ricci, and Bill Caryl, among others, were assigned to the project (these former POWs basically provided the core of the staff throughout the life of the project). It was up to us to get the exposition

Mayor Fiorello La Guardia of New York cuts the barbed wire to open the POW tour, October 1, 1945. The men in uniform include, left to right: Lt. Pete Hiltgen, Maj. Jack Fischer, Lt. Phil Melnik (with mustache), Sgt. George Adler, Greening, and Lt. Red Morgan. Edward Ozern, New York

shown in a few cities to test the likelihood of its success and find the necessary funding.

Before leaving Europe, we'd dispatched messages to the Red Cross in Geneva and the International YMCA informing them of our intentions to form a U.S. exhibition tour. The Red Cross didn't want to get involved in a partnership with us, but the YMCA took a keen interest in the project. We were particularly glad to hear of this because the YMCA had given essential aid to American servicemen, especially POWs, and we felt they hadn't been given sufficient credit. The Red Cross parcels in camp fed our bodies, while the YMCA supplies fed our hearts. America arrived in the YMCA boxes.

We thought our exposition would be an excellent means to describe the fine work accomplished by the YMCA's War Prisoners Aid section. Unfortunately, the YMCA hadn't been able to assist all POWs during the war, particularly in the

Pacific where the Japanese hampered or prohibited the efforts of neutral international aid societies. Thankfully, the YMCA had a good success rate in helping Allied prisoners in Germany and Italy.

In the United States, Terry Donahue of the YMCA's public relations staff reviewed our materials. After a conference of national YMCA officials, they agreed wholeheartedly to co-sponsor the show. As a charitable organization, they couldn't provide funding, but we didn't expect them to.

We had dispatched our public relations officer to try and get our exhibit scheduled with the Museum of Science and Industry at Rockefeller Center in New York City. He returned and told us that Rockefeller Center agreed to host the show, but they couldn't book it for 18 months and then for only a couple of days. We were terribly discouraged.

We moved our exhibit to the third level basement of the YMCA building on Madison Avenue in New York, and opened a few crates and set up a temporary display, including a terrific model of an escape tunnel. We invited Mr. Shaw, the head of the Museum of Science and Industry, to look over the exhibit. After he'd been there about thirty minutes, he told us that the museum would host our exhibit in the main display room in Rockefeller Center as soon as possible.

Shaw was so impressed that he set a deadline of October 1, 1945, to open the show. This gave us August and September to make preparations and we eagerly agreed. We were inexperienced and didn't know how hard it would be meet this deadline.

At this time, the Japanese surrendered and World War II ended. Authorities in Washington D.C. suddenly informed us that they felt the public wasn't interested in the war anymore, consequently our staff would be cut and the exposition would be canceled. I rushed to Washington D.C. to plead our case, saying that the show was needed now more than ever because there'd be thousands of veterans returning home looking for jobs, and POWs might be perceived by some citizens as not having accomplished anything positive during the war. I did a lot of talking and finally I was allowed to keep seven staff members, two trucks, and four staff cars if we could get the show on the road and find bookings.

We worked day and night getting ready for the opening at the Museum of Science and Industry in Rockefeller Center. We appeared on radio shows—*Arthur Godfrey, We the People, Hobby Lobby,* and others—and talked to Lions and Rotary clubs and other civic organizations for advance publicity. Because of questions from the audiences, some presentations lasted as long as 2 1/2 hours and were quite exhausting, but were worth the effort.

Our wives came to stay with us during this period and the housing problem was acute. Some of the time we stayed in hotels and sometimes in small apartments in the Bronx. We finally ended up at a nine-acre estate in Bronxville, which was a very fashionable community. Our entire troop was quartered there with a fine housekeeper, cook, and gardener. We became regular New York commuters.

Carol Glenn, wife of
U.S. Army musician
Eugene List, playing
Kriegie violin for
Mayor La Guardia.

We built a full sized replica of a 16-man room and a solitary confinement cell in addition to the other exhibits. Mayor Fiorello La Guardia was designated to be the guest speaker at the opening ceremony and, instead of cutting a ribbon, he'd be cutting barbed wire with a pair of prisoner-made wire cutters. The last nail was pounded five minutes before the scheduled opening time.

The exhibition's opening was hectic. Numerous newspaper correspondents were there along with YMCA officials and a band. A huge sign in front of Rockefeller Center advertised the opening of the show and thousands of people were lined up waiting to enter. Everything depended on Mayor La Guardia arriving on time, but he was 45 minutes late! The band played several tunes and we made some minor speeches to fill up the time while everyone waited.

Finally, the mayor arrived and walked up to the barbed wire. I made a short speech carried over radio and on the public address system, and La Guardia clipped the wire. He

Taken from a solitary confinement cell at Dulag Luft (transitory camp), Germany—

It's easy to be nice, boys
When everything is OK,
It's easy to be cheerful
When you're having things your way.
But can you hold your head up
And take it on the chin,
When your heart is heavy
And you feel like giving in.

It was easy back in England
Among the friends and folks
But now you miss the friendly hand
The joys and songs and jokes
The road ahead is stormy
And unless you're strong in mind,
You'll find it isn't long before
You're lagging far behind.

You've got to climb the hill boys,
There's no use turning back
There's only one way home boys
And it's off the beaten track
Remember you're Americans and that
When you reach the crest,
You'll see a valley cool and green
America at its best.

You know there's a saying that
Sunshine follows rain.
And you sure can realize that
That justice will follow pain.
Let courage be your password
Make fortitude your guide,
And then instead of grousing
Just remember those who died!

A Wartime Log

Mayor La Guardia in solitary confinement. Edward Ozern, New York

chair leg. Then the mayor walked over to the solitary confinement cell, sat on the dingy looking boards that served as a bunk, and was photographed by the news corps. Scores of wire photos were published in newspapers around the country of the "Little Flower," as La Guardia was called, wistfully sitting in solitary confinement.

He didn't really get interested, however, until he viewed the exhibit depicting escape attempts. His eyes widened and he began taking in every detail. After that, he looked everything over very closely. He examined the model planes, the knitting and printing samples, the butterfly collections, the poetry and music, the tin can knick-knacks and homemade utensils, and the numerous other items from everyday POW life.

La Guardia stayed for about 1 1/2 hours and claimed it was one of the best exhibitions of American ingenuity that he'd ever seen. He said he'd had little idea what the exposition was about beforehand. Later, he devoted an entire Sunday radio broadcast to talking about what he'd seen, which helped increase the attendance at our exhibit tremendously.

The POW show doubled the regular attendance at the museum. The director pleaded with us to extend our stay for an additional 18 months; however, we felt obliged to take the tour across the U.S. and we didn't want to stay anywhere too long. At the time, however, we still didn't have advance bookings or funding to move the show out of New York.

Just as we were beginning to focus on our funding problem, fate

In Boston on January 18, 1946, Dot and Ross examine a 12-way mousetrap invented by five POWs in Germany. This trap, baited with ersatz cheese, gives a mouse 6 chances out of 12 to escape out of the cat's mouth at the top. Associated Press photo

immediately turned around and started to walk out without saying a word or viewing the exhibit. I frantically followed him all the way out to the entrance pleading with him to see the show. I told him that this was more than a simple public affairs appearance; it was his obligation to see an exhibit of extreme importance to the American public.

He said he was an hour late to his next appointment.

In that case, I replied, it wouldn't hurt to stay a little longer. He reluctantly came back to walk through the show. La Guardia was met at the door by Carol Glenn (Mrs. Eugene List), an accomplished violinist, who played a piece for him on Lt. Claire Cline's violin made from bed slats and a

intervened in the form of Mr. Carl Fleer, vice president of the Baker Company, a large department store in Minneapolis, Minnesota. While on a business trip to New York, Fleer visited the POW exhibit and then stopped by my office to talk about possibilities. He was by nature an ingenious promoter. In just a few minutes, he outlined a plan for us to take the show across the country with advance bookings and promised he'd provide the initial financing. We named him "Boss" Fleer on the spot.

His plan was to get the big department stores in various cities to provide exhibit space and subsidize us. We liked this idea because department stores were particularly accessible to

Ross chatting with the noted entertainer, Bob Hope. Numerous other celebrities and movie stars also viewed the POW exposition, including noted film actress Olivia De Haviland.

the general public. We accepted the offer, with the proviso that at the end of the tour we'd pay him back for his advanced funding. Fleer and the YMCA agreed and we began planning for a nationwide tour, starting in January 1946.

Lt. Pete Hiltgen was sent out as our advance man and he made arrangements at department stores across the nation. Meanwhile, we made the exhibits portable and packed everything in the trucks and set out for the first scheduled showing at Filene's Department store in Boston. It was a success and Filene's claimed that our presence helped establish an all-time visitation record for them.

While I was in Boston, I received an invitation to attend the first banquet put on after the war by the famed Circumnavigator's Club of New York. I flew there with Frank Leonard. General Doolittle was to be the guest speaker. Also attending were former New York Governor Hoffman, pianist Eugene List, the famous explorer Sir Hubert Wilkins, lecturer Dean Burton Holmes, Congres-

sional Medal of Honor winner Red Morgan, Robert Ripley of "Ripley's Believe It or Not," and many others. I was excited to attend such a meeting. The room was crowded when I arrived, so I was even more thrilled when General Doolittle motioned to me to take the seat next to him at the head table.

I was quietly taking it all in when Doolittle was introduced and rose to address the audience. He went to the microphone and said, "Gentlemen, you think I'm here tonight to be the speaker for the evening. This is not the case. I'm here to introduce the speaker for the evening," whereupon he turned to me and announced my name!

I thought I couldn't possibly have heard him correctly, but when I saw the Boss looking at me expectantly, I was afraid I wouldn't be able to stand up, much less give a talk. My time to prepare a speech was exactly three steps to the rostrum. I saw a sea of faces—faces with years of experience in the world's affairs—peering up awaiting my words. I was

General Doolittle and Ross at the POW exposition.

The seven of us made a total of 1,500 radio broadcasts and 900 speeches, plus many other appearances at events and gatherings across the country. Over seven million people visited the exhibition, and we received letters from General Arnold and other Air Force generals complimenting us for our work.

One of our objectives was to help returning veterans get jobs in their local communities and we were extremely successful in this regard. In fact, we received more job offers from employers than we could fill with veterans. In Chicago alone, we generated openings for 1,200 jobs. We almost grew into a full time employment agency for ex-GIs.

Lt. Ray Brooks joined our tour in Chicago. He was the lad who'd lost a leg when captured by the Germans and our men in Stalag Luft 1 had constructed an artificial limb for him. Of course, the artificial leg became part of the display, as did Brooks himself. He also served as one of our public relations officers.

We contributed magazine and newspaper articles and gave presentations at churches and schools. We talked to senators, governors, mayors, congressmen, city officials, and celebrities everywhere. We also conducted a vigorous recruiting campaign; a number of the young men that we met later donned a U.S. Army Air Force uniform as a result.

In Omaha, Nebraska, I had the pleasure of speaking at a Negro YMCA. They gave us the wildest ovation that we

frightened and don't know what I said. Obviously I must have said something because it took me 40 minutes to do it.

I think I said that the ending of World War II didn't signify that all threats to the United States were over, and then substantiated this statement by relating my experiences with the Yugoslavian communists and with the Russians during our release from Stalag Luft 1. The only comment I remember afterwards when the meeting broke up was from Ripley, who said, "I don't believe it."

After Boston, we exhibited in Utica, Cleveland, Columbus, Chicago, Minneapolis, Des Moines, Omaha, Denver, Spokane, San Francisco, Los Angeles, Salt Lake City, Dallas, and finally concluded at Washington D.C. in September 1946. In every city, we gave presentations over the radio and at club meetings and social gatherings, telling people what POW life was like during the war. When we finished in one city, we'd frantically pack up and head out for the next booking. A typical show lasted 1 to 2 weeks.

Radio announcer interviewing Ross and two fashion models.

received on the entire tour. What's more, they came on a night that was absolutely miserable with pitching down rain and sleet. Yet they gratefully turned out for the lecture and filled the hall to overflowing.

In the nation's capitol, where we were scheduled to present our final show, some military officials told us that Washington didn't want to see World War II displays anymore and it wouldn't be popular. Regardless, we set up our exhibit for a final two-week stand in one of the city's leading department stores. As it turned out, our smallest weekday attendance here more than doubled the largest weekend attendance that we had set in any other city!

The store had to remain open beyond its regular closing time to allow the people still in line to get into the exhibit. On the tour's closing day, we were awarded a plaque from the International Barbed Wire Club, an organization

dedicated to commemorating POWs. I personally was honored, too, with the Flame of Freedom Award from the World Congress of the YMCA.

Our ability in acquiring financing for the exposition was amazing. When Mr. Fleer first offered to provide funding for the tour, we requested $6,000. A few days later, we visited the offices of the *Saturday Evening Post* magazine, which had just underwritten $1,000,000 for the Four Freedoms Campaign show that was being sent around the United States. The people at the *Post* said our POW tour wouldn't even get started for $6,000 and we'd go broke in a few days.

As it turned out, our small staff of advance men and public relations officers proved them wrong. We raised adequate monies throughout the tour and repaid Mr. Fleer with $6,000 as promised and also gave $3,000 to the YMCA. We had additional bookings or promises for bookings throughout the United States, Hawaii, and other places that could've kept the show on the road for several years. However, we wanted to get back to our Air Force careers or civilian jobs so we closed the show in September 1946.

Many of the exposition items were given back to the original owners and the rest of the exhibit was turned over to the Air Force. An exhibit was set up at Patterson Air Force Base, and then later at Reno, Nevada, as part of the escape and evasion training school.[1]

While still in Washington D.C., I experienced an unexpected personal thrill. Unbeknownst to me, Nellie Peduzzi

ASSOCIATED PRESS, *Wednesday, September 25, 1946—Hunts Her Airman. From Italy, blonde, petite Nellie Peduzzi, 29, is in the U.S. seeking one Col. Charles Ross Greening, whom she says she helped dodge the Nazis for five months after he was shot down in Italy. She is visiting relatives at West New York, N.J., from which point she is pressing the search. Now she has a report he may be in Washington, D.C., so she is going there too.*

had come by ship from Italy to stay with relatives and start a career in the U.S. She also had come to look me up, though she didn't know where I was. She was the wonderful young Italian-American woman who, with her father Toni, had provided vital assistance to me when I was on the run in northern Italy.

Nellie contacted the New York YMCA, which was the only address she had for me. Terry Donahue told her that I was ending the POW tour with a big celebration at the Hotel Raleigh in Washington D.C. The YMCA agreed to fly her there.

She'd brought the diary that I'd kept while I was hiding out in the Verona area. Nellie hoped she could personally return it to me. In this diary—which ironically had a picture of Mussolini on the cover—I'd recorded my experiences in the last half of 1943 after I'd been shot down. In about December 1943, I decided to have it secretly buried in a courtyard.[2] I'd asked Nellie to try and send it back to the United States after the war. If I didn't survive, it would tell my family what had happened to me in the five months after that fateful day over Naples.

Needless to say, I was totally delighted to meet Nellie at the airport and escort her from the plane. The two of us walked along arm in arm under an umbrella that I'd brought along because of the rain. Wire photo stories about this reunion were in newspapers all across the country. Our party at the Raleigh became a tribute to Nellie as well as a celebration of the end of the exposition. The next day, September 26, 1946, I accompanied her back to the airport for the return flight to her relatives in the New York area.

Nellie made it into lots of news stories that day too. ✦

NOTES

1. A permanent exhibit of the POW Exposition now is on display at the U.S. Air Force Museum in Dayton, Ohio.

2. See pp. 129–30 in Chapter Eleven, "Nursed Back to Health."

CHAPTER NINETEEN

RETURN TO ITALY

After the POW exposition ended, Dot and I took a long, wonderful vacation at the guest ranch in Montana with our relatives. Our partners, Dick and Margaret Hickey, were doing a great job of converting the place to appeal to families in addition to outdoor sportsmen. Dick was a trained architect who found he preferred this type of life to office work.

After I returned to duty, I was reassigned to Panama City, Florida, for jet fighter training. While in Florida, we adopted a fine young son and named him Allen Ross Greening after Dot's father. Our joy in having this child helped ease my painful memory of an infant boy or-

phaned in an Italian village when the Germans, who were looking for me, machine-gunned his parents in front of me. I later received a picture of the little boy from an orphanage in northern Italy. The photo made quite an impression on me. Just two years after we adopted Allen, Dot learned she was pregnant and soon we had another fine son, Charles William Greening, named after my father.

With the very able assistance of the Brown & Bigelow Company of St. Paul, Minnesota, I was able get my World War II paintings printed in an attractive oversize volume titled *Not as Briefed*. This 50-plate color collection with Lt. J.M. Coppinger's fine captions was distributed to my family, friends, and associates, and to the POWs who had given me their checks and IOUs while we were in the prison camp.

For a time, I served as group commander of the Ninety-first Strategic Reconnaissance Group for the Strategic Air Command, first at McGuire AFB and then at Barksdale AFB, Louisiana. In November 1949, in order to have more time with my family, I requested a transfer to the Aeronautical Chart Service in Washington D.C., where I worked with Colonel Paul Schauer and a highly qualified civilian, Melvin "Slim" Tyrell. We develop a new navigational chart holder and other aids for jet pilots, since the high speeds of the new aircraft caused problems in navigating and plotting courses.

In 1950, shortly after I'd finished my work with the jet chart holder, I attended a Doolittle Raiders Reunion in Indio, California. Hundreds of guests and noted personalities were in attendance in addition to the raiders. I was taking liberal advantage of the refreshments when, without introducing myself, I met a young man who appeared eager to talk. Being an "experienced" jet pilot with some 20 hours to my credit, I proceeded to describe to this young fellow the thrills of jet flight. He seemed to take it all in with enthusiasm, like a complete greenhorn.

After I went to the bar to replenish my drink, I noticed that several people had gathered around my new acquaintance. One of them was a good friend, Max Boyd, a public relations officer from Washington D.C. Being a gentleman, Max decided that introductions were in order.

Not knowing I'd already been talking to this fellow, Max said, "Ross, I'd like you to meet Chuck Yeager, the man who broke the sound barrier."

The orphaned Italian boy. A Wartime Log

I don't need to say how I felt. I just kept my mouth shut and downed my drink.

I next was transferred to the Pentagon for a three-year stretch with the Air Force policy division. In between times, I kept busy attending the Staff College, the Senior Staff Officers' School, the Air-War College, and finally the Strategic Intelligence School. I'd been trying to find a position in the Air Force in which I could utilize some of the unusual experiences I'd gained from my World War II days. Eventually, I found myself discussing a possible assignment as an Air Attache.

In late 1954, it was my good fortune to be posted, along with my family, to a new assignment as U.S. Air Attache in Australia and New Zealand. I was thrilled to learn that we'd be routed by air to Germany, then by train to Naples, and by ship to Melbourne. This meant that my family and I could pay a long awaited visit to my Italian friends who had sheltered me and probably saved my life many times during the war. I wired Toni Peduzzi to met us in Verona. My bonds of friendship with Toni and his family were extremely strong.

After flying to Frankfurt, we proceeded by bus and train to snow-covered Brenner Pass, and then continued south to Verona in January 1955. My emotions were running high in anticipation of meeting my Italian friends in Verona. I didn't want to disillusion them by having their "Brave Colonel," which is what they called me, breaking into tears.

We arrived at a modern, well-built station. I later learned that the United States had rebuilt it after the war. I remembered the time 12 years before when our planes dropped leaflets warning the local populace to clear the station by noon of the following day, because it would be bombed. It was gratifying to know that our armed forces would send messages like that and thereby spare lives.

I left Dot, the boys, and our seven bags of luggage in a coffee bar and began searching for Toni. I bumped into him just as he was coming up a stairway looking for me. He looked great! I'd studied Italian since the war and I think I surprised him by babbling away in Italian. Of course, I received an affectionate kiss on each cheek, a local custom I'd almost forgotten.

We gathered up Dot, the boys, and seven bags of luggage and somehow we squeezed into a small rented car and careened off in the fog towards Pescantina. The driver took us down the same street that Toni and I, tipsy with wine, had biked along to the rail station on about December 1, 1943. Dot and I realized we were embarking on the most moving and inspiring excursion of our lives.

I looked over the top of my B-4 bag jammed on my lap and saw the wonderful sight of Toni's Ristorante California coming into view. We were arriving at the same time of year as when I'd been a POW on the run. The cold was as bitter as I remembered it. We had a wonderful dinner in the main dining room, while keeping our coats on and propping our feet up on the tiny wood stove, which was trying to heat the huge room. Wood was scarce and tiny pieces were fed into the fire one at a time.

After a long evening of wine and wartime stories, we finally went to bed. During the day, Mrs. Peduzzi had kept a charcoal brazier, a "scaldaletto," burning in our bed as a warmer in an effort to drive out the chill. The local residents were accustomed to the cold temperatures and their children played outside in short pants and without jackets, but the chill overwhelmed us. To keep warm, we put on all of our underwear and warm flannels, and slept together in one bed. Dot said being here at the same time of year as I had been made her appreciate what I'd endured when sleeping outdoors in barns or under piles of leaves in caves. She realized

Home of Padre Don Amelio Pinzano in Masarolis where Ross lay ill with jaundice in a 2nd-story room (center) for three weeks. A German patrol took up residence in the house for two days during that period. Greening 1955

how vital people like Toni, Nellie, Elena, and Herma had been to my survival.

The next morning, the Peduzzis apologized for the lack of heating, but explained that this wasn't really their coldest weather. It was then just barely freezing, whereas winter lows often dropped to -10 degrees.

Later that morning, Toni took us to Rita Pavoni's home. Just days after I'd escaped from the POW train at the Bolzano rail yard in July 1943, Mrs. Pavoni was the first person who'd given me food and shelter, and then outfitted me with civilian clothes. Unfortunately, she'd passed away since the war so I had to be content with taking a picture of the hayloft where I spent the night. To me, the house had no soul without her. She was a beautiful, kindly woman who possessed great courage.

I remembered the faraway look in her eyes that night she gave me a suit of clothes. It fit me perfectly and enabled me to pass as a local. The suit had belonged to her son, who'd

Ross with Luigi Comugnero and Padre Don Amelio Pinzano at the foot of the cliff leading to the first cave. Greening 1955

been killed in action not long before I arrived on her doorstep. Her thoughts about helping an American must have been mixed at the time—maybe I'd been the pilot who had killed her son when Italian troops were being bombed.

We next were scheduled to visit my beloved friend, Angelina Righetti, and her family at San Peretto, seven miles away in the nearby hills. In late 1943, the Righettis had hidden me in their attic for 27 days at risk of death for the entire family should the Germans or Italian fascists find me. We'd informed her by mail that we were coming.

With the assistance of a translator, the Righettis sent a reply, dated November 22, 1954:

> Great Friend C.R. Greening—In this morning we have received with much pleasure your great letter. In this we have felt fine things that have given truly joy and folicity. We have felt that all you are truly well and have two gracious childs. Even we of family are well, all marred. Rinaldo with baby, Edda with three sons, Emiliana with a baby, Danila with a baby, Italo with a baby. We spend time of our life in the commerce of wool and cloth. We have a motor lorry and with this go her and there thick. In the letter we have felt of your next desiable visit. This truly causes to we great joy, in fact

we are dixious of your next meeting, to see you after much time; now the things have assumed another appearance. Come, come, we wait you sincerely and all you family, and found also hospitality of in olden times. We have with us your memoir works of wood and with this we thing at you. Come, come my very friend and found also the good and sweet wine. Even family Bustaggi are well. Giuseppe and Angelo are marred with baby. For the convoyance from Verona at Negrar is the service of the mail coach and this departs each hour. Now with the occasion we will send to you our best wished for a good Christmas Tree and for the new year. We will warn you that the time if cold. Now good by with all one's heart.— Family Righetti

On the way, we stopped at a wine shop in the picturesque town of Negrar and also took a short walk. Soon, the local citizens were turning out to meet us and we shook hands with scores of people before we left.

I remembered Angelina's tender care and prayers for me, and her terror on the day she told me that soldiers were downstairs searching the house. Now I was concerned about maintaining my composure when I saw her again.

When we arrived at San Peretto, the entire Righetti family was standing on the steps. Angelina's house was as warm of a place for my soul as my own home. Rinaldo, who was about three years my junior, greeted me with a warm hug and kisses on both cheeks. Angelina stood in the middle of her brood looking a little older, but more beautiful than I'd ever remembered. When Nellie Peduzzi visited us in Washington D.C. in 1946, she said that Angelina had told her that she had one wish—she hoped I'd come and see her one more time before she died. I felt deeply honored that anyone would feel that way about me.

Dot had been extremely anxious to meet Angelina. When they finally met, they embraced and cried as if they'd known each other all their lives. Angelina bubbled in Italian and Dot in English, but they understood each other perfectly. Even though it was raining, the entire population of the village had gathered around the house moments after we arrived. We were escorted into the Righetti's restaurant and Rinaldo brought out the family's best wine. He showed us many certificates on the wall attesting to his wine's high quality. We sat down at a table loaded with fine Italian food, and I lost count of the number of courses that were served.

During the meal, an elderly man made his way to the center of the room carrying a large bouquet of flowers. Facing Dot, he made a rather formal speech in Italian. He presented the bouquet to Dot, and then, trembling slightly, he stepped back unconscious of the fact that he was crushing his good Sunday hat under his arm. We all stood and toasted him for this lovely gesture.

Outside in the rain, villagers lined up against the windows and pressed their faces to the glass. Dot and I were enjoying a

Ross with sons Al and Bill looking into the crater of Mt. Vesuvius. Greening 1955

dream come true. The attic room where I'd hidden out for 27 days had been converted into a bedroom. We hadn't intended on staying in Angelina's house because it might be a hardship for her, but we soon learned that she'd hear of nothing else, so along with our boys, Dot and I shared my old attic room that night.

We visited the wine cellar where I'd spent many hours cleaning barrels and, incidentally, also sampled the contents. The medieval-looking barrels and stone work resembled something from King Arthur's day. Huge barrels with a capacity of several hundred gallons each lined one wall, while smaller barrels for sweet wine rested along the opposite wall.

Angelo and Beppi Bustaggi, now a U.S. Army employee in Verona, walked down from the nearby mountainside to extend their greetings. Their farm was about 1 1/2 miles away in an area where ages-old stone terraces held agricultural plots against the mountainside. I'd also hidden out at the Bustaggi home for about three weeks during the war. It was raining hard, so Dot and I decided to leave the boys with Angelina's family and we walked with Angelo and Beppi up to their home. Rinaldo and I stopped along the trail at times to recall where we'd encountered Germans or had other harrowing experiences.

It was dark when we arrived at the stone house, which loomed up ghost-like in the foggy rain looking just as it did when I'd first seen it years before. There was no electricity; the rooms were lit by oil lamp. When Mr. Bustaggi, now 86

years old, saw us, his eyes filled with tears. This elderly, diminutive hunch-backed man hugged and kissed me practically to the point of embarrassment. We'd been the closest of friends and almost constant companions during the time I hid out with them. Mrs. Bustaggi lost no time in recalling how we both almost lost our lives eating poisoned mushrooms.

A stove had replaced the open fireplace for cooking. As always, a big pot of polenta was bubbling and I couldn't resist having some again, even though a big meal was planned later at Angelina's. We toured the house, observing the wonderful handcrafted furniture that Angelo had made with homemade tools, some of which he'd made himself or inherited from his ancestors. He was one of the finest cabinetmakers in the region. The lovely bedroom sets, buffets, chairs, and other furniture, made with wood cut and seasoned by Angelo himself, contrasted rather interestingly with the simple pot of polenta simmering on the stove.

We finally said our good-byes to everyone except Angelo and Beppi, who considered it polite to accompany us at least part way down the hill. It made me think of the American custom of walking a guest to the door, or if the weather was good, perhaps to their car. It was pitch black, raining, and cold, and the trail was muddy; yet these friends walked more than half way back to assure us of their sincere hospitality. Meanwhile, Rinaldo told stories of his battles with the Germans later in the war. We were exhausted, but Dot and I agreed that this was the experience of a lifetime.

After a wonderful night, we awoke to find that the Righettis had quietly taken our mud-splattered clothes and brushed them clean. They also had provided us with soap, towels, and pails of steaming hot water. After a wonderful breakfast, we prepared to return to Pescantina with Toni. A majority of San Peretto's residents appeared from all quarters to see us off. I could keep my composure with everyone's good-bye tears until I had to face Angelina. I'd never known a more genuine and admirable person. She wasn't in the best

of health and we didn't know if we'd ever see each other again.

After saying our heartfelt farewells to the Peduzzis in Pescantina, we journeyed east by train 125 miles to Udine, where Elena and Elio Borgnolo, Herma Zamparutti, and Padre Don Amelio Pinzano were expecting us. They all looked wonderful to me. Herma was accompanied by a professor friend, Marcoline Elci, who quickly became a welcome partner in our reunion.

Herma was even more beautiful than I'd remembered her. She was an extremely good-looking woman who could raise doubts in the mind of any wife and I wondered what Dot was thinking. There'd been no cause for Dot to be concerned, but nevertheless I was very, very glad to see Herma again. She cried when we met. If it hadn't been for her, I probably wouldn't have survived jaundice or the Germans, or ever seen my wife again.

That night we visited with these friends in Udine. Elena and Elio Borgnolo, who still lived in Valle, also stayed at our hotel. While our group sat in a wine shop, Herma related some alarming information from the past to me. Jack Lang, Bob Smith, and I had always thought our cave was accidentally discovered by the German patrol that captured us. Herma, however, said the Germans had been aware of our general hiding place for some time, but they couldn't find the cave, so they finally resorted to questioning small children. A frightened 9-year-old boy pointed out the cave's location and by the next morning we were in German hands.

That 9-year-old now was 20 and was horrified to learn that I was coming back. He thought I wanted revenge. His family had moved from the mountains and now lived in Udine. I wanted to meet him and sent a message through Herma, and later through the newspapers, saying I had no interest in revenge and didn't blame him. He didn't believe me, however, and I never did get to meet the young man.

Herma also said that after our capture, the Germans had returned to the villages that had helped us. They burned homes and buildings, and executed a number of men in reprisal. Elio Borgnolo had to flee for his life and lived in a cave for a time, just as we had.

I was upset and saddened to learn this for the first time after all these years. I wondered what our reception would be like when we visited the villages, but Padre Pinzano assured us we shouldn't worry.

That evening, Italian newsmen surrounded us in a nightclub for interviews. One radio announcer even had me live on the air trying to describe my visit in Italian. When I finished, I repeated it all in English and then the reporter summarized what he thought I'd said. It must've been pretty mixed up, but people told me later that they thought it was wonderful.

That evening we met Major Quandt, commander of an American Air Force fighter squadron stationed outside of Udine. He graciously offered a military station wagon and jeep to transport our party to Masarolis, the first of the four villages we intended to visit. They also would return to pick us up after we walked back from the villages.

Fortunately, the weather cleared up nicely for our two-day trip. The Air Force drivers took us about 20 miles east to Cividale and then north a few miles over practically the same route that I'd traveled during the war. I remembered many of the sights. Just beyond Torreano, the terrain steepened and we had to switch to the jeep to snake up the narrow, steep grade. We stopped once to take pictures at Pete Comugnero's vineyard, where the German patrol had surrounded me and asked if I knew the whereabouts of an American lieutenant colonel hiding in the hills. The jeep made two trips to get our entire party up into the hills, where there still were insufficient roads and we had to proceed on foot.

We finally arrived in Masarolis, and since it was a Sunday, the villagers were gathered in the village square by the church. From a distance, Masarolis appeared picturesque and quite beautiful, but up close it was pretty rustic. Many

of the homes were built four centuries ago; no one could trace the history of the oldest buildings. We shook hands with everyone and then met the new padre. We learned that Pete Comugnero had passed away just two years ago. He'd been my close friend during the time I was hiding out in this village.

The priest took us to see Mrs. Comugnero, who was sitting in a chair in her stone house waiting for us. She was too ill to meet us in the village square. She wore a black dress and a black bandana over her head, and her eyes were deeply set into her thin face. When I saw her, I felt like I'd walked into my own home and was meeting a member of my own family. We both shed tears. I was deeply moved by seeing her again, and humbled that she was so happy to see me. We sat and talked about the events of the past eleven years. I told her I wanted to take some pictures and she bustled off to change into her best. Italians seem to love to have their picture taken.

We looked at the hayloft over the kitchen where I'd stayed; it had deteriorated over the years. Mrs. Comugnero obviously was in dire financial straits. I gave her all the money I had with me. I would have brought more, but didn't know that the villagers were still so impoverished. Clearly, conditions had remained fairly grim after the war, and folks needed additional food, medical supplies, and clothing. In spite of this, the people maintained their dignity, a respectable bearing, and a cheerful attitude. Later, Dot and I talked over plans to ask U.S. civic groups and churches to adopt these villages and make it a project to fulfill some of their needs.

Herma pointed out places in the village where the Germans had inflicted damage in reprisal for the help given to the New Zealanders and me. Fortunately, American agencies came in after the war and repaired the destruction, and even built some new structures as repayment for the assistance given to us and other Allied soldiers. It made me feel particularly proud of my country to know this.

At lunch in his home, Don Pinzano recounted how the Germans had occupied the house and he was forced to sleep on the floor while the commander took his room. The faulty latch that had delayed the German soldier from entering my second-floor room still was broken! I was sick and bed-ridden at the time, and the soldier's hesitation in fumbling with the latch allowed Herma the time to come and twice turn him away with her furious barrage of words.

After lunch, Pete's brother Luigi, a shoemaker, escorted us about a half-mile to the first cave where I'd hidden. Our boys were eager to see if the mouse that had eaten my lamp wick was still there. It's truly an amazing cavern, located on a steep slope with the entrance directly under a large bush, making the opening invisible until someone is right on top of it. The boys and I crawled around inside. After taking pictures, we returned to Masarolis and, at around 3 PM, our group made up of the Greenings, the Padre, Elio and Elena Borgnolo, and Herma and her professor friend began hiking the four miles to Valle.

Trees are sparse in these mountains and the slopes were covered by deep, green grass. Even this late in the year, it can seem idyllic almost beyond description. Dot said that at least I'd had a beautiful view in 1943–44, but I replied that this was practically the first time I'd seen this locality in the daylight. Jack, Bob, and I had mostly traveled at night to escape detection and often in rain, snow, and mud.

With the fine weather we were experiencing, we could almost see the Adriatic Sea, over 40 miles to the south. The easy trail followed along the contour of the slope, with little climbing or descending. Padre Don Pinzano was a great talker and chattered incessantly with everyone, his long black robe flowing behind in a picturesque manner. At one point he came back to me laughing. He said he'd been talking to Dot for half an hour before remembering she didn't understand Italian.

About sunset, we approached the cave that I'd shared with Jack and Bob. It was about 100 feet below the top of a 2,500-foot cliff. To get to it, we had to descend to a point level with the cave entrance, then cross along the steep cliff by clinging to rocks and brush the best we could. Elio helped one of the boys and I guided the other one; both squealed with delight. This whole trip was a great adventure to them. To be frank, I think I was just as excited as they were. I was a little homesick for that miserable hole. There still was faint evidence of the foot holes that we cut in the rock.

Dot said the cave looked exactly as she'd pictured it in her mind, even the little ledge where we often sat watching the trails below and taking in the sun. Visible far down the valley were a tiny stream and the small village that Jack, Bob, and I visited once. We climbed all over inside the cave and took pictures from every angle. Even though the Germans had dynamited the place, traces of the fireplace and bench still could be seen. I recalled that during one long, cold stretch when we were snowed in, Elio had been the first to break through the drifts bringing polenta and a pot of stew. I remembered the bitter cold when we had huddled in our straw bed. I hoped my sons would never have to experience this.

We looked down the cliff where our little sweethearts, the village children, had struggled up with their small, precious food bundles for us. In the distance, we could see Reant, which was the village closest to the cave. Herma pointed out a new American-built church that had been erected in honor of the help given to us by the villagers. After one last look from our cliff-top lookout, we continued on to Valle.

Elena's 14-year-old daughter, Renata, ran up the hill when she spied us approaching. She was hardly more than a babe the last time I saw her. I was amazed to see that she was a nearly full-grown, good looking, healthy, blond young woman. She greeted us warmly, then, as if she hadn't a minute to spare, rushed back to the house to complete her chores. I find it impossible to adequately describe the love and warmth we received in Valle. It was obvious that the

Borgnolos had carefully planned for our visit and they intended to make us feel completely welcome in their home.

Elena and Elio were leaders in the town. Their hewn-stone house was neatly laid out and spotless, and the yard was enclosed within an attractive, flower-bedecked fence. The main living room and kitchen were two centuries old, yet the furnishings were the most modern we'd seen in any of the villages. Neatly arranged inside were a beautiful wood stove, a hand-tooled table that would've created a gleam in an antique collector's eye, and a buffet and sideboard of equal quality. All of the pots and pans were gleaming. Keeping the house up this way must have taken special effort when using a wood stove for cooking and having very little indoor plumbing.

Elio's mother and cousin also assisted in the festivities. Bowls of fruit and nuts were set out near tall, enticing, bottles of wine. Flower arrangements were everywhere. Elio and his mother immediately took our muddy shoes away to brush them clean as we sat down to full cups of wine and Italian coffee.

We were served a four-course meal in elegant style—wine, liqueurs, nuts, the works! Elio's mother had to wash dishes between courses and kept the wash bucket between her legs so there was a minimum delay with the crockery. We met a few of the other local people, one of whom was the widow of a man who'd been executed by the Germans in reprisal for helping me. This remarkable woman showed no grudge toward us, and consented to having her picture taken with me.

We were served wonderful coffee from a pot that used steam pressure and then added boiled milk. After dinner, Herma, the padre, and the professor had to leave for Udine. Starting late, they became lost on the mountainside and were hours late in getting back. That evening when the boys fell asleep upstairs, we went to a wine shop at the village center.

This was "Festa" day, which meant that nearly everyone was engaged in the local pastime—consuming wine. While the men drank, the women stayed in another room and watched through the door. If a man began to slide under the table, his wife would slip in and assist him home. It seemed to be the only way they could get their men to leave.

The place was noisy before we arrived and practically turned into bedlam when we entered. This was the same wine shop in which Bob Smith and I were surrounded by a German patrol in 1944. We'd crawled up a creek bed to get out of town and evade capture. Now, in 1955, toasts and "Viva America" greeted me! The greetings continued the whole time we were there. We were treated with glass after glass of the house red wine, which left a rusty red ring around the lips and turned your teeth blood red.

I knew a great many of the people here and they all tried to tell me what had happened to them in the war. The room became rather silent as one man described the German reprisals directed against the villagers. Men had been executed in the streets for helping us and some of their widows were here in the crowd, their eyes brimming with tears. Amazingly, following these painful stories we were assured by them of their sound trust in America! They described in detail the wonderful aid that American agencies had given them when they needed it most after the war.

Many of the villagers had been pro-communist during the war, but now were condemning this doctrine. A few said they'd professed allegiance to the communist leaders only to keep them off their backs. They now were convinced that the communists had wrongly informed them for years. This was gratifying to hear, though it was easy to see that some of this was said just for my benefit. As least the American aid programs had created a desired effect in this remote area.

That night I met a young man who, when a boy of nine and with several other youngsters, would meet Jack, Bob, and me at a snowfield above our cave. We had had some devastating snowball fights and great fun. Now he was rapidly taking on the early aged look seen in so many people of the hills, the result of a hard life.

The next day we walked to Reant, just over another hill. We had many good friends in this village who helped us during the war. On the way, we passed our water hole about a half-mile from the cave. Bob, Jack, and I had taken turns carrying water back to the cave in half-gallon amounts, because that was all the containers we had.

After visiting in Reant, we walked a couple of miles along the ridge to Pedrosa, the fourth village that we relied on for assistance. We looked up Lilia, the cute little girl who, with her companion Amabile, had climbed the cliff to deliver eggs and cigarettes to us. Her beautiful eyes hadn't changed, but I was sorry to see that the insufficient diet and hard conditions were affecting her health as a young adult. Nevertheless, I was very delighted to see Lilia, and I received a warm welcome from her.

Regretfully, Lilia's father was suffering from tuberculosis. Her house, though small and dark, had the neat, scrubbed look of the others, with shining pans on the inside. After taking pictures, we walked the short distance downhill to the Borgnolo's home in Valle for a final feast before we started back to Udine.

Elio and Elena had invited the local padre and we were served the feast to end all feasts. I'm sure Elena had risen very early to prepare this meal because it seemed comparable to a king's feast in Buckingham Palace. Imagine a meal in a rustic setting beginning with antipasto, followed by a wonderful soup, a salad course, a chicken course, baked rabbit, desert, wine, cheese, fruit, nuts, and more good coffee. Renata and her cousin were kept busy in the corner washing dishes in a pail between courses.

After dinner, we were extremely sad to say our goodbyes and start the long walk back. Elena needed to return to teach school at Ancona, so she went with us. Elio came too, carrying Elena's heavy bag. It was dark when we reached the outskirts of Faedis where the Air Force station wagon was waiting to pick us up. We said farewell to Elio who had to walk the four miles back home. What a wonderful person he is, and the hospitality and love of his family will be remembered forever.

The next morning in Udine, we had breakfast with Herma and her mother at their apartment. Herma told us harrowing personal tales of the war—her sister was burnt to death, her father executed, and she had been captured but later escaped. Such were those terrible times!

After our final dear goodbyes in Udine, we spent a few days viewing the awe-inspiring sights in Venice, Florence, and Rome, but I kept thinking about what tourists were missing by not visiting Italy's little villages and wine shops. We traveled on to Naples and went up the side of Mt. Vesuvius in a cable car.

It was a moving experience to visit the scene of my bailout. I thought about the German soldier who came panting up the hill and put his rifle down to shake my hand.

I was re-telling this story to Dot and the boys when we were having refreshments at a shop halfway down the mountainside. Suddenly, a man standing nearby came up, saying, "I know! I was there and saw you land on the mountain. I thought you were going into the crater, but you drifted right across it. I can show you exactly where the plane crashed. Bits of it still are there!"

This was an amazing coincidence. I dearly would've loved to climb all over Vesuvius looking for parts of my plane, but our time was limited and I had to forego the experience.

After a brief trip to see the ruins at Pompeii, we returned to Naples and boarded the passenger ship *Orion* for the final leg of our journey to Australia.

Back in the days when I was living in the cave with Jack Lang and Bob Smith, I told them, "If it's the last thing I do, I'm going to get down to New Zealand one of these days and see what kind of a country it is that makes guys like you."

I last saw Smith and Lang in London after the war. As soon as I landed at Perth in Western Australia, I wrote to both men. I told them that immediately after arriving in Melbourne and settling my family in, I was planning on flying to New Zealand right away. Apparently, they had thought my official duties would keep me in Australia for a while before I could make the 1,200-mile flight across the Tasman Sea to see them.

I wired them that I would be landing at Paraparaumu Airport, located about 30 miles from Wellington on the south end of New Zealand's North Island. My C-47 transport experienced extremely stormy conditions during the flight. Bob and Jack arrived at the airport early, and went to the control tower and talked to me by radio as soon as my plane came in range. Though it was the southern hemisphere's warm season (in February 1955), bad weather nearly closed the Paraparaumu Airport and the fog lifted just as we came in to land.

Greening Christmas card, 1954.

Season's Greetings

Our Greetings this season from the Capital again,
No—we're not in a rut—it's a popular trend.
We're leaving the country the first of the year,
To go to AUSTRALIA—so you won't find us here.

The place where we're going resembles the U.S. a lot,
But is the language like ours?—Most certainly not!
There a Cooky's *a* Biscuit, *a* Flashlight *a* Torch,
Where tea in the evening's on the Veranda *not* Porch.
If on a date with a girl—I meant to say Lass
You've exhausted your Petrol—*don't say "Out of Gas!"*

So we change our expression from "Merry Christmas Y'all"
To "Cheerio, Pip-pip, Ripping, Ol' top, and
"Anyone for cricket?" then, "A spot o' tea from the Pot!"

DOT, ROSS, ALLEN And BILL GREENING

When I stepped out of the plane wearing my green flying overalls and grinning from ear to ear, Bob and Jack were there to meet me along with an official American delegation. Ceremonies and speeches had been planned, but when I hugged Jack and Bob, it was obvious to everyone that our joy and emotion had overpowered us and we needed time to ourselves.

Colonel Hearne of the American delegation touched me on the shoulder, saying, "I'm here to officially welcome you, but I can understand how you're situated at present, so I will see you later when you have some time." He was a fine, understanding man.

Our joyful little party went to a Wellington hotel where we spent the rest of that day and night going over the events of our lives in Italy with pictures, letters, and stories. There was an enthralled look on the faces of the many friends congregated there listening to us.

I brought with me a letter for Bob and Jack from the villagers of Masarolis. It said, in part, "When you were with us, you were like our sons. We will remember you always. Please do not forget our families."

I also brought along a fine bottle of Grappa from Italy, but it had blown its top on the way over the Tasman Sea. In spite of my official duties and press interviews, we managed to have a big party at Bob's home. I gave a running commentary of our return trip to Italy and showed pictures and color slides. The next day, I was scheduled to fly 300 miles north to Auckland where Jack lived. Unfortunately, our celebrating had aggravated Bob's serious bronchial condition, which was derived from his wartime experiences. Bob was sidelined in bed the next morning when I had to fly out.

Nevertheless, Bob's mother, who considered me to be almost like another son, came to the airport to see me off. She was in her seventies and frail from a heart attack about seven years before, but I was able to gently help her into the C-47 where I showed her the radios, extra fuel tanks, and survival gear. She sat in the pilot's seat and I described to her how to fly an airplane. She really enjoyed the experience.

Meanwhile, Jack had taken off after the big celebration party and drove all afternoon and night to get to Auckland by 5 AM. He had breakfast and then drove his family out to the Whenuapai Airport to meet me there when I flew in. I was thrilled to meet his mother, sister, wife Beryl, and their two children. I told his freckled-faced daughter, Shirley, that I really liked freckles—if she could see my two boys she'd understand why. Though I'd be stationed in Australia, I told them, "This will not be my last visit to my friends in New Zealand." I returned the next day to Melbourne, Australia.

Serving as U.S. Air Attache was the best assignment we'd ever experienced. We had a nice home, a top-notch school for the boys, and wonderful associates. I'd always hoped for a military assignment that would give me the opportunity to produce individual results outside of the usual routine of military assignments.

I launched into this intriguing job with enthusiasm. The Air Force assigned a plane to assist me in my duties. My travels took us back to New Zealand, as well as to all parts of Australia. Along with Ambassador Amos Peaslee and his wife, Dot and I embarked on a circumnavigation of the Australian continent during which time I did the flying. We visited almost every city along the way and journeyed inland to see mines and fascinating natural sights, including Ayers Rock. Everywhere, the Australians greeted us with a friendliness that was almost overwhelming.

We met many interesting people and, in fact, derived greater enjoyment from this assignment than we believed was possible. I'd always been a great believer in the law of balances. After the hardships, separations, and difficult assignments we'd suffered through, Dot and I felt this posting was destined to balance the ledger of our life in the Air Force toward the plus side. ✹

BOB SMITH'S STORY

A young man named Giovanni came up to us and said, "Follow me, I'll show you a place where nobody will ever find you." He led us back up the hill, turned along its crest, went down a slope and around a sheer cliff, and there before our eyes was a perfectly concealed cave.

"Only we locals know about this bouca" (cave) said Giovanni, "and there are all sorts of legends about it. People escaping or hiding have been using this place for generations and nobody has ever been caught in it yet."

To add to its romantic history, one could well imagine it having concealed bandits, revolutionaries, and even criminals. Extending 25 feet back into the face of a gray stone cliff, its front had gradually filled with detritus. There was a small opening of three feet at the highest point and steps leading down to the floor, which was the size of a large room. Brush concealed the opening; there was absolutely no way of seeing it until one had turned a corner and stood 10 feet from the entrance.

We had found a sanctuary. Even the climate was in our favour as the warm Italian sun shone down on these southern slopes on fine days, making it feel like spring. We called this side of the mountain "The Tropics." The other side, which faced north and never saw the sun, was "Siberia." No water was nearby, but a 15-minute return trip to Siberia remedied that. Sometimes when we were snowed in for a few days, we melted snow in a bucket on the fire.

Originally there wasn't a fireplace, but we made a good one complete with a chimney that was simply a channel dug up the face of the batter to the entrance, and covered with sticks and tamped earth to seal it. As the light gray wood smoke matched and merged into the light gray background of the cliff, this meant we could have a fire almost as often as we liked.

A pile of hay that we spread in a corner near the fire, three blankets, an eiderdown, and our two overcoats made a comfortable, warm bed. We could sing and shout to our heart's content, which we did to let off the steam generated by our weeks of enforced quietness.

After firmly establishing ourselves, we solved the livestock (lice) problem once and for all. While our underclothes were buried in the snow, then washed and dried, we spread our blankets and bedding out on some shady frozen rocks during the day. Then, sleeping in our underwear we left our outer clothes in the open air all night. That fixed the lice.

The village of Reant gradually came to adopt us and after dark we called at different houses for food. Thinking it an imposition to burden ourselves on so small a hamlet every evening, we occasionally forged afield to other villages. Initially our good friends were offended at our doing so, but were reassured when we explained why.

Our first call in Masarolis could easily have been our last. A night-time celebration was in full swing when we arrived at the local "Osteria" (wine shop). The wine flowed freely. We asked for a box of matches—we had no money to pay for them—and the girl who gave them to us said under her breath, "Take my advice boys and get out of here quick. Some of the fellows don't trust you and that group of men near the door are discussing what to do about it right now." The appearance of the men bore out her remarks.

The local inhabitants were justifiably touchy; we didn't know then that we'd been the unwitting cause of this. After some ex-POWs had been shot here a week or so before, the Germans had conducted a room-by-room search throughout Masarolis. Some men had been rounded up and the enemy kept the village under close surveillance. It seemed ridiculous to us that we'd be thought of as spies, but these villagers couldn't trust anybody till they were absolutely sure of their identity.

We didn't know it at the time, but they were particularly wary because the local schoolteacher (Herma Zamparutti) was caring for a sick American flier in a room at the priest's house. No one knew better than we that it was natural for people in these parts to regard all strangers with suspicion, so we didn't stop to argue. We went, and fast.

We avoided the villages in daylight, but occasionally met children out on the mountain slopes in the late afternoon and assisted them with odd jobs, like gathering firewood or chestnuts. Keeping much to ourselves, we tried not to burden or encumber anybody by our presence and we gradually came to be accepted by all of the neighboring villagers in the area. We eventually were welcome at Masarolis, but we never quite felt comfortable there and didn't visit this village as often. Conjure up a picture of a bandit chief's mountain hideout and you have a fair facsimile of Masarolis in wartime.

A man staggering out of the town's wine shop early one evening gave us a cheery hail. "Come and eat with me," he said. "My wife's away, but I'll cook you up something."

Wives did all of the household work and men never touched a dish. In his inebriation and eagerness he almost set the house on fire. These houses were rustic, with an open fire on a raised square hearth in the middle of the room and a hole in the wall to let the smoke out. Upstairs was the bedroom, which received the heat from the living room below. Tall adults had to walk around with head forward and shoulders stooped to keep their faces below the heavy pall of smoke. We were once in a house so blackened with smoke that its wall shone black as a coal seam in a mine. In some instances, the fireplaces had a canopy over the top with a chimney to take the smoke away. Our inebriated host set his canopy ablaze and we had to beat the fire out. At least life was never dull. There was always something going on.

As we gained entry into their homes, Jack and I maintained a courteous attitude toward adults and kindliness to children. To further gain their trust, as we were both single, we invented fictitious wives and families. The townspeople looked askance at anyone still remaining single at the ripe old age of 30. This put us in the clear with the men; the quickest way to get in trouble with them would be to get too friendly with their womenfolk. Family life was very close. Old men were the bosses, and if children misbehaved they were boxed over the ears by any adult regardless of whose child it was. Their great childhood fear was of "Lupi" (the wolf). "Watch out or old Lupi will get you" was the threat held over their heads for any misdemeanor.

The children, quite unasked, worked out a system of food supply for us. They would meet us on the outskirts of town after dark and say "Go to so and so's place tonight. They killed a pig yesterday so you will eat well." Or, "We've arranged for you to call at Mrs. Somebody Else's tonight as she brought back a special treat from Cividale today and here are some eggs and cheese we have gathered up for you to take back to the bouca."

Precious little blighters they were. It worried us that such great-hearted kids would probably grow up to nothing better than the drudgery of eking out a living in these infertile mountains. We called one of them "Bella Ochi," as she had the most beautiful blue eyes. Our simple but wholesome diet consisted mainly of cornmeal, potatoes, cheese, and onions, with occasional eggs and milk. Salt and olive oil were scarce. We never saw tea, sugar, coffee, bread, or butter.

We didn't need to go out every evening. The acquisition of an old pot ensured that we had a warm breakfast and hot meals when snowed in. When we did go out, however, the return late at night after climbing the frozen track through Siberia, then lighting a roaring fire and sitting snug in our hideout watching the flickering flames throw cheery shadows around the crannies of the cave, was like a tale out of Arabian Nights.

We heard whispers of the American flier hiding somewhere in the vicinity, but as there were always rumours flying around, we didn't pay them much attention. Furthermore, we never asked leading questions; we'd always found that minding our own business paid its own dividends.

"The American flier was a real colonel—The American flier is sick—The American flier had gone—The American flier is back," and so the stories went. If there were any truth in them, we felt we'd eventually hear about it. It was arranged that we should go to the priest's house in Masarolis to meet this mythical character.

Lt. Col. Charles Ross Greening was bombed at Bolzano when being transported by train to Germany after the Italian Armistice. Like us, he'd been on the run ever since. In roaming across northern Italy, he'd found shelter in Masarolis, but the arduous conditions under which he'd been living finally caught up with him and he suffered a bad attack of jaundice. The schoolteacher, with the priest's permission, moved Ross into the priest's home while she nursed him.

Ross was in bed when a four-man Mongoli patrol chasing Jack and me came into the village, shot other escaped POWs, and conducted a room-to-room search. The priest

had panicked and cleared out, but the schoolteacher stood firm outside Greening's bedroom door, put her arms across it, and refused to let the soldiers in saying that it was her sick cousin and the doctor's orders were that under no circumstances was he to be disturbed.

When we first met Ross, he still looked gaunt and yellow from his illness. These brave people had sheltered him at grave personal risk; if they were detected, reprisals would be brutal and summary. Although not yet fully recovered, Ross felt he should move on so as not to expose them to further danger. Normally this wouldn't have presented much difficulty, as I've never met a man more capable of looking after himself than Ross Greening. If it hadn't been for this illness, I'm sure he would eventually have made a clean getaway back to the Allied lines.

He wasn't in a reassuring situation so Jack and I suggested that if he had no other plans he should move in with us. As he was rapidly regaining health, he joined us a few days later, and from this date a new era in Anglo-American-Friuli relations dawned in this part of the world. Friuli is the regional nomenclature.

With typical American efficiency and dispatch, Ross started to improve our living standards, initiating a new project every day. In next to no time we had chairs, tables, etc. made out of trees and vines, and a hygienic latrine. Our double bed had perforce now become a triple bed, but the outsiders, due to a blanket shortage, never slept as warmly as the one on the inside—so we took turns. The man on the left had the fire's warmth to help him sleep, and in the morning it was his turn to cook breakfast.

Cornmeal made a delicious porridge as it contained its own natural sweetening. The occasional addition of pork fat gave the flavour of a meat dish. We excavated the entrance to the cave, then enclosed it properly, using an awning as a door. With the spoil we enlarged the balcony, where we could sit on warm sunny days and admire the magnificent panoramic view. We improved the trail, as on a dark night it

was possible to slip and fall down the cliff when turning the bluff approaching the entrance.

Ross Greening was a man's man by any standards. Over six feet tall and built in proportion, he'd been an athletic star at Washington State College. He was mentioned as a nominee for the 1936 Berlin Olympic Games as a javelin thrower. Humble, tolerant, and modest, Ross had the marks of greatness indelibly stamped upon him.

Being an excellent artist, he amused himself and the children by drawing their portraits in no time at all; everybody wanted his or her picture drawn. Children would arrive at the cave with eggs in one hand and a piece of paper in the other. Ross manfully obliged and dutifully signed his name as "Carlo Grini" at the bottom.

With the added attraction of having their picture drawn, the children started to play the wag from school to visit us. This was one of the small schools established by the Italians. Although Italian was the language used for instruction, Slovene was still used in the homes. The people detested the fascists; the schoolteacher who, during lessons, used Italian, immediately reverted to the native tongue when speaking to children at any other time. Truly a classic example of playing lip service only.

Although we knew the children were skipping school, we didn't have the heart to tell on them. If their parents found out what was going on, they'd apply a liberal application of the cane to deter them. It was the children's greatest delight after a heavy snowfall to gang up on us unexpectedly and engage us in a terrific snowball fight.

Naturally, the news of our presence was gradually noised further abroad, and lost nothing in the telling. We heard of a battalion of American and English soldiers in the mountains; by a process of deduction, we eventually concluded that battalion to be ourselves.

The Germans on garrison duty in Cividale regularly came looking for us. Once we didn't see them till they were walking past the cave entrance 50 yards away. Although so close, it was impossible for them to see us. Italian Fascisti used to occasionally have a go at it too. Once they were very close—right altitude, right location, but wrong spur. They tried again with some dogs to track us, so we shot up the top of a nearby mountain, picking our way amongst coarse scrub that dogs wouldn't go through.

They also would make sudden raids in the village after dark and nearly caught Ross and me on one occasion (Jack being home with a cold). As they came through the village at one end, we jumped out the other. We were in good physical condition and had little fear of being caught once we had a head start. We could scoot up a hill like hares and the quickest way down a snowy slope or a shingle slide was to take a running jump, turn, and skid sideways down on our boots as if on skis. This was a trick Jack and I had learned from the partisans.

The parents finally issued an ultimatum to their children: "no visits allowed" to the cave except on weekends, and then not by the usual track as it was becoming too well defined. This meant they had to follow a circuitous route over a hill, down a valley, then straight up a cliff, negotiable only to goats and mountain children. Imagine our mixed feelings when watching, with our hearts in our mouths, the small figure of Bella Ochi crawling upwards like a fly. Scrambling finally over the edge, she advanced towards us cupping both hands carefully round a parcel she had nonchalantly been carrying in one hand, saying, "Be careful now, don't break these eggs."

Being on the leeward side of the mountain, large overhanging snow cornices would form and sometimes it was hard for us to know where solid ground ended and soft snow began. If we misjudged, we often would flounder and start small avalanches. If it snowed too heavily, we stayed inside.

Once, after a period of several days, the Valle schoolteacher's husband, Elio Borgnolo, ploughed his way through to us laden with supplies. "I came to see if you were all right," he said, "and in case you are hungry I brought some food along."

The concern of these people for our welfare was heartwarming. Nothing was a trouble for them. They would shake their heads sorrowfully, saying "pauvre genti" (poor man), and "bruto tempo" (bad times). To be thousands of miles away from home and the comforts of family life was to them a tragedy, and they always tried to cheer us up. Waggling an optimistic forefinger a foot from our noses, they would say "Coraggio! Due mesi encora a la guerra sara finita" (Keep your spirits up. Another two months and the war will be over).

We had been hearing this "due mesi" business for months now, but it was intended as an expression of encouragement and comfort rather than to be taken literally. There were no radios, but the news would eventually seep through. When it was good, indicating a defeat for the fascists, the wine flowed freely. The price on our collective heads was 5,400 lire (about 56 pounds) dead or alive—a princely sum to these people; yet among the hundreds who knew us and our whereabouts, not one betrayed us. Although they felt sorry for us, we felt more so for them as one day we would be returning to our enlightened, prosperous countries whereas these good folks were destined to remain here impoverished till the end of their days.

We had a pet mouse that scurried around picking up crumbs. We called him "Topolino"—Italian for Mickey Mouse. A robin redbreast used to appear only when it was snowing, as food was then harder for him to gather. At breakfast, he would pop suddenly into the entrance, his little red breast making a vivid splash of colour against the background of snow, which had drifted in. We threw him crumbs as he unconcernedly hopped about eating his fill. Then he would fly away and sure enough pop back again every morning until the snow cleared. We never saw him on fine days.

Large flights of American bombers often passed overhead going north. The figure-eight vapour trails of the at-tacking Focke-Wulf fighters, the planes shot down, and the parachutes floating quietly to earth brought back memories of Hell's Corner in Kent during the Battle of Britain. To get a better view, Ross and I climbed a nearby peak, but wished we hadn't; there was no cover from bullets splattering around us from the dogfight going on above. Jack on one occasion idly picked up one of these expended bullets and put it in his pocket—an innocent act, but one which later nearly cost him his life.

We found another unexpected danger from these raids as the stray incendiaries, an incredible sight, often started brush and grass fires. The hot sunshine alternating with frozen temperatures on the hillside subjected rock outcrops to continual expansion and contraction. The extra heat of a fire occasionally caused them to explode with a loud crack.

On one occasion, such a report followed by a swishing noise caused me to hurriedly look up; "scoppio"(explosion) grinned a local man while beating out the flames. I ducked quickly to the right while a large disc-shaped boulder the size of a breadboard whistled past my left ear. These fires were a crippling blow to the peasants as they destroyed firewood as well as hay, which periodically was cut and stored in neat little haystacks for their livestock.

Seeing a young girl carrying a haystack on her head and shoulders, we offered to help. We could barely lift it off the ground. Trained from infancy, the peasants carry enormous loads; an average man hoisted 200 pounds. Many easily carried more, even up and down rough mountain tracks. It was a local saying that when a man couldn't carry 170 lbs. one mile he was getting old. Previously in Yugoslavia, Jack and I had seen young men vying with each other—they held large stones an arm's length above their heads that we couldn't even move off the ground.

The little girls—bless their hearts—had noticed that we were poorly off for socks. Unbeknown to us, they'd saved their pennies and bought some homespun wool. Each child knitted a section which, when carefully assembled under the

eye of the schoolteacher, made three pair of woolen socks, complete with coloured bands of red and blue at the top. The scene when these wonderful kiddies presented them to us quite broke us up.

The self-reliance, self-possession, and initiative of these hardy mountain youngsters were something that their city cousins could never know. So generous and spontaneous were the people in their hospitality that as a token of appreciation we arranged an "at home" one Saturday afternoon in the "bouca." Special precautions were taken and scouts were placed strategically to send a warning in case of approaching enemies. Socially it was a great success, but the hospitality was more on their side than ours, as they came bearing food, wine, and special little treats. When they left, we were laden with supplies.

We spoke Italian fairly well by this time, but Jack was the best linguist. He'd already learned Greek when on the run in Greece and had the ability to pick up a language quickly. In a discreet way, we gradually became part of the villagers' community life, and were invited to share in their celebrations. If somebody had a special feast, we were invited.

Elena Borgnolo, the schoolteacher living in Valle, taught all week at a town on the plain and returned every weekend, leaving again early on Monday mornings for the 15-mile walk back to her school. An attractive, spirited young woman, we were impressed with the contrast her well cut clothes made in the rustic village. She was most interested in the USA and in practicing her English on a real live American; to hear about his country was something in which she took delight. Saturday evenings generally would find us at the Borgnolo home as she had a vivid personality and we enjoyed her company. Women like her were only a memory and it was good to know that they still existed.

She was happily flustered on one of our visits. The fire wouldn't light so we fixed that up for her. There was a lot of mystery surrounding her activities in the small kitchen. It was a big surprise; we weren't to know. Barely containing our curiosity, we watched a sticky sugary substance bubbling in a pot. Finally, with a flourish, it was set before us. As we rarely tasted sugar, our mouths watered at the sight of such a sweet confection.

Eagerly I took a mouthful, chewed, and then glanced at Jack. Jack was looking at Ross, and Ross was looking steadily at his plate. Not a word was said. We manfully did our best to get those mouthfuls down, but it couldn't be done. What to do? We couldn't swallow. Who would be the first to spit it out and embarrass our hostess? Finally the dreadful truth dawned on Elena that not all was well with her masterpiece. The acrid flavour was burning our palates and we had to rush for water. It was lemon meringue, and lemon flavour with a vengeance—a whole bottle of it.

"But the recipe said a few drops of essence would make a delicious flavour," she wailed, "so I thought a whole bottle would be so much better."

We all set to with a will to make another one, but without the lemon flavour —fortunately there wasn't any left.

We never over-stayed our welcome, but sometimes had difficulty in getting away at a respectable hour. "Elena," we used to say, "three men can't stay late in a home with a young lady. It's not done. It's not fair to you. Moreover you're a schoolteacher and you must set a good example."

"Poof, what do I care. I can look after myself, see I am strong."

She was reared in the mountains and could lift her 170 lbs. of "fenna" (hay) up the steep tracks with the best of them. Playfully, she put her arms around us in turn, lifting and throwing us around. It was phenomenal that so feminine looking of a creature could conceal so much strength in her shapely arms and shoulders. I'd hate to be the man she took a dislike to.

Though never dissatisfied with our lot as we realized our good fortune, the enforced wait till the winter snows were over caused the hours to sometimes drag. Under Ross's tutelage, we took up wood sculpturing. Although most of the locally grown wood was unsuitable for this medium, Ross produced some most attractive figures. By way of variation and with only an old chisel and a knife to work with, he made a perfect model of a Flying Fortress, complete to the last external detail. Jack made a Spitfire, but my interest flagged early as unfortunately I wasn't much of a hobbyist.

However, I did occupy myself to some purpose. Previously I'd never had the patience to keep a regular diary, but in a notebook I'd acquired, I wrote down everything I could remember that had happened since I joined the Army in 1939. With a borrowed pack of cards, we played one continual game of Rummy. At the time of our last session, the score had reached astronomical proportions.

Our situation was known to the local partisan organization and we often acted as a halfway house to some of them passing through the area. Anybody on the run could hide with us in comparative safety. Their best known courier in these parts was a small, middle-aged, mild, hen-pecked looking fellow named Blanco. That was why he was successful, because he was so self-effacing that nobody would bother giving him a second glance. On his last periodical trip, he said he'd call for us at the end of March when winter was over and arrange to have us guided back through Yugoslavia to freedom.

The partisans suggested that we mount a machine gun at our cave entrance, but the village people wouldn't hear of it. Their enthusiasm for the resistance movement had waned by that time as it had caused them nothing but trouble. An adjacent hilltop village, two hours away, recently had been machine gunned from the air as a reprisal for partisans staying there. Five innocent men and women working in the fields were killed.

It was a fact that within a few hours of the partisans showing up, the Fascisti would be tipped off and a patrol would come after them. The fascists issued a warning that no staffs were to be carried by walkers; from a distance a staff could be confused with a weapon. The local people obeyed this warning with alacrity, as anyone seen carrying a gun by a patrol or spotter plane was immediately shot at.

The Germans knew we were in the area, but couldn't pinpoint our hiding place. It had them puzzled. We rated the honour of having an observation plane sent out to look for us; a Fieseler Storch came over and circled above. We could see its occupants quite clearly. The cave entrance and balcony were covered with brush that we'd cut, but the trail around the cliff, in spite of covering it daily with leaves, was becoming well defined. Aerial photography might spot it. Had it been summer, foliage would have shrouded our whereabouts completely.

Three lone Allied soldiers weren't much risk to the German war effort. But for us to be running around so long avoiding capture—much to the secret amusement of the country folk—indicated that the Germans didn't have complete control of the area.

The arrival of spring was heralded in mid-March with a grand Festa lasting several days. Nobody did any work and the local wine shop at Valle was the centre of revelry for the whole district. An old battered accordion on which the musician appeared to know only two tunes was the source of music for continual dancing. We danced with people of all ages, men and women, and girls and boys. It was an odd sensation to find oneself whisked onto the floor in the arms of some sprightly gent of eighty odd summers. We left in the early hours of the morning with the celebration still in full blast, and when we returned the next evening after dark they still were going strong.

Life was primitive and the Italian people took their pleasures simply—yet the stark struggle for existence lay very close beneath this surface gaiety. During the previous night, two youths had left after us to return home to their village. The wine they'd drunk told on them when they got into the cold mountain air. Being tired after all their jollifications, they rested at the side of the trail; they never woke up. Their

bodies were found frozen stiff in the snow later that morning.

We over-reached ourselves when we took part in this Festa, as it was a time when people in the whole countryside went from village to village enjoying the hospitality. In this way, our whereabouts were noised even further abroad. Elio, the schoolteacher's husband, who had become our great friend and liaison officer, suddenly became very concerned for our welfare and suggested that it was better for us to move. He showed us another cave, which, though in an inaccessible spot and otherwise suitable, had a stream of water running through it.

"There are hundreds of our people who know where you are," he said, "and though nobody has as yet given you away, it's too much to expect that the secret won't come out sometime. I've heard that the Germans are going to make an all out effort to get you."

We didn't take the advice to move from our comfortable quarters as the winter was almost over. Our cave had served its purpose in providing security and comfort, and we intended to move back through Yugoslavia with Blanco within a week or so.

Shortly after this, I was dozing off to sleep one night when something jolted me hard awake. It's the sort of thing that happens to all of us now and then, but this was a feeling of alarm and depression. Momentarily it was a feeling of panic. Something was going to happen and the dim starlight drifting through the cave entrance made the sensation more eerie.

Reassuring myself that tomorrow, perhaps, we'd better talk things over, I drifted back to sleep. Probably the next morning I would have put it down as a figment of the over-vivid imagination, which one has at sleep time. Whatever it was, I know I've never since neglected a hunch.

A fusillade of shots burst into the cave next morning while we still were in bed. To stop the grenade that I thought would inevitably follow in a second or two, I rushed outside to find myself once again close-up on the wrong end of a gun, this time held by a German a few feet away. Standing there bare feet in the snow and clad in my one article of underclothing—only a short singlet—I must have looked quite ridiculous. I certainly was cold and very scared. I spoke to him and hearing my accent his tension eased and he replied in good English.

"So! You're the English and American we've been looking for. We've found you at last. We thought it would be you as no local people would've made a hygienic latrine like you have back along the track, but we weren't taking any chances."

Seeing the disposition of the other soldiers positioned around the area and the grenades they held handy, I was glad I came out fast enough to stop them from blowing us up. He was the medical officer of an Austrian battalion, two companies of which had been detailed to search for us, having left their billets at 2:30 AM that morning. They now knew exactly where to look, but figured that their only chance was to catch us in bed. And that was how it turned out. Ross had rose at daylight to have a look out, had seen them toiling up the slopes far below, but as this had happened many times before, he paid no more attention than we usually did and went back to bed.

Well, that just about finished up our "cave-man story." It was a pity that we had to spoil the record of such a magnificent hiding place, since nobody on the run had been caught in it before. It seemed a pity too that the Germans hadn't made their attempt a week or so later, as by that time we might've been on the way back to Yugoslavia. Our captors suggested that we carry as much food and clothing as possible.

They spent an hour thoroughly searching the cave. One of the soldiers acquired an excellent war souvenir—Ross's model of a Flying Fortress. The last we saw of it, it was being swung around on a string in a realistic fashion. As we passed through Valle, the concern on everybody's face was tragic. They were sure we'd be shot, while we were sure that the Germans would exact grim reprisals on them. We looked stonily ahead, not daring to glance directly at anyone as in that way we'd betray our friends. I caught a glimpse of Elena standing back in a doorway trying to hold back her tears.

At a junction on the road below, we met a patrol of Fascisti who'd been part of the combined operation against us. Among them was a man who'd been a partisan with the anti-fascist Garibaldi Battalion. He'd been a good friend and guide for Jack, and I knew him too. Now he looked terrified. Not a flicker of recognition passed across Jack's face as he looked full at him. Although the situation now was different, Jack didn't want to turn in somebody who'd once done a friendly act. In any case, a lot of partisans had gone back to the fascists, and if we'd denounced him, he could denounce us also and we'd all be shot.

Late in the afternoon as we approached the Cividale barracks, the soldiers broke step and straggled all over the road like old Brown's cows. Perhaps these troops weren't of the same calibre as frontline soldiers, but whatever the reason, they now presented a most unmilitary sight. Loaded as we were, Jack, Ross, and I took delight in showing them up and derisively marched shoulder to shoulder with a firm military step.

During the day, I had idly removed my hat, when Ross said, "What's the matter with your head?" I put my hand up and felt my hair matted with dried blood. In the excitement and fright when those bullets came ricocheting around the cave, I hadn't noticed it, but one had cut along the top of my scalp.

The battalion headquarters was located in a large house, where we were correctly treated according to military etiquette. It appeared an easy enough place for a man to escape from, but there was more to consider than clearing out again. When visiting the toilet at night, one of us could've gone through the window on to a lean-to roof, jumped to the ground, and quickly disappeared in the nearby hills, as there

was only a picket on duty. But the two left behind would've been punished for aiding the other. I didn't suggest that it should be done. Although the matter was never openly discussed, I'm sure all three of us made exactly the same mental observation. None of us would do anything that would cause suffering to the remaining two.

Before interrogation, we agreed on the story we'd tell and not under any circumstances depart from it: "We'd never been with the partisans, the locals had never helped us, we didn't know anybody, and while on the run we'd lived solely by stealing or making threats."

We were separated early one morning for interrogation and weren't reunited till late afternoon. Jack was interrogated first. After Jack presented the usual preliminaries of name, number, and nationality, the interrogating officer said, "You have been a partisan." Jack stoutly denied this.

"Oh, yes you have, we have proof… see this," and he pulled out the expended bullet that Jack had idly picked up from the hillside during an aerial dogfight and put in his pocket. "This proves you've been with these scum and have been in action against us. It's an American bullet."

Jack explained how he came to have it in his possession.

"A likely story indeed," replied the captain. "We don't believe you. From our point of view, it's quite enough evidence to convict you of the crime of being a partisan. You'll be shot tomorrow morning."

Jack was dumbfounded, and wildly said, "You stupid fool, do you think I look like one of these locals. You can see what I am. I'm a British soldier. I've had nothing to do with the partisans. The only reason I'm here is because I escaped and want to get back to my own country."

The captain momentarily was taken aback and looked at Jack hard. "Well it's too bad. You've obviously been with them, so we'll have to shoot you. That's the penalty when any of them are caught."

Poor Jack, he thought he'd "had it," and spent a very worrisome few hours.

I was next on the list. The interrogating captain—sitting in a tastefully decorated office with green carpet, good furniture, a green-gray steel filing cabinet, typewriter, etc., all efficiently arranged—busied himself over some details and purposely ignored me. This was all routine stuff that was supposed to make me sufficiently cowed so I'd become more tractable. The Jerries were always so obvious in their attempted subtlety, or so it seemed to me. As I'd been amongst them so much, I'd come to know them well.

After the usual formalities, he suddenly said, "Where'd you get that Austrian jacket you're wearing?"

"Oh I just picked it up somewhere," I replied.

"Don't try to fool me, nobody around here can afford to buy a jacket like that and there isn't another like it within a hundred miles. You've been in Austria."

He wasn't too far off with this deduction, as we'd been in what once was part of the Austrian Tyrol. All I could do was stick to my story, to which he replied, "It's no good. You can't fool us. You've been in these parts for over six months. You've traveled a long way and we have definite proof that you've been with the partisans. However, I haven't quite decided what to do with you yet. I'll wait till we consider your case later in the afternoon."

Before leaving, I put in a plea for the people living in the mountains. I explained their difficult living conditions, of how their food was taken from them by partisans whether they liked it or not, and how in reprisals innocent people were killed. Additionally, although this wasn't true, I stated that they'd been threatened by escaped POWs who said the Allies would punish them after the war if they didn't provide food.

"Yes, I know," he said. "I feel sorry for these poor people. They do have a miserable existence, but war is war." On the day of our capture, five men were shot in Reant because it was the village closest to our cave. By way of conclusion, he said, "Tell me, how did you escape?"

"I jumped off a speeding train."

"Ah," he said with a faraway look in his eyes, "that's the way a soldier escapes."

Ross was the last to be interviewed. With his seniority in rank and by sticking to our story, he was able to handle the German captain and swing things our way. We were called together late in the afternoon and given the verdict—not guilty of being partisans, but guilty of escaping! We were sentenced to serve 30 days in solitary confinement and sent back to our quarters, where our guard was the light-heavy weight boxing champion of pre-war Germany. We were given a bottle of cognac to celebrate. We didn't drink too much, however, in case we'd inadvertently start talking. We were well treated for the few days that we were there, and given another bottle when we left.

When starting our journey north to Germany at 9 AM one morning, some well-dressed passengers were unceremoniously pushed out of a nicely appointed first-class railway compartment to make room for us. As the three of us had previously escaped from trains, we were watched very closely. Our first overnight halt was in Austria, where all the gear that we'd so laboriously carried with us was taken away during our stay.

The next day, we were taken to the Landeck punishment gaol, located at the extreme western end of the Austrian Tyrol, where we were to serve our punishment time. We were placed in solitary confinement cells, 7 feet long and 4 feet wide, with bare board beds and tiny barred windows high up near the roof. The only moveable article was a "cell utensil." Later, we were put together in an attic, where we were left alone and each given a whole Red Cross parcel in addition to the ordinary rations. This was an incredible delight and we immediately spooned off all the sweets.

After a week, we were on our way north again. When passing by Munich, we noted that the city's outskirts had been heavily bombed. The marshalling yards and railway stations were so badly battered by incessant attacks that the tracks were redirected around the edges of the city. Slave-labor camps were situated near the demolished rail yards. Even before the "all clear" signals sounded after air raids, laborers were hounded out to repair the tracks. These unfortunates suffered heavy casualties.

We stayed a night at a Gestapo gaol in Ingolstadt, Bavaria. As we marched in the moonlight toward the prison, our boots clattered noisily over the frozen surface of a Danube bridge. We were hungry and I asked for something to eat, but the wall-eyed, pimply-faced youth in uniform acting as a gaoler became abusive and started pushing me around. It was so unexpected and uncalled for that I lost my temper.

I told him in heated English that we weren't civilian criminals, but POWs in transit. Furthermore, they were losing the war and it didn't pay to be too cheeky, as I'd have him shot after it was over, or words to that effect. We all went off the handle sometimes and it was my turn to do so. Perhaps, we didn't take kindly to confinement once again after being at liberty for so long. He couldn't understand English (perhaps fortunately for me), but he wasn't much more than a kid and nothing further happened.

With no blankets or coverings to sleep under, our small cells were like iceboxes. Ross tore up an old book he'd picked up somewhere and stuffed the pages inside his jacket and trousers for warmth. Still feeling cold and having pages left over, he heaped them in piles and set a match to them to warm the place up. He nearly smothered himself in the process. Hearing yells and seeing smoke pouring from the ventilator above the door, the Jerries came shouting in alarm along the corridor. Upon opening the door, burning bits of paper were scattered about like falling autumn leaves.

Next morning, we left for an officers' camp at Eichstadt, a two-hour journey north, where I had the good fortune to be recognized as we neared the gate by Capt. George Bennett of the Maori Battalion, an old school pal. Due to his efforts, the camp POW staff saw to it that we were well looked after. During our solitary confinement there for ten days, food, clothing, and cigarettes were smuggled in to us.

We didn't have to complete our full term of punishment and left for our respective permanent camps traveling together to Nuremberg, about 100 miles northward. On the handsome concourse of Nuremberg railway station, we were separated to go our different ways, but something went wrong. Ross and Jack were kept together and I was taken in charge by an efficient looking "Oberstabsfeldwebal" (warrant officer).

We looked at each other and shrugged. "Oh well, if the Jerries want to mess things up let them go ahead. It's their business."

Traveling by rail at this stage of the war in Germany was an ordeal and every train was packed with passengers, with the main line and express services being grossly overcrowded. At the larger stations, troops scrambled through the windows headfirst even before the train stopped. On heavily used traffic lines and at the larger stations, special train police were in charge ordering both soldiers and civilians around. In addition to regulation Army uniforms and steel helmets, they wore a metal breastplate suspended by a chain around the neck on which was printed in phosphorous "Zug Polizei" (Train Police), which could be read during blackouts. With so much bombing occurring and the extreme pressure on the railway system, there was a critical need for this kind of organization to supervise operations.

The German military's love for uniforms was much in evidence. The civilians who carried the war effort on their backs looked meek and lowly by comparison. Put these same lowly civilians in uniform and they'd also probably become petty tyrants and start pushing other civilians about. This was much different from England in the early days of the war, as civilians came first there, and soldiers second.

For German civilians, normal train travel was restricted to within 100 kilometres from a person's home; special passes were required for additional travel, but only in cases of

illness or for some other pressing reason. Germany's shortage of petrol was well illustrated by the number of trucks and cars outfitted with charcoal burners, which generated charcoal gas used in place of petrol. The people seemed apathetic, bored, and listless. Only rarely was laughter or any sounds of gaiety heard.

My guard must have been an old commuter; with me in tow he'd thrash his way down aisles packed with humanity. No sluggard this fellow. He was an experienced soldier and knew all the angles. He'd been in the war from Dunkirk through the Balkans to Greece and Russia. Now he had a cushy job as a reward for long service. Although he spoke little English, and I less German, we understood each other perfectly. He loved his Fatherland, had fought hard for it, but in his opinion the writing was on the wall as far as the outcome of the war was concerned.

Previously on train trips, we'd been seated amongst civilians or packed in with soldiers. My guard did things differently. On the first train, by dint of much shoving and maneuvering, we ended up comfortably ensconced in the railway guard's compartment, which we shared with a member of the "Zug Polizei." An hour or so later, I was engaged in idle hand-sign conversation with the railway guard when I was asked where I came from.

I said, "New Zealand."

"No," said my escort, "he's an American."

"No I'm not, I'm a New Zealander."

"But you can't be, you're an American and a flier, an Oberst Lieutenant [Lt. Colonel]. I have it here on my papers."

"No, we left him back in Nuremberg."

"What?"

"Yes, he's with the other New Zealander. I'm a New Zealander, not an American."

"You mean to tell me that you're not the flier after all?"

"That's right, have another look at your papers."

He honestly thought I was the American flier and was taking me to Barth, 125 miles north of Berlin on the Baltic coast, while Ross and Jack were en route to East Sudetenland, hundreds of miles away. His disbelief changed to consternation and he hurriedly started rummaging through his satchel. After carefully checking the particulars, he pushed his cap back off his forehead, and shook and scratched his head while muttering to himself. But he still wasn't convinced.

Finally, seeing what the true situation was, he snapped his satchel shut, slapped his knee, and he and the train guard roared with laughter. Then they got busy. Above the latter's head, a shelf extending the full width of the compartment was crammed with timetables, guides, and informational booklets on the German railway system; I wouldn't have been surprised if the collection was comprehensive enough to cover the whole continent. As a captain of a ship reaches up to a similarly filled shelf in his chartroom and selects nautical volumes to assist him in determining a course, so did the guard refer to the many volumes of detailed information.

Every click of the wheels was taking me further away from Ross and Jack, who were traveling in a different direction. Finally, with a "Yah, it is gut," the railway guard, who'd made lots of notes, disappeared at the next stop to send a wire to the train on which Jack and Ross were traveling. It was midday and we began changing a lot of trains from then on. We took meals at Red Cross canteens in railway stations attended by girls in white uniforms, and at Leipzig we had a meal at the station restaurant. A young lady who spoke English joined us at the table—much against regulations, I believe—while we were having a bottle of Pilsner beer. She seemed to enjoy the opportunity to practice her English.

Normally, the German railways were a most efficient organization, but I saw enough to convince me that it was "creaking at the joints." Unquestionably, the greatest factor in the defeat of Germany on the home front was the constant battering that the transportation system received from bombing. It finally broke the back of the German war effort.

Arriving at Dresden, we walked across town to another station where we entrained for Prague. After interminable hours, I finally met Jack and Ross, both grinning, in a station waiting room. It almost was a joyful reunion, as it seemed so long since we'd parted. My guard, as he disappeared with Ross, put his fingers to his lips, and with a grin said, "Nix sprechen" (Don't say a word about this).

The last we saw of Ross, his tall, stalwart figure was striding towards a departing train. ✪

SOURCES

PRIMARY MATERIALS

C. Ross and Dorothy Watson Greening. Collection—letters, papers, documents, newspaper clippings, manuscripts, photographs, illustrations, and original artwork.

C. Ross Greening. "Doolittle Raid Diary," 1942 [China and India].

_____."Italian Diary," July to December 1943. Washington State Historical Society, Tacoma, Washington.

_____. *Not as Briefed*. St. Paul, MN: Col. C. Ross Greening and Brown & Bigelow, n.d. (limited edition) [Text and captions written by Lt. J.M. Coppinger].

_____. Original paintings. Washington State Historical Society, Tacoma, Washington.

_____. "SS *President Cleveland* Diary," summer 1933.

_____. "A Wartime Log," 1944–45 [Stalag Luft 1].

Lang, Jack. Collection—manuscripts, papers, artwork, and photographs. Jack Lang, New Zealand.

Smith, Bob. "At War in 5 Armies—The Adventurous Story of W.O.2 R.J.G. Smith." Twelve installments in the monthly *Review* (Wellington, New Zealand), 1955–56.

SOME RECOMMENDED READING

The Doolittle Raid—

Glines, Carroll V. *Doolittle's Tokyo Raiders*. Princeton, NJ: D. Van Nostrand, 1964.

_____. *The Doolittle Raid: America's Daring First Strike Against Japan*. Atglen, PA: Schiffer, 1991.

Cohen, Stan. *Destination Tokyo: A Pictorial History of Doolittle's Tokyo Raid, April 18, 1942*. Missoula, MT: Pictorial Histories, 1983.

Poggio, Chieti, Sulmona, and POW train to Bolzano—

Westheimer, David. *Sitting It Out: A World War II POW Memoir*. Houston, TX: Rice University Press, 1992 [Westheimer's best selling novel, *Von Ryan's Express*, was based primarily on the events of 1943].

German interrogation—

Toliver, Raymond F. *The Interrogator: The Story of Hans Scharff, Luftwaffe's Master Interrogator*. N.p.: Raymond F. Toliver, 1978.

Stalag Luft 1—

Richard, Oscar J. *Kriegie: An American POW in Germany*. Baton Rouge: Louisiana State University Press, 2000.

Roy, Morris J. *Behind Barbed Wire*. New York: Richard R. Smith, 1946.

Welcome to POW Camp Stalag Luft 1, Barth, Germany. Raleigh, NC: Edwards & Broughton, n.d.

Zemke, Hubert, and Roger A. Freeman. *Zemke's Stalag*. Washington, DC: Smithsonian Institution, 1991.

Wartime logbooks and USAAF POW Exposition—

Beltrone, Art and Lee. *A Wartime Log*. Charlottesville, VA: Howell Press, 1994.

Greening, C. Ross, and Angelo M. Spinelli. *The Yankee Kriegies*. New York: National Council of YMCA, n.d.

INDEX

F

Faktor, Sgt. Leland, 43
Farrow, Lt. William, 25, 67
FBI, 16
Ferguson, Major, 99–100, 103
Filene's Department Store, 231
Fischer, Maj. Jack, 227–28
Fleer, Carl, 231, 233
Flying Tigers, 47
Friuli, 249

G

Gabreski, Lt. Col. Francis, 101, 128, 179, 205–6, 219
Gallo, Captain (MD), 98, 100
Gardner, Sgt. Melvin, 12, 29, 35–37, 41–42, 49–50
Garibaldi Battalion, 255
Gay, Ensign George, 19
Geneva Convention (1929), 67, 120, 166, 193, 210, 214
Gentile, Capt. Donald, 101
Gestapo, 170, 257
Glenn, Carol, 229–30
Gooler, Lt. Col. Max, 80, 89, 91–92, 94–96
Gray, Lt. Robert, 17, 25, 43
Greening, Charles Ross [b. Nov. 12, 1914, Carroll, Iowa; d. March 29, 1957, Wash., D.C.]
  Montana years, 1
  Tacoma, WA, 1–2
  college, 1–3, 32
  Walt Disney, 2
  flight training, 3, 6
  wedding, 3–4
  early assignments, 3–9
  "The First Joint Action," 13
  Mark Twain bombsight, 14–15, 28, 55
  Sakura, Japan, 32, 34
  DFC, 44, 49
  Chinese awards, 45, 50
  Air Medal, 53
  shot down 57–59, 76, 78
  Poggio, 66, 75–76, 80
  Chieti, 78–80, 83, 98, 127
  Sulmona, 86, 94
  Bolzano, 103–16
  Verona area, 116–33
  Cividale area, 134–43
  Palmanova area, 145–46
  return to Cividale area, 147–50
  New Zealanders/the cave, 150–66
  recapture, 165–75
  Stalag Luft 1, 177–215
  "Kriegmalion," 199
  Kriegie Kraft Karnival, 201
  "Where Do We Fit," 211
  liberation, 217–24
  Thirty Seconds over Tokyo, 226
  Laird's Lodge, 225, 227
  POW Exposition, 227–34
  Circumnavigator's Club, 231
  International Barbed Wire Club, 233
  Flame of Freedom Award, 233
  jet fighter training, 235–36
  post WWII assignments, 235–36
  U.S. Air Attache, 236, 246
  revisits Italy, 236–45
  Jack and Bob, 245–46
  Australian circumnavigation, 246
  Bob Smith's story, 247–59
  "The Brave Colonel," 265
Greening, Dorothy "Dot" Watson [wife; b. Jan. 18, 1912]
  2–11 passim, 16, 19, 47, 50, 53–55, 63, 105, 107, 129–30, 180, 212, 215, 226–27, 230, 235–46 passim
Greening, Jewell [mother; Drake College]
  1, 4, 47, 55, 63, 105, 129–30, 144, 171, 212, 226–27
Greening, Charles William [father; Carelton College and U. of Minnesota Law School]
  1, 4, 29, 55
Greening, Shirley (Morgan) [sister; b. Nov. 12, 1912]
  1–2, 29, 55, 202
  Karen Morgan (Driscoll), 201
Greening, Virginia (Nisker) [sister; b. Jan. 10, 1923]
  4, 5, 55, 201, 202
Greening, Allen Ross [son]
  235, 236–46 passim
Greening, Charles William "Chuck" [son]
  235, 236–46 passim
Griffin, Lt. Thomas, 63, 67
Griffin, Worth D., 200
Gross, General William, 224
Grunta, Mr., 140, 148–51, 161, 163
guard dogs, 192, 194, 218

H

Hallmark, Lt. Dean, 18, 25, 67
Hamilton Field, California, 4
Hanford, Maj. June, 54, 129
Hankey, Lt. Col. George, 208–9, 220
Harmon, Virginia, 50
Hearne, Colonel, 246
Henderson, Commander George, 19
Henderson, Jack, 58
Hengyang, China, 44
Hickey, Dick and Margaret, 226–27, 235
Hilger, Maj. John, 8, 11–12, 18, 25, 28, 42, 46–47
Hiltgen, Lt. Pete, 228, 231
Hitler, Adolf (Fuhrer), 80, 92, 102, 173, 199, 214, 217
Hitler Jugend, 179
Holstrom, Lt. Everett, 9, 25, 27–28
Hoover, Lt. Travis, 12, 24–25, 28
Hope, Bob, 231
Hornet, 13, 16, 18–25, 30, 33, 51
Howe, Major, 104
Hubbard, Lt. Col. Mark, 67, 175, 181, 184, 193, 205, 221, 224
The Hump, 47

I

Ingolstadt, Germany, 257
Isarco River, Italy, 111
Italian Armistice, 249
Italian capitulation, 85–87, 125, 127, 141, 146

J

Johnson, Maj. Gerald, 101, 128, 205
Jones, Capt. David, 11–12, 17, 19–20, 23, 25, 28, 42, 46, 63, 67
Joyce, Lt. Richard, 14, 25, 42

K

Kane, Col. John, 79
Kappeler, Lt. Frank, 12, 23, 29–31, 35–36, 38, 41
Kelly Field, Texas, 17
Kiang, China, 44

"THE BRAVE COLONEL"

Five months after Ross was assigned to duty in Australia, he tragically developed a blood infection that attacked the valve of his heart. After a long and courageous battle, Ross passed away on March 29, 1957. Without realizing it, the corpsmen and doctors at Bethesda Hospital in Washington, D.C., gave Ross the same nickname that the Italian villagers had used during the war, "The Brave Colonel."

With friends and Doolittle raiders serving as pall bearers, Ross was buried in the hero's section of Arlington National Cemetery. Following the funeral, General and Mrs. Doolittle hosted a reception at the Statler Hotel in Washington D.C. Later, memorial services were held in northern Italy, New Zealand, and Australia. A heart research fund was established in Ross's name in Australia.

In the months before he died, Ross found deep faith and wonderful insight into the events of his life and the purpose of the cruel illness that beset him. In a letter detailing his beliefs and the happiness that he could foresee for his future, Ross gave his family more comfort and joy than they thought possible. In later years, hundreds of Ross's friends also have read this letter, receiving spiritual strength from it.